DEVELOPMENT OF ADULT, CONTINUING AND NON-FORMAL EDUCATION IN INDIA

About the Authors

S.P. Agrawal (*b*. 1929) was Director, National Social Science Documentation Centre ICSSR, Government of India and Member Secretary, Indian Association of Socia Science Institutions. He was also the Vice-Chairman of the Asia and Pacific Informatior Network in Social Science (APINESS). In 1998 he was awarded the degree of Doctor of Philosophy in Education (*Honoris Causa*) by International University Foundation. Presently, he is Member, IFLA Round Table on Research in Reading, International Committee for Social Science, Information and Documentation, Board of Studies of National Archives of India and Hindi Advisory Committee, Ministry of Coal, Government of India. He is also Fellow of the Society of Ethnobotanists. Born and brought up in the cradle of freedom movement, which he joined at the tender age of twelve, he gained an insight into social and political problems and developed a sense of responsibility which bore fruit as an information scientist. He has written extensively on various aspects of Education, Indian Polity and Library and Information Science.

M.W.K. Sherwani (*b*. 1929), former Assistant Educational Adviser of Ministry of Human Resource Development, New Delhi, has a varied and deep interest in Library Science and Education. He has worked as an Honorary Director of Library Science Course conducted by Delhi Educational Society, New Delhi, for five years. He has also worked in the Directorate of Adult Education for four years during seventies which enabled him to gain an insight into the problems of adult, continuing and non-forma education. He has also assisted Shri S.P. Agrawal, General Editor of 'Concepts in Communication, Informatics and Librarianship' (CICIL) Series, in his editorial worl relating to the publishing of books under the CICIL Series.

Meena Usmani (*b*. 1953) has been associated with Centre for Women's Developm[illegible] Studies, New Delhi. She has been actively associated with centre's documentation [illegible] bibliographical activities. She did her M.Com. from Meerut University, and M[illegible].I.Sc from Delhi University. She had earlier worked at National Institute of Publi[illegible]ooperatio and Child Development and Centre for Policy Research, New Delhi [illegible]ter other recer publication in collaboration with S.P. Agrawal is *Children's Education in India*.

Concepts in Communication
Informatics & Librarianship Series No. 87

General Editor : **S.P. Agrawal**

DEVELOPMENT OF ADULT, CONTINUING AND NON-FORMAL EDUCATION IN INDIA

S.P. AGRAWAL
former Member Secretary,
Indian Association of Social Science Institutions, and
former Director, National Social Science Documentation Centre (ICSSR)
New Delhi

MITHILESH GUPTA
former Vice Principal
Government of National Capital Region, Delhi

M.W.K. SHERWANI
former Assistant Educational Adviser,
Ministry of Human Resource Development, New Delhi

MEENA USMANI
Centre for Women's Development Studies,
New Delhi

CONCEPT PUBLISHING COMPANY, NEW DELHI-110059

ISBN 81-7022-936-7

First Published 2002

Published and Printed by
Ashok Kumar Mittal
Concept Publishing Company
A/15-16, Commercial Block, Mohan Garden,
NEW DELHI-110059

Phones : 5648039, 5649024
Fax : 091-11-5648053
Email : publishing@conceptpub.com

GENERAL EDITOR'S INTRODUCTION

Our makers of the Constitution were unrealistic and not aware of ground realities when they stipulated that the goal of education for all in India could be achieved within a decade. They did not realise several road-blocks and constraints in the way of this goal—cultural ethos of the people, particularly rural masses who resisted sending their girls to schools and were eager to marry them off at early years, the gruelling poverty of a large sections of the disadvantaged people who preferred their wards as earners to school-goers, several inaccessible and hilly parts of the country, lack of resources, lukewarm attitude of the politicians and the elites and inexperienced and unenthusiastic administrators, etc. The Sargent report (1944) was more realistic which suggested that the total literacy could be achieved only by 1984. But it is tragic to say that even after fifty years we were not able to educate even half of our population. The reasons for our dismal performance are not far to seek. Our politicians, the privileged class and the bureaucracy which have unlimited power in politics and economic development have never been sincere in the eradication of the illiteracy in the country. It may be an exaggeration, but an exaggeration of a vital truth that the political leaders were not interested in educating the masses as they feared that the educated masses could not be exploited to their ends. The financial provision which they made in wiping out illiteracy was woefully inadequate. Moreover, although we were adept in formulating ideal programmes for adult, continuing and non-formal education, yet we miserably failed to implement these programmes effectively. It is only in the 1990s that our Central Government realised that massive efforts are needed to provide total literacy in the country. As a matter of fact as a result of the 'World Conference on Education for All' which acted as global platform for proclaiming the urgent need for providing basic education for all and for achievement of a fundamental learning and life skills by a large majority and also the 'Education For All Summit of Nine High Population Countries', (held in Delhi in 1993), our government started showing increased attention for accelerating the pace of literacy development. It has now been making massive efforts in the direction of achieving the goal of 'Education For All' through a number of adult, continuing and non-formal education programmes. But it is doubtful if we would be able to realise our objective of total literacy by 2005 as envisaged by the National Literacy Mission.

The concept of adult education has undergone many changes. At a time it was mostly confined to literacy. Later on it was widened to include, in addition to literacy, other aspects of the life of the adults, their health and hygiene, their domestic, economic and social life. It was, therefore, christened as 'Social Education'. Further, in the context of change in the areas of emphasis and the contents of the programme it became 'Fundamental Education'. From 'Fundamental Education' it was again re-christened into 'Fundamental Literacy'. It too underwent a further change and was replaced with 'Non-Formal Education' which is considered as any organised programme of learning outside the formal education system and also as a means of universalising elementary education in a less formal way and in short duration. It attempts to provide educational facility to children who are school drop-outs, children in habitation without schools, working children and girls engaged in family chores. After so many changes, the adult education has regained its name. It is now adult education again. But non-formal education has come to stay. It has not been dethroned. As regards continuing education it is essentially a follow-up education. As a matter of fact it is a life-long education. Keeping all these things in view, our National Policy on Education, besides providing facility for literacy 'links adult education with national goals as poverty alleviation, national integration, environment conservation, energisation of cultural creativity, observation of small family norm and promotion of women's equality.'

The present end-publication in CICIL series gives a comprehensive view of the development of adult, continuing and non-formal education in the country. It attempts to provide information on almost all aspects of the adult education. While the First Chapter, besides defining the terms of adult, continuing and non-formal education, traces the historical development, the Second Chapter is concerned with the National Policy on Adult Education as formulated by the Central Government from time to time. The Third Chapter takes up the planning of the adult education through Five-Year Plans (from first to ninth Plan). The Fourth and Fifth Chapters are devoted to the recommendations of the Committees, Commissions, Working Groups and proceedings of the Central Advisory Board and major recommendations made by Conferences on Education respectively. The other Chapters are concerned with the National Adult Education Programme (1978), the role of the universities in the development of the programme, importance of research, evaluation and monitoring of the programme, the role of the adult education in achieving the women's equality and empowerment. The Tenth Chapter provides statistics on adult, continuing and non-formal education.

Acknowledgements

Main documentation sources are : Ministry of Human Resource Development, Department of Education, New Delhi; University Grants Commission, New Delhi; National Council of Educational Research and Training, New Delhi; National Institute of Educational Planning and Administration, New Delhi; articles appearing in important Indian journals and newspapers. We are grateful to all research institutions/ organisations, editors of journals and newspapers for using their documents/view-points in this publication.

15 August 2000 S.P. AGRAWAL

Contents

CHAPTER : FOUR

CHAPTER : FIVE

CHAPTER : SIX

Contents

CHAPTER SEVEN

ADULT, CONTINUING AND [illegible] EDUCATION IN UNIVERSITIES [illegible]

CHAPTER EIGHT

RESEARCH, EVALUATION AND [illegible]

CHAPTER NINE

OUR EDUCATIONAL [illegible] ACHIEVEMENT [illegible] 31[illegible]

CHAPTER TEN

STATISTICS ON [illegible] NON-FORMAL EDUCATION [illegible]

1

Adult Education : Concepts, Definitions and Historical Development

(A) CONCEPTS AND DEFINITIONS

(i) International Encyclopaedia of Education

The multidisciplinary nature of the field and its practitioners creates many problems in international communication. It is only recently that the concept of adult education as a discrete sector of education has been recognized in many countries; even today some societies view the education and training of their citizens from the perspective of the function such training performs or the class to which participants belong; for example, trade union education or working class education.

With the emergence of mass communication and computer technology, information sharing among professionals engaged in the education of adults has multiplied rapidly, forcing some rationalization in the technical language of the field. UNESCO's World Conferences on Adult Education and the UNESCO/International Bureau of Education's International Consultations on Adult Education Documentation have made major contributions to the international acceptance of many definitions of key concepts in the study and practice of adult education. The language will continue to evolve and develop as the profession matures.

1. *The Language of Adult Education*

All professions develop languages which facilitate communication

---

Source : Husen, Torsten and Postlethwaite, T.N., eds., *International Encyclopaedia of Education: Research and Studies*, New York, Pergamon Press, 1988, Vol. 1, pp. 115-17.

among their members. To people outside the profession, such languages may appear highly technical, specialized, even incomprehensible; sometimes the language is denigrated as "jargon". Yet the professional terms and the concepts they represent are the tools of a profession's trade, used to transmit information and to develop new knowledge. The languages become shared by all new entrants to the profession, mainly through the medium of professional education, and professional schools in many cultures will teach common concepts and use common technical terms to express those concepts.

Adult education is different in some respects from the more tranditional professions in the development of its language. The profession has been growing most rapidly in the years since the Second World War and so has its language, although such important concepts as "cooperative extension" have been part of the language for much longer. The practitioners of adult education during this period of rapid growth did not have a homogeneous background; unlike lawyers, doctors, and engineers, the professional education of these practitioners of the 1940s and 1950s was extremely varied. They gained entrance to the profession more through their practice than through a background in educational theory. No certification or examinations were required to become a member, nor are any required today to be an adult educator. These workers brought into their practice the concepts and technology of their own academic background and their previous work experience; as they began to communicate with one another, they traded concepts and ideas. So the professional language grew from diverse origins and took on meanings common in daily use.

2. *The Problem of Communication*

When the universities began to teach adult education as a field of graduate study, as early as 1930 in North America (Jenson *et al.* 1964) but later in other parts of the world, the process of absorbing the ideas and concepts used by practitioners into the study of adult education became more systematic. The multidisciplinary roots and the applied nature of adult education practice forced its practitioners and researchers to borrow theories and ideas from such fields as psychology even more than from pedagogy: this borrowing further expanded the terminology of adult education. As the field and the language developed and grew, they absorbed a flood of new concepts from business administration, organization development, operations research and psychotherapy, thereby heightening the polyglot nature of this applied field of practice.

When communicating with practitioners even within one country, problems arose in explaining the nature of the adult educator's task to the public, to legislators and policy makers, to government officials, and to other professions and groups. These problems became compounded when adult educators attempted to share experiences and ideas with practitioners in other countries and cultures. In the 1950s and 1960s, adult education in developing countries grew rapidly and technical assistance programmes at the national and international level were an important means of sharing adult education experience. Yet so often the lack of an internationally accepted or understood language of practice impeded the fullest sharing of that experience. The need to overcome some of these barriers to communication became critical as computer technology matured and made high-speed international information sharing a distinct possibility, even in fields with such imprecise and multilayered languages as the behavioural and social sciences, including adult education.

3. *The Nature of the Language*

3.1 *The Concept of Adult Education*

For many decades, educators have argued about the concept, the meaning, and the use of the term "adult education" and terms related to it. Many countries have had no concept of adult education as a distinctive sector of education, if it were to be conceived as a sector whose public, adults, is defined in terms of age, maturity, or whether persons have terminated their initial education. Countries or languages lacking such a concept described educational provision for adults from many different perspectives. For example, from the perspective of class, such terms as *education populaire, Volksbildung,* "people's or popular education", "*Scuola populare*, people's school" were used. Such terms as "vocational education", "trade union education", "social education", "citizenship education", described the concept in terms of function. Other terms were seen from the perspective of initial education, for example "*Weiterbildung*", "further education", "continuing education", and "*formation continue*".

The use of age as the determining factor of whether one is an adult is a contentious issue. When adulthood is reached depends on a person's particular culture, social or economic responsibilities, and the legal system in place. To educators, however, what matters is to be able to assist individuals to mature, to engage in and enjoy adult behaviour, to be autonomous and self-directing persons. Such a process has little to do with chromological age. In some societies with a requirement for a compulsory school attendance, once individuals reach a particular age, they attend school on a voluntary basis and thereby could be considered adults. In other societies, adult education is seen as outside the elementary, secondary, and tertiary systems entirely, whatever the age of attenders. Many writers have attempted to define adult education as a process unrelated to age, whereby persons who have terminated their initial cycle of continuous education may undertake any "sequential and organized activities with the conscious intention of bringing about changes in information, knowledge, understanding, or skills, appreciation, and attitudes".

> In everyday life, however, the expression, "adult education", is often used in another sense, as a collective term covering the institutions and procedures by which adults are enabled and encouraged to expreience the process. For many people, this mechanism is adult education.

That is what is meant when one refers to Hungarian adult education, or public adult education.

The General Conference of UNESCO in 1976 may have settled much of the confusion through having a General Recommendation on the Development of Adult Education accepted unanimously by representatives from 142 countries. It included the following definition:

> The term, "adult education", denotes the entire body of organized educational processes, whatever the content, level, and method, whether formal or otherwise, or whether they prolong or replace initial education in schools, colleges, and universities, as well as an apprenticeship, whereby persons regarded as adult by the society to which they belong develop their abilities, enrich their knowledge, improve their technical or professional qualifications, or turn them in a new direction and bring about changes in their attitudes or behaviour in the two-fold perspective of full personal development and participation in balanced and independent social, economic, and cultural development.

3.2 *Broader/Wider Concepts*

Many concepts closely related to adult education, used in the literature since the early 1960s, continue to be subject to controversy. These include "formal", "non-formal", "informal", "life-long learning", "life-long education", "continuing education" and "recent education"...

In some countries the term "non-formal education" has been used, as "social education" formerly was used, as a synonym for adult education, but this is not a fully acceptable practice since the term can and should be applied equally to children and youth... In an earlier period in North America the term "informal education" was applied almost as an equivalent of adult education but that usage has almost disappeared. Instead, now that a considerable part of adult education is formal, there is increasing pressure for more precise use of three terms: formal, non-formal and informal education as they apply to children, youth and adults so that all of them can describe the components of a total and integrated system of education. The term "formal education" is used to describe the hierarchically structured, chronologically graded system, from primary school through university and including, in addition to general academic studies, a variety of specialised programmes and institutions for full-time teaching and professional training. Informal education is the life long process whereby all individuals acquire attitudes, values, skills, and knowledge from daily experience and from the educative influences and resources in their environment—from family and neighbours, from work and play, from the market place, the library, and the mass media. Non-formal education could be defined as any organized educational activity outside the established formal system—whether operating separately or as an important feature of some broader activity—that is intended to serve identifiable learning clienteles and learning objectives.

The term "life long learning" is used internationally, but still lacks a commonly accepted definition... Cross describes the term as "slippery, strikingly inconsistent, subject to varying interpretations". Another more narrowly conceived definition appears in the reports prepared by the Lifelong Learning Project (1978). "Lifelong learning refers to the process by which individuals continue to develop their knowledge, skills, and attitudes over their lifetimes". Other writers describe the concept variously, from meaning "anything you want it to mean", to being "a banner for a movement around which various educational and social interests have rallied".

Cross says that:

> Lifelong learning means self-directed growth. It means understanding yourself and the world. It means acquiring new skills and powers—the only true wealth which you can never lose. It means investment in yourself. Lifelong learning means the joy of discovering how something really works, the delight of becoming aware of some new beauty in the world, the fun of creating something, alone or with other people.

"Lifelong education", although used often as a synonym for "lifelong learning", should more properly refer to the organized provision of opportunities for persons to learn throughout their lives. Delker makes the distinction between adult learning "as a major continuing mode of behaviour", and adult education as the "organized and sequential learning experiences designed to meet the needs of adults". Likewise, lifelong learning is the habit of continuously learning throughout life, a mode of behaviour, whereas lifelong education is "the principle on which the overall organization of a system is founded". Dave integrates the characteristics of the concept into what may be the most satisfactory description.

> Lifelong education seeks to view education in its totality. It covers formal, non-formal, and informal patterns of education, and attempts to integrate and articulate all structures and stages of education along the vertical (temporal) and horizontal (spatial) dimensions. It is also characterized by flexibility in time, place, content, and techniques of learning and hence calls for self-directed learning, sharing of one's enlightenment with others, and adopting varied learning styles and strategies.

"Continuing education" is another broad term about whose meaning there is little agreement. Thomas provides a very broad definition:

> It is a system(s) of education which includes formal and non-formal education, that is defined with respect to its various parts and agencies (elementary schools, secondary schools, colleges, and universities, for example) in terms of specific educational objectives to be fostered, rather than in terms of the ages or

> circumstances of learners. The system is available to persons of any age, part-time or full-time, voluntary or compulsory, and is financed by a mixture of private and public resources. It is distinguished from other educational activities in the society by the possession of the exclusive right to provide public recognition or certification for those completing its programmes, though not all of its programmes need lead to such certification.

It would not be agreed in all countries, however, that the system possesses the exclusive right to provide certification. A much more restricted definition of this concept has been posed in terms of its function:

> The envisaged function of continuing education is that of rounding off the individual's education, of providing further education or of retraining, so that, for example, the individual can always meet increased or new professional demands.

In the early 1970s, yet another general term came into use, first in Europe: "recurrent education" was coined to lend a more precise meaning to the concept of *education permanente*. . . It was conceived as a "comprehensive educational strategy for all post-compulsory or post-basic education over the total lifespan of the individual in a recurring way, i.e., in alternation with other activities, principally with work, but also with leisure and retirement". Another definition has been offered by Houghton and Richardson:

> Recurrent education is a lifelong process consisting of a discontinuous, periodic participation in educational programmes aimed at gradually dissolving the blocks of compulsory education and working life (front-end model).

These definitions with their overlapping tendencies and their lack of precision illustrate the phenomena of erosion of meaning and geographic specificity. Some writers use "continuing education" to mean "continuing higher (university level) education", others use "recurrent education" as a synonym for "continuing education", or "lifelong education" to signify "adult education". These habits, which function to impede communication internationally, may be modified in the near future.

(ii) By Encyclopaedia Britannica*

Adult Education

In the modern period, education has come to be strongly identified with organized preparation of the young in schools and colleges for both their personal development and their subsequent social and economic roles in society. Throughout recorded history, however, it has been recognized that to deny oneself of later adult education is to deny oneself of a great part of education that is meaningful only to grown, experienced men and women. In brief, the term adult education can thus be defined as the organized provision of facilities to enable men and women to enlarge and interpret their experiences as adults. Such facilities may be provided—and, in different places and at different times, have been provided—by voluntary action and independent agencies, by state and municipal authorities, and by commercial enterprises.

A more explicit definition is contained in a 1970 report of the National Institute of Adult Education (England and Wales), which stated:

> In the widest sense adult education is any kind of education for people who are old enough to work, vote, fight and marry and who have completed the cycle of continuous education, (if any) commenced in childhood. They may want to make up for limited schooling (or for no schooling), to pass examinations, to learn the basic skills of trades or professions or to master new working processes. They may turn to it because they want to understand themselves and their world better and to act in the light of their understanding, or they may go to classes for the pleasure they can get from developing talents and skills—intellectual, aesthetic, physical or practical. They may not even "go to classes": they may find what they want from books or broadcasts or take guidance by post from a tutor they never meet. They may find education without a label by sharing in common pursuits with like-minded people. (National Institute of Adult Education, *Provision for Adult Education, 1970).*

Varieties of Adult Education

Adult education thus comprehends such diverse modes as independent

---

**Encyclopaedia Britannica*, Vol. 1, pp. 97-101.

study consciously pursued with or without the aid of libraries; broadcast programmes or correspondence courses; group discussion and other "mutual aid" learning in study circles, colloquia, seminars or workshops, and residential conferences or meetings; and full- or part-time study in classes or courses in which the lecturer, teacher, or tutor has a formal leading role. Types of adult education can also be classified as follows:

1. Education for vocational, technical, and professional competence. (Such education may aim at preparing an adult for a first job or for a new job, or it may aim at keeping him up-to-date on new developments in his occupation or profession).
2. Education for health, welfare, and family living. (Such education includes all kinds of education in health, family relations, consumer buying, planned parenthood, hygiene, child care, and the like).
3. Education for civic, political, and community competence. (Such education includes all kinds of education relating to government, community development, public and international affairs, voting and political participation, and so forth).
4. Education for "self-fulfilment". (Such education embraces all kinds of liberal education programmes: education in music, the arts, dance, theatre, literature, arts and crafts, whether brief or long term. These programmes aim primarily at learning for the sake of learning rather than at achieving the aims included in the other categories).
5. Remedial education, fundamental and literacy education. (Such education is obviously a prerequisite for all other kinds of adult education and thus, as a category, stands somewhat apart from the other types of adult education).

In reference to the fifth category, adults frequently need to compensate for inadequacies of earlier education. If they are not remedied, they inhibit recourse to modes of education that are "adult"—adult, that is, in terms of sophistication in modern society and not in terms of age. Such education is required most extensively in societies changing rapidly from a subsistence to an industrial economy and concurrently changing politically and socially. Mass literacy acquires a new importance in these nations of Asia, Africa, and Latin America, and the establishment of universal primary education becomes a social imperative. To prevent a "generation gap" in reading skills and education while an effective school system is being created for the young, governments must attempt to provide parallel facilities for adults. Even in countries with mature systems of childhood education, however, opportunities for higher or even sometimes secondary education are unequal among various regional, occupational, and social groups. Hence there are adult programmes for completing high school or preparing for examinations normally taken at the end of secondary school. Even in so highly developed a country as Sweden it has been considered necessary in recent years not only to try to extend secondary education to more children but also to offer equivalent second chances for adults. The implication is that "remedial" adult education is needed in societies in all stages of development and not merely in the so-called developing countries.

Background of Modern Adult Education

The idea of education as a lifelong process has been expressed by philosophers and educators throughout the centuries. It is explicit in the thought and writings of Confucius, Plato, Sir Thomas More, Comenius and Benjamin Franklin, to cite only five examples widely separated in time and place. Attempts to give reality to such aspirations and to provide education for large numbers of adults, however, cannot be reasonably dated before the Industrial Revolution—and its accompanying social revolutions—of the late 18th and the 19th centuries. Changes in the ways of living—both occupationally and politically (as the franchise was extended)—produced a need for further education and re-education of adults. In the early and middle years of the 19th century these socio-economic changes were strongest in Great Britain and the United States; and it is in these countries that adult education received greatest emphasis, although significant developments also occurred in Scandinavia. Even today, the provisions for adult education in such lands as France, Italy, and Latin America are relatively small compared to what they are in the countries that pioneered further education.

Early Programmes: The rise of organized adult education in Great Britain is generally dated from the late 1790s, when the first adult school and the foundations of the first mechanics' institute were established, in Nottingham and Glasgow, respectively. In the next 50 years adult schools created generally by religious people to reduce adult illiteracy and mechanics' institutes designed to spread among artisans knowledge of science and its applications in industry, all dependent on voluntary effort and voluntary finance, were founded in many parts of England. Both declined later in the 19th century, although the adult schools revived and were active in the 20th, and the institutes often became technical colleges or reading and lecture societies.

In the 1840s the early cooperative societies in Great Britain undertook adult education work that still continues, and the industrial and social conditions that inspired Christian socialism and other humanitarian movements also prompted the founding of people's and workingmen's colleges. The first of these was established in Sheffield in 1842, but the most influential was the London Working Men's College (1854). Others were short lived, and none was residential until Ruskin College was founded at Oxford in 1899 to equip workingmen for their respondibilities as citizens and trade unionists.

Meanwhile, in the United States, the first half of the 19th century was a period of national adjustment and the rich development of educational institutions, each one unique and often unrelated to the others but all providing new channels of learning. Most important were the lyceums, local associations of men and women who had had some formal education and were concerned both with their own further learning and with the creation of a public school system; their education came chiefly through hearing debates and lectures on timely topics. Paralleling the growth of the lyceums and to some extent developing out of them were libraries, museums, mechanics' institutes, lecture series, endowed institutions, publicly supported evening schools, and a host of other institutions, many of which became permanent.

The second half of the 19th century, particularly during and after the Civil War, was another period of America's readjustment and therefore, another era of growth for organized adult education. Both the land-grant colleges and the U.S. Department of Agriculture were created, thus laying the groundwork for their later collaboration in the teaching of scientific agriculture and home economics to farmers and their wives. Institutions developed earlier gained strength; the most notable development of this sort perhaps was the growth of the public library, greatly stimulated by the benefactions of the steelman and philanthropist Andrew Carnegie. Sporadic university lecture series for the general public evolved into systematic programmes of "university extension"—educational courses for adults who are not full-time students. (The idea that a university owed responsibility to a wider constituency than its enrolled students was first officially endorsed, however, in England at the University of Cambridge in 1873.) A new variation on the lyceums was the "chautauqua", a nationwide movement that was inspired by the example of the annual summer-camp meetings of teachers, social workers, and others at Chautauqua Lake in New York State, where lectures, study workshops, and popular entertainment were offered for moral and intellectual improvement. (The popularity of the Chautauquas did not decline until the mid-1920s.)

National Variations: Although the British and American programmes in adult education were the ones to influence most strongly the development of adult education elsewhere in the world, the folk high schools in Scandinavia represent a noteworthy national development. These residential schools for young adults were first founded in Denmark in the middle of the 19th century to foster a sense of cultural unity, and they became a powerful instrument of national regeneration after the country's defeat by Germany in 1864. The man whose personality and writings stimulated their development in Denmark as well as the other Nordic nations was N.F.S. Grundtvig, who has been called the "father of the folk high school" and whose interests were unquestionably more political and nationalist than industrial or commercial. A theologian as well as an educationist, he stressed the need for a thorough knowledge of the mother tongue and of national and biblical history, and he put forward the idea that the years after 18 are those of real awakening to life. Such was the inspiration for the folk high schools in which young people of every class were to be encouraged to educate themselves and one another.

Even when such efforts in Scandinavia, Britain, the United States, and elsewhere were aimed at the educationally least privileged; however, several factors at first limited their success. The planners took insufficient account of the inadequacies of elementary education, and, in the absence of public subsidies or other aid the programmes were frequently priced beyond the capacity of working men and women. They tended to appeal more effectively to those with already established educational appetites and to be eyed with suspicion by articulate workers attempting to institutionalize political and economic protest through trade unions, cooperative societies, and independent political parties.

Moreover, even though its importance has often been publicly affirmed, adult education has seldom in the past engaged the attention of legislatures. The most notable exceptions have been in the Scandinavian countries, in the eastern European countries under Communist regimes, and most recently in some of the newly emergent nations, such as Tanzania. In free enterprise economies and pluralistic societies, the interplay of philanthropy and social reformism and the promotion of particular religious, political, and social interests have all contributed to the creation of adult learning opportunities. But government action has largely resulted from the efforts of these independent pressure groups seeking official recognition and public financial support; thus, specific legislative acts have usually not been concerned with a general theory or broad programme of adult education so much as with the solution of particular problems brought forward by special interests. (Such a pragmatic or problem-oriented approach is illustrated by the setting up of agricultural experimental stations in the United States under the Hatch Act of 1887, which provided the basis for federal extension services in agriculture and home economics).

The Scandinavian countries are unique in the numbers of legislators who claim personal experience of adult education, particularly in the folk high schools, and who are thus favourably disposed toward adult education. They are also the countries in which democratic practices are most deeply imbedded in a wealth of popular movements to which the state has come to entrust relatively large amounts of money for the development of adult education. One of the most recent examples is the Danish legislative act of June 1968 concerning "leisure time instruction". This act provides aid for youth schools, leisure-time activities for children and young people, leisure-time instruction for adults, supplementary cultural arrangements (that is, lectures, art exhibitions, concerts), university extension activities, correspondence schools, leisure-time instruction for seamen. Although the act specifies in detail the conditions that must be fulfilled by voluntary organizations and municipalities in order to qualify for state financial support, there is no attempt to define curricula or to restrict educational and ideological objectives. Similar "democratic" programmes exist in all the Scandinavian countries.

In Great Britain, which continued in the early part of the 20th century to be a more distinctly hierarchic or class-structured society, adult education was frequently a case of the "privileged" accepting a responsibility for helping the "underprivileged". Some individuals with an elite education in independent schools and universities were willing to apply their education, example, and moral suasion to help the working classes to help themselves. Thus, the Workers' Educational Association (WEA), founded in 1903 "to promote the higher education of working men and women", drew upon the services of tutors from the universities—in effect, broadening the activities of university extension. Emphasis on continuous academic study in small groups under the guidance of highly qualified tutors largely replaced the earlier tradition of lectures to large audiences. From almost the beginning the national board of education offered grants toward the teaching costs of such classes, and especially after World War II there was a rapid and substantial increase in the work of the WEA and of the university extension services based on increased grants from the new Ministry of Education (today entitled the Department of Education and Science). In addition, there were established a number of new institutions concerned with adult education. Prominent among these were some 30 new residential colleges, some provided by universities, a small number by voluntary effort, but the majority by local education authorities. They all differed from Ruskin College and several others established earlier in that they provided only short courses, lasting from a weekend to a few weeks or occasionally two or three months. At the same time, local education authorities were increasingly fostering liberal studies in technical colleges and other institutions.

Traditions of Voluntary Participation and Curricular Freedom

Two traditions in adult education thus established themselves in the countries that pioneered adult education, the tradition of voluntary participation and the tradition of freedom from state control in matters of curricula and educational goals (even though the state might fund the programmes). This contrasts with practices, for instance, in the U.S.S.R., which has put heavy emphasis on adult educational programmes. According to an anonymous but trypical text, *Education of Adults in the U.S.S.R.,* dated 1960, "The transformation of society into a Communist society now making headway in the U.S.S.R. involves the education of the wide masses of people, the development of their consciousness and the raising of their political and production activities". The provisions made to achieve these ends are impressive, but the key words here are *masses* and *society*—ignoring *individuals.* Adult education is promoted to enable people en masse to understand and adjust to change, not to enable them to exercise individual judgment about the character and direction of change.

Another kind of of contrast exists between the Scandinavian and Anglo-American countries on the one hand and France and other Latin nations on the other, where the Napoleonic aftermath of central direction of education is most marked. The public education authorities have taken little notice of adult education. As one English observer has noted:

> Those accustomed to the provision made for non-vocational adult education in the English speaking countries have long found French practice in this sphere so foreign as to be incomprehensible... In France, educational opportunities for adults are highly decentralised and informal, in the hands of a vast number of private societies, large and small, run by unpaid, part-time labour, whose records are often sketchily kept and whose finances are complicated... The scene is further obscured because adult education is not considered as an independent branch of education as we tend to see it and the term itself is little used. For the French it forms only a part of a wider activity, called *education populaire* or *culture populaire*, which in its widest sense is defined as any communal non-vocational activity of a social, recreational, sporting or intellectual nature, carried on outside home, school, or work, which enriches and develops the personality. (Colin J. Titmus, *Adult Education in France*, Pergamon Press Ltd., 1967).

Irrespective of modes of provision and direction, however, adult education is also affected by the quantity and quality of education available in childhood and youth. Quite simply, the more education that people receive the more they are likely to want and the more likely they are to actively seek information about its provision. Raising the overall school-leaving age and increasing the proportions of young people proceeding directly to higher or continuative education are clearly associated with a rising demand for adult education for personal and social reasons. The same kind of increasing demand is associated with high economic productivity and the accelerated technological obsolescence that accompanies it. This sets in motion the need for vocational retraining in adult life that must be included in the modern concept of adult education.

Agencies and Institutions

Varieties of Schools and Programmes

Any classification of agencies and institutions involved in adult education must necessarily be arbitrary, given the great variety found not only among nations but within single nations. The following are the general types:

The folk high schools, first established in Denmark and now found in all Scandinavian countries, are residential schools in which young adults who have completed formal schooling and usually have had some subsequent work experience pursue at least several months of study. The study aims at furthering both moral and intellectual development and instilling an understanding of local and national traditions and conditions, thus still reflecting Grundtvig's original concept. Although at first they were independent or separate institutions, they are now frequently promoted or supported by communal boards of education. Although rarely exported with success in their pure form, the folk high schools have influenced the development of residential forms of adult education in countries as diverse as Canada, Kenya, India, and The Netherlands.

Non-resident adult education centres, the most widely distributed specialized institutes for adult education, are represented by "workers academies" in Finland, "palaces of culture" in the U.S.S.R. and some other Communist countries, "workers' universities" in Yugoslavia, "peoples' high schools" in West Germany and Austria, "adult education centres" in Great Britain, and "people's universities" in The Netherlands, Italy, and Switzerland. The distinguishing characteristics of these institutions are that they are independent of the general education authorities, at least in terms of programmeming; that student attendance is voluntary and part-time; and that teachers and administrators are either volunteers or professionals offering mainly part-time services. Traditionally, these schools do not prepare students for examinations or offer training in advanced vocational skills. Typically the curriculum includes instruction in practical and domestic crafts, fine arts, music and drama, familial and social problem solving, and modern languages, as well as instruction designed to reinforce primary and secondary education. The workers' universities in Yugoslavia probably go furthest in trying to fuse these elements into an overall programme to equip workers to play a role in the self-management of industrial and commercial enterprises.

Agricultural extension services, though almost wholly an American development, are conducted on a scale great enough to rate separate mention. The extension service of the U.S. Department of Agriculture conducts agricultural, home economics, and even public affairs programmes in every county in the United States. It has had special significance in developing "demonstration" as a method of adult education, in emphasizing the adoption of new practices, and in providing a possibly appropriate model for newly developing countries.

The open university, a new British institution, is significant for its new dimension and sharp break with previous degree programmes for adults. In some educationally advanced countries—such as Australia, New Zealand, Canada, and the United States—adults have long had opportunities to pursue part-time education leading to the award of university degrees, but these programmes have usually been carbon copies of programmes offered to regular undergraduates. The open university, in theory at least, aspires to a kind of universal higher education. It is intended to service only mature or older adults studying part-time; it has no standardized entry requirements; and it attempts to combine various educational technologies and techniques—correspondence instruction, mass-communication media, personal counselling, and short-term residential courses.

Commercial enterprises have provided correspondence courses or class instruction (part- or full-time) for adults who are usually seeking some form of vocational qualification (but who may, however, be simply seeking "self-improvement", as in speed-reading programmes). Such schools may be licensed or supervised by state agencies (as in Sweden and The Netherlands), or they may be self-policing through associations offering accreditation. Some schools are non-profit organizations. One interesting development has been Switzerland's *Klub-Schulen* ("club schools"), supported through the philanthropy of a commercial concern, the Migros trading organization, but operated on a non-profit basis; the programmes, furthermore, have no particular vocational emphasis.

Extension services include both public school programmes for adults and the unviersity extensions mentioned earlier. The school programmes are administered by the public school systems, and they are popularly termed night schools because ordinarily they are housed in the same school buildings used in the daytime for school-age youth and also because some of the same teachers are often involved. (Much of the teaching, however, is also done by subject specialists not employed as school-teachers.) Though often originating in efforts to remedy or supplement inadequate childhood education, many of these programmes now cater to the same range of interests served by the "non-resident adult education centres" cited above. They often retain elements of vocational preparation at a less specialized level, generally for younger adults—for example, in commercial and trade skills.

The difficulties inherent in trying to provide adequate services to adults as a kind of marginal addition or after-thought to the education of children have led some local education authorities in Britain and the United States to design schools that can be used specifically for adults as well as children. The "village colleges" in Cambridgeshire and the Mott Foundation programme in Flint, Michigan, involve a pattern of separate staffing for adult and child education and of comprehensive planning that enables a very large adult programme to be provided within the school system. Such developments require the recruitment and training of larger cadres of full-time adult education teachers than have been customary in the past. The further growth and sophistication of public provision is likely to be a marked feature of adult education in the future.

The extension services offered by institutions of higher learning are of two broad types. The British tradition, influential in most Commonwealth countries and former colonial territories, has emphasized the provision of non-credit courses of "liberal" studies. The North American tradition, found in countries influenced by the United States and Canada, places a larger emphasis on credit programmes duplicating courses offered to regular undergraduates; such programmes are offered via television or correspondence or in separate "downtown" (urban) colleges. Both traditions seems in the process of modification—the British in the direction of offering more credit-earning and vocation-related refresher courses, the North American toward a wider acceptance of the provision of general liberal studies for the public at large and for specialized vocational groups. It is everywhere apparent that universities are assuming more responsibility for the continuance and renewal of education for the highly educated.

Organisations, libraries and museum servicing adult activities

In addition to the various schools or services listed above, there are countries organizations whose main purposes may not be adult education but that offer some kind of instruction or leisure-time activities for adults. They include such bodies as the Young Men's Christian Association, the Young Women's Christian Association, political parties and labour unions (often operating through especially constituted "workers educational associations"), women's organizations like the Norwegian Housewives League, and temperance organizations like the International Order of Good Templars. Such a list could be almost endless. Other agencies for which adult education is a related rather than a primary function are libraries, museums, botanical gardens, and the like. Not only do these agencies provide the means of individual self-education but also they frequently promote group activities or put their accommodations and resources at the disposal of adult education agencies. Finally there should be mentioned the advisory and instructional services offered by various social and welfare agencies in the fields of health, safety, marital guidance, family planning, and so forth.

Future Perspectives

Acceleration in the rate of change in human affairs is so much a cliche of contemporary discussion as not to require elaboration. It is summed up in the aphorism attributed to American anthropologist Margaret Mead that "no man today will die in the world in which he was born". The inescapable consequence is the need for continual renewal of learning in all forms of employment and in various phases of life. As one example of the problems involved, in those fields of advanced technology (such as aerospace and nuclear engineering) in which it is impracticable to duplicate some operational plant in a separate educational milieu, education may have to be integrated with the productive process itself. Moreover, initial education in many fields is now so specialized and demanding on the time and energy of the young that a broad, general education may be impossible unless the whole of life, not merely the formative years, is accepted as time for learning.

Encouragement is given to these trends and to more widely ranging concepts of adult education by professional associations in adult education—associations whose objects are to promote cooperation between different schools and agencies, to foster enquiry and research, and to disseminate information. With differing structures and varying levels of development such organizations exist in Australia, Canada, Denmark, England and Wales, Finland, India, Ireland, The Netherlands, New Zealand, Norway, Scotland, Sweden, Switzerland, and the United States. Intercommunication beyond national boundaries has been encouraged by the United Nations Educational, Scientific and Cultural Organization (UNESCO) and by such regional bodies as the European Bureau of Adult Education, the African Adult Education Association, and the Asian-South Pacific Association for Adult Education. Still largely dependent on the personal efforts of a few individuals, these bodies are an index to the growing awareness of the importance of adult education throughout the world.

Bibliography. Much of the literature of adult education is to be found in journal articles and in pamphlets, frequently issued in small editions and only accessible in specialized libraries, although sometimes now available on microfilm or microfiche. Some important general works, however, are: Thomas Kelly (ed.), *A Select Bibliography of Adult Education in Great Britain*, 2nd ed. (1963), a bibliography of works published to the end of 1961; and *A History of Adult Education in Great Britain*, 2nd ed. (1970), on the development of both formal and informal means of adult education from the Middle Ages to the mid-20th century; J.F.C. Harrison, *Learning and Living, 1790-1960: A Study in the History of the English Adult Education Movement* (1961), a text starting with the experience in England as the first industrial society and ending with the post-World War II search for social relevance; John Lowe, *Adult Education in England and Wales: A Critical Survey* (1970), a recent general work on the English educational system; Edmund De Schweinitz Brunner *et al., An Overview of Adult Education Research* (1959), an inventory of research in non-vocational adult education made by the Bureau of Applied Social Research, Columbia University, that attempts to achieve valid generalizations applicable to the broad field of adult education; C. Hartley Grattan, *In Quest of Knowledge* (1955), a short sketch that concentrates on the western European background from primitive man to the Industrial Revolution and then focuses on the American experience, with a brief resume of that in Britain; Cyril O. Houle, *The Inquiring Mind* (1961), a comprehensive study of the adult student; and J.R. Kidd, *How Adults Learn* (1959), a synthesis of theory and practice in the field of adult education; Malcolm S. Knowles, *The Adult Education Movement in the United States* (1962), an informed, comprehensive study, containing a bibliography of general sources; Coolie Verner and A. Booth, *Adult Education* (1969), a well-documented basic text.

(iii) By International Encyclopaedia of Social Sciences

The term "adult education" has come into general use within the last half century to identify two different but related phenomena: a field of social activity and an emerging discipline in social science. Although different, these phenomena are interdependent. The discipline finds its subject of study in the field, which is, in turn, dependent upon the discipline for its development.

The field of adult education has been identified and designed in various ways. Most definitions include all learning by adults, from the casual incidental learning that may occur in the natural societal setting

---

International Encyclopaedia of the Social Sciences, MacMillan, New York, 1968, p. 100.

to the systematic learning accomplished in a formal instructional setting. Thus, the field of adult education may include "all the activities with an educational purpose that are carried on by people engaged in ordinary business of life". This aspect of adult education may be designated by several alternate synonyms: continuous learning, adult schools, education of adults, lifelong learning, night schools, further education, extension, and continuing education.

The discipline of adult education is concerned with the study of those educational activities for adults that occur in the formal instructional setting. Consequently, it can be defined more precisely: "Adult Education is the action of an external educational agent in purposefully ordering behaviour into planned systematic experiences that can result in learning for those for whom such activity is supplemental to their primary role in society, and which involves some continuity in an exchange relationship between the agent and the learner so that the educational process is under constant supervision and direction".

(iv) Adult, Continuing and Non-Formal Education*

Introduction

It is indeed a matter of great responsibility to be writing a trend report on a group of topics like Adult Education. Continuing Education and Non-formal Education (NFE). To some it may sound as though they are conceptually one and the same topic, if seen in a global perspective. Indeed, this is true to some extent. If adult education is seen as an activity of educational endeavour outside the ambit of organised and structured school or collegiate activity, then conceptually it is very much a part of non-formal education. Similarly, if continuing education is defined as educational pursuit as a part of lifelong education, it is certainly a part of non-formal education. There seems a lot of overlap and sometimes confusion in the terminologies that we use, and that, too, very often interchangeably. It is, therefore, necessary to have some kind of definition or operational definition in the Indian context because these are understood by educators as three distinct domains. Therefore, it would be necessary to clearly understand the three terms in our own perspective.

---

* N.K. Ambasht, Adult, Continuing and Non-Formal Education, In *Fifth Survey of Educational Research 1988-92: Trend Reports*, Indian National Council of Educational Research and Training, New Delhi, 1997, pp. 541-45.

Adult Education

It may be mentioned that in India adult education has travelled a long way, at least in programme implementation. In the early fifties it was known as the 'Social Education' programme. Then came a change in the areas of emphasis and the contents of the programme were given a slant. The changed programme came to be known as 'Fundamental Education', as citizenship education in a nascent democracy became of prime importance. Still further, down the line in the time perspective, in the mid-sixties it underwent a metamorphosis to become 'Fundamental Literacy'. Still further, it assumed the nomenclature of 'Non-formal, (Adult) Education' to ultimately revert back to 'Adult Education'. As may be apparent, it is the shift in emphasis on the approach and content of the programme that has necessitated the change in nomenclature. So, if we have to go into the historicity of the programme, we will have to look at everything that went under the names of social education, fundamental education, functional literacy, adult education and non-formal (adult) education.

Adult Education has now been defined as the education of those who are illiterate and are in the age-group 15-35 years (though older age-groups are also included but the emphasis is on 15-35 years) in the skills of literacy, functionality and awareness. Here literacy includes the three R's. But it should be clearly understood that the 3 R's are not the sole objective; it also includes learners' awareness of social, economic and political realities (conscientisation efforts) and the functional use of the skills learnt, including the 3 R's.

The nature of adult education is quite confusing in the sense that adult education denotes two levels of activity: one, educating the adults, and two, educating the adult educators. While at the first level it is the practice of adult education, at the second level it is theory and understanding of the basic concepts of adult learning. In other words it can be labelled as 'adult education as practice' and 'adult education as a discipline'. Those who are engaged in teaching and research in the field of adult education may be easily caught in the status trap because it is still an evolving field. It may be pertinent to point out that it is a discipline in the same sense as medicine or law or engineering. It is very much a subject worthy of academic study. Like medicine, law or engineering it is a discipline which draws its substance from various other disciplines and is related to a set of practices—to a profession. The Adult Education studies are linked to one profession—a profession directly related to serving the human society. The nature of adult education is such that it draws heavily from various disciplines like psychology, sociology, linguistics, philosophy, history, and so on. But at the same time the adult educationists (theoreticians) and the adult educators (practitioners) are not concerned with the whole of psychology or sociology, etc., but with that part of it that may be relevant to the needs of adult education.

Thus, one expects different scholars to refer to adult education using different terms and concepts, depending on who they are, the culture they represent, etc. To elucidate, in India, the adult education programme is primarily addressed to the age-group 15-35 years, and yet legally those in the age-bracket of 15-18 years are not adults for they are not eligible to vote. Adults have been variously defined in different cultures. Sometimes the roles performed by an individual in a society may be the criteria of adulthood; sometimes it is the physical conditions (puberty, etc.); and sometimes the age prescribed by law.

As mentioned earlier, the unsystematic nature of adult education terms and concepts is the product of cultural differences and scholars have defined adult education as a product of culture. Friedman, G. (1972) defined it thus:

> Adult education is a process which is part of cultural development, primarily the means of communication between the cultural systems of transmitters (inventors, researchers, creative minds, etc.) and the cultural system of receivers (i.e., the groups for whom adult education is intended).

Education being a macro-term encompasses many components (nursery, kindergarten, primary, secondary, senior secondary, tertiary, etc.), refers to all kinds of learning that take place, whether formal or non-formal (and some would include informal also). In this sequence, adult education can be regarded as a micro-term, since it refers to learning that takes place among the adults. Liveright and Haygood proposed that:

> Adult education is the process whereby persons who no longer (or did not) attend school on a regular and full-time basis undertake sequential and organised activities with the conscious intention of bringing about changes in information, knowledge, understanding or skills, application and attitudes; or for the purpose of identifying and solving personal and community

problems.

There are many scholars who tried to define adult education in the context of literate societies. Some of them are M. David, Edmund Bruner, Bryson, Scott Fletcher, Reeves, Fensler and Houle, Ohlinger and Morgan, etc. The Canadian Association of Adult Education also held a similar view as stated above. They all considered a situation where the percentage of literacy was very high, as a result of long experience of universal compulsory education up to the high school level. Under such circumstances only the very minimum number of population in such societies needed a basic literacy programme, while a large percentage was expected to take either remedial or continuing education or training to qualify themselves for jobs, to spend leisure wisely, and to acquire new knowlege and skills in the case of knowledge explosion. Thus, the concept of adult education of the Western scholars is only meaningful when it is examined in the background of the participants referred to by them.

Similarly, in developing countries the situation is no different. Here also, the cultural and educational background determines the nature and content of adult education. High illiteracy rates lay the greatest emphasis on literacy skills as the content of the adult education programme; the problem of free and compulsory primary education, and ignorance and conservatism, lead to the nature and content of the adult education programme in these countries.

The *International Directory of Adult Education* (UNESCO 1952) states:

> Adult education has been associated with the teaching of literacy and such remedial measures as night schools for adults who have missed the opportunity for schooling. The concept of adult education has been broadened considerably so as to cover the activity of a wide range of institutions or agencies and to include a content as wide as life itself.

The most typical defintion offered is by the National Institute of Adult Education (England and Wales) in 1970, which is quoted in the *Encyclopaedia Brittanica*, 15th Edition. It states that:

> It is any kind of education for the people who are old enough to work, to vote, to fight and to marry and who have completed

> the cycle of education (if any) commenced in the childhood. They want to make up for limited schooling (or no schooling), to learn the basic skills of trades or professions or to master new working processes. They may turn to it because they want to understand themselves and their world better and to act in the light of their understanding or they may go to the classes for the pleasure they get from developing talents and skills, intellectual, aesthetic, physical or practical. They may not even go to the classes. They may find what they want from books and broadcasts, or take guidance from a tutor they never meet. They may find education without a label by sharing in common pursuits with like-minded people.

Finally, it seems that the UNESCO definition of 1976 has come to stay in most parts of the world. According to it, adult education:

> denotes the entire body of organised educational processes, whatever the content, level and method, whether formal or otherwise, whether they prolong or replace initial education in schools, colleges and universities as well as in apprenticeship, whereby persons regarded as adults by the society to which they belong, develop their abilities, enrich their knowledge, improve their technical or professional qualifications and bring about changes in their attitude or behaviour in the twofold perspective of full personal development and participation in balanced and independent social, economic and cultural development.

Continuing Education

Continuing education, as the term indicates, is essentially a follow-up education. Its starting-point, unlike that of adult education, is undefined because it depends on from where one wishes to take off and continue one's education in whatever field one wants. It can be in the nature of post-literacy to post-postgraduation programmes or anything in between. But in most cases it could be highly flexible and unstructured—a point closer to the nature of non-formal education. Continuing education is obviously a component, or let's say an essential strategy, in lifelong education concept.

It may be seen that the concept of Continuing Education, which can be termed, to some extent, as lifelong education, is almost embraced under the definition of 'adult education' as given by UNESCO (1976). However, there are subtle differences. For example, that concept of lifelong education has both deliberate and non-deliberate education but in Continuing Education there is only the deliberate component which is involved. It may be either through formal or non-formal means.

Ambasht, N.K. while presenting a paper for the Programme Area-3, under action plan of 'Education for All' for the SAARC countries, made a distinction between adult education and continuing education thus:

> (Adult education) has a basic input of literacy activity, the (Continuing education) takes on from where the formal education and/or adult education leaves a learner. Therefore, the starting points for continuing education may be many—neo-literates, school drop-outs with permanent literacy skills, secondary school leavers, college and university leavers and those who have completed college/university education.

In the Indian context, the problem of continuing education is more pronounced at three levels, namely, neo-literates (to reinforce the literacy skills to make them permanent), school drop-outs and the secondary school leavers. For the college and university leavers or those who have completed these, there is a necessity of continuing education, though not as acute as to warrant priority over the neo-literates, and school drop-outs with permanent literacy. Women's welfare programmes and their related educational components are also included in this.

There have been myriad efforts with success in preparation and dissemination of post-literacy materials, more specifically under the National Literacy Mission's post-literacy programmes. Seen in the perspective of continuing education, quite a few agencies other than education have been engaged in this activity. Agriculture, health and family welfare departments, cooperatives, banks, etc., have been producing materials for their extension programmes which could also be used for continuing education purposes. Similarly, for the school leavers there is a lot of scope for material preparation in areas like "Do It Yourself", Vocational Education materials and materials for small-scale entrepreneurship programmes. Mention must be made of the systematic work in this regard of the NCERT which produced vocation-based-materials primarily meant for the senior secondary stage but which can be very well used for the continuing education programmes for school leavers.

Further, the Culture Centres established in the different regions of the country also provide a potential avenue to further the cause of continuing education. However, these have not been visualised as continuing education agents and whatever agencies have been responsible for these programmes have viewed them from their own perspective and have not considered them as an activity of continuing education; at least they have not said so.

Non-Formal Education

Non-formal education, as defined by Ahmad, M. and Coombs, P.H. is:

> Any organised educational activity outside the formal education system—whether operating separately or as an important feature of some broader activity—that is intended to serve identifiable learning clientele and learning objectives.

It may be noticed that this definition embraces all learning activities which is organized and is outside the formal educational system and, therefore, would embrace what is known as adult education, distance education, continuing education, lifelong education including hobby courses, etc. Earlier, Coombs, P.H. had put Non-formal Education as:

> Any organised programme of learning, carried on outside the framework, the rules and logistics of the formal-education system.

This definition also includes any educational activity irrespective of stages of education. Naik maintains that non-formal education includes all sectors of education outside the formal system. He includes adult education when he mentions four approaches to non-formal education. Paulsten, R.G. defined non-formal education as:

> Structured systematic non-school educational and training activities of relatively short duration in which sponsoring agencies seek concrete behavioural changes in fairly target population.

Adiseshiah, M.S. characterised non-formal education as:

> The out-of-school programmes which are learner-centred, whose tools and technologies are centred on the learner, and are as varied, disaggregated and diversified as the learning interest, need and capacity of each individual participant.

Rawat, D.S. and Majumdar, H.B. saw non-formal education as a means of universalising elementary education in the Indian perspective. Therefore, the target group, according to them converged to only 6-14 years age-group population.

Ambasht, N.K. gave an operational definition which was the basis of the entire approach of the National Policy of Education (1986) of the Government of India. He operationally defined non-formal education as:

> Planned and deliberate educational activities, or programmes for out-of-school children of 6-14 years age-group, leading to learning outcomes comparable to that of elementary schools.

He acknowledges that flexibility is the key word of non-formal education.

(B) HISTORICAL DEVELOPMENT

(a) (i) Introduction

The history of adult education in modern India is not very old. The mass movement for national feeedom provided the motive force for adult literacy and adult education. Gandhiji was the greatest worker in this cause. He knew that illiteracy constitutes a heavy drag on freedom and progress, and limits the mental horizon not merely of people but also their posterity.

He said, "I would have adult education, nor as we ordinarily understand it, but the education of parents so that they can undertake adequately the moulding of their children".

Prior to 1937, the literacy campaigns, though not of much quantitative importance, helped to create public interest in the problem. In 1937, with the advent of Congress ministries in the provinces, large-scale campaigns to liquidate adult illiteracy were launched, but the enthusiasm petered out after the resignation of the ministries in 1942. The Central Advisory Board of Education in 1939, appointed a Committee of

Adult Education which recommended that the objectives of the movement should be to teach the illiterate adult the three R's, and to impart knowledge closely correlated to his working life and give him a grounding in citizenship. The Board incorporated several recommendations of the Committee in its *Report on the Post-War Educational Development* (1944). The Report made the following observations: the main emphasis, for sometime to come, should be on literacy, although some provisions must also be made for adult education proper; instructions must be intelligible and interesting to the students and closely related to their occupations, personal interests, social and economic conditions; fullest possible use of visual and mechanical aids should be made; it is necessary to provide adequate libraries; the state must accept primarily responsibility for tackling the problem, though every effort should be made to enlist the help of voluntary agencies; and universities should expand and popularize the work of their extramural departments.

With the Independence of the country in 1947, a new phase began. The Central Advisory Board of Education in 1948 set up a sub-committee under the Chairmanship of Shri Mohan Lal Saksena. The sub-committee emphasized the need for general education of the common masses, the provision of funds by the provincial governments for adult education and the removal of 50 per cent illiteracy in the next five years. The Central Advisory Board of Education in its 15th meeting (1949) designated adult education as 'Social Education'. Since then, many new experiments have been made in the states and many new paths have been forged. West Bengal and Bihar emphasized recreational and cultural activities; Madras and Mysore laid stress on the organization of libraries; Bombay has given a successful trial to a new experiment known as Gram Shiksha Mohim movement. The role of the Central Government in the promotion of adult education programmes is very much limited. It can at best stimulate action in the field of adult education through research, pilot projects and clearing house functions.

A National Board of Adult Education has been established on the recommendation of the Education Commission. In the Presidential Address to the first meeting of the National Board held in May, 1970, Prof. V.K.R.V. Rao, the then Union Minister for Education and Youth Services posed the crucial problem of adult education and suggested a solution :

> Looking back, we find that the percentage of literacy in India has risen from 6.2 to 33 during the period 1901 to 1969. But the

> number of illiterates, which was 298 million in 1951 has now increased to 349 million in 1969 ... What I am really concerned about is the population in the age-group 15-44. As I have said earlier, the illiterate among them is likely to be 150 million or so. By using conventional norms of making an adult literate, we will need something like over Rs. 4,500 million to make this age-group literate. We have no resources of this order available today, nor do I imagine, will we have these resources available in the near future. What do we do then? Can we not launch upon a big national movement in our country, where all educated people in every mohalla, village, taluka, district, city and town, factories and farms, take a pledge that they will make their brothers and sisters literate?

He concluded with a appeal to his country :

> On this red-letter day, in the history of adult education, I would like to appeal to my friends here and countrymen to realise the gravity of this situation and to take up the task of liquidation of illiteracy in India and lend their support in terms of their time, energy and other resources. Let us ensure that light spreads throughout the length and breadth of this country. Then only can we breathe a really fresh air of hope and fulfilment and thus usher in real freedom to our country.

(a) (ii) Movement for Adult Literacy

Before 1921

No significant measures were taken to liquidate adult literacy. There were only a few primary schools conducted at night primarily for the part-time education of children who were employed, and incidentally of those adults who would like to attend. In spite of the recommendation of the Indian Education Commission (1882-83) that night schools be encouraged wherever practicable, very little was done. The period between 1902 and 1917 marked a large decline in the number of night-schools. The question of adult education began to engage public attention during 1917-22, as the interest in the problem was stimulated by the discussion on the franchise and the passing of Government of India Act, 1919. The United Provinces, the Punjab, Madras, Bombay and Bengal took a lead. The work in the night-schools, however, continued to be largely experimental.

1921-1937

The movement made considerable progress after the transfer of education to the control of Indian ministers in 1921. In 1927, there were 11,158 institutions for men and 47 for women. Unfortunately, the interest in the problem waned with the economic depression that set in after 1927. The number of adult night-schools declined so much that in 1937, there were only 2,016 institutions for men, and 11 for women. Nevertheless, the sixteen years of the diarchical rule (1921-37) were significant because this was the period when valuable spade-work was done for the future development of adult education, when the spirit of service to expand the movement was mobilized among the students and the local bodies, and co-operative societies were energised to assist in the work.

1937-1947

When the Congress Ministries accepted office in 1937 they organized large scale campaigns to liquidate adult illiteracy. The objectives of the Adult Education Movement Act : (1) to teach the illiterate adult, and (2) to impart knowledge closely correlated to the working life and to give him a grounding in citizenship. Mere literacy without the broader aspects of education was not considered enough, as it would not equip an adult to lead a better and fuller life. The work was taken up with great zeal in the States and the Provinces, but unfortunately the movement slowed down with the resignation of the Congress Ministries in 1940. The work was restarted as soon as the popular ministries assumed office in 1946, and the succeeding period recorded great progress in the field.

After 1947

After Independence the Government of India could no longer remain indifferent to the movement. In 1948, the main objectives and techniques of adult education were formulated on the conviction that mere literacy was not enough, that the adult should be made a responsible citizen to the new society. To distinguish it from the earlier campaign of literacy and to stress its socializing aspect, the term 'adult education' was gradually abandoned in favour of 'social education'. Up to the end of the First Five-Year Plan, the social education activity was mostly confined in the state sector though a few central schemes were initiated as pilot projects in selected areas by setting up community centres, janta colleges and library service. In the Second Five-Year Plan, the National Fundamental Education Centre for the training of district social education officers was set up. A country-wide library service was also introduced.

1. Adult Education as part of Elementary Education was included in the Minimum Needs Programme in the Sixth Five-Year Plan. The target was 100 per cent coverage of the age-group 15-35 years by 1990. Eradication of adult illiteracy with the help of students and voluntary agencies is an important element of the Twenty Point Programme. During the first two years of the Sixth Plan (1980-81 and 1981-82), a total coverage of 56,89,724 adult illiterates in the age-group of 15-35 was achieved.

2. Although the implementation of the programme rests largely with the States, the Centre plays a crucial role in a number of respects. The Centre provides full financial assistance for the 386 Rural Functional Literacy Projects (RFLP), spread across the various States and UTs. These projects can cover at an optimum level 30.50 lakhs of adults in a year. The projects are mainly located in districts with a literacy rate below the national average of 36.17 per cent. During 1983 total enrolment was about 21 lakhs. It is necessary to step up the enrolment so as to come closer to the anticipated coverage. Besides, the states have their own State Adult Education Projects (SAEP). During 1983-84, the enrolment was about 17.22 lakhs. Unfortunately, a number of States have not given adequate priority to adult education and have not matched what the Government of India spends in the respective states. Steps need to be taken to ensure SAEP does not fall short of the Central Programme of RFLP.

3. The Centre has also provided assistance to voluntary agencies for conducting Adult Education Centres and to State Resource Centres (SRC) for training, preparation of literacy materials, research and evaluation. Currently, 68 Universities and 705 Colleges are involved in student run Adult Education Centres. The expenditure on this account is met from the budget of the University Grants Commission. The number of Centres so run is nearly 9,000 and the number of learners covered is 2.5 lakhs. It is estimated that if we succeed in overcoming the difficulties faced by students in running the programme and in instilling enthusiasm in a larger number of students, the coverage can be doubled in the current year and expanded further in the years to come.

4. The Central Directorate of Adult Education functions as a

National Resource Centre, intimately involved in training activities, curriculum development, preparation of the materials, evaluation, use of the media and guidance and counselling as needed. Over the years, the directorate has developed considerable expertise in these areas. The Ministry also keeps in close touch with the States through the Area Officers who are senior officials of the Ministry entrusted with specific States or Union Territories for the purpose of close monitoring through systematic visits and discussions. Apart from the programmes of the Ministry of Education, some amount of adult literacy work is also carried on through a programme known as Functioning Literacy for Adult Women (FLAW) which is a component of the Integrated Child Development Service (ICDS) of the Ministry of Social Welfare.

5. Some of the major difficulties that are met within the running of Adult Education Centres are : (i) Inadequacy of Instructors, especially women and those belonging to Scheduled Castes and Scheduled Tribes, (ii) Insufficient facilities in backward areas in regard to accommodation, lighting, etc., and (iii) Difficulties of adult learners in attending the literacy classes regularly, on account of having to migrate in search of employment.

(b) Non-Formal Education (Adult and Social Education)*

During the last century no attempts were made to make the masses literate. *Charles Wood, in 1854*, proposed a policy for combating ignorance and making efforts towards adult literacy, but no concrete steps were taken. The Indian Education Commission of 1882 pointed the existence of night schools in Madras, Bombay and Bengal. But by the start of the present century their number had declined. The Government of India Act of 1919 came into force in 1921. Under this Act, Indian Ministers took interest in solving problems of adult education. In 1929, the Hartog Committee claimed that there were 11,000 institutions for adult education in British India and nearly 300,000[1] people were attending these institutions.

In 1939, the Adult Education Committee[2] of the Central Advisory Board of Education made a few recommendations on adult education. Some of the most important ones were as follows : (i) efforts should be directed in the beginning to persuade illiterates voluntarily to undergo

---

**Source* : Kuldip Kaur, *Education in India (1781-1985): Policies, Planning*, Centre for Research in Rural and Industrial Development, 1985.

Note : Table numbers have been given to conform chapter number.

instruction, failing which, ways and means of bringing pressure to bear on illiterates should be explored; (ii) the form in which instruction was given must be intelligible and interesting to the student and the instruction should be closely related to his occupation, his personal interest and the social and economic conditions under which he lived; (iii) if necessary, separate classes should be organised for boys between twelve and sixteen and those attending evening classes; (iv) the possibility of making a period of social services obligatory on all students in universities and pupils in the proper forms of High Schools should be carefully examined; in the meantime an appeal should be made "to all educated persons, and in particular to government servants, to render voluntary service in connection with the literacy campaign" and (v) mechanical aids to learning such as the radio, the cinema, the gramophone and the magic lantern could be used with great effect in adult education.[3] During the short-lived regime of the Congress Ministries, adult education made rapid progress.

The Central Advisory Board of Education brought out *in 1944 a comprehensive Plan of Post-War Educational Developments in India, popularly known as the Sargent Plan*. Among its recommendations on adult education, the following were important: (i) although the main emphasis in the beginning might be placed on the liquidation of illiteracy, adult education in the full sense must be provided for those already literate, and this should progressively increase as illiteracy disappeared; (ii) even with the introduction of a universal system of social education there would remain over a crore of illiterates (age-group 20-40); hence the need to regard adult education as complementary to free and compulsory primary education; plans should be made to solve the problem of adult education within twenty years, the first five years being devoted to the training of teachers and other necessary preparations; (iii) the responsibility for adult education must rest with the State but every efforts should be made to ensure the aid of suitable voluntary organisations whenever available; and (iv) comprehensive arrangements on the lines set out in the Adult Education Committee's report should form an integral part of any national system of education. The proposals of the Sargent Plan were estimated to cost a little less than Rs. 3 crore during the entire period of twenty years needed for the complete liquidation of illiteracy. But due to the financial constraints the Sargent Plan was never put into operation.[4]

The Central Advisory Board of Education appointed the *Adult (Social) Education Committee in January 1948 under the*

Chairmanship of Mohanlal Saxena. It recommended that Provincial Governments should accept the aims and objectives of social education and set up Social Education Councils to assist Directors of Public Instruction. The Councils were to suggest legislation or other administrative action of conscripting students, government employees and refugees to promote the social education. The target was to set up one education centre in each primary school and two in each secondary school. The scheme for social education was designed to impart education to people between the ages of 12 and 45. The recommendations of the Committee were approved by the Central Advisory Board of Education at its 15th meeting held at Allahabad in January 1949.

The work of social education gathered momentum once again when, *in 1949, the Central Advisory Board of Education adopted the following twelve-point programme especially for Delhi*: (i) the village school will be the centre of instruction, welfare work, sports and recreation for the entire village; (ii) separate time will be allotted to children, adolescence and grown-ups; (iii) certain days in the week will be reserved exclusively for girls and women; (iv) a number of motor vans fitted with projectors and loud-speakers will be secured to visit each village school atleast once a week to show films and magic lanterns and play recording of talks played; (v) schools will be provided with radio sets and arrangements will be made for broadcasting special programmes for school children, adolescents and grown-up people in the light of the scheme of social education; (vi) popular dramas will be organised in the schools and from time to time prizes given for the best plays produced; (vii) there will be provision for teaching national and community songs; (viii) arrangements will be made for giving simple instruction in some craft or industry suited to the locality; (ix) lectures will be arranged in co-operation with the Ministries of Health, Agriculture and Labour to instruct villagers in the simple laws of social hygiene, methods of agriculture, cottage industries and co-operative activities; (x) in co-operation with the Ministry of Information and Broadcasting suitable films and slides will be shown from time to time, arrangements will be made for visits of public men to speak to the villagers on problems of national importance and help and assistance of public bodies interested in constructive work will be sought to give effect to the programme of social education; (xi) arrangements will be made for organising group games and competitions will be held from time to time between different schools and villages; and (xii) periodic exhibitions, fair and excursions will be organised. The same year a Conference of Provincial Education

Ministers was summoned to consider the implementation of the scheme.

The Conference met in New Delhi in February 1949 and accepted the proposal of the Government of India that out of the sum of Rs. 1 crore earmarked by the Centre for social education, Rs. 10 lakh should be reserved for central activities and the remaining Rs. 90 lakh should be distributed among the provinces in proportion to the number of illiterates in them. In Delhi, the scheme of social education was in operation for several years. In 1949, one hundred and twenty-five centres of social education were established and the Adult Education Department of Delhi Municipality also made arrangements for the training of social workers.

In April 1951, the Ministry of Education of the Government of India called a Conference of eminent educationists to discuss the production of suitable reading material for neo-literates. Many useful suggestions were made and the Conference agreed that there was need for the following types of literature: (i) daily news-sheet; (ii) an illustrated fortnightly or monthly, which would contain material on sports, health, hygiene, agriculture and world news; (iii) graded primers; (iv) general literature for adults; (v) guide books for teachers. Some State Governments drew up programmes for producing suitable literature for adults.

The Committee on Social Education Literature, appointed by the Government of India in 1952, discussed this subject further. Its most important recommendations were that the Central Government should produce a teachers' handbook (preparation of this was undertaken in 1952), guide-books for teachers and a bibliography on social education books in various Indian languages. It was of the opinion that the publication of social education periodicals and production of graded primers should be left to private publishers, the State Governments being responsible only for laying down specifications and standards. It was also suggested that writers should be encouraged to write through competitions and prizes. The recommendations of the Committee were noted by the Central Advisory Board of Education in March 1952.

The *First Five Year Plan 1951-56* expressed the opinion that social education in the country was essentially experimental and needed central guidance. It proposed that the work should be co-ordinated with similar activities in Basic Education and common committee of experts should advise the Centre in the matter of initiating and financially aiding experimental work in both these fields in the states and guide it, assess the results and make them available to other States. A common national platform, where the various agencies could meet at intervals for mutual discussion was so necessary for evolving a common outlook and securing co-ordination of different agencies, had already been provided by for the Indian Adult Education Association. The Director of Social Education in state should be a man highly trained in community organisation and should be able to advise and help the state in the matter of public participation in its various development programmes. He should have a body of advisers representing important non-official agencies.

At the field level it was mostly a task of reorganising and co-ordinating existing agencies rather than of creating new ones. The problem was different in rural and urban areas. In rural areas the following measures were proposed to be taken: (i) educational institutions should become examples of self-help, democratic community living, co-operative labour and intelligent handling of economic activity. Education should centre on agriculture and cottage industries and educational institutions should be well equipped with agricultural farms, craft workshops, etc. Educational institutions should thereby become excellent centres for spreading ideas for improving social and economic life. Basic schools which had already been conceived on the above lines, had special significance in this regard. All facilities should, therefore, be provided at the basic training centres so that the teachers were trained as first class social education workers; (ii) the village level workers, wherever provided, should also be stationed in a school, as far as possible. Under his guidance even an ordinary school could begin to make some contribution, which would also prepare it for ultimate conversion into a basic school; (iii) besides the above agencies, the state should provide, wherever possible, community organisers, at least one for 50 villages, to make use of help, guide and co-ordinate the activities of all agencies working in their respective spheres. These should also be attached to educational institutions.

In urban areas quite a large number of agencies existed and the key problem was to co-ordinate their activities for a comprehensive programme of social education. For this purpose City or Town Social Education Councils were to be instituted, where they did not exist already, each consisting of representatives of the various agencies operating in the town concerned. This Council was to distribute items of social education work among the various agencies, according to their capacity and willingness to undertake it. Social education in industrial areas in towns had special importance in view of the dull and drab conditions of life prevailing in urban areas. Here the employer and the labour unions were expected to co-operate to achieve the desired end.

The different proposals led to the formulation of a new programme of social education. On the administrative side the Ministry of Education took upon itself the functions of co-ordination, guidance and financial assistance to the states, though some programmes, on a limited scale, were assigned to the Ministries of Labour, Railway and Defence. The CABE appointed a Standing Committee on social education. On the execution side, 116 Model Community Centres and 454 School-cum-Community Centres were established. A scheme for integrated library service, and for starting Janata Colleges for training teachers and social education workers was introduced. The progress of the schemes under this head can be judged from the Table 1.1.

Table 1.1: Progress of Adult Education

(Figures in 000's)

	1950-51 Actual	1954-55 Estimates	1951-55 Estimates
1. Social Education/ Literacy Centres/ Adult Schools	48.6	57.0	8.4 (additional)
2. Number of Adults on Rolls	1,580.8	1,150.0	4,424.0 (total)
3. Number of Adults made literate	600.6	490.0	1,955.0 (total)
4. Literacy Teachers	40.5	43.0	2.4 (additional)

Source: *First Five Year Plan: Progress Report*, 1954-55, Planning Commission, 1956, p. 185.

The State Government received grants for opening Janata Colleges and Social Education Centres. Grants were also given for production of literature for neo-literates in the regional languages, books for children and general books. Other fields of development included integrated library service for each state, district and central libraries, youth camps, inter-university youth festivals and youth hostels. A few minor schemes were also put into operation, such as centres for the blind, promotion of rural higher education, assistance for social and child welfare, building national theatre and opening a National Centre of Basic Education.

During the plan period nearly five crore of rupees were spent on social education. A National Fundamental Education Centre for research and training of higher personnel in the field of social education was set up towards the end of the plan and departments of social education in a number of states were strengthened. During the period 1951-55, the Ministry of Education helped the establishment of 145 Model Community Centres and 454 School Community Centres, 25 Integrated Library Services, 21 Janata Libraries and 137 District Libraries, etc.[5]

The Census of 1951 showed that only 16.6 per cent of the population were literate and if children below 10 years were excluded the proportion went-up to 20 per cent. Apart from the low percentage of literacy there was serious disparity in literacy between men (24.9 per cent) and women (7.9 per cent) and between the urban population (34.6 per cent) and the rural population (12.1 per cent). Rapid social and economic progress along democratic lines and widespread illiteracy are rarely compatible with each other. As essential reforms proposed in the system of education were to be carried out, facilities for continuation classes and social education classes at various levels were to be developed. The State Plans provided for the opening of literacy and social education centres, training social education workers and organisers, libraries, publication of literature, audio-visual education and establishment of Janata Colleges. The total allotment in the plan for social education was about Rs. 15 crore, including about Rs. 10 crore in the National Extension and Community Development Programme.[6] An expenditure of Rs. 1 crore was incurred during 1959-60 as against Rs. 70 lakh spent in the previous year. The Community Development and National Extension Service Programmes also covered social education schemes. The National Fundamental Education Centre continued its research on social education workers.

The National Fundamental Education Centre was established on the recommendation of the CABE and with the co-operation of UNESCO. It had the following objectives: (i) training district social organisers; (ii) producing literacy and audio-visual material; (iii) co-ordinating the work in different states; and (iv) conducting research and providing information. Besides, a Worker's Social Education Institute was set up at Indore with Central aid. A National Book Trust was established at Delhi. Financial assistance was given for the production of literature for neo-literates and organising literacy workshops for authorship pertaining to adult education literature. The total number of adult literacy centres started was 1,62,600 and the number of adult illiterates converted into literates was 40,54,530. The percentage of literates increased from 17 to 24 during the decade 1951-1961[7] and 28.6 per cent in 1966.

Social education and adult literacy had to be developed as extension activities undertaken by educational institutions, especially village schools, in collaboration with panchayats and cooperatives and voluntary organisations. The broad aim of the Third Plan was that wherever a group of persons sufficient to constitute a class desired to attain literacy, the requisite facilities by way of teachers and teaching materials were to be made readily available. Every educational institution was to be involved in this effort, and individual teachers participating in it were to be given suitable honorarium. At the same time, the village panchayats and other agencies were to make their due contribution towards the effort, while Social Education Organisers, Block Education Officers and individual educational institutions were to work closely together to place the facilities needed at the service of local communities. The Panchayat Samities, Village Panchayats and voluntary organisations were to be primarily responsible to create and maintain popular enthusiasm and develop adult education and literacy on a continuing basis in a manner related organically to their own needs and conditions. At every step the local leadership, the teachers and the voluntary workers were to be drawn into the movement for the expansion of literacy both among men and women. Proposals for a large scale programme of adult literacy on these lines were drawn up by the Ministry of Education in consultation with the Ministry of Community Development and Cooperation, and it was hoped that appreciable progress would be realised during the Third Plan. The Third Plan provided a sum of Rs. 62 crore under Social Education, against only Rs. 2 crore spent in the first four years on such items as the development of library services in Delhi, National Book Trust and training of social education workers. The main provision for social education was included in the Community Development budget. Unfortunately, the impact of the emergency, in the field of general education, was pronounced on cultural programmes and social education.

The Third Plan continued by and large the schemes launched by the Second *Five Year Plan*. These included in establishement of social education institutions (Janata Colleges) at various places, running of community centres, starting of Youth Clubs (like Gram Raksha Dal, Farmers' Club), running Mahila Samitis in each development block, training of social education workers, organising seminars, providing post-literacy facilities, setting up public libraries, producing and using documentary films and producing literature for neo-literates. Maharashtra started the Gram Shikshan Mohim. Teachers, students and other educated persons offered their services on a voluntary basis and the expenditure was borne by the Panchayats. This was a model scheme for other State Governments. The Central Government strengthened the library service. Delhi Public Library was started in 1952, and State Governments were given assistance to start State libraries. Thirteen States had started district libraries. A Hindi encyclopaedia (Hindi Vishva Bharati) in 10 volumes was published. Twenty workshops for training authors were organised. Delhi University started correspondence courses in 1962. The Universities of Mysore, Poona and Rajasthan also organised Adult Education Departments. The Indian University Adult Education Association was also set up. A new term, 'Functional Literacy' came into existence.

The Mysore State Education Council organised six Vidya-Peeths as centres of education in better methods of agriculture and farms industries. Jaipur University started the Adult Education Department to provide facilities for higher learning for adults. The Indian Adult Education Association, New Delhi, organised a number of seminars. The All India Radio broadcast programmes for villagers from 30 stations under a joint project with UNESCO. A television series on popular topics were also started. Programmes on farmers' education and functional literacy were also extended to 100 districts in the different states.[8]

In 1963, the Union Ministry of Education published a pamphlet defining the concept of adult and social education: (i) social education meant adult education; (ii) social education was a subject for necessary social change; (iii) social education was meant for the development of the social, economic, political and moral life of the individual as well as the society; and (iv) social education was a subject for better work, better rest, better use of leisure and better recreation, etc.

The Indian Education Commission 1964-66, appointed by the Government of India, under the Chairmanship of D.S. Kothari was the first body to give serious thought to the problem of social education. It discussed this issue, however, under adult education. It recommended that an effective programme of adult education in the Indian context should involve: (i) liquidation of illiteracy; (ii) continuing education; (iii) correspondence courses; (iv) libraries; (v) role of universities in adult education; and (vi) organization and administration of adult education.[9] According to this Commission, there should be 80 per cent literacy by the year 1976. But this target has not yet been achieved.[10]

During the *Fourth Five Year Plan 1969-74* efforts were proposed to be made to spread literacy amongst adults through the mobilisation of voluntary workers and local community resources. Pilot projects were to be initiated in selected districts to begin with and the programme was to be extended to other areas in the light of experience. For the development of the programme, assistance was to be sought from industry, students working under the National Service Scheme, and from voluntary organisations which were to be assisted financially and given technical guidance. The programme of Farmers' Education and Functional Literacy, in the high yielding variety areas, was to be extended to 100 districts and was to cover 10 lakh adult farmers. Adult education was to continue to be an integral part of the community development programme. The University Departments of Adult Education were to be helped to take up pilot projects, to conduct research and organise extension and extra-mural lectures. The National Board of Adult Education was set up to advise Government on the development programmes and for enlisting the cooperation of the interests and agencies concerned. Further development of television and the experiments with satellite communication, which were to begin from 1972-73, were expected to provide significant experience for education, especially adult education.[11]

Functional literacy was the main programme to be developed among farmers. It was to be integrated with plans for increased agricultural production. The centrally sponsored schemes included the following: (i) assistance to voluntary organisations; (ii) production of literature for neo-literates; (iii) farmers' education and functional literacy; and (iv) social education workers' institutes. The unfortunate part of the Fourth Five Year Plan was that a very meagre share was allocated to social education. Out of a total outlay of Rs. 809 crore, social education received only Rs. 10 crore, a mere 1.2 per cent.

During the Fourth Five Year Plan, the most important development in the field of social education was the formation of the National Board of Adult Education by the then Union Minister for Education and Youth Services, under the Chairmanship of V.K.R.V. Rao. The programme of farmers' education and functional literacy were extended to 100 districts. About 100 Nehru Yuvak Kendras were constituted for implementing programmes of national development. New literature was prepared for the neo-literates with the help of UNESCO. Awards were given to 419 books, and an adult encyclopaedia was published under the title

"Gyansarovar". Workshops were conducted as a part of literacy camps.[12] The Central Education Advisory Council, at its 31st meeting set up standards for adult education. These were: (i) recognition of about 350 words; (ii) ability to write numerals upto 100; (iii) ability to read simple charts, posters, etc.; (iv) knowledge of objects of daily utility; and (v) ability to write simple sentences and names. All these suggestions were implemented in the different adult education centres run by Government or private bodies.

The Committee of Members of Parliament on Education appointed by the Ministry of Education, Government of India in 1967, reviewed the recommendations of the Indian Education Commission 1964-65. It also suggested that in order to reduce new additions to the ranks of adult illiterates, part-time literacy classes should be organized for grown-up children (age-group 11-17), who did not attend school or had lapsed into illiteracy. It further recommended that all employees in large commercial, industrial and other concerns should be made functionally literate within a prescribed period of their employment and a lead in this direction should be given by the industrial capitalists in the public sector. Similarly, teachers, students and educational institutions should be actively involved in literacy campaigns, especially as a part of the social or national service programme. The achievement of literacy should be sustained by providing the neo-literates attracting reading material and library services. The Committee also recommended that adult or continuing education should be developed through facilities for part-time or own-time education and through the expansion and improvement of library services, educational broadcasting and television. The development of extension services in the universities was considered to be of great significance in this context. It was suggested that the universities in particular should organise special extension programmes to train rural leadership.

The Government of India through the National Policy of Education announced in 1968 virtually endorsed the recommendations concerning spread of literacy and adult education put forth by the Committee of Members of Parliament. It, however, laid special emphasis on the education of the young practising farmers and on the training of youth for self-employment.[13] The National Policy on Education stressed that there was a great need for the development of part-time education and correspondence courses not only for university students but also for secondary school students, teachers, agricultural, industrial and other workers.[14]

In 1970, the National Board of Adult Education made the following recommendations: (i) national compaigns for literacy should be launched every year; (ii) there should be an intensive follow-up of these efforts through the publication of literature for neo-literates and the establishment of well furnished libraries; (iii) the Ministry of Education should give priority to programmes concerned with eradication of illiteracy and take necessary follow-up action with regard to the adult education programme; (iv) pilot projects on Adult Education should be started in various parts of the country; (v) State Governments should adopt Gram Shikshan Mohim as started by Maharashtra Government for the eradiction of adult illiteracy; (vi) more time should be given to adult education programmes over the radio; (vii) Boards of Adult Education should be established in all the States and Union Territories; (viii) training for adult education should be imparted to the teachers and workers by universities and other concerned institutions; and (ix) adequate funds should be provided for the development of adult education and expenditure in this respect should be considered under the head of national development. Most of the recommendations are being implemented.

The statement, issued by the Conference on Continuing Education and Universities in Asian and the South Pacific Region on December 26-30, 1970, spelt out the role that universities should play in continuing education, and suggested the following programmes: (i) professional courses designed to up-date the knowledge of teachers, scientists, doctors, engineers, etc.; (ii) courses in human relations, leadership and executive skills and in decision making processes; (iii) courses in the humanities and liberal arts; (iv) courses of remedial or re-conversion nature; (v) action research and training; (vi) the production of curriculum materials for continuing education; (vii) training programme for leaders in continuing education, community development projects and in voluntary organizations; and (viii) education for political understanding. The Conference recommended the steps the Universities should take to fulfil the above tasks: (i) establishment of a department, division or unit of continuing education, ascertaining the needs of the community; (ii) setting up a broad-based Advisory Committee to the department headed by the Vice-Chancellor; (iii) making available the necessary physical facilities, such as libraries, laboratories, residence halls etc.; and (iv) involving the community in the planning and conduct of programmes.[15]

The International Commission on the *Development of Education*

1971-72, established by UNESCO under the Chairmanship of Edgar Faure, laid special stress on non-formal education. It pointed out that there could be many methods and means of education, such as full-time education, part-time education, education by correspondence and also many forms of self-education making direct use of information sources. Uninterrupted study was, therefore, certainly not the only conceivable method. Individual should have the freedom to make choice as to the means and methods of education—formal or non-formal. The Commission recommended: (i) each person should be able to choose his path more freely, in a more flexible framework, without being compelled to give up using educational services for life if he leaves the system; (ii) artificial or outmoded barriers between different educational disciplines, courses and levels, and between formal and non-formal education should be abolished; recurrent education should be gradually introduced and made available, in the first place, to certain categories of the active population.

The Commission was also seized of the problem of adult education and literacy. It observed that the normal culmination of the educational process was adult education. It, therefore, recommended that educational strategies in the coming decade should include rapid development of adult education, in school and out of school, as one of their priority objectives. The Commission pointed out that adult education did not merely consist of literacy. It observed that literacy training was only a 'moment' and an element in adult education. For the spread of literacy, it, however, recommended "in all areas where there is widespread illiteracy, programmes organised for the adult population must include a strong literacy campaign. Action must be taken in two ways: it must aim firstly at functional literacy among strongly motivated sections of the working population; and secondly, at mass of literacy when conditions are appropriate and, above all, when social development conditions—political, economic and cultural—are suitable for active large scale participation by the people". The Commission stressed that in order to avoid past disappointments, the literacy programmes should be linked to basic education on civic life and the world of work.[16]

Providing basic education to the primary producers is a highly desirable aim for a democratically functioning society. Past experience in the field of social education needs to be combined into an effective strategy which should optimise the use of available resources, mobilise community support and develop and exploit fully the potentialities of adult education for economic and social development. For this purpose, adult education should be linked effectively with such key national tasks as elementary education, health and family planning, agricultural extension, cooperation, etc. To strengthen the motivation of the adults, their education should be effectively linked with their activities. The modern mass media should also be pressed into service and educational institutional brought into the programme of adult education, especially through the National Service Scheme.

The framers of the Fifth Five Year Plan 1974-79 proposed to integrate adult education with all development programmes where large masses were involved as producers or beneficiaries. The agencies concerned should be responsible for organising adult education programmes for their clientele. They were to be assisted by the Education Departments which were to produce literature suitable for neo-literates. The programmes of adult education and functional literacy were to be supported by a network of village and block libraries. The programmes already started by different organisations, such as the Vidyapeeths of Mysore, Polyvalent Centres of Bombay, Central Social Welfare Board, Jamia Milia Islamia, Delhi, the Gram Shikshan Mohim of Maharashtra were to be expanded. Extension education for occupational adjustment and personnel development were to be promoted by the universities. Youth centres/clubs, set up in the urban and rural areas, as also the Nehru Yuvak Kendras were also to become the focus for informal education. The expansion of book production programmes, accompanied by an equal emphasis on ensuring sales of the materials produced, were to receive emphasis. A quick survey was to be carried out to ascertain the current position and to help produce books at low prices on subjects of interest. High priority was to be given to the publication of original works in the Indian languages by top level subject specialists.

Machinery had to be set up at the central level, on the pattern of the one for the coordination of work in the Hindi-speaking states to coordinate the work of the production of university level books in the non-Hindi speaking states. National and regional training institutes were to be set up for training personnel in editing, translation, illustration, production and sales to support the expansion of the book production programme. These institutes were to carry out research and surveys as well various fields of publishing. The National Book Trust was to concentrate on the production, promotion and distribution of books and the training of personnel involved in publishing. Surveys and studies were to be conducted to provide basic data and information to help formulate and implement effectively the national policy of book development. The National Book Development Board was to be strengthened suitably to implement the Fifth Plan schemes.

The library programmes were to be stepped up. Central and State libraries were to be strengthened in respect of buildings, acquisition of books, staff, etc. The deficiencies of the district, block and village level libraries were to be removed. The attempt was to develop a library system at the district level so that the district library was properly linked to the smaller units and could feed them. The States were also to be assisted by the Raja Ram Mohan Roy Library Foundation to strengthen the district, block and village level libraries with the strengthening of existing programmes of non-formal education, about 16 lakh participants were expected to be covered and the existing programmes were intended to be reviewed.[17]

The Sabanayagam Working Group on Adult Education 1977 was appointed in August 1977 to review developments in the field of adult education, advise on the approach and priorities for the *Sixth Plan 1978-83*, formulate proposals indicating financial implications and structural arrangements, and to apportion the areas of responsibility among the Centre, States and voluntary agencies. The working group suggested that under the adult education programme, special priority should be given to women, scheduled tribes, schedules castes, etc. It also recommended that Central and State Governments, political parties and other associations, voluntary organisations, educational institutions, employers and local bodies should be involved in the nation-wide awakening regarding adult education programmes. These recommendations were to be implemented through a net work of projects.

Soon after the Janata Government came to power, the then Education Minister, P.C. Chunder declared in Parliament that the government's decision was to accord the highest priority to universalisation of primary education and adult education. He held long discussions with the educationists and field workers in adult education and a Draft Policy Statement on adult education was formulated in June 1977. The Ministry of Education prepared an outline of the National Adult Education Programmes in October, 1977. The National Board of Adult Education was constituted and at its first meeting, held in November, 1997, the National Adult Education Programme was considered elaborately.

The Draft National Policy on Education 1979 estimated that 2300 lakh of our adult population were illiterates belonging mostly to the poorest and the most neglected sections of the nation. Their contribution to national well being could have been far greater than it was if they received some education. Their condition was such that they were unable to take advantage of the benefits available to them under the development plans and continued to be exposed to exploitation and social disabilities. The nation should deem it its important duty to give education to them. The Draft Policy maintained that the National Adult Education Programme should be implemented with urgency and sustained vigour. The immediate target should be to educate under this programme 1000 lakh in a period of five years, so that universal literacy could become a reality in our country within the shortest possible time. The adult education programme should mean not only acquisition of literacy and numeracy, but also functional development and social awareness, with a view to cultivating the habit of self-education.

Adult education was made an integral part of the Revised Minimum Needs Programme, whose thrust was: (a) to reach the poor people, (b) coordinate all such programmes with developmental activities, and (c) to integrate them with area planning. The RMNP, including adult education could not be considered the sole responsibility of one ministry, department or agency. Since this massive programme stipulated a large investment, its operational strategy had to be carefully worked out. The most important point that had to be kept in view was that the programme had to be community oriented. Agencies and instruments for this programme had to be so identified that the maximum coordination took place between the local community and the government.

The programme was to be started through multiple agencies with priority to voluntary agencies in so far as they were available. The involvement of teachers, students, trade, industry, youth and women's organisations, social workers, developmental departments, municipalities, panchayats and other local bodies was to be ensured right from the beginning. Since the real problem of adult illiteracy existed in the rural areas, special efforts would have to be made to involve the rural community and teachers in the rural areas to conduct this programme. A special effort should be made to activise Mahila Mandals and youth organisations. Some input from the community would be desirable to make it a continuing programme. Since the programme was not meant only for abolishing illiteracy but also to create awareness about other problems, it would be necessary that such programmes as family planning, health and nutrition, child and mother care should be built into this programme. For this, it would be desirable that the newly appointed instructors for this programme should be women as far as possible.

Besides removing illiteracy and creating awareness, adult education programme had to have some developmental content. It should also aim at improving the skills of the target groups so that their productivity can be improved. For this, institutions of vocational education should be put into service. The adult education programme should include techniques for continuing education to sustain the interest of those adults who had taken advantage of it and to enable them to develop knowledge and skills with their own efforts. These techniques should include low-priced books and literature, village libraries, material put out through the mass media, etc. The development of a rural library system was considered necessary to support the programme of continuing education.[18]

The *Sixth Five Year Plan* had laid emphasis on minimum essential education for all citizens, irrespective of their age, sex and residence. The approach to achieve this objective was to be characterised by flexibility, inter-sectoral cooperation and inter-agency coordination. Technocracy was to be adopted as the major instrument for the spread of literacy, numeracy and practical skills relevant to the economic activities of the people concerned. It would be supported by post-literacy continuing education through a network of rural libraries as well as instructional programmes through mass communication media, particularly after the INSAT was launched in orbit.

Non-formal education for adults, particularly in the *productive age-group, 15-35 years, was to receive priority in the Sixth Plan*. The programmes of adult education, which had been initiated in the previous plans and which formed part of the minimum needs programme of elementary education were to be made more effective and extended in cooperation with the other developmental activities and the employment agencies. The programmes would aim at extending appropriate educational support to the concerned groups of individuals and development departments, through carefully designed group-specific and work-based curricula, which were to be an integrated part of development activity. They were also to take advantage of the cultural and other group characteristics in the process of involving the learner groups to participate in, and benefit from adult education programmes. While designing the programme, the weaker sections such as women, Scheduled Castes, Scheduled Tribes and agricultural labourers, as wel as slum dwellers, were to be given priority. The framers of the Sixth Plan also proposed to cover 650 lakh adults in the following manner: (i) first year—15 lakh; (ii) second year—45 lakh; (iii) third year—90 lakh; (iv) fourth year—180 lakh; and (v) fifth year—320 lakh.

For the success of the programme, it was considered necessary to motivate the adults, properly select and train workers, prepare good learning materials, adopt dynamic methods of learning through doing and living, organise a mass movement, and provide adequate supervision and guidance. These aspects were to be given attention during the Sixth Plan period.[19]

Besides the National Board of Adult Education established at the Centre to guide programmes of adult education at the national level, suitable agencies were also to be constituted with the same object at the State, District, Block and Local community level. The launching of the National Adult Education Programme was an important achievement of the early period of the Sixth Five Year Plan. By the end of December 1984, 1,86,510 centres were functioning in 31 States including Union Territories with an enrolment of 55,34,763 adult leaners. A comprehensive scheme to make adult education a mass programme has been proposed for the Seventh Five Year Plan. Special emphasis will be laid on areas which require more attention.[20] Eradication of illiteracy by 1990 is a National Programme included in the Seventh Plan, which implies turning nearly 11 crore illiterates in the 15-35 age group into literate. Major thrusts for this programme would be a target group approach for disadvantaged groups of the society, involvement of voluntary agencies and educated youths in this massive programme of adult education. Electronic and folk media for motivation and promotional purposes will be utilized.[21]

It is evident, however, that the process of all round national development in India has changed the concept of adult education significantly. It is no longer confined to traditional literacy in 3R's alone. While determined efforts are being made to universalise elementary education up to the age of 14 years, educational facilities are being extended to the adult population to remedy their educational deprivation and to enable them to develop their potentiality. The National Adult Education Programme formally launched on October 2, 1978, aims at providing education facilities to cover about 10 crore *adult illiterate persons in the age group 15-35*, between 1978-79 to 1983-84. To advise the government in the formulation of policies, a National Board of Adult Education and State Boards of Adult Education have been set up at the national as well as state-levels. District level Committees have also been set up in most of the states to ensure proper coordination and for overseeing the implementation of the programme at the local level. Assistance to voluntary organisations working in the field of adult/non-formal education is one of the most successful programmes of the government which started in 1980-81. Several agencies have been approved for financial assistance to run 29,000 centres in the country. Under the scheme of Rural Functional Literacy Projects, Central financial assistance to 241 projects is continuing.[22]

Recently, Education Minister K.C. Pant urged the States to make women the focal point of their adult literacy campaign. Inaugurating the second meeting of the National Board of Adult Education, K.C. Pant said that of the 1100 lakh illiterate adults, as many as 680 lakh were women. About 100 lakh were covered during the Seventh Plan, leaving the onerous burden of bringing 580 lakh women under the campaign in the Seventh Plan. He suggested that 50 per cent of all fresh enrolments for the adult literacy drive should be made up of women. The Scheduled Castes and Scheduled Tribes, who were still to be lifted up educationally should account for 30 per cent and 15 per cent respectively of the fresh enrolment. Of the 402 districts in the country, as many as 243 had literacy levels below the national average of 36.23 per cent. This indicated the stark dimensions of the work that remained to be done. Presently, students from 2086 colleges affiliated to 74 universities were associated with programmes covering 3.86 lakh learners. He said students and voluntary agencies could help in motivating the illiterate adults in the rural areas to join the literacy classes for them.[23] Despite all these efforts, the need for social and adult education in our country is still very great. It is evident that the efforts of government for the education of adults have not met with much success. Even its emphasis on the education of workers in the programmes of adult education has not resulted in any significant success so far. This may be because, by and large, these have concentrated on a narrow objective of literacy, making only token concessions to the idea of delivering relevant knowledge to the target population, for improving their economic performance as well as their quality of life. Moreover, Adult Education cannot be persued with any vigour without the participation of the masses in initiatives for social, economic or political change. Since the rationale and the dynamism of Adult Education programme comes from the perceived imperative that it is a pre-requisite for development and survival, it seems necessary to consider how the national goals can be advanced through it.[24]

REFERENCES

1. Styler, W.E., *Adult Education in India*, Oxford University Press, 1960, p. 20.
2. *Report of the Adult Education Committee, 1939*, CABE, Pamphlet No. 28, 1946, pp. 31-33.
3. *Ibid.*, p. 32.
4. *Report of the Post-War Educational Development in India*, 1944, pp. 58.
5. *First Five Year Plan: Progress Report, 1954-55*, Planning Commission, 1956, p. 186.
6. *Second Five Year Plan, 1956-61*, Planning Commission, 1956, pp. 516-17.
7. *Third Five Year Plan, 1961-66*, Planning Commission, 1961, p. 599.
8. *Third Five Year Plan: Progress Report, 1963-65*, Planning Commission, 1967, p. 152.
9. *Report of the Indian Education Commission, 1964-66*, National Council of Educational Research and Traning, 1971, para 17.06, p. 779.
10. *Education in Retrospect, op. cit.*, pp. 77-78.
11. *Fourth Five Year Plan: Draft, 1969-74*, Planning Commission, 1969, p. 286.
12. *Fourth Five Year Plan: Summary, 1969-74*, Planning Commission, 1971, p. 117.
13. *Report of the Indian Education Commission, 1964-66, op. cit.*, p. XXI.
14. *Education in Retrospect, op. cit.*, p. 83.
15. *Ibid.*, p. 85.
16. *Ibid.*, p. 87.
17. *Fifth Five Year Plan*, 1974-79, Planning Commission, 1976, p. 77.
18. Quoted in *Education Commission and After, op. cit.*, pp. 215-17.
19. *Sixth Five Year Plan*, 1980-85, Planning Commission, 1980, p. 356.
20. *Employment News*, Vol. X, No. 14, July 6, 1985, p. 1.
21. Better Education, Better Nation by R.K. Bhandari, article published in *Yojana*, Vol. 29, No. 7, April 16-30, 1985, p. 6.
22. *India—A Reference Annual, 1983 and 1984, Publication Division, New Delhi*, p. 53 and pp. 62-63.
23. *Hindustan Times*, May 26, 1985, p. 13.
24. *Challenge of Education—A Policy Perspective, 1985*, Ministry of Education, New Delhi, August, 1985, pp. 91-92.

2

National Policy on Adult Education

(A) NATIONAL POLICY ON EDUCATION (1968)

Spread of Literacy and Adult Education

(a) The liquidation of the illiteracy is necessary not only for promoting participation in the world of democratic institutions and for accelerating programmes of production, especially in agriculture, but for quickening the tempo of national development in general. Employees of large commercial, industrial and other concerns should be made functionally literate as early as possible. A lead in this direction should come from the industrial undertakings in the public sector. Teachers and students should be actively involved in organising literacy campaigns, especially as part of the Social and National Service Programme.

(b) Special emphasis should be given to the education of young practicing farmers and to the training of youth for self-employment.

The above National Policy is based on the *Report of the Committee of Members of Parliament on Education (1967): National Policy on Education,* Parliamentary Committee Report is as follows:

7. *Spread of literacy and adult education :* The liquidation of mass illiteracy is essential. Plans to accelerate the spread of literacy should therefore be prepared and intensively implemented.
8. *Education of girls:* There is still a wide gap in the enrolment of boys and girls at all stages. It is necessary to eliminate this gap at the primary stage, and to narrow it at the other stages.
9. *Education of the weaker sections of the community:* It is

Notes : (i) The para numbers refer to page numbers of the document.
(ii) Table numbers have been provided to confirm to Chapter number.

necessary to expand and extend the existing special educational facilities and concessions to the scheduled castes and scheduled tribes.

(B) ADULT EDUCATION—A POLICY STATEMENT (1977)

Genesis : The Janta Government declared that the highest priority in adult-education should be given to the illiterate persons. It was estimated that about 100 million persons in the age-group 15-35 were illiterate in 1977. A policy statement was made on the floor of Parliament on April 5, 1977 declaring that along with universalisation of elementary education, higher priority in educational planning would be given to adult education. In pursuance of the policy, the National Adult Education Programme was launched on October 2, 1978. An immediate target was fixed to educate 100 millions in a period of five years so that universal literacy became a reality. The yearwise coverage of the programme was proposed as under:

Table 2.1: Coverage of the Programme : Yearwise

Year	Annual coverage in millions	Cumulative coverage in millions
1978-79 (year of preparation)	1.5	1.5
1979-80	4.5	6.4
1980-81	9.0	15.0
1981-82	18.0	33.0
1982-83	32.0	65.0
1983-84	35.0	100.0

Policy Statement

1. Exclusion of a vast majority of the people from the process of education is a most disturbing aspect of educational and social planning. This has been uppermost in the consideration of the present government ever since it assumed office in March 1977. While determined efforts must be made to universalize elementary education upto the age of 14 years, educational facilities must be extended to adult population to remedy their educational deprivation and to enable them to develop their potentiality. Indeed, universalization of elementary education and of adult

literacy are mutually inter-dependent.

2. The government has resolved to wage a clearly-conceived well-planned and relentless struggle against illiteracy to enable the masses to play an active role in social and cultural change. Literacy ought to be recognized as an integral part of an individual's personality. The present thinking on adult education is based on the assumptions (a) that illiteracy is a serious impediment to an individual's growth and to country's socio-economic progress; (b) that education is not co-terminous with schooling but takes place in most work and life situations; (c) that learning, working and living are inseparable and each acquires a meaning only when correlated with the others; (d) that the means by which people are involved in the process of development are at least as important as the ends; and (e) that the illiterate and the poor can rise to their own liberation through literacy, dialogue and action.

3. Adult education should emphasize imparting of literacy skills to persons belonging to the economically and socially deprived sections of society. However, such persons often lack motivation for sustained participation in literacy and follow-up programmes. In this context, stress should be laid on learning rather than teaching, on use of the spoken language in literacy programmes and on harnessing of the mass media. Motivation also depends on an awareness among the participants that they can transform their destinies and that the adult education programmes will lead to advancement of their functional capability for the realization of this objective. Moreover, a literacy programme unrelated to the working and living conditions of the learners, to the challenges of the environment and the developmental needs of the country cannot secure an active participation of the learners; nor can it be an instrument of development and progress. Adult education, therefore, while emphasizing acquisition of literacy skills should also be relevant to the environment and learners' needs; flexible regarding duration, time, location, instrumental arrangements, etc.; diversified in regard to curriculum, teaching and learning materials and methods; and systematic in all aspects of organization.

4. Highest priority in adult education needs to be given to the illiterate persons. In the post-Independence period, the achievements in the field of literacy have been far from satisfactory. In 1947, the rate of literacy was 14 per cent, which rose to 34.65 per cent (excluding the age-group 0-4) in 1971. Yet, owing to population increase and half-heartedness of the past effort, the number of illiterate persons has risen from 247 million in 1951 to 307 million in 1971. According to the census

of 1971 the total number of illiterate persons above 14 years of age is 209.5 million, of which 97.1 million are in the age-group 15-35, which is likely to be about 100 million at present. A massive programme should be launched to cover this vast segment of population in 15-35 age-group as far as possible within five years of its launching. This implies organization of special programmes for women and for persons belonging to scheduled castes and scheduled tribes. The regions which have a concentration of illiteracy will also require special attention.

5. While the conceptual position stated in paragraphs 2 and 3 needs emphasis, the need to view the programme as a mass movement must also be underlined. From the organizational.point of view it is of utmost importance that elaborate preparations are made before launching a massive programme. Identification and motivation of the instructors, preparation of curriculum and teaching/learning materials and training have been the main areas of deficiency in adult education programmes in the past. A satisfactory level of preparedness in those areas must be reached before the programme is to be launched. Besides, adult education must cease to be a concern only of the educational authority. It should be an indispensable input in all sectors of development, particularly where participation of the beneficiaries is crucial to the fulfilment of development objectives. A pre-requisite of an adult education movement is that all agencies, governmental, voluntary, private and public sector industry, institutions of formal education, etc., should lend strength to it. Voluntary agencies have a special role to play and necessary steps shall have to be taken to secure their full involvement. Instructional work shall have to be done by the teachers, students and unemployed men and women. It would be of great advantage if unemployed or underemployed youth having the potentiality to organize adult educational programmes are provided necessary training and then entrusted with the responsibility for organizing such programmes. To ensure effectiveness and systematic analysis of the problems, the programmes should have built-in mechanisms for monitoring and evaluation as well as for applied research. Finally, importance must be laid on follow-up measures such as production and distribution of reading materials, organized learning and group action.

6. Adequate financial and adminstrative support will be essential for organization of the massive programme. Provision shall have to be made for a programme comprising literacy as well as environmental and social education, extending to approximately 300-350 hours or about 9

months, and also taking into account other costs. The required resources shall have to be provided by the government, local bodies, voluntary agencies, trade and industry, etc. A realistic assessment should be made of the size and capability of the administrative and professional apparatus which would be necessary for the programme and necessary steps taken to create it.

7. In addition to organizing a massive programme for adult illiterates, it is necessary to provide special programmes for special groups based on their special needs. For example, programmes are needed for:

— Urban workers to improve their skills, to prepare them for securing their rightful claims and for participation in management;
— Government functionaries such as office clerks, field extension workers and police and armed forces personnel to upgrade their competence;
— Employees of commercial establishments such as banks and insurance companies to improve their performance;
— Housewives to inculcate a better understanding of family life problems and women's status in society.

Programmes for these and several other categories of persons could be organized through classroom participation, correspondence courses or mass media, or by a combination of all these.

8. It is of the greatest importance that implementation of adult education programmes is decentralized. It would also be necessary to establish agencies of co-ordination and centralisation. A National Board of Adult Education has been established for this purpose by the Central Government and similar Boards should be established at the state levels. Suitable agencies should also be created at the field level for co-ordination and for involvement of the various agencies in the programme.

(C) NATIONAL POLICY ON EDUCATION (1979)

Incentives

2.6 Incentives such as mid-day meals, free textbooks, stationery and uniforms should be provided to poorer pupils. Special attention should be given to the education of girls and children of Scheduled Castes and

Scheduled Tribes.

School and the Community

2.7 The school should function as a focal centre for the development of the neighbourhood. The community in its turn should involve itself in the educational effort. Skills available within the community should be utilized for education programmes in the school.

Common School System

2.8 Beginning with the elementary stage, steps should be taken towards the common school system. The effort should be to provide education of good quality. It should be ensured that in all schools, the medium of instruction is the regional language and fees and rules of admission are uniform.

Neighbourhood School Plan

2.9 The neighbourhood school plan will be the main feature of the common school system by which the schools in the area will be required to enrol all the children in the neighbourhood. This will promote common interests and social integration.

Adult Education

Need for Adult Education

3.1 It is estimated that 230 millions of our adult population are illiterate. These form mostly the poorest and the most neglected sections of the nation. Their contribution to national well-being could be far greater than it is, if they received some education. Their condition is such that they are not able to take advantage of the benefits available to them under the development plans and continue to be exposed to exploitation and social disabilities. The nation should deem it its solemn duty to impart education to them. The National Adult Education Programme, which has been organized, should be implemented with urgency and sustained vigour. The immediate target should be to educate under this programme 100 millions in a period of five years so that universal literacy becomes a reality in our country within the shortest time.

Concept

The Adult Education Programme should mean not only acquisition of literacy and numeracy, but also functional development and social awareness with a view to cultivating the habit of self-education.

Revised Minimum Needs Programme

3.2 Adult Education is an integral part of the Revised Minimum Needs Programme (RMNP) whose thrust is : (a) to reach to the poor people, (b) to co-ordinate all such programmes with developmental departments, and (c) to integrate them with area planning. The RMN Programmes, including adult education, cannot be the sole responsibility of one ministry, department or agency.

Agencies

3.3 Since this massive programme stipulates a large investment, its operational content has to be carefully worked out. The most important point to be kept in view is that the programme is community oriented. Agencies and instruments for this programme have to be so identified that the maximum interaction takes place between the local community and the government.

3.4 The programme will be conducted through multiple agencies with precedence of voluntary agencies in so far as they are available. The involvement of teachers, students, trade, industry, youth and women organizations, social workers, development departments, municipalities, panchayats and other local bodies will be ensured right from the beginning.

Emphasis on Rural Areas

3.5 Since the real problem of adult literacy exists in the rural areas, special efforts will have to be made to involve the rural community and the teachers in the rural areas to conduct this programme. A special effort should be made to activise Mahila Mandals and Youth Organizations. Some input from the community would be desirable to make it a continuing programme.

Women Instructors

3.6 Since the programme is not meant for removing illiteracy alone but its aim is also to create awareness about other problems, it would be desirable that such programmes as family planning, health and nutrition, child and mother care should be built into this programme. For this, it would be desirable that the newly appointed instructors for this programme should be women as far as is possible.

Skill Development

3.7 Besides removing illiteracy and creating awareness, adult education programme has to have some development content. It should also aim at improving the skills of the targeted groups so that their productivity can be improved. For this, institutions of vocational education should be pressed into service.

Post-literacy Programmes

3.8 The adult education programme should include measures for continuing education to sustain the interest of those adults who have taken advantage of it and to enable them to develop knowledge and skills on their own. These measures would include low-priced books and literature, village libraries, material put out through the mass media, etc. The development of a rural library system is necessary to support the programme of continuing education.

(D) DRAFT NATIONAL POLICY ON EDUCATION (1986)

Adult Education

4.9 Our ancient scriptures define education as that which liberates i.e., provides the instruments for liberation from ignorance and oppression. In the modern world, it would naturally include the ability to read and write, since that is the main instrument of learning. Hence, the crucial importance of adult education, including adult literacy.

4.10 The critical development issue today is the continuous upgradation of skills so as to produce manpower resources of the kind and the number required by the society. Since participation by beneficiaries in the developmental programmes is of crucial importance, systematic programmes of adult education linked with national goals such as alleviation of poverty, national integration, environmental conservation, energisation of the cultural creativity of the people, observance of small family norm, promotion of women's equality, etc. will be organised and the existing programmes reviewed and strengthened.

4.11 The whole Nation must pledge itself to the eradication of illiteracy, particularly in the 15-35 age-group. The Central and State Governments, political parties and their mass organisations, the mass media and educational institutions must commit themselves to mass literacy programmes of diverse nature. It will also have to involve on a large scale teachers, students, youth, voluntary agencies, employers etc. Concerted efforts will be made to harness various research agencies to improve the pedagogical aspects of adult literacy. The mass literacy programme would include, in addition to literacy, functional knowledge and skills, also awareness among learners about the socio-economic reality and the possibility to change and improve it.

4.12 A vast programme of adult and continuing education will be implemented through various ways and channels, including:

(a) establishment of centres in rural areas for continuing education;
(b) worker's education through the employers and concerned agencies of government;
(c) post-secondary education institutions;
(d) wider promotion of books, libraries and reading rooms;
(e) radio, television and films, as mass and group learning media;
(f) creation of learner's groups and organisations;
(g) programmes of distance learning;
(h) organizing assistance in self-learning; and
(i) need and interest based vocational training programmes.

Non-Formal Education

5.8 A large and systematic programme of non-formal education will be launched for school drop-outs, for children from habitations without schools, working children and girls who cannot attend whole-day schools.

5.9 Modern technological aids will be used to improve the learning environment of NFE centres. Talented and dedicated young men and women from the local community will be chosen to serve as instructors, and particular attention paid to their training. Steps will be taken to facilitate their entry into the formal system in deserving cases. All necessary measures will be taken to ensure that the quality of non-formal education is comparable with formal education.

5.10 Effective steps will be taken to provide a framework for the curriculum on the lines of the national core curriculum, but based on the needs of the learners and related to the local environment. Learning material of high quality will be developed and provided free of charge to all pupils. NFE programmes will provide participatory learning environment, and activities such as games and sports, cultural programmes, excursions, etc.

5.11 Much of the work of running NFE centres will be done through voluntary agencies and panchayati raj institutions. The provision of funds to these agencies will be adequate and timely. The Government will take over-all responsibility for this vital sector which is not yet fully established.

A Resolve

5.12 The New Education Policy will give the highest priority to solving the problem of children dropping out of school and will adopt an array of meticulously formulated strategies based on micro-planning, and applied at the grassroots level all over the country, to ensure children's retention at school. This effort will be fully coordinated with the network of non-formal education. It shall be ensured that all children who attain the age of about 11 years by 1990 will have had five years of schooling, or its equivalent through the non-formal stream. Likewise, by 1995 all children will be provided free and compulsory education upto 14 years of age.

(E) JANARDHANA COMMITTEE ON NATIONAL POLICY ON EDUCATION (1991)

Review of Ramamurti Committee*

Introduction

Appointment of the Committee

The National Policy on Education (NPE) was adopted by Parliament in

Note: The numbers given in parentheses at the end of each recommendation is the para number of the Report of the Committee under which that recommendation appears.

* Report of the CABE Committee on Policy, Department of Education, Ministry of Human Resource Development, Government of India, New Delhi-1992.

May 1986. The Policy was followed up by an elaboration through the Programme of Action (PoA) which was adopted by Parliament in August 1986. Para 11.5 of NPE envisages a review of the implementation of various parameters of the Policy every five years. The Central Government had in May 1990, appointed a Committee to review NPE, 1986 (NPERC), under the chairmanship of Acharya Ramamurti. The Committee submitted its report on 26th December, 1990. The report was tabled in both the Houses of Parliament on 9th January, 1991. The Central Advisory Board of Education (CABE) in its meeting held on 8-9 March, 1991 examined the procedure to be adopted for consideration of the report of the NPERC and decided that a CABE Committee be constituted by the Chairman, *viz*., Union Minister of Human Resource Development, to consider the recommendations of the NPERC.

In pursuance of the above decision, the Chairman of the CABE appointed a Committee on 31st July, 1991, to review the implementation of various parameters of NPE taking into consideration the report of the NPERC and other relevant developments since the Policy was formulated and to recommend modifications to be made in NPE. Following is the composition of the Committee:

Chairman

Shri N. Janardhana Reddy
CM and Minister of
Education, AP

Members

1. Shri Vikram Verma
   Minister of Education, MP,
2. Shri Geegong Apang
   CM and Minister of
   Education,
   Arunachal Pradesh
3. Dr. Ram Chandra Purve
   Minister (SE and PE), Bihar
4. Shri R.M. Veerappan
   Minister of Education,
   Tamil Nadu
5. Shri S.S. Chakraborty
   Minister (Higher Education),
   West Bengal
6. Shri E.T. Mohammad
   Basheer
   Minister of Education,
   Kerala
7. Dr. (Smt.) Chitra Naik
   Member (Education)
   Planning Commission
8. Prof. G. Ram Reddy
   Chairman
   University Grants
   Commission
9. Dr. M.S. Adiseshiah
   Chairman
   Madras Institute of
   Development Studies
   79, Second Main Road,
   Gandhi Nagar Adyar,
   Madras-600 020

10. Dr. Radhika Harzberger
Director
Rishi Valley School
PO Madahapalli,
Distt. Chittoor,
Andhra Pradesh

11. Dr. A.P. Mitra
Bhatnagar Fellow
New Delhi

12. Smt. Jaggannathan Krishnammal
Secretary
Land for Tillers Freedom (LAFTI)
Kilvelur-611104
Tanjore District
Tamil Nadu

13. Dr. Ram Dayal Munda
Professor of Regional Languages
Ranchi University, Ranchi

14. Shri Habib Tanvir
Director
Naya Theatre
D.D.A. Staff Quarters
Bar Sarai,
New Delhi-110016.

Member Secretary

15. Dr. R.V. Vaidyanatha Ayyar
Joint Secretary (Planning)

Union Education Secretary (Shri Anil Bordia), Director of NCERT (Dr. K. Gopalan) and Director of NIEPA (Prof. Satya Bhushan), were permanent invitees to the meetings of the Committee.

Summary of Recommendations

Overview

1. The concept of participatory educational order should go beyond involvement of education institutions and should extend to the community itself. (Para 2.2)

2. While very little of policy requires reformulation, the PoA needs to be revised considerably. (Para 2.3)

Education and Women's Equality

3. While the NPERC had rightly reiterated the importance of women's education, the NPE policy frame is adequate and the Programme of Action (PoA) should be revised to take into account the recommendations of the NPERC. (Para 3.5)

Education of the Scheduled Castes, Scheduled Tribes and Other Educationally Backward Sections

4. A single focal agency should be identified in each State for the purpose of monitoring the programmes and reporting to the Central Government. (Para 4.4)

5. A Standing CABE Committee on education of SCs, STs and other educationally backward sections should be constituted, educationists from these groups should have representatives in that Committee. (Para 4.4)

6. While instruction should be child-centred and cater to individual differences, it is not advisable to differentiate students in the matter of syllabus and curriculum. (Para 4.5)

7. Monitoring of the implementation of the guidelines for recognition of minority-managed educational institutions is better left to the State Governments, as they are deeply conscious of the need for proper monitoring and many organisations like the Minority Commission already exist for the purpose of monitoring. (Para 4.6)

8. No policy reformulation is necessary; all recommendations of the NPERC on education of the SCs, STs and other educationally backward sections, except R. Nos. 69 and 80, should be taken into account while revising the PoA. (Para 4.8)

Education of the Handicapped

9. No policy reformulation is necessary; the recommendations of the NPERC on education of the handicapped shoule be built into the revised PoA. (Para 5.3)

Common School System

10. Effective measures need to be taken to implement the provision of NPE 68 and NPE in regard to Common School System. To this end, disparities between schools should be ended as early as possible by upgrading the quality of ordinary schools and providing amenities for achieving minimum levels of learning. Both the Centre and the States should take determined action in this regard. The privileged schools should accept social accountability by sharing their facilities and resources with other institutions, taking up community activities, and

facilitating access to children of the disadvantaged groups. (Para 6.6)

Navodaya Vidyalayas

11. The scheme should continue and a NV should be set up in each district as originally envisaged. Further, the following measures are suggested:

(i) constant review to keep the scheme as cost effective as possible;
(ii) ensuring the continued validity and reliability of the admission tests by periodic evaluation and appropriate modification of admission procedure; and
(iii) more particular attention to the pace-setting role of these institutions. (Para 7.5)

12. It is also necessary to begin thinking about the future course of the scheme after NVs have been established in all districts with the requisite facilities and investment. A choice has to be made between establishment of new institutions and expansion of facilities in the existing institutions. Planning has also to begin for catering to the higher educational needs of students who pass out of NVs. A scheme needs to be formulated for Central financial support to residential schools. In this scheme priority should be given to ST areas and areas predominantly inhabited by SCs. (Para 7.9)

Early Childhood Care and Education

13. The scope of Article 45 of the Constitution need not be enlarged. (Para 8.8)

14. ICDS and other CSS relating to ECCE should continue as Centrally-sponsored Schemes during the Eighth Five Year Plan. The Anganwadi workers should play an expanded role and should be the focal point for a number of activities and support services for women and children, such as child care, family welfare, nutrition and health. The recruitment and training of Anganwadi workers should be so organised as to ensure that they have the necessary skills and motivation to discharge the expanded role. (Para 8.8)

15. The other recommendations of the NPERC which broadly relate to implementation modalities should be taken into account for reviewing PoA. (Para 8.8)

Universalisation of Elementary Education

16. What is needed is not so much a Constitutional amendment as suggested by the NPERC as the manifestation of a national will to achieve UEE. The Central and State Governments should bestow overriding priority to adult literacy and UEE, and provide the programmes in these two areas total support—financial, adminstrative and political—a support which is commensurate with the priority. (Para 9.2)

17. No further refinement of the policy relating to access and enrolment is required; what needs to be done is large scale operationalisation of important components of the strategy outlined by NPE/PoA such as community mobilisation, school mapping and microplanning. (Para 9.5)

18. MLL should be a thrust area. (Para 9.6)

19. The NPE approach to non-formal education is more practical and realistic than that of the NPERC. (Para 9.13)

20. Expeditious and effective action is required to tone up the management system and the learning environment of NFE so as to ensure that the quality of NFE is comparable with that of formal system in all respects. The Centre and the States should closely and continuously monitor NFE programmes in order that the programmes are effective. (Para 9.13)

21. Operation Blackboard, being one of the priority strategies for UEE, should continue during the Eighth Plan, in an expanded and extended form. (Para 9.15)

22. Till operational models of an educational complex are developed, tested and tried out, it is not feasible to link the Scheme of Operation Blackboard with the educational complex; nor is it feasible to entrust the planning and minitoring of UEE to the educational complex, as suggested in R. Nos. 169, 171, 173 and 175 by the NPERC. (Para 9.15)

23. Para 5.12 of NPE, which laid the targets for UPE and UEE, needs to be revised. Every effort should be made to ensure that the constitutional obligation of providing free and compulsory education upto the age of 14 years becomes a reality before we enter the twenty-first century. (Paras 2.6 and 9.17)

24. The following points deserve priority during the Eighth Five Year Plan in the area of UEE:

(i) Universal enrolment of all children, including girls and persons belonging to SC/ST;

(ii) Provision of primary school for all children within one kilometre of walking distance, and of facility of non-formal education for school drop-outs; working children and girls who cannot attend schools;

(iii) Improvement of ratio of primary school to upper primary schools from the existing 1:4 to 1:2, this being a pre-condition for larger opportunity for widening girls' participation at upper primary stage;

(iv) Reduction of drop-out rates between Classes I to V and I to VIII from the existing 45 per cent and 60 per cent to 20 per cent and 40 per cent respectively;

(v) Improvement of school facilities by revamped Operation Blackboard, to be extended to upper primary level also;

(vi) Achievement of minimum levels of learning by approximately all children at the primary level and introduction of this concept at the upper primary stage on a large scale;

(vii) Local level committee, with due representation to women and teachers, to assist in the working of primary education and to oversee its functioning; and

(viii) Improvement of the monitoring system for universalisation of elementary education to see to the achievement of above-mentioned goals.

NPE and PoA may be revised accordingly. (Para 9.18)

Adult and Continuing Education

25. The "dual-track approach" of promoting simultaneously UEE and adult literacy should continue to inform educational planning; the special needs of women and of disadvantaged groups like SCs and STs should be specially attended to. (Para 10.1)

26. The NPERC's perception of Mahila Samakhya (MS) as an alternative model is not valid. (Para 10.4)

27. Events since December 1990, when the NPERC submitted its report, have established that NPERC had underestimated the significance of the "Ernakulam experiment". The TLC approach is a potent and viable model which could help achieve a significant breakthrough in the literacy scene in the Eighth Five Year Plan. (Para 10.6)

28. Programmes of post-literacy and continuing education should be

planned for neo-literates and youth passing out of primary education system (through the school system or non-formal education programme) and these programmes should be planned simultaneously with literacy campaigns and be made effective as soon as large number of persons complete literacy courses. (Para 10.9)

Secondary Education

29. The policy should be reformulated to bring about the new initiatives that are required in secondary education. (Para 2.7)

30. It would be necessary to bring about a planned expansion of secondary education facilities all over the country in order to cope with new demands for secondary education. (Para 11.3)

31. Efforts should be made to bring about uniformity in the management structure for secondary education in all the States. (Para 11.4)

32. It is necessary to reorganise the Boards of Secondary Education and vest them with autonomy so that their ability to provide academic inputs to secondary education is enhanced. (Para 11.5)

33. Time-bound measures should be taken by the Central and State Governments to implement the directions contained in Para 10.7 of NPE and to empower the Headmasters with administrative, academic and financial powers. Training of the heads of institutions requires particular attention. (Paras 11.6 and 17.5)

34. Teacher training in secondary education requires no less importance than in primary education. (Para 11.8)

35. The ongoing programme of CLASS needs to be revamped. (Para 11.9)

36. Open learning should be given utmost encouragement and that the National Open School should play the same lead role within the open school system as IGNOU with open universities. (Para 11.11)

Vocationalisation of Education

37. The existing vocational stream at the +2 level may be suitably strengthened and wherever possible the vocational courses may be started from Class IX also. (Para 12.12)

38. The idea of a core vocational course, mooted by the NPERC, is attrative. Generic vocational courses may be introduced on a selective basis; to begin with generic vocational courses may be tried out in about

ten per cent of the schools. (Paras 2.5 and 12.12)

39. The Work Experience programme may be systematically implemented by allocating 12.5 per cent to 20 per cent of the school time for these activities; the activities should have a practical orientation in relation to various subjects under this programme. The vocational "core" would find place at the secondary and higher secondary stages; Work Experience/SUPW would relate to elementary education. (Para 12.12)

40. The other recommendations of the NPERC relating to implementation of the scheme of vocationalisation of education may be taken note of while revising PoA. (Para 12.12)

41. Greater rigour should be brought to bear on the planning and implementation of the scheme. (Para 12.12)

Higher Education

42. It is not advisable to set up a national level statutory mechanism to regulate the opening of non-standard and sub-standard universities and colleges. The proliferation of colleges without adequate facilities can be curbed to a large extent if the universities exercise rigorous control and insist on creation of necessary infrastructure and if the State Governments respect the decision of the universities in these matters. The establishment and operationalisation of State Councils of Higher Education will go a long way in the planned development of higher education. (Para 13.3)

43. Efforts should be made to secure involvement of teachers and students in extension work such as literacy. Adequate facilities should be provided to ensure that all students participate in one or the other existing schemes, particularly National Services Scheme (NSS), and National Cadet Corps (NCC). Specific schemes should be formulated to encourage out of school youth to participate in national service and development. The feasibility and financial implications of a two-year composite programme for students who complete the +2 stage, comprising paramilitary service, development of vocational and professional skills, and extension work in rural areas be studied. An important feature of the programme would be that the students would be required to participate in these programmes outside their home state with a view to promoting national integration. (Para 13.4)

44. NTS should undertake the conduct of tests so that it acquires the required expertise and develops into a competent resource centre. (Para 13.5)

45. A Central Council of Rural Institutes is necessary to provide the

much needed fillip to rural education on Gandhian lines; it should be set up immediately. (Para 13.6)

46. The recommendation of the NPERC (R. No. 219) on NCHE is sound and Para 5.34 of NPE should be reformulated. (Paras 2.5 and 13.7)

47. There is no need for appointment of full-time members in the UGC. (Para 13.10)

48. Regional offices of the UGC should be set up at the earliest, with adequate authority and functions. (Para 13.11)

49. Since most of the universities are affiliating universities, R.No. 201 of the NPERC can be implemented only when most of the colleges become autonomous or when a system of internal evaluation gradually replaces a terminal examination or when an independent State level examining body is set up to conduct common examinations for all undergraduate courses. (Para 13.12)

50. The UGC may consider augmenting research facilities in selected colleges within the available resources. (Para 13.13)

51. The Scheme of Curriculum Development Centres should be continued; however, to allay any misgivings the UGC may reiterate that the universities have full freedom to adapt model curricula. The UGC should also consider specific requests from the universities for curriculum development. (Para 13.15)

52. The UGC may closely monitor the implementation of the Scheme of Academic Staff Colleges. (Para 13.16)

Technical and Management Education

53. It is not advisable to regulate through a statute the emigration of graduates of IITs and RECs. All efforts should be made to ensure that environment for science and technology in the country is attractive enough for talented persons. (Para 14.2)

54. A detailed evaluation of the thrust area schemes should be taken up in 1994-95, the third year of the Eighth Plan (1992-97). (Para 14.3)

55. The Department of Education, Government of India (GOI), should take early decisions on the report of the Kalbagh Committee on Community Polytechnics. (Para 14.4)

56. The Department of Education, Government of India, should take early decisions on the report of the IIT Review Committee. (Para 14.5)

57. The AICTE Act should be amended and Para 6.19 of NPE should be reformulated. The Regional Committees of the AICTE should

be adequately staffed and that the Chairman of the Regional Committee should be an Education Minister of a State from the region by rotation. The Regional Committee should have the power to make recommendations on the opening of new institutions, starting of new courses and enhancing the intake within the framework of the guidelines laid down by the AICTE. The State Governments and the universities should issue the necessary approvals based on the recommendations of the Regional Committees only. (Para 14.6)

58. The recommendations of NPERC relating to improvement of quality and standard, upgradation of infrastructure facilities, industry-institution linkages, technology watch and manpower planning, promotion of R&D, special programme for the disadvantaged entrepreneurship development and continuing education and retraining programmes should be given due consideration in the revision of PoA. (Para 4.7)

59. All the recommendations of the NPERC in the area, except R. Nos. 239 and 246 are useful and should be taken into account in the revision of PoA. (Para 15.3)

60. The merger of KHS, CHD and CSTT is not desirable. (Para 15.4)

61. A fresh linguistic survey is not desirable. (Para 15.5)

Content and Process of Education

62. The recommendations of the NPERC on value education should be taken into account while revising the PoA. (Para 16.3)

63. The recommendation of the NPERC on educational technology should be followed up by the Central and State Governments and it be taken into account while revising the PoA. (Para 16.4)

64. There is need to progressively expand facilities for computer education in schools, particularly at the secondary stage. (Para 16.5)

65. The suggestions on Youth and Sports may be taken into account, while revising the PoA. Students should be required to participate in one or the other existing schemes, such as NSS and NCC, as envisaged in Para 8.22 on NPE. (Para 16.7)

66. Rather than leaving examination reforms to the individual initiatives and inclinations of the examining bodies, a strong and coordinated effort should be made by the Centre and the State Governments in this area. *Inter alia* the following measures are suggested:

(i) Preparation of a status report of examination reform measures undertaken by the examining bodies;

(ii) Preparation of a National Examination Reform Framework to serve as a set of guidelines to the examining bodies which would have the freedom to innovate and adopt the framework to suit the specific situation;

(iii) Developing an effective mechanism for coordination, monitoring and evaluation of the implementation of the examination reforms by the different examining bodies; and

(iv) Documentation and dissemination of innovations and measures for examination reforms. (Para 16.11)

67. While the load of the school bag is a valid concern, one cannot afford to ignore the requirements of modernisation and relevance. (Para 16.12)

68. The NPE provisions and the National Curricular Framework should be followed faithfully so that the problem of the load of the school bag will be mitigated. The teachers of the expensive private schools in urban areas should be reoriented so that they give up the habit of prescribing unnecessarily a large number of books. (Para 16.13)

Teachers and Students

69. Licensing of teachers as suggested by the NPERC is not desirable. (Para 17.2)

70. The selection system, whether for teachers or teacher trainees, should be objective and immune from undue inducements, thereby fostering the credibility of the selection process. (Para 17.1)

71. The suggestion of the NPERC on the content and process of teacher education are commended to NCTE, NCERT and SCERTs for consideration whenever the curriculum is reviewed or renewed. (Para 17.4)

72. First degree in teacher education should not be given through correspondence courses. (Para 17.5)

73. The NCTE should be immediately provided, as envisaged in the NPE/PoA, with necessary resources and capability. (Para 17.5)

74. An expert body like the NCTE should study the internship model of teacher training as suggested by the NPERC and guide the SCERTs and teacher education institutions. (Para 17.6)

75. Regarding NPERC's recommendation on the syllabus for the

B.Ed. courses, NCTE may take necessary action in consultation with States/UTs. (Para 17.6)

76. The attributes of teacher education identified by the NPERC may be kept in mind by the NCERT while preparing special programme for teacher educators. (Para 17.8)

77. Training and management of a in-service training programmes for elementary teachers should be the responsibility of the DIETs only. (Para 17.9)

78. State Governments should give emergent attention to fill up all the posts in the teacher training institutions and to frame recruitment rules for them. (17.10)

79. Emergent steps should be taken for operationalising the teacher education institutions for which financial assistance was provided by the Government of India; further financial assistance should be denied to those States in which the physical progress and utilisation of funds are unsatisfactory. (Para 17.11)

80. Every DIET should be a distinct identity with enough operational flexibility. (Para 17.12)

81. The State Governments and universities may take appropriate action on the recommendations of the NPERC on students, taking into account the specific situations. (Para 17.15)

Management of Education

82. The idea of educational complex may be tried on an experimental basis in selected areas. (Para 18.2)

83. The District Boards of Education should be set up and operationalised expeditiously. (Para 18.3)

84. It would be necessary to hasten the process of consultation with States and to give concrete shape to the idea of IES with due regard to the views and concerns of the States. (Para 18.4)

85. On Centrally-sponsored Schemes the decisions of the 43rd meeting of the NDC held on 23-24 December, 1991, are reiterated. Launching of new CSSs in some priority areas not so far covered, such as advancement of educationally backward minorities, are also suggested after due process of consultations with the States. (Para 18.7)

86. Constitution of specialised State Level Educational Tribunals is desirable. The details of setting up of these tribunals may be worked out in consultation with the State Governments. (Para 18.8)

87. "Making the System Work" has to be treated as non-negotiable.

Formulation and implementation of an Action Plan to put into practice the strategy outlined in Para 7.3 of NPE is strongly recommended. (Para 18.10)

Resources for Education

88. The practice of treating education as a residual sector in the matter of allocation of resources should be reversed; Para 11.4 of NPE should be implemented forthwith. Need-based financing requires to be provided for priority areas like Universalisation of Elementary Education. Adult Literacy and Vocationalisation. (Para 19.4)

89. Higher budgetary allocation for education should be complemented by other measures such as :

(i) Prioritisation within the Education Sector in the matter of allocation of governmental resources;
(ii) Progressively making higher education and technical and management education largely self-financing by revising the fee structure with appropriate support to the needy students by way of student loans;
(iii) Institutional finances for development of educational infrastructure;
(iv) Incentives to academic institutions to augment income by way of consultancy and other studies;
(v) Encouraging community and the cooperative sectors to financially support education. The time and effort given by thousands of unpaid volunteers in the Total Literacy Campaigns is a concrete demonstration of the possibility of raising social capital without any cost; and
(vi) Efficiency and effectiveness of expenditure which would imply that programmes should be judged not only with reference to the financial expenditure or coverage in terms of geographical area or number of beneficiaries but also in terms of outcomes. (Para 19.5)

(F) REVISED NATIONAL POLICY ON EDUCATION (1992)

Introduction

In pursuance of its election manifesto, the National Front Government appointed on 7th May, 1990 a Committee with Acharya Ramamurti as its Chairman, to review the National Policy on Education (NPE), 1986. The Committee submitted its report to the Minister of State in the Ministry of Human Resource Development on 26th December, 1990. The report was tabled in Parliament on 9th January, 1991. During this period political changes of far reaching consequences took place. Shri V.P. Singh's Government was voted out on 7th November, 1990 and Shri Chandra Shekher became Prime Minister on 10th November, 1990. Shri Chandra Shekhar's Government lasted for a very brief period between 10th November, 1990 to 6th March, 1991. Thereafter, he worked as a caretaker Prime Minister till 20th June, 1991. Shri P.V. Narsimha Rao assumed office of the Prime Minister of India on 21st June, 1991, after the victory of his party at the polls. It was, therefore, natural that under the changed situation, the Ramamurti Report could not receive government patronage.

The recommendations of the Ramamurti Review Committee Report were examined by the Janardhana Committee appointed by the Central Advisory Board of Education in July 1991. The Janardhana Committee submitted its recommendations in Junuary 1992. The CABE considered the Janardhana Committee Report in the first week of May 1992 and finalised the revised NPE.

The Revised NPE was presented in both Houses of Parliament on 7th May, 1992 by the Human Resource Development Minister Arjun Singh. In his statement the Minister said the NPE, 1986 has stood the test of time and enunciated a comprehensive framework to guide the development of education.

(G) CABE COMMITTEE ON NPE (1992)*

Introduction

The Government of India, Ministry of Human Resource Development, Department of Education, appointed a National Policy on Education Review Committee (NPERC) in May 1990 to review NPE, 1986, under the Chairmanship of Acharya Ramamurti. The Committee submitted its report on December 26, 1990. With a view to examining the report of the Ramamurti Report Committee, the Central Advisory Board of Education (CABE) appointed a committee with Janardhana Reddy, Chief Minister

* Ministry of Human Resource Development, Department of Education, New Delhi, 1993.

and Minister of Education, Andhra Pradesh, as its Chairman. The Committee gave its report in 1992.

Extracts from the Report

Overview (Chapter 2)

After a careful consideration of the recommendations of the NPERC as well as development since, NPE, we have come to the conclusion that while very little of policy required reformulation, the POA needs to be revised considerably. (2.3)

Education of the SCs/STs and other Educationally Backward Sections (Chapter 4)

A standing (CABE) Committee on Education of SCs, STs and other educationally backward sections should be constituted; educationists from these groups should have representation in that Committee. (4.4)

Adult and Continuing Education (Chapter 10)

The "dual-track approach" of promoting simultaneously UEE and adult literacy should continue in educational planning; the special needs of women and of disadvantaged group like SCs and STs should be specially attended to. (10.1)

Programmes of post-literacy and continuing education should be planned for neo-literates and youth passing out of primary education system (through the school system or non-formal education programme) and these programmes should be planned simultaneously with literacy campaigns and be made effective as soon as large numbers of persons complete literacy courses. (10.9)

(H) NATIONAL POLICY ON EDUCATION, 1986: PROGRAMME OF ACTION (1992)

2. Education of Scheduled Castes and Scheduled Tribes and Other Backward Classes

2.3.1 Adult education programmes will be an integral part of educational micro-planning in all tribal areas.

2.3.2 Under the total literacy campaign SC and ST populations will be the major focus for achieving total literacy. Special attention will be paid to adult illiterate women.

2.3.3 Post-literacy centres will be set up in SC/ST areas where literacy campaigns have been carried out in order to provide facilities for continued literacy for adult neo-literates women specifically.

5. Adult and Continuing Education

1. Present Situation

5.1.1 The National Literacy Mission (NLM) was launched as a societal and technology mission on 5th May, 1988 with the objective of imparting functional literacy to 80 million illiterate adults in 15-35 age group by 1995. Built on an objective assessment of the strength and weaknesses of the National Adult Education Programme it has imparted a new sense of urgency, new emphasis and seriousness to the problem of eradication of illiteracy in the country. The implementation of the programme of adult literacy and education in a Mission mode during the last four years has confirmed more than one sense that eradication of illiteracy is possible and achievable. This has been demonstrated by the provisional figures of 1991 census which revealed that the literacy rate for the population aged 7 years and above in the country increased from 43.56% in 1981 to 52.11% in 1991, registering an increase by 8.55%. The country achieved for the first time the distinction of having larger number of literate persons (352 millions) than that of the illiterate ones (324 millions). After experimenting with successive alternative models of literacy programmes, we have settled down to one which is known as campaign for total literacy which is area-specific, time bound, volunteer based, cost-effective and outcome oriented. This has given us lot of hope and faith that illiteracy is not a fatality and can be overcome in a time bound manner with planned, concerted and coordinated efforts. Mass campaigns for total literacy have been launched in 156 districts (either fully or partially) during the last 2-3 years. Even though the emphasis under NLM is on imparting functional literacy to illiterate adults in the age-group 15-35, potential learners in the age-group 9-14 and above the age of 35 have also been enrolled in most of these campaigns. Taken together, about 55 million potential learners are presently covered in these campaigns. While the total literacy campaigns have made some impact in few parts of the country, the States of Bihar, Rajasthan, Arunachal Pradesh, Madhya

Pradesh, Uttar Pradesh, Andhra Pradesh, Meghalaya and Orissa and UT of Dadra & Nagar Haveli are significantly below the national average of 52.11%. Intensive efforts have, therefore, to be made and special strategies to be adopted to improve literacy situation in these States/UTs with special emphasis on persons belonging to SCs/STs and women.

2. *Strategies of Implementation—Mass Campaign Approach to be the Dominant Strategy*

5.2.1 The mass campaign approach is based on mass mobilisation and support of government (both Central and State), district administration, non-governmental and voluntary agencies, people from all sections of the society and all walks of life with a tinge of voluntarism, a compact, well-knit and efficient management structure with an inbuilt monitoring system. The efficiency of this approach has been established beyond doubt inasmuch as it has succeeded in transforming a fully government-funded and government-controlled traditional centre-based programme (which was also honorarium-based) into a mass campaign leading towards a people's movement for total literacy and a new awakening. The Total Literacy Campaign (TLC) approach constitutes the principal strategy of NLM and would continue to be so for such time till the goal of universal literacy has been fully achieved.

5.2.2 As a result of the evolution of the programmes of literacy, post-literacy and continuing education during the past four years or so under the NLM, a clear and comprehensive conceptualisation of the total programme has already emerged and would be adopted for future work. This will include the following:

(i) Basic literacy for about 200 hours spread over about six months which will basically be a guide learning programme;

(ii) Systematic post-literacy programme for about 50 additional hours spread over two months which will start with guided learning and will culminate into self-learning by making the learner self-reliant; and

(iii) Self-directed continuing education in the perspective of life-long learning through library service, newspapers for neo-literates, charcha mandal, and such other activities. This may also include the skill development programme for personal, social and occupational development.

3. Process

5.3.1 The process involved in implementation of the mass campaign for total literacy strategy would include the following:

(a) Persuading the State Governments/UT administrations to formulate detailed action plans for the state as a whole as also for each district for achieving total literacy before 1997-98. The imperatives of literacy would be built into the educational and developmental planning process at all levels.

(b) Orientation of political parties, as also representatives of the people (MPs, MLAs, MLCs, Chairmen, Zilla Parishads, Panchayat Samitis, Mandal Panchayats/Panchayats, Municipalities, notified area councils, etc.) to come together, plan together, work together and pledge their unqualified solidarity and support to the campaign experiment despite their ideological and political differences.

(c) Orientation of officers of all departments (of both Central and State Governments) at the state and district level in the campaign approach so as to secure their co-operation and support to the campaign at all stages of its operationlisation.

(d) Registration of Saksharata Samitis in the districts/areas where mass campaigns for total literacy are to be taken up with representation of officials, non-official members, voluntary agencies, educational institutions and opinion leaders in the community/society.

(e) Mass mobilisation of all sections of the society like teachers and students of educational institutions, employers, trade unions, members of disciplined forces, ex-servicemen, banks, cooperatives, educated unemployed youth, voluntary agencies and the volunteers mobilised by them for combating illiteracy. The important role of voluntary agencies in mass-mobilisation will be continued and strengthened.

(f) Peoples' participation in environment building, planning and operationalisation of the campaigns by assigning specific roles to key resource persons, resource persons, master trainers, volunteers, etc. and by serving on various committees at the district, Panchayat Samiti/Mandal Panchayat/Panchayat and village levels. This should lead to emergence of various grass-roots level community institutions, including the Village

Education Committees.

(g) Creation of people oriented, well-knit management structures at the district, taluka, block, mandal/panchayat and village levels consisting of both officials and non-officials to function in a decentralised, debureaucratised and participative mode with a view to ensuring participation and support of people at all levels. For this purpose, services of experienced and committed personnel would be obtained from educational institutions, Central and State Government Departments, Central and State public sector undertakings, autonomous bodies, etc. preferably on secondment basis.

(h) Effective involvement of good, committed and reliable voluntary agencies interested in taking up campaigns for total literacy in small and compact areas where total literacy campaigns are not being implemented and bringing them under the umbrella of TLC, wherever, a TLC is being undertaken with a view to securing their support and services for the campaign.

(i) Mobilising and harnessing all components of the educational system at the university, college/school level for promoting literacy as part of their social obligation.

(j) Elaboration of the present NLM norms into appropriate and specific competencies in literacy and post-literacy for ensuring effective achievement.

(k) Insistence on the preparation of teaching/learning material on the motivation centres technique of Improved Pace and Content of Learning (IPCL) in the campaigns supplemented by readers on host of development messages such as health, family welfare, immunisation, nutrition, maternity protection, child care, protection of environment, small family norm and women's equality, etc.

(l) Insistence on all institutions/agencies/individuals interested in literacy work to work with understanding, rapport and bonhomie and carry out specific assignments related to material production, training and environment building under the leadership and direction of the concerned saksharata samiti.

(m) Ensuring implementation of the total literacy campaigns in accordance with the guidelines of the National Literacy Mission Authority (NLMA) combined with such flexibility and freedom as may be necessitated by local conditions.

(n) The Central/State Governments/UT Administrations and

Central/State public sector undertakings to make available the personnel at various levels to work for the campaigns as and when requested to do so and to ensure a reasonable continuity in their tenure so as to avoid a dislocation in pace and momentum of the TLC.

4. Environment Building—A Continued Necessity

5.4.1 Both the literate and the educated will be sensitised to take literacy work with a sense of pride, patriotism and social obligation. The community of learners will be motivated and mobilised for literacy to perceive the need for literacy and internalise this need for their collective well-being. For this purpose, environment building activities would continue to be undertaken through organisation of jathas, street plays and nukkad nataks, wall writings, literacy songs and slogans, articles in newspapres and magazines by creative writers, thinkers and opinion leaders, etc.

5.4.2 Media would be used in literacy promotion as a tool of dissemination of information, as a tool of mobilisation, motivation and sensitisation, as a tool of learning by sharing information, ideas and experiences and as a tool of social action for change. For this purpose, discussion on various aspects relating to literacy would be arranged on Doordarshan and Radio, spots and motivational films would be produced and shown on TV and classes conducted through radio. Both print and non-print media, including the traditional folk arts, would be fully harnessed for disseminating the message of literacy and for creating a positive climate for literacy.

5. Integration with other Development Departments

5.5.1 With a view to ensuring that acquisition of literacy actually enables the neo-literates to participate in various processes of national development, the NLM would be geared to the nationally accepted goals by way of development of an effective linkage between literacy and other development programmes. In particular, the endeavour of the NLMA would be on the following:

(a) All development departments/agencies would be fully oriented to literacy and sensitised to improve and strengthen the delivery mechanism for which they are directly or indirectly responsible with a view to meeting the natural demand and sometimes heightened aspirations of the people (arising as a result of the campaign for literacy) which in turn will sustain the need for literacy.

(b) Benefits available under various protective and anti-exploitative laws, institutions as well as development schemes would be made available to learners with a view to alleviating their poverty and deprivation, promoting general and economic well being to the extent possible and ensuring an effective participation in the affairs of family, community and society as also larger affairs of the nation.

(c) Social, emotional and linguistic integration, communal harmony, tolerance of and respect for each others' faith and belief which has been achieved to a fair extent in many of the campaign districts would continue to be sustained and invigorated.

(d) Literacy campaigns would take up activities related to protection and conservation of environment with a view to generating intensive awareness for such conservation and formation of groups, wherever, possible which will provide the nuclei for all activities which go with conservation. Such activities will be integrated into the content of primers, content of materials for neo-literates, curriculum and course content of training and orientation of all functionaries, transaction of instructional lessons, evaluation, etc. This will enable the learners and neo-literates to assimilate, imbibe and internalise the message related to conservation.

(e) Propagation of the message of small family norm which has been yet another issue of national concern as also one of the sub-themes of all literacy campaigns would continue to be accelerated. This, along with other measures like importance of delayed marriage, proper spacing, changing existing social biases in favour of the male child in our society, etc. will be integrated into the content of the primer, content of materials for neo-literates, curriculum and course content of training and orientation of all functionaries, transaction of instructional lessons, evaluation, etc.

(f) Promotion of women's equality will be a major area of focus in literacy programmes. Working towards this objective will have following implications for planning and implementation of

TLCs:

(i) Enabling the participation of women in the decision making processes of the campaign and developing organising skills.
(ii) Ensuring widest possible participation of women as teachers and learners in the teaching-learning process.
(iii) Organising activities specifically designed to bring about attitudinal change amongst men, thereby developing a greater sensitivity towards the difficulties faced by women in Indian society. This should lead to collective action to remove such difficulties wherever possible.
(iv) Promoting the formation of women's organisation which will take up issues relating to women's rights.
(v) Providing suitable avenues of gainful employment of women and ensuring their participation in every stage of the developmental process.
(vi) Ensuring that society as a whole is sensitised to the need to translate assurances of equality into concrete action such as payment of equal wages for equal work.
(vii) Designing and promoting innovative and imaginative schemes which consciously work towards women's equality and empowerment. Existing models such as the Women's Development Project (WDP), or the Mahila Samakhya concept, would be enlarged in scope and ambit, and integrated with literacy campaigns.
(viii) Creating structures, and facilitating mechanisms by which the concept of women's equality and gender justice is integrated at all levels with the work of the Saksharta Samitis—be it in training, content or participation.

(g) An important and positive fallout of the campaigns is that parental demand for enrolment and retention of children in the formal school system has increased manifold. Endeavour would be made to positively respond to such demand by opening new schools, adding rooms to the existing school buildings, appointing additional teachers and arranging their orientation and training and improving the operational efficiency of the delivery system so that it can absorb the growing demand. Simultaneously efforts would be made to provide appropriate and needbased non-formal education to working children in

9-14 age group so that they do not, after reaching adulthood, add upto the ranks of illiterate adults. For this purpose, an effective linkage would be established with programmes/activities related to UEE, including NFE.

(h) Messages of basic health care and programmes formulated thereunder, both protective, curative and preventive with special emphasis on health care programmes for women and children, would be integrated into the content and process of campaign materials, training, environment building, actual teaching learning phase, etc. in the same manner as small family norm, conservation of environment and women's equality.

6. Academic and Technical Resource Support

5.6.1 In view of the increasing responsibilities of the State Resource Centres (SRCs) in the wake of TLCs having been launched in 156 districts in the country and similar campaigns likely to be launched in about 200 additional districts during the 8th Five Year Plan, the SRCs, which have been providing academic and technical resource support to the literacy and adult education programme, would be suitably equipped, strengthened and stabilised so as to enable them to shoulder their responsibilities in an effective manner and without any uncertainty. The services of District Institutes of Education and Training (DIETs) and District Resource Units (DRUs) would also be suitably used in providing academic and technical resource support to the campaigns for total literacy particularly at the district and block levels. Wherever considered necessary, their working will be reviewed and revamped in such manner as would admirably serve the purpose for which they have been set up.

5.6.2 Additionally, with a view to making orientation and training programmes for functionaries of the total literacy campaigns at various levels more effective and further improving other aspects of academic and technical resource support to the programme, the following measures would be taken:

(i) Establishing a national pool of resource persons for covering various elements of the NLM strategy, by drawing upon the stock of expert personnel already available in practically all the States, in universities, SRCs, State-level and national institutions of education and social sciences and eminent non-governmental organizations engaged in education and development activities at the grassroots level.

(ii) Establishing a state-level pool of scholars and resource persons to enable the SRCs and other State-level resource organizations to avail of their expertise so as to build up effective programmes of resource support to literacy, post-literacy and continuing education at the State and district levels.

(iii) Utilising the services of experts from all over the country for the preparation of orientation plans and development of materials for the guidance of resource persons. In this connection, activities at the national level would be closely inter-linked with similar activities to be undertaken at the State level, in a flexible manner and with active participation of state-level experts in order to respond to varied needs and situations in different States.

7. Post-Literacy and Continuing Education

5.7.1 Literacy *per se* is a minimal and imperative entry point to the world of information and communication. It is a basic step towards adult education which is a process of life-long learning. This entry point will have to be carried forward, sharpened and refined to enable learners to enrich their knowledge, to acquire skills for improving their functional capability keeping in view the latest developments and to apply literacy skills for solution of their day-to-day problems and improve their well-being. Post-literacy and continuing education programmes would be organised keeping these objectives of adult education in view. The main features of the post-literacy and continuing education programme to be implemented under the Mission would include the following:

(a) Keeping in view the wide variations in the levels of literacy and numeracy achieved by those who are supposed to have become literate and keeping in view the possibility that a substantial proportion of persons who have acquired basic literacy skills through the total literacy campaigns will tend to relapse into illiteracy, different strategies for post-literacy and continuing education would be evolved and used in different parts of the country keeping in view the local needs and priorities, levels of achievement in the basic literacy phase and the situation in which most of the learners are placed.

(b) The planning for each post-literacy programme would be

initiated much in advance and preferably in the middle of the basic learning phase of the campaign so that the time-gap/interregnum between close of the basic literacy phase and commencement of the post-literacy phase is minimised.

(c) Post-literacy would be a planned, structured and coordinated effort and would preferably be implemented in a campaign mode as in the TLC. The Saksharta Samiti at the district level and similar peoples' committees at the block/mandal panchayat, panchayat and village level would continue to provide leadership and direction for the post-literacy campaigns as in the TLC.

(d) The three important goals of post-literacy programme would be *remediation* by way of starting a bridge course of 30-40 hours' duration, *continuation* of learning activities through facilities of libraries and reading rooms, supply of reading material suiting the felt needs and interest of learners and application of literacy skills to actual living and working situations.

(e) As the frame-work of the Jana Shikshan Nilayam (JSN) as a strategy designed to cater to the post literacy and continuing education needs of the neo-literates of the centre-based programme may not be of universal application, particularly in the areas covered by total literacy campaigns, it would not be the only mode of post-literacy. It would be the endeavour of the NLMA to provide an institutional frame-work in the form of learning centres in every village/habitation/urban slum in as decentralised and debureaucratised mode as possible. Irrespective of the form the learning centres may take, it would be ensured that the community is fully involved in planning and implementation of the post literacy programmes, the ultimate objective being to organise the unorganised. Functioning of JSNs would be reviewed with a view to making them more effective and ensuring that they subserve the purpose for which they have been set up. Where JSNs and other forms of learning centres co-exist, an effective linkage between the two would be established.

(f) Each post-literacy programme would be suitably integrated with programmes of other development departments. These departments would provide facilities for location of the learning centres, impart training to the beneficiaries of the post-literacy programme and would provide literature on activities/

programmes being undertaken by them, besides meeting and talking to the learners at the post literacy centres to understand the existential reality of the situation in which they have been placed and to provide support services to minimise the rigour and hardship of their existence.

(g) Schemes/programmes of TRYSEM, DWACRA, SCYTES, etc. would be suitably interlinked with post-literacy and continuing education so that the facilities under these schemes are available to the neo-literates.

(h) Newspapers for neo-literates, neo-literates' newsletter, wall papers, periodicals, magazines, etc. would become a part of supportive learning strategy.

(i) The library movement like the Kerala Granthshala Sangam would be converted into a mass movement and a programme of mobile libraries would be evolved and implemented in consultation with the State Governments. Facilities available through the Raja Ram Mohan Roy Library Foundation and other institutions/agencies working in this area would be extended to the post-literacy centres, to the extent possible.

(j) For promoting reading habits, the learning centres would be encouraged to set up penfriend clubs, reader clubs, etc. Book voyage will be integrated with post-literacy programme at the local, district and state levels.

(k) Government support to post-literacy programme would continue for a period of at least two years before the community takes it over for implementation on a long-term basis.

(l) The employers, trade unions and the government departments/ undertakings would be expected to provide facilities of reading rooms, libraries, etc. for the neo-literates/learners, and their employees/members, etc. The Central Board of Workers' Education would be involved in organising learning centres for the workers in the industrial establishments.

(m) The National Book Trust, State Resource Centres, voluntary agencies and the private publishers would be encouraged to bring out books of common interest to the learners at subsidised rates. The educational institutions would be persuaded to allow the neo-literates to make use of the facilities of their libraries.

(n) The University Grants Commission would be involved organically and effectively in literacy and post-literacy movement by galvanising the entire higher educational system to discharge its social obligation.

(o) Radio, television and films would be used with creativity and innovative skills to encourage efforts in the districts covered by the total literacy campaigns to sustain literacy, particularly reading and numeracy skills. Specially designed audio-visual learning material would be prepared for use in the JSNs and post-literacy centres. Serials, particularly for the neo-literates, would be developed and shown/broadcast through TV/radio.

(p) Use would be made for extending local radio net-work being set up by AIR to design curricula in different vocational and other life skills for the neo-literates in the TLC districts. Radio programmes would be supported by print and other materials which may be prepared locally to cater to the particular needs of the area.

(q) All other avenues of learning of appropriate levels would be provided to the neo-literates, the ultimate objective being creation of a learning society.

(r) Industry, trade, commerce and banks would be impressed upon the need to provide avenues for continuous learning to their employees, particularly the neo-literates.

8. Skill Development

5.8.1 Skill development would be integrated in each programme of post-literacy and continuing education. In particular, the endeavour of NLMA would be on achieving the following objectives in close collaboration with other departments/agencies which will be requested to assume specific responsibilities:

(a) Enabling the neo-literates to acquire skills for economic self-reliance, such skills also including managerial and entrepreneurial skills.

(b) Opening of additional Shramik Vidyapeeths in urban, semi-urban and rural areas and promotion of more agencies/ institutions in the non-formal sector for the purpose of imparting vocational skill information to the neo-literates and conducting such programmes.

(c) Enabling the educational institutions to start vocational courses for neo-literates, without the educational qualification being a condition precedent for admission in such courses, which could be run in the evening.

(d) Creation of enabling structures for working neo-literate women in the form of creches, day care centres, etc. by the village level agencies and other development departments/ organisations.

(e) Imparting skills like communication skills, survival skills and skills aimed at upgrading the functional capability of the neo-literates.

5.8.2 Based on the needs voiced by women neo-literates, wide range of interventions in terms of information sharing on availability of schemes/programmes, bank credit, appropriate technology, marketing channels, availability of materials, etc. would be executed. With a view to enabling them to become self-employed/better employed, formation of cooperatives of women neo-literates would be facilitated.

9. Research

5.9.1 The National Institute of Adult Education (NIAE) which has been set-up as a technically independent, administratively autonomous, professionally competent and a highly specialised body with research and academic orientation would undertake, good quality action research on various aspects relating to adult education programmes of all descriptions. The emphasis in programmes and activities of NIAE would be on creative and innovative work and on collaboration and net-working with other agencies in India and abroad, working in the field of adult education. The other agencies/organisations interested in taking up such research would also be encouraged to do so.

10. Targets

5.10.1 It is estimated that at the beginning of the 8th Five Year Plan the number of adult illiterates in the age-group 15-35 was 104 million. Whereas, 80 million adult illiterates would be covered by total literacy compaigns to be taken up in 350 districts in the country by the close of the 8th Five Year Plan, the remaining 24 million illiterates would be imparted literacy through programmes to be taken up by voluntary agencies, educational institutionals, Nehru Yuva Kendras, etc. It would be the endeavour of NLMA to cover about 21 million persons in the age-group 15-35 in each year of the 8th Five Year Plan.

5.10.2 Whereas, persons in the age-group 9-14 would also be covered in the total literacy campaigns where the Saksharta Samitis so propose, it would be ensured that after the first phase of basic literacy in the total literacy campaigns, appropriate arrangements are made for learners in this age-group so that they complete prescribed course of non-formal education and acquire the minimum levels of learning prescribed for non-formal education. As the priority age-group under NLM is 15-35, it would be difficult to make an estimation about the number of persons in the age-group 9-14 which would be covered under the total literacy campaigns.

11. Continuation of the Mission

5.11.1 Launched in May 1988 with the objectives of imparting functional literacy to 80 million illiterate adults by 1995, the NLM has now come to stay, and the need of literacy for improving the overall well-being of the illiterates and enabling them to make an effective contribution in all processes of national development has been fully realised. The time span of National Literacy Mission was initially fixed upto 1995 so as to coincide with the terminal year of the 8th Five Year Plan (1990-95). Since, however, the 8th Plan could not start from 1990-91, as was originally planned, the time span of the Mission would be extended upto 1997 which would be the terminal year of the 8th Five Year Plan (1992-97). It would be imperative to retain and strengthen, if considered, all the structures of the Mission at the national, state and district levels, as have already come into operation and which, with their combined efforts, have succeeded in covering 156 districts in the country by the literacy campaigns.

12. Monitoring and Evaluation

5.12.1 A detailed monitoring system to facilitate timely flow of information on the pace and progress in the implementation of the programme from the field to the national level, which has already been evolved, would be made more effective in the light of the experience that may be gained for about a year or so. It would be ensured that both qualitative as well as quantitative aspects of the programme are monitored.

5.12.2 Evaluation under the NLM would be systematic, simple and intelligible and technically sound. It would be participatory, supportive and non-threatening. The important features of the evaluation system under NLM would be the following:

(a) It would provide basic information on the achievement of the literacy campaigns from the point of view of social accountability, providing feed-back to the organisers, securing political support and injecting an awareness and respect for education in general and literacy in particular.
(b) Scores for competencies achieved in reading, writing and numeracy skills would be clearly defined.
(c) While conducting evaluation, the wide variations in regard to the rate of literacy in different parts of the country and the situation in which most of the learners are placed would be kept in view.
(d) The findings of the evaluation would be shared with the representatives of the people, learners, volunteers and all those who have worked for the campaigns.
(e) A manual on evaluation techniques, including design of training modules would be prepared and a number of parallel tests would be evolved and indicated in the manual.
(f) Well defined criteria would be evolved for the purpose of declaring an area fully literate.
(g) The literacy scenario in the country is characterised by wide-spread disparity in both relative and absolute terms in respect of a State as also a district(s) between urban and rural areas, between males and females. It is quite likely that as a result of operationalisation of the TLCs, the position will undergo qualitative change resulting in substantial reduction of this disparity. Agencies undertaking evaluation studies in respect of TLC districts would be asked to reflect this in the evaluation study reports so that the situation obtaining before the commencement of the programme and after the conclusion of the programme could be known and shared with the masses.

3

Planning of Adult Education: Five-Year Plans*

1. First Five-Year Plan (1951-52 to 1955-56)

Social Education

The concept of adult education, which was mostly confined to literacy, was found to be too narrow to be able to meet the various needs of the adults. It was, therefore, widened to include, in addition to literacy, the health, recreation and home life of the adults, their economic life and citizenship training; and to denote this new concept the term 'social education' was coined. Social education implies an all-comprehensive programme of community uplift through community action.

In rural areas the point at which the social education programme in a locality can begin will of course depend on the condition prevailing in the given area. Attempt should, however, be made at the earliest opportunity to organise an economic activity on co-operative basis... Similarly, programmes of health education and health services should also be organised on co-operative lines.

2. Second Five-Year Plan (1956-57 to 1960-61)

Social Education

The census of 1951 showed that only 16.6 per cent of the population were literate and even if children below 10 years are excluded the proportion

*Planning Commission, Government of India, New Delhi.

Note : Para Numbers refer to para numbers of the document.

rises to 20 per cent only. Apart from the low percentage of literacy there is serious disparity in literacy between men (24.9 per cent) and women (7.9 per cent) and between the urban population (34.6 per cent) and the rural population (12.1 per cent). Rapid social and economic progress along democratic lines and widespread illiteracy are scarcely compatible with each other.

As essential reforms proposed in the system of education are carried out, facilities for continuation classes and social education classes at various levels should be developed. Plans of States provide for the opening of literacy and social education centres, training of social education workers and organisers, libraries, publication of literature, audio-visual education and establishment of Janata colleges. The total allotment in the Plan for social education is about Rs. 15 crores, including about Rs. 10 crores in the national extension and community development programme.

3. Third Five-Year Plan (1961-62 to 1965-66)

Social Education and Adult Literacy

As was stated in the First Plan, social education implies an all comprehensive programme of community uplift through community action. Social education, thus, comprises literacy, health, recreation and home life of adults, training in citizenship and guidance in improving economic efficiency. Between 1951 and 1961 literacy has increased only from about 17 to about 24 per cent. The introduction of Panchayati Raj at the district and block levels and the important role assigned to village panchayats render it imperative that in as short a period as possible a substantial proportion of the adult population should become capable of reading and writing. This is essential in their own interest as in that of the community as a whole. As sufficient progress has not been achieved so far in this direction, the problem is now being studied afresh with a view to working out means for the rapid expansion of adult literacy.

Programmes of the Ministry of Education provide for the further development of the National Fundamental Education Centre as a part of the National Institute of Education, production of literature for neo-literates, assistance for voluntary organisations in the field of social education and expansion of library facilities. The educational plans of states provide for libraries and continuation classes and, to a limited extent, for adult schools and other schemes for promoting adult literacy. The main provisions for social education are made under the community development programme through the schematic budget. Altogether, in the Third Plan, about Rs. 25 crores are expected at present to be available for social education.

During the Third Plan, steps will be taken to set up or develop all the four National Libraries at Delhi, Calcutta, Bombay and Madras. There are provisions also for strengthening libraries at the state headquarters and for increasing the number of libraries at the disrict and taluka levels. Besides these, educational institutions have libraries of their own. These will be improved and strengthened during the Third Plan.

4. Fourth Five-Year Plan (1969-70 to 1973-74)

Adult Literacy

Efforts will be made to spread literacy amongst adults through mobilisation of voluntary effort and local community resources. Pilot projects will be initiated in selected districts to begin with and the programme will be extended to other areas in the light of experience... The National Board of Adult Education has been set up to advise Government on the development programmes and for enlisting the co-operation and interests of the agencies concerned. The further development of television and the experiments with satellite communications, which are to begin from 1972-73, may have significance for education, especially adult education.

5. Fifth Five-Year Plan (1974-75 to 1978-79)

Non-formal Education

With the strengthening of existing programmes of non-formal education, about 16 lakh participants are expected to be covered under these programmes.

6. Sixth Five-Year Plan (1980-81 to 1984-85)

Adult Education

Techniracy would be adopted as the major instrument for the spread of literacy, numeracy and practical skills relevant to the economic activities of the people concerned.

7. Seventh Five-Year Plan (1985-86 to 1989-90)

Adult Education

10.37 Eradication of adult illiteracy and the development of a programme of continuing adult education is a major thrust area of the Seventh Plan. The task of covering all the illiterates in the age-group 15-35 years by 1990 is a formmidable one. As motivation of the learner is crucial for success and as the number to be covered is about 90 million, the strategy to achieve the goal can only be through a mass movement involving social institutions, voluntary organisations, students, teachers, employers and the community. This programme will also have to be linked effectively with various development programmes especially the Integrated Rural Development Programme (IRDP). Active participation of village panchayats, mahila mandals, community centres, etc. is essencial. Employers will be required to impart necessary functional education to all their illiterate employees. The programmes of Nehru Yuvak Kendras (NYK) and the National Service Scheme (NSS) will also focus on eradication of illiteracy. Programmes for motivating the learners by holding community meetings and through publicity through posters, films, broadcasting, etc., will be implemented on an adequate scale and with sufficient intensity to create a conducive climate. A network of libraries and the development of literature for neo-literates will also be initiated as a follow-up programme to avoid lapse into illiteracy. Community participation in all literacy programmes will be an essential feature from village level upwards to give proper direction and orientation and lend effective support to this national programme.

10.38 Another aspect of education of adults relates to training in functional skills relevant to their respective economic activities. Programmes for this purpose will be strengthened and adequate resource support provided for organising technical and vocational skill-based courses for the benefit of adult learners through Shramik Vidyapeeths and other similar institutions. As a part of the post-literacy and follow-up services, short-duration condensed training courses will be organised for upgrading the skills of the neo-literates and for increasing their awareness of various social events. The existing programmes on rural functional literacy and State adult education programmes and various training programmes for adult learners will be consolidated and dovetailed in the new mass movement programmes of adult education. Citizenship education including adult education, will be a necessary part of the entire education system, and will be specially promoted.

8. Eighth Five-Year Plan (1992-93 to 1996-97)

11.16 The NPE and the Programme of Action (POA) envisaged that the Adult Education Programme (AEP) would cover 4 crore illiterates by 1990 and another 6 crores by 1995. With the launching of the National Literacy Mission (NLM) in 1988, the targets were reformulated and strategies recast. Accordingly, 3 crores illiterates were expected to be covered by 1990 and 5 crores by 1995. While Rural Functional Literacy Programme (RFLP), the post-literacy the teaching-learning process were modified, new strategies like area-specific and time-bound approach to achieve 100 per cent Total Literacy (TL), massive participation of Non-governmental Organisations (NGOs) and students and effective utilisation of traditional and folk theatre forms in literacy work were evolved by 1991-92. The post-literacy programme was institutionalised in the form of 32000 Jan Shikshan Nilayams (JSN). Apart from the introduction of Improved Pace and Content of Learning (IPCL) method, which reduced the duration of learning from 500 to 200 hours, technology demonstration programmes were initiated in 42 selected districts. The scheme of Shramik Vidyapeeths (SVs) was reviewed, suggesting a need for expansion. The number of State Resources Centres (SRCs) increased from 19 to 20. A National Institute of Adult Education (NIAE) was set-up in January, 1991 to augment the technical and academic resource support to adult education and to undertake quality and evaluation studies.

11.17 Area-specific and time-bound mass campaigns for TL first launched in Kottayam town and Ernakulam district in Kerala in 1989 with the active participation of students and voluntary agencies have been extended to other districts. By March 1992, twenty-five districts had achieved total literacy (in the sense of 85 per cent literacy) and TL campaigns were at different stages of progress in 80 districts in Andhra Pradesh, Bihar, Gujarat, Haryana, Himachal Pradesh, Karnataka, Madhya Pradesh, Maharashtra, Orissa, Punjab, Rajasthan, Uttar Pradesh and West Bengal covering over 3 crore illiterates with the help of about 30 lakh volunteers.

Adult Education

11.5.15 Literacy programmes will be launched in districts/regions which are educationally backward or have high concentration of SC/ST population or have low female literacy. By the close of the Eighth Plan, 345 districts including about two-thirds of all districts in the educationally backward states would be covered by the TL campaigns, while the Centre-based approach would be gradually phased out and confined to hilly, tribal and sparsely populated regions. The strategy for backward districts would be two-fold. First, a few blocks would be selected where the literacy campaign can achieve success within a reasonable period. The demonstration effect of the blocks would influence the backward blocks which, in course of time, could develop appropriate literacy programmes. Secondly, the voluntary base in educationally backward districts being somewhat weak, ways and means of identification, strengthening and expansion of the same would be evolved in consultation with the respective State Governments. It is also necessary to develop technical competence among voluntary agencies so that the partnership between the Government and the operating agencies becomes meaningful.

11.5.16 The responsibility of further enhancing contributions from community especially in urban areas and industrial towns would be explored so that apart from voluntary services, at least 20 per cent of the total expenditure on campaigns may be met.

11.5.17 In states, where library movement is strong, rural libraries should be integrated with JSNs which are envisaged as innovative post-literacy and continuing education courses. Reputed NGOs, educational institutions, distinguished individuals, ex-servicemen, war widows, award winning teachers etc. will be encouraged to setup and run JSNs. Particular attention would be paid to the availability of a variety of quality materials in adequate quantity to the neo-literates. Reputed printing presses and publishers would be motivated to print gratis literacy materials, posters and charts.

11.5.18 The academic and technical support to Adult Education programmes would be provided by the newly set up NIAE, which would be involved to a greater extent in various aspects to training, action research and monitoring so that the Directorate of Adult Education can be phased out by the end of the Eighth Plan. At the State level, the State Resource Centres will be strengthened.

11.5.19 The scheme of SVs, which provide a variety of training programmes to the industrial workers and their families would be extended to cover workers in unorganised sector and would also experiment with a variety of training models including distance education.

11.5.20 The contents of adult education would also include inculcation of values like secularism, national integration, scientific temperament, small family norm, concern for environment conservation, cultural appreciation and so on. Even a society with a literate population is required to provide many avenues for continuing education in the context of the march towards a learning society, in which open schools and open universities would play an important role.

9. Ninth Five-Year Plan (1997-98 to 2000-2001)

3. HUMAN AND SOCIAL DEVELOPMENT

3.3 Education

SECTION I

Issues and Strategies for the Ninth Five-Year Plan

Introduction

3.3.1 Education is the most crucial investment in human development. Education strongly influences improvement in health, hygiene, demographic profile, productivity and practically all that is connected with the quality of life. The policies and approach to investment in the Education sector and its development in the Ninth Plan assume considerable significance from this standpoint.

Adult Education

3.3.4 Adult literacy and further education of the literates, being as great an area of concern as universal elementary education, more intensive efforts will be made to spread literacy in the rural and tribal areas which

---

Notes: (i) Para numbers refer to the para numbers of internet printout.
(ii) Table numbers have been provided to confirm to Chapter number.

are lagging behind, with special attention to women and such marginalised groups as small and marginal farmers, landless labours and educationally neglected tribal groups. For this purpose, a disaggregated and decentralised mode of planning and implementation will be adopted. Inter-linkage of the adult education programme with income generation, better health and nutrition, women's empowerment and overall rural development will be focused upon. At the grassroots level, people's participation will be emphasised in planning and implementing local programmes for "Education for All".

Adult Literacy

3.3.19 Considerable progress has been made in making India's population literate as the following statistics show:

Table 3.1: Literacy Rates

(In percentages)

		Rural	Urban	Total
	1	2	3	4
1951				
(Total Population)	Male	19.0	45.1	24.9
	Female	4.9	22.3	7.9
	Total	12.1	34.6	16.7
1991				
(7 years and above)	Male	57.9	81.1	64.1
	Female	30.6	64.1	39.3
	Total	44.7	73.1	52.2

3.3.20 As in other cases, there are wide variations in literacy levels among the States from a low of 38.6 per cent to a high of 89.8 per cent (1991 census). The variations for males and females were respectively 55 per cent and 93 per cent and 20.4 per cent and 86.1 per cent. Within the States, literacy rates vary between males and females and between urban and rural areas.

3.3.25 The scheme of Adult and Continuing Education and Women's Studies were initiated in order to promote greater involvement of institutions of higher education in socio-economic and cultural development. As many as 104 universities have set up departments of adult and continuing education. In addition, more than 2600 colleges have set up Adult Education Units, while 22 universities and 11 colleges have set up centres for womens' studies.

Adult Education

3.3.36 The effort to make adults literate has not been commensurate with the growth in population. Elementary education has not made the expected dent on the eradication of adult illiteracy due to high drop-out rates. Consequently, though the rates of literacy have increased, there is an increase in the number of illiterates—from 267.32 million in 1961 to 328.88 million in 1991.

(vii) *Mahila Samakhya :* The project aims at empowerment of women through their mobilisation and change in their perception about themselves and the society. The programme was launched in 1991 in 10 districts of U.P., Gujarat and Karnataka. It was extended to Andhra Pradesh. It now covers 5000 villages in 35 districts in 7 states. An evaluation, conducted in 1993, has indicated that the project has laid the foundation for empowerment of women at the grassroots level.

(viii) *Non-formal Education:* In pursuance of the National Policy on Education 1986, the Central Government is providing assistance for the establishment of non-formal education centres. Assistance is given to the extent of 60 per cent of the expenditure incurred on Centres established by State Governments and 100 per cent for Centres established by voluntary organisations. The Centres, exclusively meant for girls, are eligible for 90 per cent assistance. At present 2.79 lakh Centres—2.40 lakh of the State Governments and 39000 of voluntary agencies are functioning. The enrolment in these centres is estimated to be 70 lakh. The Centres provide education through condensed courses of 2 to 2½ years' duration.

Adult Education Thrusts

3.3.54 The thrust in the Eighth Plan was on sustainability of literacy skills and on remediation. Learning of useful skills and their application in actual living and working situations was emphasised in the programmes. The main strategy emphasised an area-specific approach along with the campaign mode, with particular attention to women, the disadvantaged groups and backward rural areas. The National Mission, with State Literacy Missions, provided the main mechanisms for the implementation of literacy and post-literacy programmes. The services of non-governmental organisations were utilised for various literacy and post-literacy activities, including skill development among the adults.

Major Achievements

3.3.55 During the Eighth Plan, the organisation of campaigns and adoption of areas for intensive work constituted the two elements of the strategy. So far, 428 districts have been covered under the literacy phase and 188 districts under the post-literacy programme. About 93 million have been enrolled, out of which 61 million are estimated to have been made literate, consisting of 62 per cent females and 38 per cent males. 22 per cent are scheduled castes and 12 per cent are reported to be scheduled tribes.

3.3.56 The strategy of total literacy campaign was reviewed in 1993. The approved modifications include: the target of making the entire country literate by 2005 with 100 million persons of age group 15-35 being made literate by 1998-99; funding the Tribal Area Sub-Plan between the Centre and the State Governments in the ratio of 4:1, instead of the earlier ratio of 2:1; launching of an Operation Restoration Programme in those districts where total literacy campaign had not taken off due to various causes.

3.3.57 The Shramik Vidyapeeths, which offer specially designed non-formal programmes by integrating literacy, general education and skill training for identified groups, was expanded by establishing 25 new Vidyapeeths during the Plan period. The Centre provided assistance to State Governments for strengthening of administration and to voluntary organisations for various activities.

Adult Education Issues

3.3.88 Adult literacy and further education of the literates is as great an area of concern as universal elementary education. Adult illiteracy is the result of the failure of the primary education system in reaching the socially and economically disadvantaged segments of society. Adult literacy programme has, therefore, to be looked upon as 'operation restoration' for granting everyone the fundamental right to education. It was with this object in view that the National Literacy Mission was established in 1988. Its mandate was to mobilise all possible financial and human resources within and outside the Government in order to eradicate adult illiteracy through decentralised district-level action, in a time-bound manner. Although the achievements of the Mission have been considerable, the pace of literacy movement needs to be accelerated and the goal of full literacy needs to be achieved within the next few years. More intensive efforts are required to spread literacy in the rural and tribal areas which are lagging behind, with special attention to such marginalised groups as women, small and marginal farmers, landless labour and educationally neglected tribal groups.

3.3.89 The problems of universal adult literacy and universal primary education are similar. In both, the coverage of the accessible and socio-culturally motivated groups through normal educational programmes has been easy. However, the inaccessible and deprived segments have not been reached through the full-time conventional system of education. Therefore, various alternatives in educational provision and approaches are necessary to reach the goals of 'Education for All' as accepted by the country. For this purpose, voluntary agencies and the Government need to collaborate and adopt a disaggregated, decentralised mode of planning and implementation. The human resource development policy of investment in the education of people would pay the expected dividends in the area of adult education if the expenditure on administration and infrastructure is kept at a moderate level and greater support is given to the educational process, including skill acquisition for income-generation and inter-linkage of the adult education programme with programmes of health and nutrition, poverty alleviation, tribal development, overall rural development and women's empowerment at the grassroots level through the PRIs. Adult literacy, further education and universal primary education need to be integrated in decentralised planning. Experimentation in this behalf must be promoted by the National Literacy Mission under the auspices of the Government, voluntary agencies, rural entrepreneurs and similar partners. In this efforts, close involvement of rural development personnel is necessary.

3.3.90 While the main aim of adult education should be to increase the incomes of the poor, the need to mobilise the rural community for utilising the skills of these persons for sustainable community development should also be stressed. The most important issue of ensuring the marketability of their skills and their products, as also moving towards modernisation of the traditional skills, should also be considered as the guidepost for continuing education for overcoming 'income poverty'. At the same time, the 'legal poverty' of the people must be overcome by informing them about the land laws, the labour laws, social legislation, the rules and regulations of cooperative enterprises and so on. In addition, the 'political poverty' of the rural, tribal and other marginalised groups must be removed so that they understand the rights granted to them by the Constitution and their role as citizens in the political system of the country. A strong component of science and technology must be included in the continuing education programmes. As technology application is going to be the main stimulator of rural productivity, this will require change in the traditional roles of women to adapt to knowledge about modern tools and processes of production. Continuing adult education with S&T inputs would thus be a major thrust towards economic, political and cultural renovation of rural India. The task before the National Literacy Mission is thus a formidable one which would require a substantial financial and socio-political support.

3.3.91 The main objective of the Ninth Plan is to make 100 million adults in the age-group 15-35 literate by 1998-99. The thrust of the strategy would include: decentralisation and disaggregated planning and implementation; devolution of authority to State Literacy Mission Authorities; empowerment of local bodies, particularly the Panchayati Raj Institutions so as to make adult education a people's programme; focus on the needs of special groups like Scheduled Castes, Scheduled Tribes and minorities; reduction of disparities between males and females and urban and rural areas; convergence of various programmes and avoidance of parallel management and administrative structures; emphasis on skill development to promote income generation capabilities among adults; and utilisation of different media for motivational purposes and for widening the reach of literacy and post-literacy activities. Post-literacy programmes will receive particular attention so that the gains accrued are not lost.

3.3.92 It is proposed to cover 90 uncovered districts under literacy campaigns and 300 districts under the post-literacy campaigns, particularly in States like Arunachal Pradesh, Nagaland, Mizoram and Sikkim and the Union Territories of Lakshadweep and Andaman & Nicobar Islands which have so far not been covered under the programmes. The norms for funding will be suitably modified for both the literacy and post-literacy phases. The post-literacy phase will emphasise skill development. Those, who wish to pursue further education, will be enabled to enrol in courses offered by the National Open School and the State Open Schools. It is proposed to set up continuing education centres to serve a population of 1500-2000 and 500 neo-literates through the agency of Zila Sakhshtra Samitis. Non-governmental organisations and local authorities will be encouraged to undertake continuing education programmes, providing facilities for further education and skill training. The scheme of Shramik Vidyapeeths will be recast on the basis of the recently conducted evaluation study.

3.3.93 The State Resource Centres will be supported for conducting surveys, preparation of teaching-learning materials related to literacy and post-literacy activities, training of functionaries and monitoring and evaluation of programmes. The National Literacy Mission Authority and the State Literacy Mission Authorities will be the principal agencies for promoting and coordinating adult education programmes.

4

Committees, Commissions and Working Groups: Their Recommendations Pertaining to Adult, Continuing and Non-Formal Education*

(A) ADULT (SOCIAL) EDUCATION COMMITTEE OF THE CENTRAL ADVISORY BOARD OF EDUCATION (1948)

Genesis : The Central Advisory Board of Education, at its 14th meeting held at New Delhi in January, 1948, expressed the view that the organization of Adult Education in India had become imperative after the attainment of freedom. The Adult Education had been confined to literacy work. The value of the ability to read and write was much recognized but the Board felt that the immediate task should be to improve the standard of life and culture of the adult. With this end in view the Board set up a Committee on the 13th January, 1948, under the chairmanship of Shri Mohan Lal Saksena to prepare scheme of Adult Education and to make their recommendations on the subject.

Chairman
Shri Mohan Lal Saksena, Minister for Relief and Rehabilitation.

Members
Prof. Humayun Kabir, Joint Educational Adviser; Dr. Mata Prasad, Principal, Royal Institute of Science, Bombay; Mr. K.G. Saiyidain, Educational Adviser to the Government of Bombay.

Terms of Reference : To prepare the Scheme of Adult Education for the country.

---

* Report of Adult (Social) Education Committee of the Central Advisory Board of Education, Ministry of Education, Government of India, New Delhi.

Major Recommendations

1. In view of the far-reaching implications of the scheme, it should be called 'A Scheme for Social Education' instead of 'A Scheme for Adult Education and Literacy'. A new orientation must be given to schemes for the education of the adult. Till now, adult education has been largely confined to literacy work. The immediate task is to improve the standard of life and culture of the adult and turn him into a healthier, happier, and better citizen. The work of literacy must go on and special efforts must be made to achieve the target of 50 per cent literacy in the course of the next 3 years. Even greater emphasis must, however, be placed on the social aspects of education.

2. The objectives of such social education may be defined as follows:

(a) To instil a consciousness of the rights and duties of citizenship and foster a spirit of service to the community;
(b) To develop a love for democracy and impart an understanding of the way in which democracy functions;
(c) To disseminate knowledge of the outstanding problems and difficulties facing the country and the world today;
(d) To develop love for and pride in our cultural heritage through the knowledge of our history, geography and culture;
(e) To teach the simple laws of personal and community health and develop habits of hygiene and cleanliness;
(f) To foster the growth of the co-operative spirit as a way of life;
(g) To provide training in crafts both as a hobby and as a means to economic betterment;
(h) To provide cultural and recreational facilities by way of folk dances, drama, music, poetry, recitation and other ways of spontaneous self-expression;
(i) To provide through these various activities as well as through reading and discussion groups, an understanding of the basic moral values;
(j) To give a reasonable mastery over the tools of learning—reading, writing, simple arithmetic—and to create an interest in knowledge;
(k) To provide facilities for continuation of education through libraries, discussion groups, clubs and institutions like People's Colleges.

3. The Provincial Governments should be requested to prepare schemes for social education for making at least 50 per cent of the adult population of the province literate in the course of the next three years.

4. The Provincial Governments should entrust the working of the scheme in their respective provinces to an experienced educational officer, preferably the Director of Public Instruction.

5. The scheme for social education should be designed for the purpose of imparting education to the population between 12 and 45 years.

6. The Central Government should be requested to appoint a Board of experts and technical men to examine the Provincial schemes, to recommend to the Government of India the payment of necessary grants for these schemes from the Central Revenues, to advise on and make arrangements for the preparation of literature and audio-visual aids for use throughout the country.

7. Besides utilizing the services of students and teachers, an all-out effort should be made to utilize the services of refugees and other Government employees who are superfluous or have been retrenched.

8. Legislation for compelling employers to provide facilities for the education of their employees should include a provision to the effect that the cost incurred by the employers on the education of their employees may (subject to the approval of the Provincial Education Department) be admitted as legitimate charge on the expenses of establishment of the concern, for the purpose of assessment of income-tax.

9. One Education Centre should be started in each primary school and at least two such centres in each secondary school and adequate remuneration be given to the teachers for the additional work.

10. Research in the methods of teaching the adult should be encouraged.

11. On the recommendations of the Provincial Education Department, special allotment of paper be made for writing, publication of books, journals etc., for the purpose of social education.

The Provincial Governments should provide increased facilities for printing books and other literature connected with Social Education at the Government Press and should encourage the preparation of literature for use by adult literates and other workers in social education.

(B) EDUCATION COMMISSION (1964-66)*

Major Recommendations on Social Education

ADULT EDUCATION

1. Liquidation of literacy : (1) Every possible effort should be made to eradicate illiteracy from the country as early as possible and in no part of the country, however backward, should it take more than 20 years. The national percentage of literacy should be raised to 60 by 1971 and to 80 by 1976.

(2) As a first step to arrest the growth of illiteracy the following measures should be taken :

(a) Expansion of universal schooling of five years duration to the age group 6-11;

(b) Provision of part-time education to those childern of age-group 11-14 who either miss schooling or drop prematurely out of the school;

(c) Provision of part-time general and vocational education to the younger adults of the age-group 15-30.

(3) For the liquidation of illiteracy a two-fold strategy comprising the selective approach and the mass approach should be adopted.

(4) Under selective approach, programmes should be adopted for specified groups of adults which could be easily identified, controlled and motivated for intensive literacy work. All employers in large firms and commercial, industrial, contracting and other concerns should be made responsible, if necessary, by law, for making their employees functionally literate within a period of three years of their employment.

(5) Under mass approach, all available educated men and women in the country should be mobilized for raising a force to combat illiteracy and utilize it in a well-planned literacy campaign. In the organisation of mass campaign, the teachers and students and all educational institutions should be actively involved (17.7-24).

2. Part-time Education: Educational institutions of all types and grades should be encouraged and helped to throw open their doors outside the

Note: The figures within brackets at the end of each recommendation indicate respectively (1) The number of chapter in the Report, and (2) The number of the paragraph.

* Report of Education Commission (1964-66), Ministry of Education, Government of India, New Delhi.

regular working hours to provide such courses of instruction as they can to those who are desirous of receiving education. A parallel part-time system of education should be created to provide adults with opportunities for taking the same diplomas and degrees as students in schools and colleges. (17.32-35)

3. *Corresponding Courses*: (1) In order to bring education to those who are unable even to attend part-time courses, widespread organisation of correspondence courses should be organised.

(2) Students taking correspondence courses should be provided to meet the teachers occasionally, they should be given the status of recognised students, and where possible be attached to some colleges in order to enable them to make use of the library and other facilities.

(3) Correspondence courses should not be confined to preparing students for the university degrees but should also provide agricultural, industrial and other workers such special courses of instruction as would help them to improve production.

(4) Correspondence courses should be made available for those who desire to enrich their lives by studying subject of cultural and aesthetic value.

(5) Opportunity to take examinations conducted by the Secondary Education Board and Universities in the country should be made available to those who wish to work on their own without any assistance. (17.44-56)

4. *The Libraries :* The recommendations of the Advisory Committee on libraries relating to the establishment of a network of libraries throughout the country should be implemented. (17.57-58)

5. *Role of Universities* : The universities in India should assume a much larger responsibity for educating the adults. (17.61)

6. *Organisation and Administration* : A National Board of Adult Education on which all relevant Ministries and agencies would be represented should be established. (17.68)

(C) COMMITTEE OF MEMBERS OF PARLIAMENT ON EDUCATION (1967)*

Report on National Policy on Education

Spread of Literacy and Adult Education

The liquidation of mass illiteracy is essential, not only for accelerating

* Committeee of Member of Parliament on Education, 1967, Report on National Policy on Education, Ministry of Education, New Delhi, 1967.

programmes of production, especially in agriculture, but for quickening the tempo of national development in general. Plans to accelerate the spread of literacy should therefore be prepared and intensively implemented on several fronts. With a view to reducing new additions to the ranks of adult illiterates, part-time literacy classes should be organized for grown-up children (age-group 11-17) who did not attend school or have lapsed into illiteracy. All employees in large commercial, industrial and other concerns should be made functionally literate within a prescribed period of their employment and a lead in this direction should be given by the industrial plants in public sector. Similarly, teachers, students and educational institutions should be actively involved in literacy campaigns, especially as a part of the social or national service programme. The achievement of literacy should be sustained by the provision of attractive reading materials and library services to the neo- literates.

Adult or continuing education should be developed through facilities for part-time or own-time education and through the expansion and improvement of library services, educational broadcasting and television. The development of extension services in universities is of great significance in this context. In particular, the university should organize special extension programmes to train rural leadership.

(D) WORKING GROUP ON ADULT EDUCATION FOR MEDIUM TERM PLAN 1978-83 (1977)*

Chairman	Shri P. Sabanayagam.
Official Members	Dr. Ajit Mazumdar; Dr. B.D. Sharma; Smt. P. Ramachandran, Dr. Ishwar Das; O.P. Gautam; Shri C.G. Rangbhashyam; Shri C.S. Shastry; Shri M.P. Baizbarua; Prof. Satya Bhushan; Dr. S.N. Saraf.
Non-official Members	Dr. Ramlal Parikh; Dr. Malcolm S. Adiseshiah; Shri Kishore Saint; Shri K.S. Radhkrishnan; Dr. (Smt.) Chitra Naik; Shri S.N. Maitra; Dr. T.A. Koshy; Smt. Elaben Bhatt; Shri Mushtaq Ahmed; Father Gjousalves; Dr. Anil Sadgopal; Shri G.K. Gaokar.
M. Secy.	Shri Anil Bordia.

Notes : * (i) Ministry of Education and Social Welfare, New Delhi, 1978, p. 30 (Summary).

(ii) Table numbers have been provided to confirm to chapter number.

Appointment

The Working Group on Adult Education appointed by the Ministry of Education and Social Welfare, Government of India in 1977.

Terms of Reference

(a) To review the developments in the field of adult education;
(b) To advise on the approach and priorities for the Sixth Plan 1978-83;
(c) To formulate concrete proposals indicating financial implications and structural arrangements; and
(d) To apportion the areas of responsibility among the Centre, States and voluntary agencies.

Contents

Adult Education and Development; The Perspective and Strategy; Special Priority; The Organisational and Promotional Agencies; The Instructional Agencies; Resource Development; Post-literacy and Follow-up Programmes; Monitoring, Evaluation and Research; Planning and Adminstrative Structures; Programme Planning; Financial Arrangement and Phasing; The International Dimension; Appendices from I to V.

Recommendations

The Perspective and the Strategy

1.The attention paid in the successive five-year plans in the past has shown a declining awareness towards this sector of education.

2. *The Literacy Scene :* An analysis of the literacy scene for age-group above 14 years shows that while the percentage of literacy has increased in 1951, 1961, 1971 and 1977 from 19.26, 27.76, 34.08 to 38.00 the number of illiterate persons has also increased during this period from 17.39, 18.70, 20.95 to 22.66 crores. The segmental dimension of the problem is even more serious. In 15-35 age-group, out of a total of 9.71 crores of illiterate persons the rate of literacy among rural females is only 18.80 per cent and there are vast variations between rural and urban and between scheduled castes and scheduled tribes on the one hand and the remaining population on the other. These disparities will continue to rise unless arrangements are made to bridge this gap.

3. *The Operational Strategy :* The National Adult Education Programme recognises the importance of giving special priority to these segments of society, and lays importance on the 15-35 age-group because it is during this phase in life that people make families and have to upgrade their skills and understanding in the socio-economic perspective. In the first couple of years, rather than organising programmes on a massive scale, programmes of smaller size which are carefully planned would be taken up. Adult education programmes would be implemented through a network of projects. Every agency intending to take up the programme would determine the area which would be covered by it. As far as possible the project area could coincide with CD blocks, or in tribal areas with integrated tribal development projects. The effort would be to take up a contagious compact area and to organise as many adult education centres as feasible.

Special Priority

4. *Women:* Women form a substantial and integral segment of the labour force. An understanding about the role and status of women in society will, therefore, be an essential part of all programmes organised under NAEP. Adult education programmes for women may also have to be separately organised and, as a part of the post-literacy and follow-up programme, they may have to be encouraged to form their own groups for learning and to strengthen their participation and voice in the developmental process. As far as instructional responsibility is concerned it shall have to be borne by women teachers and other educated women in rural areas. A large programmes of condensed courses and training shall have to be organised.

5. *Scheduled Tribes:* Elimination of exploitation of the tribal people is an important task of development and this can be achieved only by building up the inner strength of those communities. Only education can provide this crucial inputs. In the organisation of adult education programmes for the tribals, the special characteristic of their society must be kept in mind. These programmes should (a) help them to acquire skills so that they may be able to negotiate effectively with the world around them and compete with outsiders in job situation and business dealings; (b) it should assist them in acquiring appreciation of their vibrant culture and conserve their environment; and (c) be inter-woven with the rest of the development programmes being organised through integrated tribal development projects. Within the vast tribal areas, there are some to

which higher priority needs to be given : the regions where industrial and mining activity is increasing, the pockets of particularly low levels of illiteracy and areas with large population of landless labourers.

6. *Scheduled Castes :* Persons belonging to the scheduled castes are scattered through the length and breadth of the country. Some of the issues in connection with organisation of adult education programmes are as follows:

(a) Though not desirable, it may be necessary to organise separate classes for these persons;
(b) As far as possible, if there is only one adult education centre in a village, it should be for person belonging to the Scheduled Castes;
(c) Even if the enrolment in a Scheduled Caste centre is thin, a centre should be orgainsed for them making an effort to bring enrolment to an optimum levels as soon as possible;
(d) Efforts should be made to improve their skills and techniques and if possible enable them to rise above their traditional occupations;
(e) Programmes of occupational diversification should be organised, such as poultry farming, plantation of fruit trees, animal and sheep husbandry, khadi and village industries;
(f) In the course of the adult education programmes as well as follow-up, organisations with fair representation of persons belonging to Scheduled Castes should be created. Where mixed organisations are not feasible, separate organisations should be set-up; and
(g) In regions where organisations of persons belonging to Scheduled Castes can lead to serious social tensions, the district authorities should be kept well informed about it, so that creation of such orgainsations may not lead to conflicts resulting in further deterioration of the condition of these people.

The Organisational and Promotional Agencies

7. *The Central Government*: As a part of its responsibility for social and economic planning the Central Government has naturally to provide leadership in NAEP. It should have special responsibility for involvement of the various agencies, particularly the voluntary organisations and universities/colleges, and taking up of programmes such as training,

production of teaching and learning materials and evaluation. The Ministries and the Departments of the Central Government, as well as their various autonomous organisations and other agencies, should explore ways to relate their programmes with NAEP.

8. *The State Governments:* In planning and implementation of NAEP the states have a pivotal role to play. Integration of adult education with development can take place only by a firm resolve of the State Governments. The State Governments will also have to take responsibility for identification of various agencies and managerial structures. As in the case of Central Government, NAEP in the States also cannot be the concern only of one department : all departments who organise programmes in which the involvement of beneficiaries is crucial to the success of the programme ought to look upon education a method for such involvement.

9. *Political Parties and other Associations:* No accoumt of promotional agencies can be complete without a mention of the impotance of :

— the leadership of political parties and their mass organisations of women, youth, workers and peasants;
— all-India cultural, religious and youth organisations;
— federations/associations of teachers, employees and of trade and industry.

These agencies can help in transforming of NAEP into a mass programme and they can also create the environment which would motivate the functionaries as well as the learners. The role expected from these agencies is to catalyse their members and affiliates, rather than taking up the field programmes themselves.

10. *Voluntary Organisations:* They have a place of precedence among the organisational agencies. These agencies should organise field adult education programmes. Voluntary agencies also have special responsibility in resource development, particularly training, production of teaching and learning materials and evaluation. The all-India voluntary organisations should be encouraged to organise orientation programmes for voluntary agencies. Agencies entering the field of adult education for the first time should ordinarily begin with a small programme which might be enlarged after an evaluation of their work. The Government must also replace the mechanisms which obstruct involvement of voluntary agencies by enabling mechanisms. Voluntary organisations

should be non-political and non-communal in nature in order to become eligible for assistance to implement programmes.

11. *Educational Institutions:* Introduction of national and social service at all stages of education is now the accepted policy. Involvement of educational institutions in NAEP would provide to them a well-defined means to interest students in service; it would also provide to NAEP a large number of dedicated workers. Although it needs to be emphasised that educational institutions should organise field adult education including literacy programmes, there are large number of other things which also they can do. These would include:

(a) creation of an environment;
(b) surveys;
(c) preparation of curriculum, teaching/learning materials and organisation of training, etc.;
(d) supplemental programmes of instruction through audio-visual means, cultural programmes, sports and games, etc.;
(e) facilitating women participants by taking care of their children;
(f) post-literacy and follow-up programmes;
(g) construction of adult education huts in villages where facilities for organisation of adult education activities are not enough; and
(h) evaluation and research.

12. *The Employers:* In respect of all their employees, all employers should be expected to organise adult education programmes including literacy, skill training, etc., Government being the biggest employer has a special resposibility. In large construction works, such as railways, irrigation dams, scarcity relief operations, roads, etc., arrangements of adult education should be provided for the workers. Apart from Government, the organised sector including factories, mines, plantation, etc., engage very large sized work-force. It should be the responsibility of the employers, in cooperation with the Central Board of Workers Education or other concerned agencies of labour welfare, to organise adult education and literacy programmes. Employers in the semi-organised sector also should be encourged to organise such programmes.

13. *The Local Bodies:* Municipalities and the Panchayati Raj Institutions can also play an important role in the organisation of adult education programmes in their areas. In particular the municipalities will have to take full responsibility for post-literacy and follow-up programmes in cities.

14. *Considerations in Selection:* In the past, there has been excessive reliance on elementary school teacher to function as instructors in adult education centres. This happened not because there was a deliberate decision regarding their suitability but by a force of habit. This uncritical method must be replaced by well-considered decisions, keeping in view the various possibilities and considerations, which would include:

— *voluntariness:* all persons to be involved as instructional agencies should participate on a purely voluntary basis;
— *motivation:* motivation among the instructors is a pre-condition of motivation among the learners;
— *communication:* the potential instructors should have the linguistic capability to communicate as well as attitude of equality towards the learners.

15. *Village Youth:* Owing to the possibility of natural communication, existence of un-emloyment and under-employment amoung the villagers and the possibility of creation of a new kind of rural leadership, the village youth need to be preferred as the instructional agents. A majority of the village youth would prefer to work on full-time basis, it would be worthwhile to continue the part-time adult education work with either the non-formal elementary education work or as a part of the various programmes of rural development.

16. *School Teachers :* Although school teachers have some advantages, such as being accustomed to organisation of educational programmes and their training in handling of teaching and learning materials, the formal system of education has become a part of their lives. They tend to be authoritarian and rigid and are seldom able to deal with villagers in a spirit of equality. Yet, such of the teachers as volunteer to participate in the programme should be welcomed. Besides, it should be possible to appoint unemployed persons who have had teacher training. They could be paid a meagre subsistence allowances, and can be entrusted responsibility for organisation of non-formal eductional programmes for children and for adults for a well defined community.

17. *Students:* Students at + 2 stage and in institutions of higher education should be encouraged to take responsibility for organisation of adult education centres, including literacy. This would necessitate continuous work for 200 to 350 hours a year, depending on the type of programme organised. It would be necessary for teachers to involve

themselves in NAEP if students are to be so involved. Representative organistions of students can also play a vital role in this connection.

18. *Developmental Fuctionaries:* It would be of immense advantage if village level developmental functionaries could take responsibility for organisation of adult education programme. While this would be good for adult education, it would also facilitate the work of those functionaries. Even, when development fuctionaries do not themselves organise adult education centres they should contribute to the programme as a part of a team. Keeping in view the importance of village revenue record keepers (Patwari, Lekhpal) and their role in land reforms, their participation in the programme would be of immense value.

19. *Retired Personnel:* A large number of ex-servicemen are discharged every year and can function as adult education instructors. In addition to ex-servicemen there are several other categories of retired personnel who can take instructional responsibility.

Resource Development

20. In the context of NAEP, resource development is intended to mean the instrumentality for transforming the concept and the objectives of the Programmes into a learning system. Its elements include curriculum development, preparation of teaching/learning materials, training and evaluation. Resource methodology has to be based on the principles of:

— flexibility and openness;
— devolution; and
— efficiency.

21.*Curriculum Development:* Curriculum in NAEP has to be related to the identifiable needs of the groups of learners, and, therefore, would ordinarily be preceded by a survey of such needs. The curriculum:

— should enable the learners to get a basic understanding of the social and physical environment in which they live,
— should develop an attitude of self-reliance and initiative,
— should encourage them to constructive action,
— should prepare them for parenthood and family life,
— should enable them to realise their rights and responsibilities, and
— should impart skills in literacy and numeracy so that self-

reliant learning may take place. The duration of the adult education programmes, including literacy, should be of 300 to 350 hours.

22. *Teaching/Learning Material and Training*: Teaching and learning materials, based on the curriculum, should help participants in entering into dialogue and mutual communication. The language to be used in the materials should be the spoken language of the pariticipants and special material should be prepared for linguistic minorities. The size and diversity of NAEP will necessitate well-organised training for all functionaries. The training of instructors should be organised by the project agency using locally available resource persons. Training of district adult education officers, project officers and supervisors should be the responsibility of a specially designated training institution, which would generally be established with a voluntary agency or an autonomous organisation. The training of State-level functionaries, heads of major voluntary agencies and other key personnel would be the responsibility of the Directorate of Adult Education.

23. *The Resource Structure:* At the apex of the resource structure is the Directorate of Adult Education, the National Resource Centre. In each state there is to be a State Resource Centre, which is critical level in resource development. A SRC is not expected to be a large unwieldy institute, it should use available resources within the state and make effort to devolutionise resource capability at the district and project levels. A district resource consortium should be organised to support the project agencies, which themselves would have substantial resource capability. Ultimately, each village where there is to be an adult education centre will have to develop its resource system, so that the programmes are related to the local needs and problems.

Post-Literacy and Follow-up Programmes

24. *The Educational Continuum:* If adult education and literacy have to play a germinal role, then the programme cannot be a one-time programme of 8 or10 months, or 300 or 350 hours. It must be a part of a continuous process of education leading to action and action needing further education. The post-literacy and follow-up programmes will mean that the learners will reinforce their literacy, will gain a more critical understanding of the impediments which are blocking their way. At the same time they will have a clearer idea about what economic programmes

can be taken up, how to utilise different government and non-government schemes, how to grasp effectively the facilities which are provided by banks and other institutions, how to organise cooperative societies and how to form and upgrade relevant skills.

25. *Organisation of Continuing Education Centres:* The responsibility of organisation of post-literacy and follow-up programmes will rest with project agency. Each project will have a Project Library Centre and a network of village continuing education centres would be created. In the urban areas the responsibility for organisation of continuing education would rest with municipalities and educational institutions. A continuing education centre would also serve as the focus for creation of village organisations. Besides, short duration training courses and condensed courses could be organised to raise understanding and levels of skills in regard to the occupational, health and civic issues. Mass media and folk culture can provide valuable means of recreation and learning.

Monitoring, Evaluation and Research

26. *Central level:* The past experience leads us to the realisaton that the system of monitoring, evaluation and applied research should aim at improvement of the management of the programme at all levels. Besides, evaluation of training outcomes, monitoring of progress and impact studies are special areas to which all exercises at evaluation must apply themselves. In organisation of evaluation and monitoring, the Directorate of Adult Education will play an important role, on the one hand establishing cooperative relationship with a number of appropriate management and research agencies as well as institutions of higher education and on the other hand preparing agencies in the states and districts to develop capibility for evaluation and applied research.

27. *Field level:* It is important that the progress of the programme, with reference to specfic determinant points, is regularly and systematically reported. This shall be the responsibility of the adult education instructor and the project agency. The second aspect of parties monitoring and evaluation would be a system of data audit, through creation of parties in practically every district who would draw samples in a prescribed manner and would undertake a check of the information furnished. The district parties could comprise teachers in universities, colleges and higher secondary schools or research workers. The third aspect is an examination regarding the extent to which programme

conforms to the objectives, its impact in the field and the reaction among the participants and other members of the community. Finally, on the basis of study of impact, measures for improvement of the programmes will have to be identified and disseminated to the implementation agencies.

Planning and Administartive Structures

28. *Project level:* NAEP is to be implemented through projects, which are visualised as the key unit for planning and implementation of the Programme. Ordinarily the area of a project would be co-terminous with one or two CD blocks and the number of adult education centres to be organised per project would vary from 100 to 500. Agencies taking up the programme for the first time could take up smaller projects also, but generally not less than 30 centres. There should be close and dynamic link between the project and the various development programmes in a project area. A project visualised in a spirit of autonomy, and the project administration should have not only sufficient financial powers and power to appoint intructors, but it should also organise training of instructors, prepare or moderate teaching/learning materials and organise evaluation and monitoring. Post-literacy and follow-up activities would be an essential part of the project activity. The administrative structure of a project would comprise a project office, in the case of large project generally assisted by an assistant project officer and a continuing education organiser, a certain number of supervisors and instructors.

29. *District level :* At the district level the primary responsibility for the programme shall rest with the Collector/Chief Executive Officer. The Government project agencies would be supervised by the District Collector and he would also organise coordination, monitoring and general supervision over all agencies in the district. The Collector/CEO would be assisted by a district adult education officer. There would be a district adult education board/committee, presided over by the Ditrict Collector/CEO, of which all project officers would be members, in addition to district-level development officers, public workers, etc. The district level agency would normally examine the proposal of a voluntary agency and would make suitable recommendation to the State Governmant. The Committee would also oversee the work of all projects running in the district.

30. *State level :* At the apex in each State would be the State Board of Adult Education, presided over by the Chief Minister or the Education

Minister. The State Board would provide policy guidelines and would periodically appraise the progress of implementation. For ensuring coordination between the development programmes and adult education, to oversee programme formulation and to receive periodic reports regarding implementation, a Steering Committee would be set up under the Chairmanship of the Chief Secretary. A State adult education office shall have to be set up in each State. The office would be headed by a senior official who should be a head of the department, either working under the director of the department dealing with adult education or independently.

31.*Personnel policy :* In appointment of personnel at various levels—project, district and State—certain general considerations should be kept in view. The scales of pay of staff working in adult education should normally be comparable with appropriate levels in education or development departments. Rather than, appointing persons by routine promotions or non-selective transfer, suitable selection should be made from any department the staff of which can have experience or expertise in the field of adult education. Preference in appointment should be given to women and to persons belonging to Scheduled Castes and Scheduled Tribes. Arrangements should be made to retain good workers, and when promotions become due to them, they should be provided opportunity within the sphere of adult education.

Programme Planning

32. *Objective:* The ultimate aim of programme planning process is to create village and mohalla adult education units which would take their own decisions regarding duration of programmes, persons, to be entrusted instructional responsibility, teaching/learning material to be used, post-literacy and follow-up programmes, etc. Right from the beginning, effort should be made to create such units.

33. *Projects as the Level of Programme Planning:* The vital level of programme planning at this level can be divided into : (i) preparation for starting of the programme, (ii) organisation of adult education centres, and (iii) post-literacy and follow-up activities.

34. *Preparatory Action :* Preparatory action should begin with appointment of project officers and supervisors, which would take place about three months before the centres are to be established. Their first month would be spent in training. The instructors would ordinarily be appointed a month after the appointment of project officers and

supervisors and a training would be organised for them in the second month. The third month, which would be the month preceding establishment of adult education centres, would be spent on survey, identification of places for establishment of adult education centres, securing of supplies including teaching/learning materials, creation of environment and establishing communication with the people of the community where the centres are to be established.

35. *Implementation Stage :* With the starting of the adult education centre, systematic enrolment of learners should be made and no adult, whatever his age, who wishes to participate in the programme, should be refused enrolment. Simultaneous steps should be taken to involve the development and revenue functionaries and a beginning should be made with discussion around problems of land, production programmes, health and child-care, etc. There is need to create a special consciousness among the instructors and supervisors regarding the measures to be taken to sustain the interest of the learners. Accurate progress reporting measures of self-evaluation in which learners might also be involved, and systematic supervision have to be ensured. Preparatory action for the next batch should start a couple of months before conclusion of a particular batch.

36. *Follow-up : Concurrent Action :* Action for post-literacy and follow-up programmes should also start before conclusion of the first batch. This would involve establishment of a village Continuing Education Centre, identification and training of continuing education worker and involvement of a large number of agencies for organisation of a short-duration training programmes, cultural and recreational activities and formation and strengthening of village organisations.

Financial Arrangements and Phasing

37. *Central Responsibility:* The responsibility of the Central Government in financing of NAEP should be for involvement of voluntary agencies and youth, taking up of model pace-setter projects (the on-going Farmers' Functional Literacy Programme and Non-formal Education for 15-35 age-group to be merged from 1979-80) and for establishment of institutional structures for training and resource development. Besides, funds for strengthening of planning and administrative structures may also be provided by the Central Government. The rest of the financial responsibility must rest with the State Government and, speaking of the overall five-year outlays, the expenditure to be incurred

through the States should match the expenditure to be incurred by the Central Government.

38. *Costing :* The cost per person enrolled in adult education programme has been calculated at the rate of Rs. 60. Since, approximately one-third of the participants may drop out, the effective cost per learner comes to Rs. 90. However, as the duration of some of the programmes may be shorter, and some voluntary contribution may also be made, the effective cost per learner has been assumed at Rs. 80. This, however, does not include the expenditure on planning and administrative structure, on evaluation and monitoring and on post-literacy and follow-up activities. Assuming that the effective target for the Five Year Plan period would be 650 lakhs, as indicated in the Draft Five Year Plan document, the requirement of funds for the period 1978-83 would work out as follows:

Table 4.1: Requirement of Funds for 1978-83

6. 50 crores × Rs. 80. 00	Rs.	520	crores
Add 10% (Administrative cost)	Rs.	52	crores
TOTAL	Rs.	572	crores
Add 20% (follow-up cost)	Rs.	114. 4	crores
GRAND TOTAL	Rs.	686. 4	crores
		or say	
	Rs.	686	crores

The Yearwise Phasing of the Target would be as follows:

Table 4.2: Phasing as the Target : Yearwise

Year	Annual coverage (in millions)	Cumulative coverage (in millions)	Cost (rupees in crores)
1978-79 (year of preparation)	1.5	1.5	15.84
1979-80	4.5	6.0	48.52
1980-81	9.0	15.0	95.04
1981-82	18.0	33.0	190.05
1982-83	32.0	65.0	336.95
Total Cost:			Rs. 686.40 crores or say Rs. 686 crores

39. *Multiple Agency Funding* : Only Rs. 200 crores have been provided for this programme in the Five Year Plan 1978-83. In this contest, it may be mentioned that the Planning Commission has observed that this provision is only one source of funds for programmes of adult education and that funds for this purpose would also become available in other developmental sectors such as tribal development plans, rural development programmes and programmes of agricultural development. The Planning Commission has also stated that the present outlay indicated will be stepped up if necessary on the basis of the experience gained in the year to year implementation of the programme.

The International Dimension

40. *The International Dimension* : Keen interest has been evinced by a number of international agencies and other countries in supporting NAEP as well as in obtaining the services of Indian experts in the programmes, being organised by other developing countries. While appreciating the offers made in this behalf, it would be advisable to base NAEP on country's own financial resources. Some of the areas in which the Indian search and experimentation needs to be supplemented include : (i) integration of adult education and development; (ii) functionality of adult literacy; (iii) problems of linguistics; (iv) the manner in which programmes oriented towards liberation of the illiterates and poor persons are to be organised; and (v) evaluation and applied research. The countries from which we should seek short-duration experts would be mostly developing countries. It might be of greater advantage for Indian field workers and experts to visit foreign countries and observe their experiences and learn from them. There may be need to secure support from international agencies or on bilateral basis for training and audio-visual equipment and paper. At the initial stage it would be desirable to channelise international cooperation through UN agencies. Close contact should also be established with International Council of Adult Education, directly by Government as well as through all-India voluntary agencies.

APPENDIX II

Functional Chart I

National Adult Education Programme
National Board of Adult Education

Ministry of Education and Social Welfare, Directorate of Adult Education, U. G. C., Shramik Vidyapeeths, Nehru Yuvak Kendras, N. S. S Voluntary Organisations	State Board of Adult Education	Dev. Ministries/ Departments Agriculture, Labour, Information and Broadcasting, Cooperation, Industry, Home (Tribal Dev.) Etc.
State Deptts. of Education (or Deptt. Dealing with Adult Education), Directorate of Edu./Adult Education, State Resource Centre, Universities Voluntary Organisations		State Development Deptts., Agriculture, Animal Husbandry, Dairy, Labour, Industry, Information and Publicity, Cooperation, Tribal and Harijan Welfare, Community Development, etc.
	District Adult Education Committee	
Distt. Edu./Adult Education Office		Distt. Offices of Dev. Deptts.
	Project Officer	
	Supervisors Instructors	Field Functionaries

APPENDIX III

Functional Chart II

State Level Agencies

1. **State Board of Adult Education**

   (a) Laying down of policy guidelines.
   (b) Certain of Environment.
   (c) Periodic appraisal of the Programme.

2. **Steering Committee**

   (a) Plan formulation.
   (b) Coordination between adult education and various sectors of development.
   (c) Coordination among various implementation agencies—Government, voluntary agencies, educational institutions, employers, etc.
   (d) Monitoring of the programme.
   (e) Advising the State Board.

3. **Education Department or any other Department dealing with Adult Education in Secretariat**

   (a) Establishment of management system.
   (b) Laying down of financial pattern—delegation of financial powers.
   (c) Coordination between adult education and formal system of education—involvement of universities, colleges and schools.

4. **State Adult Education Office**

   (a) Preparation of plans, project formats, methodological guidelines.
   (b) Encouraging voluntary agencies to participate.
   (c) Direction and overall supervision over Government programmes.

(d) Overseeing and coordination of programmes taken up by various agencies other than Government.
(e) Selection and placement of personnel.
(f) Monitoring and evaluation.

5. State Resource Centre

(a) Organisation of seminars, symposia, etc., for wide understanding of the concept and objectives of NAEP.
(b) Development of methodological guidelines for curriculum preparation.
(c) Preparation of teaching/learning materials, and devolution of this capability.
(d) Training support to the Programme.
(e) Preparation of guidelines for post-literacy and follow-up action, production of material for neo-literates.
(f) Evaluation, research and innovation.
(g) Publications.

APPENDIX IV

Functional Chart III

District Level Agencies
Collector/Chief Executive Officer
District Adult
Education Committee/Board
District Adult
Education Officer

(a) Coordination

(i) between adult education and development agencies,
(ii) between adult education and formal system of education,
(iii) between adult education and revenue and law and order agencies,
(iv) among various adult education agencies—earmarking of area of operation and creating a consortium for resource development.

(b) Training

(i) training of instructors—in projects where the project officer and supervisor need supplementation of their capability,
(ii) inter-learning among project officers and supervisors of various agencies in the district through seminars, workshops.

(c) Control over Government agencies—allowing as much autonomy to them as feasible.
(d) Processing of the applications of voluntary agencies for financial assistance, periodic appraisal of the progress of their work.
(e) Monitoring and evaluation.
(f) Conduct of enquiries necessitated by the direction of State-level or national-level agencies.

APPENDIX V

Functional Chart IV

Project Level

1. Project Officer

(With the assistance of Assistant Project Officer and Community Education Organiser)

(a) Identification and appointment of instructors.
(b) Training of instructors.
(c) Securing supplies for instructional arrangements.
(d) Preparatory action for starting of adult education centres curriculum, teaching/learning materials.
(e) Establishment of contact with the field.
(f) Supervision over and guidance to supervisors, and instructors wherever possible.
(g) Contact with district level agencies.
(h) Contact and liaison with block level development revenue and law and order functionaries.
(i) Management of office, maintenance of accounts, etc.
(j) Monitoring and evaluation.
(k) Planning and organisation of post-literacy and follow-up activities, including setting up of a project library centre.
(l) Preparation of periodical project reports.

2. Supervisors

(a) Assistance of project officer in resource development, particularly training—recurrent training of instructors in monthly meetings.
(b) Supervision over and guidance to instructors.
(c) Establishing a living rapport with the people of the area where adult education centres are being run.
(d) Liaison with local development functionaries, extension officers—and institutional structures such as youth clubs, Mahila Mandals, cooperative societies, panchayats, schools, etc.
(e) Ensuring payment to instructors and availability of supplies.
(f) Ensuring that timely returns are submitted by instructors.
(g) Post-literacy and follow-up activities.

(E) REVIEW COMMITTEE ON THE NATIONAL ADULT EDUCATION PROGRAMME (1979)

Chairman Prof. D. S. Kothari

Members Dr. M. S. Adiseshiah; Smt. Ela Bhatt; Shri J. P. Naik; Shri V. Siddharthacharry; Dr. Surajit Sinha; Shri Habib Tanvir; Shri B. G. Verghese

Member Secretary Shri Anil Bordia

Appointment

The Review Committee on the National Adult Education Programme was appointed by the Ministry of Education and Culture, Government of India in October 1979.

Terms of Reference

(a) To review the working of the NAEP in all its aspects, and to recommend any modifications that would improve its implementation, quality and impact;

(b) To recommend any changes in the priority assigned to adult education that may be called for in the light of the review by the Committee; and

(c) To examine if any economy could be effected in the allocations for the NAEP by better implementation and more effective participation of educational institutions and non-official agencies.

Contents

Letter from the Chairman to the Union Education Ministers; Members of the Review Committee; Introduction; Adult Education; Objectives and Organisation, The Role of Adult Education in Educational System; Adult Education for Development; Preconditions for Organisation of a Nation-wide Adult Education Programme; The National Adult Education Programme; A Review; Early efforts; Development since independence; The National Adult Education Programme (1978); Progress of the NAEP

Source : New Delhi, Ministry of Education and Culture, Government of India, New Delhi, 1980, p. 127.

(1978-80); Recommendations; The Future Programme; Scope and Organization; Magnitude of the Programme and Annual Projections; Widening and Deepening of the Content; Motivation; Participation of Priority Groups; Organization; Evaluation, Monitoring and Research; Implementing Agencies; Resources Development and Media; Implementing Agencies: The Instructor; Supervisors and Project Officers; Resource Centres; Production of Instructional Materials; Communication and Culture; Finance and Implementation; Conclusions and Recommendations; Appendix—State Resource Centres as on 31-3-1980; Statistical Tables from IA to IE and IIA to IIH.

Recommendations

7.1 In the modern world, education and development, and indeed survival, go together. Good education promotes development—economic, social and moral. Bad education is counter-productive and can seriously harm national interest and welfare. Mahatma Gandhi assigned the first place in education to character-building. The education of the people was upper-most in the mind of Jawaharlal Nehru. He said: "The country cannot make progress worth the name till we are able to remove illiteracy from among our masses".

7.2 There is an increasing realisation of the crucial importance of adult education. Yet in determination and effort for its promotion has been hardly commensurate with the colossal magnitude and extreme urgency of the task. The literacy rate for the country is still only 35 per cent. Even, if a hundred million people were covered by the NAEP in five years—an extremely difficult task—the national literacy percentage would still be below 60 per cent.

7.3 A preliminary review of the NAEP, as operating at present, shows that it has evoked an encouraging reponse. Nothing should be done to undermine this. The present programme has both strengths and shortcomings. Despite commendable work done in several areas, the review also brings out many weaknesses. For instance, more careful preparation is needed in the formulation of State and district plans, preparation of annual projections, training of instructors, and greater participation of all priority groups. The duration of the programme is too short and provision for follow-up activities is inadequate. The link between the education and development components of the programme is lacking. The feasibility of the programme and the tangible benefits flowing from it are not clear. *An uncertain programme cannot be a mass movement.* The more crucial a programme for national development, the greater is the need for thorough preparation.

7.4 The Programme needs to be radically modified and strengthened. Our specific recommedations are:

(1) Priority

(a) In the plans of national development, along with universalisation of primary education, adult education should receive the highest priority. Adult education should be an integral part of the Basic Minimum Needs Programme (Paras 2.13 and 2.16).

(b) All illiterate persons of the age-group of about 15 to 35 should be covered in the shortest time possible by a programme of adult education. Nothing should be done to weaken the momentum generated for the NAEP. The Programme should be continued, and steps taken to radically modify and strengthen it.

(2) The Future Adult Education Programme

(a) State and district plans of adult education and annual projections should be prepared. With determined efforts, most States and many districts in all States would be able to complete the programme in five years. Some would take longer. But even in these areas the programme should be completed in not more than ten years.

(b) Pending the finalisation of the plans, the number of illiterate persons to be covered in the year 1980-81 may be retained for the present at nine million, as visualised in the NAEP.

(c) The content of the programme—consisting of literacy, functionality, and awareness,—should be deepened and widened. An adequate level of literacy should be insisted upon with emphasis on the learners improving their vocational skills and taking organised action for the improvement of their condition.

(d) Sustained effort should be made to link litercay with development.

(e) The duration of the programme should be about three years, divided into three stages of about a year each.

(f) The programme should be flexible and closely related to the needs of the learners and the local environment (Paras 4.2 to 4.11).

(3) Participation

(a) In organisation of the programme special attention should be paid to creation and sustenance of motivation among the learners.

(b) Emphasis should be laid on participation of women in the programme. Measures should be taken which would influence social attitudes and remove pratical difficulties which women face in attending adult education classes. It would be desirable to arrange adult education for women as part of their work.

(c) Women should be adequately represented on advisory committees at all levels. Their recruitment as instructors and at other levels should be substantially raised.

(d) The programme for the Scheduled Castes should pay attention to their special problems. Adult education centres common to all are desirable, and efforts should be made to move in that direction. Where necessary, separate classes for the Scheduled Castes should be organised in their localities.

(e) The adult education programmes for the Scheduled Tribes should use tribal languages where necessary and pay special attention to their special cultural heritage and crafts.

(f) The involvement of Scheduled Castes and Scheduled Tribes should be emphasized. They should be made aware of the Government schemes for their amelioration and be enabled to utilize them.

(g) The Scheduled Castes and Scheduled Tribes should be represented on all advisory committees. Their recruitment as instructors and at other levels should be encouraged in every possible way.

(h) Special attention should be paid to the organisation of adult education programmes for the physically handicapped (Paras 4.13 to 4.27).

(4) National Board of Adult Education

The National Board of Adult Education should be autonomous, with the Union Education Minister as Chairman. There should be a whole time

Vice-Chairman and two or three other whole-time members. It should be responsible for planning, financing and implementation of the Programme at the Centre and for giving it the necessary leadership and support. The NBAE' s responsibility would also include support to and development of the SRCs, monitoring, evaluation and research and, generally, improvement of the quality and coverage of the Programme. The funds provided in the Central budget for adult education should be placed at its disposal. The Board should make an annual report to the Parliament (Paras 4.28-4.29 and 4.39 to 4.42).

(5) State Boards of Adult Education

Autonomous Boards of Adult Education (SBAE) should be eastablished in every State. They should be responsible for planning, financing and implementing the Programme and for its coordination at the State level. They should make intensive efforts to expand and improve the Programme (Para 4.30).

(6) District and Field Organisation

(a) Every district should have an Adult Education Committee.
(b) The District Adult Educaion Officers should be responsible to the SBAE. Their duties would include planning and implementation of the Programme. They should have adequate powers and support for the purpose.
(c) The Project should be smaller in size than at present, ordinarily consisting of 100 to 200 centres. The project officers should have wider powers than at present.
(d) The organisation of the adult education centres should be flexible enough to suit the learners' needs, local conditions and availability of resources (Para 4.31 to 4.36).

(7) Implementing Agencies

A number of agencies are making or could make an important contribution to the Programme. In respect of them, we recommend as follows:

(a) *Voluntary Agencies:* The associations with the programme of voluntary agencies engaged in social service, education, rural development, village industries, health-care and such other activities, should be continued and they should be given all encouragement and assistance. Whether they should continue to be assisted directly from the Centre or through the State Governments would need further examination by the National Board of Adult Education (Para 5.11 to 5.13).

(b) *Universities and Colleges:* Universities and colleges should be involved to the greatest possible extent, through NSS or otherwise. Involvement of Women's colleges would help in increasing the participation of women learners in the programme. In the long run, participation in social service, including adult education, should become a part of the academic course (Paras 2.14, 5.14 and 5.15).

(c) *Schools:* Involvement of schools should be increased. Eventually, every school should be developed into a community centre for the education of children as well as adults (Para 5.16).

(d) *Panchayati Raj Institutions and Municipalities:* Panchayati Raj Institutions and Municipalities should be involved in the programme, wherever and howsoever possible. They should also take responsibility for running reading rooms and libraries (Para 5.9).

(e) *Cooperatives:* The NBAE should prepare, in consultation with the National Cooperative Union of India, a detailed programme for participation in adult education of the members of cooperative societies and also of their families, if possible (Para 5.10).

(f) *Employers:* Employers in the organised sector, public and private, should be required to provide adult education facilities for all their employees, and if possible, for the members of their families. A lead should be given by Government and the public sector undertakings. In this, trade unions and Central Board of Workers' Education should be associated (Para 5.17).

(g) *Individuals and other Groups:* Every effort should be made to involve dedicated individuals, housewives and youth clubs, *Mahila Mandals* and Sainik Boards, and other interested organizations (Para 5.18).

(8) Involvement of Political Parties and certain other Organisations

The NBAE should examine, as soon as possible, the question of ineligibility of political parties and certain other organisations—such as trade unions, associations of teachers and students, all-India cultural organisations, etc., to receive grants from Government. Till then, the present practice may continue (Paras 5.19 and 5.20).

(9) Need for Vigilance

Appropriate mechanisms should be evolved for ensuring that misuse of funds for adult education is prevented (Para 5.21).

(10) The Instructor

Every effort should be made to attract the best possible persons as instructors. Steps should be taken to increase the pool of persons available for recruitment as instructors, especially in remote and backward areas. Training of instructors should be improved and the best available persons should be involved in it. The honorarium of the instructor should be raised to Rs. 75 per month in Stage I and to Rs. 100 and Rs. 125 per month respectively for Stages II and III. The appointment of instructors should be for the duration of the project (i.e., 3 or 4 years), subject to satisfactory work. There should be adequate opportunities for their advancement (Paras 5.22 to 5.29).

(11) Supervisors and Project Officers

There is need to improve the opportunities of advancements for supervisors and project officers. The gap between the remuneration of instructors, supervisors and project officers should be reduced (Paras 5.30 and 5.31).

(12) Resource Centres

The Central Directorate of Adult Education and the SRCs should be strengthened. A Resource Centre, should be established for the North-Eastern Region. District Resource Units should be established. Full use should be made of universities and other institutions for resource development (Paras 5.32 to 5.36).

(13) Instructional Material

Material of good quality, including teaching aids, need to be produced in larger numbers for the instructional programme, especially for functionality and awareness and for Stages II and III. Materials are also needed for training of instructors, supervisors and project officers, and for promotional and motivational purposes. While production of material is a responsiblity of the Central Directorate of Adult Education and the SRCs, there is need for serious involvement of universities and other institutions of proven capability (Paras 5.37-5.40).

(14) Traditional and Folk Media

A programme of people's education should lead to a renaissance of the people's culture. There is need to support traditional and folk arts *per se* and also for their fuller and wider use in the furtherance of literacy and adult education programmes. Suitable schemes for this purpose should be prepared (Paras 5.42 and 5.43).

(15) The Modern Media

The potential of the electronic media and film should be exploited for the Programme. This needs close collaboration between the authorities concerned with education, INSAT, Films, Doordarshan and AIR. The National and State Boards should have Media Councils and the AIR and Doordarshan should have adult education and distance learning cells at their national and regional headquarters (Paras 5.44 to 5.49).

(16) Libraries and Continuing Education

Steps should be taken to produce literature needed for post-literacy and continuing education. A nation-wide network of libraries should be organised and linked closely to the adult education programme (Paras 5.50 to 5.52).

(17) Finance

(a) The cost per person covered under the modified programme, on a rough estimate, works out to Rs. 150. The present figure is a little over Rs. 100 (Paras 6.8).

(b) On the above basis, the total cost of the programme for 100 million persons will be Rs. 15,000 million (or Rs. 1500 crores). Of this, the amount needed in the next five years would be about Rs. 9,000 million (or Rs. 900 crores).

(c) A major part of this sum of Rs. 9,000 million should be provided in the Plan of the Education Sector. The rest should be in the other sectors of development to enable the development agencies to include a component of adult education in their programmes. It should be earmarked for adult education.

(d) The existing arrangement of equal sharing of expenditure between the Central and State Plans should continue. However, special additional provision should be made in the Central Plan to provide support for tribal hill and desert regions and for such priority groups as women, Scheduled Castes, Scheduled Tribes, and the Physically handicapped (Para 6.19).

(18) Financial Procedures

(a) There should be no diversion of funds provided for adult education to any other stage of education or to any other sector of development.

(b) It is essential to devise procedures which will ensure that funds reach the projects agencies in time and to delegate adequate financial powers to the project officer to enable him to deal effectively with the day-to-day problems (Para 6.10).

(19) Economy

An important method of economy is to improve the efficiency and quality of the programmes. Other means would include the involvement of the community and harnessing the idealism, dedication and commitment of the people, especially the youth (Para 6.11).

(20) Implememtation

The first step should be a statement by the Government regarding acceptance of the main recommendations contained in the Report. The National Board of Adult Education should be set up as early as possible to give effect to the modifications needed in the Programme. Meanwhile, action should be taken to implement recommendations such as improvement of training of instructors and instructional material, special attention to priority groups, greater involvement of voluntary agencies and local bodies, cooperatives, and employers and expansion of the participation of teachers and students (Paras 6.12 to 6.15).

APPENDIX

State Resource Centres (as on 31-3-1980)

Address of the Institutions	*States Covered*
1	2
1. Department of Continuing Adult Education, Osmania University, Hyderabad	Andhra Pradesh
2. Deepayatan, 32-A, New Srikrishnapuri, Patna	Bihar
3. Gujarat Vidyapeeth, Ahmedabad	Gujarat
4. State Resource Centre, Chandigarh	Haryana
5. Centre for Continuing Education, Punjab University, Chandigarh	Himachal Pradesh Punjab, UT of Chandigarh
6. Department of Education, University of Kashmir, Srinagar	Jammu & Kashmir
7. Karnataka State Adult Education Council Krishnamurthipuram, Mysore	Karnataka
8. Kerala Association for Non-formal Education and Development, Trivandrum	Kerala
9. Indian Institute of Education, 168/2 Karve Road, Kothrud, Pune	Maharashtra
10. Utkal Navjeevan Mandal Angul, Distt. Dhenkanal	Orissa
11. Rajasthan Adult Education Association, 38, Jobner Bagh, Jaipur	Rajasthan
12. Tamil Nadu Board of Continuing Education, 2, Adams Road, Madras	Tamil Nadu
13. Literacy House, P. O. Alambagh, Lucknow	Uttar Pradesh
14. Bengal Social Service League, 1/6, Raja Dinendra Street, Calcutta	West Bengal

(F) WORKING GROUP ON NATIONAL INSTITUTE OF ADULT EDUCATION (1995)

SECTION I

Introduction

The idea of establishing a national institution devoted to adult education was initially mooted in the National Policy on Education,1986 and further specified in the accompanying Programme of Action. Following this, the NIAE was established as an autonomous organisation under the Societies Registration Act in 1991.The Institute formally began functioning from September 1991.

After the recruitment of faculty and other staff, the first annual plan was prepared for the year 1992-93 and on the basis of which, programmes and activities were designed and initiated. The programmes were duly examined and approved by a Programme Advisory Committee. However, the PAC could again meet only in September 1993; also, no meetings of the GB and the EC were held thereafter creating a state of uncertainty for the activities of the Institute.

The period of uncertainty continued as the terms of the GB and EC expired in the beginning of 1994. It is only recently that the EC was reconstituted under the Chairmanship of Mr. Mushtaq Ahmed. In its first meeting held on 28 September 1995, the EC took serious note of the continued uncertainty of the Institute and the confusion over its specific roles and responsibilities, and set up the present Working Group consisting of the following members to examine the whole issue and make suitable recommendations to the EC.

(1) Dr. Anita Rampal - Convenor
(2) Ms. Nishat Farooq
(3) Dr. Venkatesh Atreya
(4) Dr. R. Govinda
(5) Dr. Veena Mazumdar
(6) Dr. Anita Dighe

The specfic Terms of Reference of the Working Group were:

(i) To make a quick assessment and review of the work done by NIAE;

(ii) To define the Role of the NIAE in the present context of the nature and progress of the literacy movement; and

(iii) To specify the function of the NIAE against this background.

The Working Group had several rounds of meetings during the last three months and examined the documents available on the functioning of the Institute. In addition, the members of the group also held a meeting with the Faculty of the Institute to elicit their perceptions of the future role and functions of the Institute. Informal discussions were also held with the Director of the DAE and the DG, NLM. An attempt was made in these meetings to understand the current nature and volume of work in the sphere of literacy and spell out the distinct roles that could be played by NIAE, DAE and other bodies operating at the national level. An attempt was also made to delineate the inputs required to address the immediate issues faced by the literacy campaigns, while maintaining a broader focus on the long term perspective essential for continuing and life long education for all citizens in the country.

SECTION II

Brief Review of the Work of NIAE

The review of work presented here is not an exhaustive and in-depth analysis of the work done by the faculty members of the institute. What follows is, therefore, a quick overview of the various kinds of activities—research, training programmes, publications, carried out by the Institute till now. Based on a quick analysis, some broad observations have been made indicating the future directions in which the Institute may proceed, while formulating and executing various activities during the years to come. The basis of the review is mainly the annual reports of the Institute, a quick reading of the published and unpublished material produced by the faculty, and a broad spectrum discussion with the faculty members.

An Overview of Work Done

The tasks assigned to the institute according to the Memorandum of Association included : (1) providing academic and technical resource support for implementation of NLM and adult education programmes of all descriptions; (2) organizing training programmes and academic courses keeping in view the manpower required for the adult education programmes; (3) supporting the improvement of content and processes of adult education programmes; (4) preparing media material and harnessing traditional and non-traditional media; (5) undertaking research, and monitoring activities; (6) liaising and coordinating with various categories of institutions and agencies for the furtherance of these objectives.

Keeping the above objectives in view and based on the Task Force Report (1988) on NIAE, five thrust areas were identified at the intial stage. These were subsequently modified towards the end of 1991 through internal discussions among the faculty members, possibly in view of the background and experience of the professional staff who had by then joined the Institute. These were:

> (1) Gender Equity in Literacy; (2) Media and Communication; (3) Evaluation Issues; (4) Social Sciences in Adult Education; (5) Population Education; and (6) Post-Literacy and Continuing Education.

Following this, an approach paper was prepared by the faculty which was then used as the basis for the first annual plan of action for 1992-93.

Based on the proposals made in the annual plan, several research studies were initiated in the Institute. These researches were originally intended to provide technical feedback to the on-going activities of the NLM in a need based manner. However, the outputs have largely remained in a draft form and no feedback seems to have flown to the field level activities. It would have been of great value if the work done in the areas of 'Literacy Primers' and 'Action Research on Continuing Education for Women' had been brought to a final shape and the findings made available to the NLM, and also to the TLCs which needed such inputs. Indeed, the outcomes of the field-based appraisal and evaluation of TLCs, undertaken by a few of the faculty members seem to be the only sets of information which have been disseminated through direct communication to the NLM and/or through publication in academic journals by individual faculty members.

It is difficult to make evaluation judgments on the quality of research done based on the draft versions of the reports available. However, it needs to be stated that work in certain areas, such as, population education lack any interface with the field level requirements of the NLM. It is also recommended that the thrust areas of the Institute mentioned earlier are thoroughly re-examined to make them more relevant to the current state and essential requirements of literacy programmes of the country.

Emphasis on exploiting modern technology for promoting literacy activities is quite desirable and is a part of the basic task of the Institute. However, this should be done keeping a close watch on its relevance, cost effectiveness and feasibility at the field level, to match the consciously adopted frugal funding pattern of the TLC approach. Moreover, one should perhaps desist from developing national level prototypes to be adopted at the grassroots level; instead it is more desirable to promote such activities in a decentralized and need-based fashion.

Initial documents brought out by the Institute, including the approach paper evolved by the faculty members, underline the need for adopting an inter-disciplinary perspective in designing various programmes of the Institute. However, this is not quite evident from the research activities carried out by the Institute. Contrary to the proposals made in the approach paper, individual faculty members, their background and expertise seemed to have determined the nature of work carried out. Another related problem one could notice is the absence of sustained net-working arrangements with field based organizations.

The Institute seems to have kept training programmes completely outside its purview. This is a bit paradoxical as the expanding programme of NLM has brought into the field new sets of actors who need professional orientation and training on a continuous basis. The few programmes conducted by the Institute have only been in the form of seminars and workshops. Many of these again formed a part of the research projects initiated by individual faculty members. It is needless to say that a national institution has to play a more significant role in building capacities through meaningful training and orientation programmes, and also generate innovative ideas that can provide new directions to policy and programme formulations in the area of adult education.

Documentation and dissemination activities by the Institute have remained a virtual non-starter. An impressive plan was intially drawn up for setting up a comprehensive documentation facility at the Institute. But no follow-up could perhaps be taken up due to the ensuring uncertainty about the Institute and absence of funding for developmental activities. Consequently, the Institute altogether failed to reach out to the field with its expertise and understanding.

Observation on the nature of activities carried out and directions for the future

There is a need to evolve an institutional perspective which can guide the formulation of training and research activities. Some attempt has been made in the approach paper prepared by the Faculty. Yet the paper appears to be too broad and does not concretely explicate the common thread that would run through the programmes of the institute. This was of course the first attempt and there is a need that the faculty jointly works on such a perspective document before it again goes for examination and approval by the EC. The perspective should effectively translate the basic objectives of the NLM into a programmatic framework, from which concrete research and training activities can be derived, and a plan of action charted out.

We realize that a common perspective on the Institute's activities has to evolve through a process of continuous interaction among the faculty members and outside professionals over a reasonable stretch of time. However, it is essential that a conscious effort is made to overcome the problem of individual research interests taking precedence over the institutional perspective. This is particularly important in the intial stages of development of the Institute.

An important instrumentality for the emergence of a common perspective will be the designing of activities, particularly in the form of relatively long term training programme, which become occasions for collaborative action by all the faculty members of the Institute. They have to be designed keeping in view the pooled expertise available, not only individual interests and expertise. While one or two faculty members may become task organizers, involvement of several others in each programme should be considered imperative. This would be logical, as the number of faculty members in the Institute at present is very small.

We find that the exclusion of training and capacity building activities from the purview of the Institute has deprived the faculty of very useful and organized occasions to interact with the field level functionaries and thereby enhance their own understanding of the on-going developments in this field. Future activities of the Institute have to incorporate training and capacity building as important components of the Institute's programme. In particular, the Institute has major responsibility in building academic and technical capacities among the staff of the SRCs and SLMAs. This would also give the faculty an opporunity to evolve and experiment with innovative approaches of training and orienting field level functionaries thereby influencing the quality of field level operations.

Activities of the Institute have to be, on the one hand, intimately linked to the current programmes and actions in adult education in the country, and on the other, it has to look beyond in a proactive manner, on the policies and programmes of adult education in the country. Again, the Institute has also to build professional linkages with similar institutions within the country through programmes of professional collaboration.

SECTION III

The Current Context of Literacy and the Role of NIAE

A changed scenario : New demands and unprecedented challenges

In the last five years the national agenda for literacy has dramatically enlarged and also undergone a marked shift. The National Literacy Mission (NLM) has promoted a time-bound 'misson' approach to literacy and adopted the Total Literacy Campaign (TLC) model formulated out of the Ernakulam district experiment. Unlike the earlier centralized model involving regular adult education centres with paid instructors, the TLC approach is decentralized to the district level and is based on people's voluntary efforts. An autonomous Zilla Saksharta Samiti is formed to formulate the project, and is expected to spearhead a mass participatory campaign, through continuous environment building activities, and by mobilizing volunteers to conduct classes, while constantly monitoring and sustaining the momentum of the programme over a short period of 1-2 years.

The TLC model had been proposed to the NLM by peoples' science groups, which had decided to concentrate on mass literacy as part of their efforts towards social change. The Bharat Gyan Vigyan Samiti (BGVS), supported by the NLM, began as a voluntary body to coordinate the countrywide mobilization jatha in 1990 to promote 'literacy and science for self-reliance'. The jatha mobilized the first few districts to take up a TLC on the lines of the Ernakulam model. In the last three years there has been an immense expansion of the TLC programmes to cover almost 350 districts, and it has become increasingly difficult to cope with the pressures of rapid expansion as well as the associated tendency to 'bureaucratize' the programme, in the absence of appropriate preparation and strong local groups. Correspondingly, various tasks,

such as, orientation and training, initiating local groups and providing resource support in material production, appraisal and review of the project implementation, etc. have become much more complex, and the need for more professional organizations to provide umbrella support to field based endeavours is now felt even more.

The TLC emphasis on decentralization to the district level and on people's campaigns has placed new demands on the local administration as well as on the traditional structutres and institutes engaged in adult education. To have the district collector playing a nodal role and yet encourage democratic functioning of committees with real participation from capable people has been a difficult task for the administration, which is normally accustomed to issuing directives and exercising complete control over government-run programmes. Similarly, state institutes and departments of adult education have normally played a centralized role in monitoring, training as well as material production and dissemination, and have not always been able to make a smooth transition to the new requirements. It is in this context that the role of a national institute like NIAE assumes significance, for, this institute must now help steer away from a 'centralizing' ethos and infuse the essential spirit of 'decentralization' and 'participation' within the existing framework, while providing rigorous academic support to the programme.

The current context of literacy is characterized not only by immense 'expansion' but also by 'diversification'. For instance, in the various TLCs the actors involved no longer fall within homogeneous groups of adult education officers, local functionaries or instructors. There are now millions of new actors of all kinds, ranging from local administrators, ZSS members, BGVS activists, cultural and academic resource persons, trainers, to volunteers of all ages and backgrounds. Interacting creatively with these diverse sets of actors and devising orientation and training programmes for them is a demanding task, which the present institutions, such as, the DAE, and the SRCs are burdened to handle all on their own. A national institute like NIAE would need to address itself to this task, and actively network with a host of other agencies to provide essential support to the DAE and SRCs for this purpose.

The landmark decision of the NLM to encourage every district to produce its own teaching learning materials reflecting the concerns and needs of its own people, in more than one language or script if so required, has presented many new challenges and also called for intensive academic support as well as research insights. More significantly, it has called for a changed mind-set and a radically differnt mandate and methodology of providing resource support. In consonance with the earlier approach, the DAE and SRCs have functioned on the of premise of themselves formulating the curriculum and producing 'exemplar' or 'generic' teaching learning materials, which they were expected to disseminate further. In fact, the mandate for the NIAE, spelt out by the Task Force Report (1988), is guided by the same 'centralized' model. It expects the NIAE to generate "basic and generic material containing accurate information in simple language using limited vocabulary with an appropriate blend of national and social values", and also " to prepare some prototype training material which could be used in field 'as it is' "(p. 18). The current canvas of TLC experiences is splashed with a plethora of diverse colours—and the most marked of these is related to the creative use of language, an area which has also raised a lot of unresolved questions, but has gone far beyond the earlier accepted notions of centrally produced 'exemplar' materials, 'simple language' or even 'limited vocabulary' for non-literate learners. In this context, it is worth mentioning that there is an urgent need to collate and critically analyze the wide diversity of experiences gained through TLCs, in order to review and revise some of the assumptions and IPCL norms regarding adult teaching learning processes. This is one task that still remains undone, and the NIAE would need to enlist the efforts of a host of capable people to undertake such work.

The NIAE plan in retrospect

The literacy scenario in the country was different and more limited when the NIAE was first planned in 1987. There was no model of the TLC kind, and the NLM was still working on a centralized plan for a mission-directed approach. It was then envisaged that instead of having two separate bodies it might be desirable to convert the Directorate of Adult Education into the NIAE, which would then serve as an umbrella for all academic and technical support to the NLM. It was also looked upon as a composite organization that would, on the one hand, provide managerial, administrative and technical support, and on the other, engage in and promote academic and research activities to scaffold the literacy programmes with sound professional inputs.

The Report of the Task Force (1988) on the setting up of NIAE had gone into details of the functions of the DAE and the proposed NIAE, and had recommended that "the structure of the Institute will have to be such that it permits a judicious combination of the Old Directorate and the new Institute, to retain the strong and positive aspects of the Directorate while maintaining the vigour and enthusiasm of the Institute." However, in hindsight, and in the light of the present expanded TLC terrain, it is now clear that it is not advisable to try to deliberately forge a 'judicious combination' of the two agencies, and that the two have their own roles to play through often distinct modes of functioning. We have seen that the attempts to merge the two agencies have been detrimental to both, and have negatively influenced their separate identities and responsibilities, often threatening to place them in unpleasant situations of mutul suspicion. Moreover, the work pressures and demands are so enormous that both these bodies, even when they function at optimal levels of efficiency, would be overstretched with the requirements of NLM's present programmes and activities. In addition, both would need to work on their own long-term agendas for guiding the MHRD and other ministries in the crucial task of ensuring 'continuing and lifelong' education for all adult citizens of the country.

In addition, the Task Force had made perceptive comments regarding the status of the DAE as a subordinate office of the Ministry and had noted that, on the one hand, "it gave it an edge in dealing with different state governments". However, on the other, its identity and the government restrictions it was bound by tending to limit and circumscribe "its freedom to initiate, to decide, to experiment and innovate in its professional areas and support services" (pp. 10-11, *Task Force Report*). Therefore, now after five years, it would not at all be desirable to push the Institute back into the government fold, by merging it with the DAE, and thus deny NLM of the opportunity to ensure that academic innovation and freedom to experiment do indeed find a place in its programmes.

The NIAE was expected to function as an autonomous organization so that it "would have much greater flexibility, accessibility and openness" and could generate the requisite creative organizational ethos and culture "distinct from that of an organization which is primarily involved in efficient and effective operations management" (pp. 13 & 22, *Task Force Report*). It was supposed to have a full-time Director, an eminent educationist who could provide leadership and also help create an ethos which encouraged innovation and initiative. However, in the absence of this, and in the ambiguous situation of the proposed DAE-NIAE merger, the NIAE has not been given a chance to fully establish itself and play its role in the current literacy context. It is now hoped that once the uncertainty in status of both these bodies is cleared, and doubts regarding the precedence of one over the other are laid to rest, and after each is given a clear mandate to carry on the immense tasks before them, they would be invigorated to forge ahead.

Before proceeding to spell out the major tasks and the respective roles envisaged for DAE and NIAE, it is important to point out that all this is contingent upon the basis that NIAE would institutionally gear itself to provide such support to the NLM and actively engage itself with the problems and requirments of TLCs. The Institute will immediately need to reinforce itself in terms of personnel with experience and expertise in specific targeted areas, including a full time Director who can help shape the requisite institutional framework and prepare a detailed plan of action. It will also need to move beyond its present research agendas to explicitly address immediate issues and problems at hand. While it is true that the Institute has not been allowed to function autonomously, it is also important for it to shape itself not only as a 'research' institution but also as a major 'resource' institute, actively engaged with and intervening in literacy and adult education programmes, while continuing to give them a new direction.

The distribution or sharing of tasks between the DAE and NIAE

1. Monitoring the Implementation of NLM Programmes

The DAE has continued to perform this important task, and the demand for further strengthening of its role is felt with the rapid expansion of the TLCs. The main responsibility of the DAE would be to function as the executive arm of the NLM, and to develop as effective and credible Management and Information System, with provision for continuous feedback and also immediate corrective mechanisms. In addition, there is need to impose checks on tardy projects and operationalise withdrawal of sanctions where necessary. Optimal use of the NICNET and other network facilities need to be explored and district functionaries trained for the purpose.

The NLM scheme to appoint interested academics as voluntary consultants, to regularly appraise and provide resource support to the districts, was a laudable one but could not be sustained for lack of proper coordination. The DAE would need to have a special cell that provides administrative support to the consultants, while the NIAE would need to evolve mechanisms to provide constant academic and motivational support to them, so that such academics could contribute fully to the literacy programmes.

2. Project Formulation

Presently, the issue of project planning and formulation is left to the districts without much resource support in the form of professional guidance. As a result, the district administration often comes up with a poorly copied version of an earlier approved project document, without necessarily understanding the intricacies of the TLC model and the specific needs of their own area. Moreover, the Project Approval Committee (PAC) of the NLM is burdened with the task of scrutinizing, correcting and later re-examining the projects submitted by the ZSSs. This guiding role should ideally have been played by State level organizations such as, the proposed SLMAs or even the SRCs. However, since the SMLAs are not yet functional and the SRCs need to be strengthened, NIAE could act as a national resource body for training and capacity building within these organizations. Moreover, this task is going to become even more diversified and challenging now that many of the TLCs are entering the Post-Literacy (PL) phase, and would need to encompass in their projects long-term programmes for sustained continuing education.

3. Material Production

This is undoubtedly one of the critical areas of work in the literacy programmes. The DAE has been reviewing and approving basic literacy (IPCL) primers and PL materials according to the norms and guidelines laid down by the NLM. As mentioned earlier, developments during the last few years which have focused on locally relevant materials, in many different languages and dialects, have thrown up new challenges in dealing with questions of diversity and plurality at the grassroots level. Some ZSSs and associated NGOs have been trying out various creative approaches to meet this challenge and they often need the initial support, reassurance and guidance from an innovative resource institute. NIAE could fit this role effectively by initiating programmes of review, reflection and innovation in material production, in close collaboration with SRCs and the district organizations.

4. Training and Orientation

Within the NLM context there are broadly two kinds of training activities. One is with a managerial focus, for literacy functionaries and government administrators who are directly involved in the implementation and monitoring of the programmes. This task is largely performed by the DAE and the SRCs. The second kind of training consists of professional enrichment and capacity building for a wide range of persons involved in different tasks at the district level, such as, mobilizing the community, training volunteers, producing materials, implementing and evaluating the programmes. It is with regard to designing new methodologies for such training programmes that the NIAE can play an important role. Secondly, in addition to strengthening the training capacities of SRCs, NIAE can also organize intensive professional development programmes for them. NIAE would also collaborate with the DAE in orienting relevant personnel in other development departments involved in literacy activities.

5. Research

A large variety of difficult issues and problems have been thrown up, such as, those related to language and scripts, linkages of numeracy teaching with folk or street mathematics, different processes of adult learning, effective and practical methods of evaluation and so on. While some of these areas may offer problems for long term research, there are others that require analysis and understanding within a limited time frame so that research insights could actually feed into ongoing programmes of the NLM. Moreover, such research would need to be cost effective and consciously in consonance with the frugal funding pattern of the literacy programmes.

The NIAE must serve as the national agency for conducting and also promoting others to conduct research in relevant areas, which has an immediate impact on the ongoing programmes on the one hand, and also sets new directions for future activities in adult education in the country. In addition, it will need to network with SRCs and build their research capabilities, while also collaborating with field level agencies and other research organizations.

6. Evaluation

The DAE has commissioned evaluation studies by external experts and agencies to assist the ongoing programmes of the NLM. The DAE also receives a large number of internal evaluations, especially regarding learner achievement, from various ZSSs. The National Group for

External Evaluation is enlisting various organisations and research institutes to conduct further studies. The DAE would need to systematically review and widely disseminate such evaluation studies.

Most studies are essentially designed in a norm-based fashion according to set criteria. However, there are many aspects of evaluation which go beyond norm-based assessment of achievements, and there have been various influences and spin-offs on the field that have not necessarily been captured by standard procedures of evaluation. In order to generate a new framework for field level 'process' evaluation, which allows space for innovative action, the NIAE could set up mechanisms of close collabration with other agencies, including both research institutions as well as field based groups. There is also need to carry out sub-sectoral evaluation studies on literacy materials, methods for learner assessment, efficacy of training programmes, etc., with the involvement of SRCs.

7. Documentation, Dissemination and Publication

The DAE has been playing an important role in this area with regular dissemination of information through its periodical bulletins and other publications. However, proper 'process' documentation of the developments in TLCs has been generally neglected area. Indeed, the current literacy campaigns represent a unique phenomenon in cultural and social action and proper documentation of this experience in an inter-disciplinary perspective will be an invaluable contribution. Moreover, establishing a comprehensive documentation and resource centre has been a felt need that NIAE should be able to fulfil. Publication and proper dissemination is also an area that has not received adequate attention which, of course, demands the involvement of a large number of agencies. Nevertheless, NIAE could act as a nodal point in reviewing and promoting publication activities in the area of literacy and adult education.

8. Media and Communication

The DAE sponsors and provides promotional and motivational media support to NLM, and has also held occasional writers' workshop or sponsored theatre camps. The TLC approach has made extensive use of folk media for its environment building and motivational activities. However, there has been a need to continuously enrich, sustain and upgrade the abilities of the local activists through professional support, while also evolving newer methodologies for their environment building pogrammes. It is clear that the area of work is so vast that not only NIAE but many more agencies need to be brought in to augment this effort.

The NIAE could play the important function to facilitate close interaction between creative artists and media persons with talented field level activists, through regular camps and intensive workshops.

The NIAE would need to conduct and promote effective media impact studies. It must also help train SRCs in basic communication studies, and provide fresh inputs to strengthen their training programmes.

Since the mainstream media has not provided an in-depth and sustained coverage of the literacy campaigns, NIAE would need to continuously liaise, collaborate and actively feed into media efforts at all levels.

In short, while the DAE would essentially serve as the executive arm of the NLM, providing managerial and technical support to the TLCs, the NIAE would be required to provide in-depth academic resource support to a variety of persons involved. In the fast expanding and diversifying literacy scenario, the SRCs need to be reoriented and strengthened academically so that ultimately they can provide requisite academic support to the DRUs and the ZSSs. NIAE would need to extend considerable academic and professional support to them by effective networking and conducting regular programmes for capacity building in specific areas of creative and innovative action.

It is clear that in all the areas and responsibilities listed above, it would not be possible for DAE and NIAE, however, distinct their roles might be, to provide all the necessary technical and resource support to the NLM. It would therefore be necessary for NIAE to act as a nodal *networking* agency to enlist academic and research support from universities and other institutes, to collaborate with NGOs and other voluntary organizations at the field level, and to enlist active cooperation of creative artists, writers and media persons.

SECTION IV

NIAE in a Broader Perspective

Adult education has traditionally confined itself only to literacy. But as TLCs are completing the basic literacy phase in a large number of districts, it is becoming apparent that there is a need to have an extended and expanding view of adult education. As a matter of fact, the concept of life long learning is becoming increasingly important as new educational needs are getting articulated and also as the changing socio-economic scenario is generating new demands for education.

With the increasing number of adults and youth becoming literate, the demand for appropriate coninuing education programmes is getting enhanced. Alongside there is also a need for constant upgradation of knowledge and skills, especially as the rapid changes in economic programmes and policies threaten to make the existing skills of large number of people soon obsolete. The challenge ahead would therefore be to design and develop relevant continuing education programmes to cater to the emerging demands of varied clientele groups.

Adult education will also have to be viewed in relation to the broad framework of formal as well as non-formal education (NFE) in the country. There will thus be need for an interface with the NFE and also the efforts to attain universal elementary education (UFE), as well as with the various open learning systems. Already it has been seen that a large number of neo-literates who are coming out of the TLCs are aspiring either to enter directly or get accreditation and certification from the formal system, and the National or State Open Schools are faced with the challenging task of designing appropriate curricula and methods of assessment.

On the other hand, the educational aspirations of vast segments of neo-literate adults are getting raised as they begin to participate more effectively in various development activities and programmes. If development has to take place 'by the people and for the people' suitable educational interventions will have to be designed whereby it is the aduts themselves who can intervene and exercise control over the content pace of their learning. In addition, elected members of the newly constituted Panchayati Raj institutions would require training and educational inputs to enable them to perform their roles more effectively. Special educational needs of women will have to be paid attention to.

With the shifting trends in higher education, with increasing costs and most youth getting marginalised from the benefits of higher learning, there is a growing demand for restructuring of courses to make them relevant to employment patterns. There would be need for university departments of adult and continuing education to work closely with other departments to design new courses which address such requirements and creatively combine academic with vocational learning.

A professional organization such as the NIAE could play a

facilitative and enabling role with regard to the educational need suggested above. Besides innovative programme formulation in collaboration with other agencies and organizations and catalyzing their support, an important dimension would relate to research, experimentation and documentation, so as to influence policy directions. This would require liaising with principally three types of agencies so that sustained partnerships can evolve between them. These would be: (1) Institutions that can provide human resources, such as universities/ colleges, research institutes, NGOs etc., (2) Grassroots organizations that are trying to promote functionally oriented training and educational activities (through such development schemes such as TRYSEM, DWCRA, JRY, etc.) and (3) Funding agencies meant to support such programmes (such as Central Social Welfare Board, DGE&T, Department of Rural Development, Department of Women and Child Development, Department of Science and Technology, etc.). One, this would help promote and design sustainable programmes for post-literacy and continuing education in a broader developmental context. It would also be in keeping with the larger mandate of the National Policy on Education for an expanded vision which links education and development in a life-long perspective.

SECTION V

Conclusions and Recommendations

1. *DAE and NIAE to play distinct roles:* With the rapid expansion of NLM activities and with greater stress on diversified and decentralized approaches, the demand for institutional support has increased tremendously. Within this context, both DAE and NIAE have distinct roles to play often through different modes of functioning. It is necessary to nurture them as independent but collaborating institutions.
2. *Need for a stable institutional structure for NIAE:* There is an urgent need to create a stable institutional structure for NIAE, including the appointment of a full time Director who is an eminent educationist capable of providing leadership to the Institute at this important juncture.
3. *NIAE to provide academic leadership:* The NIAE would need to provide essential academic leadership to the newly constituted SLMAs, the SRCs and the ZSSs in adapting to the current NLM ethos which emphasizes decentralization and a participatory

mode of operation.

4. *An appropriate institutional perspective for NIAE :* One of the priority tasks would be to develop an institutional perspective and prepare a plan of action that addresses both short-term and long-term needs in the field of adult education. In this context, it would be necessary to reconsider the current thrust areas of NIAE.
5. *Research agenda that also addresses NLM objectives :* The research agenda has to be carefully drawn up keeping the institutional paln of action in view. Deliberate effort would be required to match the current needs of the NLM in designing research activities of the Institute.
6. *To function as a Resource Institution :* NIAE has to function not only as a research institute but also as a resource institution to provide active academic and professional support to the NLM.
7. *Training and capacity building functions of NIAE :* Training and capacity building have to be important components of NIAE activities. NIAE has to play a major role in strengthening the academic and professional capacities of SRCs. The Institute could actively collaborate with field level agencies in developing new methodologies of training and orientation in a decentralized framework.
8. *Continuous contact with the field :* Activities of the Institute would need to have clear focus on the challenges and démands emerging from the field. For this, it would need to operate in close collaboration with various field level agencies.
9. *Partnership and networking :* With the large agenda placed before the NIAE and the expanded areas of operation visualized, it would need to develop partnership and networking mechanisms with other national and state level professional institutions.
10. *Shaping policy directions:* It is envisaged that the professional activities and research programmes of NIAE will enable it to function as the focal agency for generating new ideas and influencing policy directions in the area of literacy and adult education. More significantly, it would need to immediately engage in providing academic and technical support to shape the policy guidelines of the newly constituted State Literacy Mission Authority (SLMA) in different states.

The following chart provides a brief summary of the various distinct roles and tasks that need to be shared between the DAE and the NIAE

Sharing of Essential Tasks in Relation to the Current Literacy Context

TASKS	*DAE*	*NIAE*
1. Monitoring the impelmentation of NLM Programmes	Main responsibility of DAE to function as the executive arm of the NLM; to develop an effective MIS feedback and corrective mechanisms.	Supplementary role in appraisal and monitoring.
	To provide administrative support to academics meant to function as NLM Consultants to give feedback on TLCs.	To provide academic and motivational support to such NLM Consultants.
2. Project Formulation	Supportive Role.	Training and orientation of SLMAs and SRCs for formulation of TLCs and PL projects.
3. Material Production	Reviewing and approving basic literacy (IPCL) and PL materials; providing technical support to SRCs and ZSSs.	Support and guidance to ZSSs engaged in curriculum development in collaboration with SRCs. Critical review, reflection and innovation on participatory material production.
4. Training	Training literacy functionaries and government administrators for the implementation and management of TLCs.	To provide academic inputs for professional development and strengthen training capacities of SRCs; critically review and evolve new methodologies for ZSS training of resource persons and volunteers.

(Contd.)

TASKS	DAE	NIAE
5. Research		To conduct and promote research activities to help NLM objectives, in collaboration with field level agencies and other research organisations: net-work with SRCs and build their research capacities; to also ensure that research inputs feed into ongoing programmes.
		To orient and assist such external agencies.
6. Evaluation	To review and disseminate evaluation studies by agencies commissioned by the National Group for External Evaluation.	To itself undertake and encourge other agencies to conduct process and programme evaluation studies; to evolve new methodologies and frame-works for evaluation of field based activities under NLM.
7. Documentation, Dissemination and Publication	Disseminates through periodicals, bulletins and other publications.	To establish a comprehensive documentation centre; to conduct process documentation of TLCs to promote publication and dissemination activities.
8. Media and Communication	Sponsors and provides media support to NLM.	Conduct media impact studies; evolve different media strategies for evnironment building, training of SRCs and literacy activists in communication methodologies;
		To facilitate close interaction between creative artists and media persons with field level activists.

(G) COMMITTEE FOR REVIEW OF NATIONAL POLICY ON EDUCATION (1986)

7.1.0 The perspective on adult education has been spelt out in the NPE in paras 4.10 to 4.13 and Chapter VII of the Programme of Action-1986. Apart from facilitating creation of ability to read and write the policy links adult education with national goals such as poverty alleviation, national integration, environment conservation, energisation of the cultural creativity of the people, observance of small family norm and promotion of women's equality. Adult Education has also been spelt out as a responsibility of the whole nation—all sections of the scoiety involving teachers, students, youth, employees, voluntary agencies, etc., apart from Central and State Governments and political parties and their mass organisations. Functional literacy has been considered as another important concern of adult education. A massive programme of adult and continuing education was envisaged for implementation through various modalities.

Committee's Perspective

7.2.1 The Resolution setting up the Committee to review NPE, *inter alia*, states:

> "Depite efforts at social and economic development since attainment of Independence a majority of our people continue to remain deprived of education, which is one of the basic needs for human development. It is also a matter of grave concern that our people comprise 50 per cent of the world's illiterate, and large sections of children have to go without acceptable level of primary education. Government accords the highest priority to education—both as a human right and as the means for bringing about a transformation towards a more humane and enlightened society. There is need to make education and effective instrument for securing a status of equality for women, and persons belonging to the backward classes and minorities. Moreover, it is essential to give a work employment orientation to education...".

7.2.2 The perspective of the Committee as regards Adult Education cannot be presented more effectively than by the following extract of the

Perspective Paper on education released by the Committee in September, 1990.

> "The content and process of adult education, as distinct from adult literacy, is to be reorganised. The questions of survival, development and justice are to be interwoven into content, pedagogy and learning situation of adult, letting literacy come in organically in the process when, and if, it becomes the felt need of the adult learners. This understanding would help in avoiding the dispropotionate emphasis on literacy campaigns. A major objective of these campaigns should be to enthuse the adult illiterates to send their children for school education. Other objectives may include education for democracy and Pachayati Raj and for eschewing violence, casteism, communalism, gender bias and all other forms of discrimination..."

Post Policy Implementation

7.3.0 In pursuance of the policy, a National Literacy Mission was established in 1988. In quantitative terms, the Mission seeks to impart functional literacy to 80 million illiterate persons in 15-35 age-group; 30 million by 1990 and an additional 50 million by 1995. The emphasis of the Mission is not on more numbers but on attainment of certain pre-determined norms and parameters of literacy, numeracy, functionality and awareness, under this Programme. 2,84,000 Centres are functioning in the country with an estimated involvement of 84 lakh adult learners (about 35 lakh men and 49 lakh women). Six lakh literacy kits have been delivered to students, volunteers. Over 30,000 Jan Shikshan Nilayams have been sanctioned to provide Post-Literacy Programmes. Over 300 Voluntary Agencies have also been involved in the process. A mass campaign under NLM was launched by the then Prime Minister in May, 1988. Similar campaigns were launched by 24 States and UTs on the same date and after. The Director General, NLM in his presentation before the NPERC stated that the programme had suffered due to shortage of funds. As against the barest minimum requirement of funds amounting to Rs. 139 crores during 1989-90, the actual amount provided was of the order of Rs. 76.17 crores. The position was somewhat improved in 1990-91 when a sum of Rs. 96 crores was provided. Considering the magnitude of the problem of illiteracy the large uncovered area and the need for mobilisation (A total of Rs. 227

crores was spent under NLM during the years 1987-88 to 1989-90). Much more funds are required even for implementing a purely volunteer based, campaign-oriented plan of action than what has been provided. The DG, NLM further informed the Committee :

— In conformity with the area-specific and time-specific approach for complete eradication of illiteracy, plans have been drawn up/ implemented for complete eradication of illiteracy as shown below:

- Kottayam city Kerala made fully literate in 100 days (April-June, 1989).
- Eranakulam district, Kerala made fully literate in one year (January - December, 1989).
- Projects for total literacy have been launched in Kerala, Goa and Pondicherry.
- Saksharatha Abhiyan was launched by Gujarat Vidyapeeth on 1st May, 1988 with the involvement of over 400 voluntary agencies and 1.5 lakh volunteers to make 35.00 lakh illiterates literate by 1991. Two hundred villages out of 1000 covered are reported to have been made literate as a result of this Abhiyan.
- A mass campaign for complete eradication of illiteracy was launched in Karnataka to make 4 lakh illiterates literate by 1990-91.The evaluation of the outcome of mass campaigns has shown that out of 4 lakh illiterate adults, 70,000 became fully literate and 1.30 lakhs partially literate at the close of 1989-90. Bijapur and South Kanara districts in Karnataka have been taken up for total literacy by 1991.
- A scheme for whole village literacy was adopted in 1986-87 in Rajasthan according to which one village in every district was to be made literate every year. Against a target of 60 villages to be made fully literate by 1989-90, 20 villages have been made fully literate. A project of Education for All by 2000 AD is being taken up with SIDA assistance and will be launched soon.
- Twenty CD blocks in West Bengal have been taken up for total literacy from 8th September, 1989 (to be completed in one year). The plan is being implemented by the panchayats while the funding has been shared between

Central and State Governments 50 : 50.

- Seventy CD Blocks in Orissa have been taken up for full litetracy by 1991.
- Nine Mahanagars and 8 hill districts in UP are being taken up for full literacy in 1990-91.
- The Bihar Education Project encompassing UEE, NFE and AE for total literacy with UNICEF assistance is being launched shortly.
- The Bhagavatula Charitable Trust, Yellamanchill (Andhra Predesh), has launched a project known as 'India Literacy Project' for total literacy in Visakhapatnam district with a coverage of one million illiterates. This project is proposed to be jointly funded by the Government of India, Non-Resident Indians and foreign donor agencies. Mandal motivators who will be full time workers in the projects, are the kingpin in the programme.
- A plan from total literacy has been launched in Coimbatore district, Tamil Nadu. The Coimbatore Literacy Mission Society (COLIM) has been recently constituted with the District Collector as the Chairman. The Society has drawn-up an action plan for imparting functional literacy to 5.25 lakh illiterate adults in 21 Blocks and 6 corporations municipalities of the district. It is proposed to involve 50,000 voluntary instructors in the projects which is to be implemented during April, 1990 to March, 1992.

Past Experience

7.4.0 Adult education programmes have been unsuccessful in the past mainly for the following reasons :

- Efforts are made to begin with adult literacy; this is most often not perceived as a felt need; the adult doesn't respond; adult education centres are attended often largely by young persons.
- Adult literacy is not placed within a wider social context. The whole gamut of the developmental needs of the adult—of survival, employment, health, etc.—are not addressed. There is failure to realise that illiteracy is but a form of marginalisation or exclusion of those who are unable to secure for themselves

minimum standards of well-being.

— The problem has been viewed more in the context of teaching methods and of learning to read and write.

Present Scenario

7.5.0 It is a matter of serious concern that half of the world's illetrates would live in India at the turn of the century. This fact belies all our claims to progress and development. While 53 per cent of the male population was reported to be illiterate in the 1981 census, the level of illiteracy among the women was as high as 75 per cent. This gender disparities in the literacy rate is another issue of national concern. The gap in the literacy levels of SCs *Vs* non -SC / ST communities and STs *Vs* non-ST/ SC communities had widened further during the sixties and seventies and as of 1981 census. The literacy rates among SC/ST women are appallingly low, with the ST women in Rajasthan existing at the pre-literate level of 1.2 per cent.

Programme of NLM

7.6.1 Notwithstanding the phenomenal effort put in by NLM and a number of determined voluntary agencies during the last three years, there is wide-spread cynicism regarding what has so far gone on under the banner of literacy programmes. The cynicism is the result of a general observation that the majority of the literacy effort, whether by the Government or the voluntary sector, has not demonstrably contributed to increasing the literacy rate. Before the formation of NLM, the Ministry had commissoned 56 research studies to reputed social science research organisations around the country. The Committee analysed 33 of these reports. By and large, the reports had shown that most of the literacy classes rapidly fizzled out due to high drop-out rate. Often there were no objective criteria for finding out the attainment level in terms of literacy at the end of the class, run normally for ten months. The Committee noted that a general practice had been (it continues in many states even today) to declare a person literate merely if she/he did not drop-out for a period of three to four months, even if the attendance was irregular. The question of actual attainment in literacy was not considered.

7.6.2 However, in the context of the scenario presented earlier, the Committee acknowldged that it would be plainly unjust if almost 250 million people in the plus 15 years age-group are left to spend their entire productive life without literacy, a powerful tool for acquiring knowledge and enabling effective participation in democratic polity of India. Clearly, like UEE, adult education with a strong literacy component has to be one of the central items on the national agenda. Therefore, the formation of the National Literacy Mission (NLM) in pursuance of NBE was a welcome development on the Indian Education scene.

NAEP to Mass Campaign

7.6.3 The Committee held detailed deliberations with the representatives of both the Ministry and NLM on the issue of the methodology used in the adult literacy programme. An attempt was made to understand the reasons why the pre-NPE National Adult Education Programme (NAEP) started in 1977-78, did not make significance difference in the rate of literacy among the adults. A Committee found that NAEP mainly relied upon what has come to be known as the centre approach. A centre is organised with one paid instructor and attends to about 30 adult learners, primarly in the 15-35 age-groups. The learning materials like slates and pencils and premises were provided free of cost to each learner, besides other support material including a lantern. The general experience was not hopeful. The attendence of the enrolled learners was irregular and the drop-out rates fairly high. A centre, after a few weeks or months, either had only handful of learners left or most of the learners attending were children below 15 years. There were reports of a large percentage of centres closing down due to low response. Other could never get off the ground. Taking this experience into account, the NLM adopted a modified strategy which differed from NEAP. Since early 1989 the Department of Education indroduced the Mass Campaign strategy—that is, from the time total literacy efforts was taken up in Ernakulam district of Kerala State. Under the stratergy, the entire community's support is mobilised in a given area through mobilisation programmes such as Jathas, street plays etc. Volunteers for imparting adult education as well as those who are to be given adult education are identified. The identified instructors themselves secure the avenues where adult education would be imparted. The services of the voluntary agencies are involved significantly in this strategy. This strategy also helps in the total discontinuance of the centre based approach to adult education and thus is meant to be less costly. At present the campaign method is being followed in 62 districts in the states of Kerala, Goa, Pondicherry and Gujarat. The proposal is to add 50 districts per annum to the target for coverage by campaign method.

7.6.4 The NLM officials shared their conviction with the Committee that their modified approach involving mass campaign and reliance on voluntarism has the necessary elements for overcoming the barriers faced by the previous programmes. It was stated that the campaigns were likely to generate a level of enthusiasm that would enable the illiterate adult to cross her/his threshold of resistance *vis-a-vis* literacy. They placed before the Committee several success or near success stories from different parts of India, though no supporting documentary material as such was provided. Indeed, the Committee has taken note of the positive response the mass campaigns have generated amongst the educated youth, reportedly primarily from the middle class for literacy work. Optimistic signs of such responses have been reported from Bijapur in Karnataka, Pondicherry, Durg in M.P., Midnapore in West Bengal and some other districts in other states as well.

7.6.5 This campaign method, even according to the thinking in the Department of Education, is not capable of universal application as of now. The reasons are:

— A total shift from centre based project approach in one shot is not feasible because of the serious disruptions that it can bring about in the on-going process of adult education.
— The campaign strategy cannot be applied in all parts of India principally becuase of the differing levels of awareness in different States.
— There may be pockets where the number of illiterates will be small; covering those pockets to handle small groups of learners will not be cost effective.
— The campaign method cannot also be introduced universally without appropriate evaluation of the impact it makes in areas where it is being followed as of now.

7.6.6 It remains to be seen whether the enthusiasm generated by these early campaigns in different pockets would be eventually translated into effective literacy classes and then into literacy attainment. Whatever may be the end result, there is no denying that NLM has succeeded in placing adult literacy on the national agenda and also in generating a level of enthusiasm for literacy work among the youth at least in certain pockets.

Ernakulam Experiment

7.7.0 During Commttee's deliberations, the experiment of Ernakulam district in Kerala was discussed at length. The report of the District Collector shows that the benchmark level of literacy in Ernakulam before the start of the campaign last year was above 90 per cent. In a major and well concerted drive, this level has been raised to about 98 per cent within a matter of less than one year, thus giving Ernakulam district the status of being 100 per cent literate—the first one in India. While this is commendable, it is doubtful whether lessons could be drawn from this experiment for application elsewhere. The high literacy rate to start with in Ernakulam, a result of successful school education programme, provided favourable socio-cultural conditions which cannot be expected in most parts of India where literacy rate ranges between twenty to thirty per cent. This situation is particularly acute and distinguishable from Ernakulum in the case of the ten educationally backward States, particularly the Hindi speaking States of UP, Bihar, MP and Rajasthan. Ernakulam, for that matter entire Kerala, exemplifies how literacy is linked with development and socio-cultural factors. In our plans for eradicating illiteracy from India before the turn of the century, we may not be able to wish away the hard ground realities that have been so far responsible for alienating large masses of Indian people from the benefit of education.

Mahila Samakhya Model

7.8.0 In this context the Committee looked at an alternative model of adult education being promoted by the Ministry itself. This alternative can be seen in the design of *Mahila Samakhya*, a scheme of the Ministry to empower women in pursuance of NPE. The POA chapter on Education for Women's Equality states, "as majority of women in this age-group (*i.e.* 15-35) are workers, literacy *per se* may not have any relevance for them" (para 14). Accordingly, the *Mahila Samakhya* programme primarily emphasises the issues of development and social justice such as health services, minimum wages, water etc. In contrast to NLM's approach of starting and focusing upon literacy the *Mahila Samakhya* is designed to being with life-related issues and weave in processes that would motivate the participation towards the desire for literacy. In *Mahila Smakhya*, therefore, one would move towards literacy as and when it becomes the felt need of poor women groups as a result of raising awareness of their changing role in society.

UEE to Pre-empt Adult Illiteracy

7.9.0 The low rate of literacy in India is a direct consequence of continued failure to universalise Elementary Education, a constitutional directive. In this context, a comment is necesary about Kerala, where the literacy rates have almost reached the level of 90 per cent or, in certain parts, even higher. The Committee observes that the success in Kerala on the literacy front is a result of more than a 100 years of sustained effort by various segments of society in promoting school education. Same can be said about Mizoram, where, too, the literacy rates are far ahead than in most parts of India.

Recommendations

(i) Imparing of literacy should be placed in the context of the developmental needs of the adult. Adult education programmes should be accompanied by a wide range of measures relating to health, nutrition, housing and employment needs. They should also address themselves to issues of fundamental rights, laws secularism and democracy. After creating awareness in respect of these essential needs and issues the adult learner himself should be expected to ask for adult literacy as a felt need. Instead of starting with adult literacy, the start should be in respect of creation of awareness for essential needs and from there work backward to adult literacy.

(ii) While the mass campaign strategy may be tried out further, the alternative model being employed by the Department of Education through Mahila Samakhya may be closely monitored and its application for adult literacy examined—considering that the objective of this project is to create awareness regarding issues of survival and thereby generate felt needs.

(iii) The mass campaign strategy as well as the *Mahila Samakhya* model may be objectively evaluated to look for meaningful lessons for the future.

(iv) On most of the developmental problems and matters relating to fundamental rights, social justice etc., the majority of the illiterates more often than not find themselves in positions of conflict with the official authorities. Therefore, genuine initiatives for adult education programmes, voluntary agencies community groups, political parties and their mass organisations should be facilitated.

(v) While NLM goes ahead with its planned literacy campaign in the Eighth Five Year Plan period, an independent study group should be commissioned to evaluate the programme, particularly with a view to arrive at an understanding of what may be appropriate strategies to remove adult illiteracy in the quicker possible time. The evaluation may also look into the various alternative models and study their relevance with respect to diverse socio-cultural and political conditions in different parts of India. The minimum objective of this study should be to find out on objective basis what approaches do not yield results, so that, five years later, at least those models may not be encouraged.

(vi) The Department of Education should coordinate with the Department of Rural Development and Ministry of Labour and organise programmes for vocational skills for the adult illiterates —facilitating flow of funds from programmes like TRYSEM (Training of Youth for Self-Employment). Community Polytechnics should also be involved in a large scale in imparting vocational skills amongst the adult illiterates. (This will enhance the employability of the adult illiterates and thereby create awareness regarding basic needs and issues of life, in the process generating demand for adult literacy as a felt need).

(vii) The neo-literates should be placed in an environment in which they have constant interface with the challenge of the written word.

(viii) Illiterate adults are those who have either not had access to education or having had access, have been unable to complete their schooling. A person has to remain in school atleast for a minimum of four years to attain a relatively irreversible level of literacy. Literacy should be a form of basic training making it possible for the adult to acquire some knowledge as may be necessary. It is imperative that Universalisation of Elementary Education is given top priority in educational planning and resource allocation. The objective should be to ensure that no child in the early nineties shall grow into an illiterate adult in the next century. (If this can be achieved, we would have then succeeded in controlling the chief contributor to illiteracy in India, *i.e.* low rate of participation in school education.)

(H) CENTRAL ADVISORY BOARD OF EDUCATION (CABE) WORKING GROUP ON ADULT EDUCATION AND LITERACY* (1991)

We declare that the attainment of mass literacy is linked to the attainment of the national objectives of eradication of poverty, the achievement of full employment and realisation of the values of national concern, namely national integration, women's equality and employment, small family norm, protection and conservation of environment.

1.1 *Magnitude of the Problem of Illiteracy*

The number of illiterate adults should be shown on the basis of the Census of 1991 instead of projecting them on the basis of 1981 Census.

1.2 Factors contributing to the phonomenon of rising illiteracy in the country.

These include :

* Inadequate coverage of children of school going age in schools due to poor infrastructure and unwillingness of parents.
* Majority of the children, particularly belonging to the under-privileged and in educationally backward areas, not staying long enough in the school to acquire the minimum levels of learning on account of social and economic compulsions caused by poverty and deprivation.
* Adult Education/Literacy programmes not being able to counter

* Committee for Review of National Policy on Education 1986 : Towards an Enlightened and Humane Society, Ministry of Human Resoure Development, Government of India, New Delhi, 1991, pp. 193-201.

the pulls and compulsions resulting in large scale drop-out of adult learners before achieving minimum levels of literacy.

* Inadequate and unsatisfactory arrangements failing to enthuse neo-literates to take up post-literacy and continuing education programmes and preventing them from relapse into illiteracy.
* Growth in literacy (both in rate as well as in absolute number) not keeping pace with rise in population (both rate of growth as well as in absolute number).
* Educational backwardness of specific areas (desert areas, slum areas, tribal and forest areas and other interior and inaccessible areas), poverty, social deprivation, economic exploitation, unemployment, irrelevance of the educational system to the larger needs of life, absence of a positive and conducive learning environment and general absence of society which values and prizes literacy.

1.3 *Strategy for Reduction in Illiteracy*

This would include the following measures :

* Universal enrolment and retention of children in schools upto 14 years of age.
* Improvement of socio-economic conditions including creating conditions for ameliorating the plight of socially and educationally disadvantaged groups and creating an environment which will facilitate learning and reinforce the teaching-learning process.
* Improvement in the quality of education imparted in the formal school system.
* Provision of non-formal education of good quality to those who cannot join regular primary school.
* Provision of opportunities to illiterate adults in 15-35 age group to enable them to become functionally literate.
* Overriding priority to female literacy.
* Provision of opportunities and facilities for post-literacy and continuing education.
* Outlining a special strategy for areas which are actually disadvantaged from the point of infrastructure, communication, transport, etc. as also other educationally deficient areas.

1.4 Findings of Institutes of Social Science, Research and Management on evaluation of the impact of the Adult Education Programme conducted by them.

The summary of the findings of evaluation studies as brought out in the agenda was noted. These include the following :

* Lack of stress on the time-bound plan for eradication of illiteracy.
* Lack of adequate planning and preparation with special reference to environment building prior to actual commencement of the Centre-based programme.
* Wrong selection of staff.
* Lack of back-up support by training and continuing education of functionaries.
* Delayed supply of teaching-learning materials.
* Deficient physical teaching-learning environment.
* Excessive emphasis on quantitative rather than on qualitative achievement.
* Lack of credible and effective management information system.

It was emphasized that while these deficiencies be made good in the current programme, they should not be allowed to repeat themselves in the future Centre-based programmes.

1.5 *Shift from Institutionalised Centre-based Approach to Campaign Approach*

Determination and unqualified support of State Governments and UTs to literacy campaigns.

The welcome shift which is taking place from the traditional Centre-based approach to the Campaigns approach, which is area-specific-time specific, volunteer-based, cost-effective and result-oriented, is endorsed. For this, there is need for total political will, commitment and unqualified support of the State Governments. and UTs as preconditions for the success of these campaigns and suggested that such involvement and support may be secured in the following manner:

In respect of districts where campaigns have already been launched

* An energetic and committed district administration will have

to be the focal point of mobilisation of social forces as well as coordination of all such forces to act in synergy for the success of the campaign. The State Government, in addition to creating conditions for such a synergy, will also have to ensure continuity of tenure of the functionaries at various levels of district administration who are closely invloved with the campaign and particularly of the District Magistrate who provides the principal driving and coordinating force for the campaign in the district.

* Voluntary Agencies are grassroot level organisations which have flexibility of structure and operations and have volunteers who have intimate knowledge of and contact with field conditions. They have, therefore, a very special role to play in a campaign for total literacy. The State Government and the District Administration will have to create conditions in which the VAs can make their voluntary contribution to the campaign more meaningfully and effectively. Such involvement and support of VAs can be secured in a number of ways such as giving them representation at various committees, assigning specific responsibilities such as resource support through training, evaluation and conducting of literacy programmes, etc.
* Involvement of State Government would also mean total emotional involvement of development functionaries in the campaign. Such an involvement is also necessary to convert the campaign for total literacy into a campaign for immunisation, maternity protection, child health care, protection and conservation of environment, small family norm, etc. In addition to issuing instructions in clear and unambiguous terms to Secretaries to Government, Heads of Development Departments, Revenue Divisional Commissioners, Collecters and all other independent bodies (including statutory and corporate bodies) regarding release of personnel and provision of logistic support to the campaign, the State Government also needs to monitor the pace and progress of such involvement.

In selection of new districts for launching campaigns afresh

* Campaigns can become a part of our stratery for total eradication of illiteracy only if State Governments develop faith in the efficacy of the campaigns approach and create

conditions for their success. One of the factors which can contribute to this purpose is selection of TLC districts with imagination and far sight. The following broad criteria may be kept in view for selection of the TLC districts :

— A rich folk culture and tradition which can be harnessed for environment building.
— A confluence of creative forces and energies which can be harnessed for providing resource support such as training, monitoring and evaluation of the campaign.
— A team of energetic and committed officials and non-officials at all levels.

Campaigns for total literacy have, as their clientele, persons in different age-groups such as 6-60, 9-45, 15-35, 14-45 etc. Of these, children belonging to the age-group of 6-8 and 9-14 will have to be covered in the NFE programme, which has a duration of two years for achieving the minimum levels of learning as against the duration of 6 months or 200 hours for adults. While children in these age-groups can be covered in the campaigns by providing separate curriculum instructional materials, training and separate teaching-learning places for them, the State Government will have to take a policy-decision in regard to extension of the NFE programme (Centre-based) beyond the campaign period with a view to ensuring minimum levels of learning for children covered in the campaign.

Ensuring adequate media coverage and support to the developments in campaign districts

While sizeable media coverage and support will have to come from the Ministry of I&B and the autonomous bodies thereunder, such as AIR and Doordarshan the State Government can contribute a lot in (a) preparing and disseminating success stories of ongoing campaigns in districts; (b) identifying creative thinkers, writers and artists and encouraging them to contribute by way of regular writeups in the local press to disseminate the message of literacy in its correct perspective as well as to dispel the mistaken notions about such campaigns for total literacy and (c) placing the services of the District Information and Public Relations set up at the disposal of the campaign authorities for intensive publicity and propaganda for reporting the pace and progress of the campaign as well as the outcome thereof.

Mass Mobilisation

It was noted that significant achievement has been made both in regard to coverage as well as creation of a positive environment for literacy by Bharat Gyan Vigyan Jatha as well as Paidal Jatha of Gandhian and Sarvodaya workers in October-November 1990. It was also noted that a large number of area-specific concrete action plans for total literacy have been formulated as a result of the positive environment which has been created and total literacy campaigns are being implemented in a number of districts. In view of the imperative need for reinforcing and sustaining, it is suggested that similar initiative may be launched on a large scale all over the country. It is also suggested that necessary measures be taken to secure large scale involvement of students and teachers in the environment building as well as campaign effort by designing appropriate motivation strategies for them.

The new initiative taken by Prof. Yash Pal, former Chairman, UGC and a number of like-minded persons on the subjects of Mass-Action for National Regeneration by large scale involvement of students in schools, colleges and universities for one year to deal with the problems of illiteracy and mal-development was welcomed. It was noted that for the current year, a beginning is to be made by extending the summer vacation during which students and teachers will work intensively for literacy on the one hand and by integrating literacy as an integral part of the curriculum in the school, collegiate and university system on the other. It was further noted that this has been endorsed by the Council of the National Literacy Mission Authority in its recent meeting held on 15th February, 1991.

Priority to Women's Literacy

Keeping in view the close linkage between the female literacy and the status of the women in society, maternity protection, child health care and its impact on reduction of infant mortality rate and birth rate and also in view of the abysmally low rate of female literacy in several parts of the country, the Group suggested a number of measures for giving an effective boost to female literacy (both in terms of rate as well as absolute number), such as involvement of women functionaries in adult education and literacy programmes in large number, designing curriculum (both teaching-learning and training) as well as conducting the progrmme in a manner which will enthuse and motivate women to participate in the programme in large numbers, etc. It was noted with satisfaction that a good deal of linkage has been established between the campaign for total literacy in some of the districts and the new programme for women's equality and empowerment, know as '*Mahila Samakhya*'. The functionaries of *Mahila Samakhya* in these districts, in addition to helping in creation of a positive environment for literacy have also acted as resource persons in training and mobilisation of women. While recommending extension of the *Mahila Smakhya* project to larger number of districts, reinforcement of the nexus between *Mahila Samakhya* and Campaign mode for total literacy was also emphasised.

Involvement of Voluntary Agencies

The voluntary agencies will also have to be persuaded to adopt the new approach which is area-specific, time-bound, volunteer-based, cost-effective and result-oriented as far as possible and practicable. This would require considerable efforts on the part of the Central and State machinery in-charge of implementation of the programme in (a) organisation of workshops for VAs for their large scale familiarisation with the area-approach and IPCL techniques; (b) assisting the VAs in formulation and reformulation of action plans for total literacy in specified areas; and (c) extending continuous encouragement, support and help to VAs to enable them to run the programme in a climate of total freedom and spontaneity.

The Director-General, National Literacy Mission stated that in the wake of the *Paidal Jatha* undertaken by a large number of Gandhian and Sarvodaya workers in the 5 States of Assam, Orissa, Bihar, UP and MP a good number of good and reliable VAs have been mobilised and motivated to come up with concrete action plans for total literacy in specific areas. A workshop was held at Sevapuri near Varanasi with representatives of 30 such voluntary groups, which was attended by him and the Educational Secretary, Government of India, and the need for creating a decentralised set-up and mechanism for processing of such proposal from the VAs, with utmost speed and expedition on the one hand and also to provide continuous encouragement, guidance, leadership and support on the other, was felt. It is in this context that need for constituting a State level body to assist the VAs in formulation and reformulation of action plans, sanction and release of funds, monitoring and all other promotional activities related to the VAs, was felt. He indicated for information of the Group the consensus which had emerged from the workshop about the broad composition of such a state level body. The composition would be as below:

> *Chairman:* a distinguished civil servant serving or retired, of sufficiently high seniority in the hierarchy who has empathy and sensitivity to the voluntary sector and who is acceptable as such,
> OR
> an otherwise eminent person in public life.
> *Secretary :* Should be full time to be taken on deputation from the State Government (Dev. Deptt.). Should be acceptable to the VAs.
> *Members :* 3 local VAs of whom atleast one should be a woman.
> 1 VA from outside the State.
> 1 representative from Government of India.

The State level body would be registered as a Society under the Societies Registration Act and may be named as "Sampoorna Saksharta and Gram Swarajya Samiti " or by such other name as may be considered locally appropriate. In addition to scrutiny and sanction of proposals of VAs, this body would also function as a promotional and development body vested with mobilisation and leadership development functions. While endorsing the suggestions regarding constitution of such a State level body for the specific purpose as indicated above, it was recommended that Director, Adult Education of the State and Director, State Resource Centre should also be made members of the society.

1.6 *Flexibility in Approach*

The new thrust, intiative and awakening in the direction of mass campaigns for total literacy was noted and the following suggestions made :

* Mass mobilisation and campaigns for total literacy should be taken up wherever possible. A campaign for total literacy would mean mass mobilisation, voluntarism and learning outcome

according to NLM norms as its cardinal principles. This would also require for its success designing, good training modules, and effective Management Information System (MIS) and an effective system of evaluation of the learning outcome.

* The traditional Çentre-based programme should be totally frozen in those districts where mass campaigns for total literacy have been launched.
* The traditional Centre-based programmes should be progressively phased out even in districts where mass campaigns for total literacy have not been launched but by adopting other alternative approaches like involvement of women coordinators, prerak/instructor centred approach etc.
* In areas, such as border areas, desert areas, tribal and forest areas, inaccessible areas and other disturbed areas where it is not possible to go in for mass campaigns for total literacy, a more flexible approach or mixed approach (both Centre-based and Volunteer-based) could be adopted, as may be relevant to the specific needs of that region (it being noted that in the same area, the Centre-based approach and the Volunteer-based approach should not be adopted).
* The Group noted that we should be a little guarded and cautious about the continuance or replication of the scheme of payment for results, as has been introduced in the 20 CD Blocks of West Bengal and the Ex-servicemen projects in the States of Tamil Nadu, UP, MP and Rajasthan.

2.1 *Post-Literacy*

In districts where mass campaigns for total literacy, have been launched, it was suggested that alternative mechanisms could be designed for an effective post-literacy and continuing educaion programme, which would take into account :

(i) Continued Non-Formal Education of children in the 9-14 age group until they achieve the minimum levels of learning;
(ii) Retention and strengthening of literacy skills of those persons (neo-literates) who have achieved the NLM levels of literacy with a view to making them permanent;
(iii) Continued basic literacy skills for those persons who have

during the course of the campaigns, not quite achieved the NLM levels of literacy; and

(iv) A programme of literacy for those persons who were for various reasons not able to participate in the basic literacy campaign.

It was felt that adequate steps should be taken to design graded post-literacy materials and making available these materials in sufficient quantity for the neo-literates through libraries and other institutionalised avenues. It was felt that priority in organising the post-campaign and post-literacy strategies should be given to continuing education for women. It also noted that a series of meetings/workshops are being planned with a view to evolving strategies for post-literacy and continuing education in the campaign context. It was also felt that it may be necessary to organise training programmes in skills including vocational skills in which opportunities for self-employment as well as wage-employment are locally available. Illustratively simple and short duration training could be organised on health and nutrition, common ailments and inexpensive remedies, information about proper upkeep and maintenance of productive assets, measures of safe storage of water, growing and storage of vegetables, introducing devices which can minimise hardships and drudgeries, particularly in the lives of rural women (smokeless *chullahas*, bio-gas, solar cooker, etc.). Such training could also be organised to provide access to legal literacy, such as provisions of labour, tenancy laws and welfare laws, etc.

We, the students, teachers, working people in Government, business concerns, firms and factories, men and women of all ages pledge to devote ourselves wholly beginning this year for the attainment of total literacy which is the hallmark of progress and development.

Participants in the Group on Adult Education and Literacy

Chairman

1. Dr. Malcolm S. Adiseshiah
   Chairman
   Madras Institute of Development Studies.

Rapporteurs/Members

2. Shri A.J. Shukla
   Director (AE and PE)
   Governement of Gujarat.
3. Shri Mohd. Abdul Bari
   Minister-in-Charge
   Mass Education and Extension,
   West Bengal
4. Shri Prem Bhai
   Secretary, Banwasi Seva Ashram, Govindpur,
   Sonbhadra, Uttar Pradesh.

5. Shri Vijendra Kabra
Director, Indian Institute of Rural Works,
Aurangabad.
6. Shri Harivallabh Parikh
Chairman, Anand Niketan Ashrama,
Rangpur, Baroda, Gujarat.
7. Smt. Sarva Sridevi
Sitaphalmandi,
Secunderabad.
8. Shri J.C. Ranganayakulu
Director of Adult Education,
Government of Andhra Pradesh.
9. Smt. Tilottama Barooah
Additional Director, Adult Education,
Government of Assam.
10. Shri S.G. Amonkar
Director,
State Literacy Mission and Adult Education,
Government of Goa.
11. Shri M. Madan Gopal
Director, Mass Education
Government of Karnataka.
12. Shri P.K. Sivanandan
Secretary,
(Local Administration) and Secretary, Kerala Saksharta Samiti,
Government of Kerala.
13. Shri R. Kar
Director,
Teacher Education,
Government of Orissa.
14. Shri M.C. Mathur
Director, Education,
Government of Sikkim.
15. Shri G.P. Upadhayaya
Deputy Director, Education Department,
Government of Sikkim.
16. Miss. Gauri Dhar
Additional Director, SW and Social Education,
Government of Tripura.
17. Dr. K.A. Pandey
Director, Adult Education,
Government of Uttar Pradesh.
18. Shri M. Roy
Director, Mass Education and Extension,
Government of West Bengal.
19. Shri Narendra Prasad
Commissioner-cum-Secretary (Education)
Delhi Administration.
20. Shri Lakshmidhar Mishra
Joint Secretary (AE) and Director General (NLM),
Department of Education,
Ministry of H.R.D.

Recommendations and Observations of CABE on Adult Education

The report of the Working Group on Adult Education and Literacy was presented by the Chairman of the group Dr. Malcolm Adiseshiah. The following points were made in course of discussion :

(a) The initiative taken by Prof. Yash Pal, former Chairman, UGC and a number of like-minded persons to involve school and college students in national issues like eradication of illiteracy was welcome;

(b) Concrete steps should be taken to revive the Vidyapeeths set up in Karnataka under the auspices of Karnataka Adult Education Council;

(c) There is need for greater linkage of the adult education programme with the system of libraries. Systematic programmes need to be undertaken for ensuring that neo-literates do not relapse into illiteracy; and

(d) In the planning of literacy and post-literacy programmes special attention should be paid to habitations with SC/ST concentration.

With these observations the CABE adopted the working group report.

(I) EXPERT GROUP ON NATIONAL LITERACY MISSION* (1993-94)

Introduction

The Ministry of Human Resource Development constituted in 1993, a 6-member Expert Group consisting of the following Members to undertake a Status-*cum*-Impact Evaluation of Literacy Campaigns as a mid-term assessment of the National Literacy Mission which was launched in 1988.

1. Prof. Arun Ghosh, Ex-Member Planning Commission.
2. Prof. Vina Mazumdar, Centre for Women's Development Studies.
3. Prof. Andre Beteille, Professor of Sociology, Delhi School of Economics.
4. Prof. U. R. Ananthamurty, President, Sahitya Akademi.
5. Prof. S. M. Kansal, Indian Statistical Institute, New Delhi.

---

* Reproduced from S. P. Agrawal and J. C. Aggarwal, *Third Historical Survey of Educational Development in India. Select Documents 1990-92*, Concept Publishing Company, New Delhi, 1994, pp. 348-59.

6. Shri Achin Vanaik, Fellow, Nehru Memorial Museum and Library.

The report submitted in 1994 touched upon the importance of mass involvement and strong political commitment to make a success of NLM. It has been suggested by them that primers for teaching be reassessed and all materials that send negative messages to learners be removed. As far as evaluation is concerned, they think it is more important and practical to have high success rate than "total literacy". Apart from these, the Committee has dwelled at length on one major problem that today confronts the literacy campaign—Post Literacy/Continuing Education.

Major Recommendations on Literacy Campaigns

General

The Group has made recommendations on decentralisation of procedure for pre-appraisal and sanction of projects, constitution of state level core groups to guide, monitor and assess projects and also to recommend to the Central Government for release of grants, on the need to further improve the primers specially with regard to their content reflecting on the status/image of women and to ensure that the content does not lower the self-esteem of the learners and made some special recommendation on implementation of the campaigns in the major Hindi-speaking States.

According to the Group, a strong political commitment to the cause of literacy, existence at the State and district level of a strong core group fully committed to the Literacy Campaign, village level mass involvement/popular enthusiasm, adequate pre-launch preparations and an atmosphere of a popular movement are the minimum pre-conditions of a Literacy Campaign. The Group, therefore, recommended as follows:

* A State level core group of 4-5 pesons including some from outside the Government known for their full commitment to literacy campaigns must be constituted. This group should provide an adequate framework for preparations/monitoring at the State level before District level Literacy Campaigns are launched.
* There should be orientation courses for Collectors and senior administrators not only relating to the *nitty gritty* of the programme but also on the conceptual aspects of a literacy

campaign.

* The present system of sanctioning literacy campaigns at the Centre should be replaced by the following procedure : On the basis of a preliminary proposal for Literacy Campaign in a district for environment building and preparatory activities, some funds should be released for such activities. At the end of this phase, the State level core group should assess the adequacy of preparation for launching the teaching-learning phase and they should recommend further release of the grants by the Centre.
* The Group has welcomed the NLM strategy of sanctioning a PLC when 25% of the learners or 50,000 learners, whichever is less, have completed primer-II. The Group has recommended that the concept of "total literacy " at 80% level of success be given up. The target approach of achieving "total literacy" should be given up and the objective should be to seek to achieve high success rates rather than "total literacy". A success rate of 35-60% among identified non-literates should be considered to be a good success rate.
* The resources should be utilised to make the 9-45 age group literate rather than higher age groups. There should be a graded range of learning outcomes such as outstanding, excellent, very good, good, mediocre and poor.
* There should be a second cycle of literacy campaign in low literacy/difficult areas after another round of motivational campaigns so as to reinforce the achievement of the first cycle of the literacy campaigns and also achieve substantial results.

Primers for Teaching/Learning

* The NLM in collabration with SRCs should organise reassessment of the content of primers to remove materials which patronise learners and send messages that lower the self-esteem and those which have a general bias against women. The ZSSs will have to play a sensitive monitoring role in this.

Hindi-Speaking States

* Regarding the Hindi belt the Group has recommended that

attention should be given to ensure commitment particularly to Universal Primary Education and eradication of illiteracy;

* Stability of administration including stability of tenure of Collectors has to be ensured in these States; and
* Adequacy of prepration in districts in these States should include the following :

  (a) Each village should have as identified activist as a key-organiser who would have already distinguished himself/herself in the early part of the environment building phase; and

  (b) In States with low political commitment, there is need to ensure such full timers who would be available for the duration of the Literacy Campaigns and great care should be taken to select only those with proven dedication and commitment.

* It should be ensured that the basic education projects in these States are coordinated with the Literacy Campaign projects.
* Particular attention should be paid to integrate literacy and development even during the course of Literacy Campaigns in these States. At least one government development scheme should be coordinated with the introduction of a full Literacy Campaign project; and
* Programmes and resources of the government should be pooled right from the Literacy Campaign stage. This will ensure linking of socio-economic development with the literacy campaigns.

Recommendations on Post-Literacy Measures

The Group has suggested a framework for post literacy and continuing education programmes. They have specifically mantioned that carrying out successful PL/CE remains the single most difficult problem confronting the NLM and the whole of the literacy programme. Following recommendations have been made :

* The Group holds a strong view that PL/CE should not be attempted in the 'campaign mode'. New forms of institutionali-sation, new agencies of organisation, new

attitudes towards the PL/CE phase fundamentally different from the literacy campaign phase are required.

* At least one PL/CE centre per village or even per Tola or for a cluster of Tolas is essential. The current policy of one JSN per 5,000 learners which tends to serve a cluster of villages has not been recommended.
* The literacy campaign and the PL/CE phases must be integrated and should be one continuum.
* Organisational control of the PL/CE should be different from the structure in the literacy campaign phase. *Mahila Mandals*, women members of Panchayats and staff of primary and secondary schools should play a more prominent role than the traditional village hierachy in controlling PL/CE activity. Since the literacy campaign and PL/CE are to be integrated, the organisational structure for running the PL/CE must emerge and operate alongside the organisational structure for running, the literacy campaign.
* To begin with, the PL/CE centre could become an 'information window' in the village. Information about various schemes *e.g.*, for education, for training, for services rendered by different cadres of functionaries is seldom available at the district level and hardly at the village level. Pooling and dissemination of such information is critical for both neo-literates and planners to widen their own choices, vision and courage for innovation as well as for making literacy as a means of enhancing 'access' and 'capability'.
* The Group has strongly recommended that access to knowledge about basic laws and legal procedures should be an essential component of PL/CE. A great deal of experience and material already exists as a result of the activities of the Committee for Implementation of Legal Aid Schemes (CILAS) in 80s. The Committee has recommended simplified literature to be produced as in the case of literature for development schemes.
* The library is critical for the success/expansion of PL/CE activities. Support in the acquisition of material and a full time paid Prerak libraraian and caretaker for such PL/CE centres has been suggested. Necessary training for PL/CE librarians on a group basis could be arranged at the block/district levels.
* On the whole, there should be a structured and an unstructured

part of PL/CE. There should be both mopping up operation and an element of continuing education. The structured part of PL/CE should be the function of information window for all government/non-government programmes, legal literacy etc. The unstructured part of the programme should be left to each local community to fill in. Resource mopping may be first introduced in few areas and extended to become a part of the structured part of every PL/CE programme. This should be in the shape of "information system" and a motivating factor for education.

Monitoring and Evaluation of Campaigns

The Group has broadly endorsed the need for and utility of bringing out Status Reports on a regular basis at the national level as is being done now. These reports are, however, based on internal information being provided by the campaigns. Therefore, there is need to considerably tighten up the system and current practice of external evaluation about which strong reservations have been expressed. It has been emphasised that proper internal evaluation is a must in every case which should be corroborated/validated by external evaluations.

Approach to Evaluation

The approach to evaluation should be a participatory approach involving participants in programme implementation and should be non-threatening in nature. In this context, it has been recommended that the concept of "total literacy" may be abandoned so that a target centred approach does not lead to undesirable pressures leading to manipulation of figures. The group has specifically mentioned that increasing the literacy rate in a district from 15 per cent to 50 per cent would be deemed to be quite credit-worthy as compared to a progression from 50 per cent to 85 per cent. This is so becuase the size of the literate population providing volunteers in the former case is much less than in the latter.

Design for External Evaluation

This has been suggested based on the basic principle to ensure that every member of the target population gets an equal chance of being included in the sample and also special groups of learners belonging to SCs, STs, minority community, other backward castes etc., get a fair representation. It is important to cover varying social demographic and regional characteristics of the district and different organisational features of the campaign.

Internal evaluation should be conducted for all learners on 100 per cent basis and should conform, as closely as possible, to the standards set for external evaluation. This would also help to provide baseline information to chalk out all PC/CE strategies and activities. The internal evaluation data should be properly stored at appropriate levels.

Impact evaluation studies should be conducted after 1-2 years of the literacy campaign adopting a 'household survey' approach by selected social science institutes/departments of universities.

Strengths

Among the strengths highlighted by the Expert Group are:

(i) Literacy campaigns have been more of a movement than a programme; (ii) There has been an overwhelming impact on women who constitute between two-thirds to three-fourth of adult illiterates; (iii) Inter-mixing of social strata has had a positive impact on castes and communal relations; (iv) Greater demand had been generated for primary education and a new determination to enrol girls; (v) Direct interaction between the volunteers and the poor has resulted in generation of social activists with the concern for developing a just, humane society; (vi) TLC has helped to sensitize the bureaucracy to the concern of ordinary village fold especially those who are the most deprived; (vii) Literacy has been placed on the national agenda and the transparency of the programme has been greater than for any other government programme.

Weaknesses

Among the weaknesses the group has pointed out the following :

(i) Owing to pre-occupation with "Total Literacy", quality of the programme has sometimes suffered; (ii) The levels of literacy attainment are fragile posing serious problems of relapse; (iii) Because of easy availability of funds there has been a tendency to meet "politically committed" targets that is total literacy by the year 2000 leading to sanction of projects which are not prepared to take up campaigns; (iv) Bureaucratisation or 'top-down' approach leading to 'volunteer fatigue' in some cases; (v) In the Hindi belt states, especially in U.P. and Bihar, progress achieved has been patchy and sometimes doubtful because of the problems of large size of illiterates, small size of the pool of literates, lack of literacy, traditional/movements, low political commitment, etc.; and (vi) Poor progress in urban areas where the problems are infinitely more difficult for diverse reasons.

5

Conferences on Education : Their Recommendations Pertaining to Adult, Continuing and Non-Formal Education

(A) STATE EDUCATION MINISTERS' CONFERENCES (1949-1984)

(i) First Conference of Provincial Education Ministers held at New Delhi on 19th and 20th August, 1949 under the Chairmanship of Maulana Abul Kalam Azad, the then Minister of Education.

Genesis : At the meeting of the Central Advisory Board of Education held at Allahabad on 6th to 9th January, 1949, the Report of Adult (Social) Education Committee appointed in 1948 was adopted with a few minor modifications and it was proposed to call a meeting of the Provincial Education Ministers for the purpose of considering the implementation of the scheme. Accordingly, for the first time, a meeting of the Education Ministers was called. It, however, did not form part of the regular series of the State Education Ministers' Conferences. In August 1949, another meeting of the Provincial Education Ministers was called. This was later regarded as the First State Education Ministers' Conference in the series of such conferences.

Gist of Chairman's Address

The Hon'ble Maulana Abul Kalam Azad said that making an immediate start with the scheme of Social Education and the training of teachers was urgently needed for the spread of basic education. In spite of the fact the country was faced with financial difficulties, the need for the spreading of education among the masses could not be minimised. The education of the adults should not be confined to the imparting of literacy alone, it should also provide them with training in the element of citizenship. The Ministry of Education was willing to extend the financial assistance to the provinces for training a large number of basic education teachers.

Some Significant Resolutions/Recommendations

The Conference made the following major recommendations:

1. Social education in the provinces should be carried out by the combined efforts of both teachers and volunteers, the latter requiring the teaching only for two months in summer camps.
2. One teacher should teach 90 adults in a year in 3 batches of 30 adults.
3. The provinces should review their own scheme of social education so that to bring them in line with the scheme approved in the conference.
4. Normally schools and training colleges should include in their courses the theory and methods of teaching adults.
5. The government should encourage the use of visual aids.
6. The provinces should start circulating libraries.

(ii) Twelfth Conference of State Education Ministers held at New Delhi on 13th and 14th July, 1978.

Adult Education : The Conference considered the paper on the detailed action to be taken by the State and Central Governments in regard to implementation of the National Adult Education Programme and the recommendations of the Working Group on the subject. The Conference endorsed the general approach and recognising significance of the programme resolved to give the highest priority to it. It also called upon all concerned to make necessary preparations to launch the programme with effect from October 2, 1978. The Conference wanted the disbursement of funds to voluntary agencies to be routed through the State Government.

(iii) Thirteenth Conference of State Education Ministers held at New Delhi on 2nd June, 1981 under Chairmanship of Shri S.B. Chavan, the then Minister of Education.

Adult Education

— That adult education programme should be directly related to life situations and closely linked to needs, interests and aspirations of the adult learners and to national goals of socio-economic development;

— That such a massive programme cannot be successfully implemented exclusively through government's efforts and must involve educational institutions, employers and voluntary organisations which play a vital role in the field;

— That the adult education programme must give special priority to women and weaker sections of society.

(iv) Fourteenth Conference of State Education Ministers was held at New Delhi on 23rd and 24th May, 1984.

Some Significant Resolutions/Recommendations

1. The Conference is of the view that all possible low-cost strategies, like providing part-time teachers, use of educational technology, etc., should be fully availed of for attacking the problem of low enrolment and high drop-out rates by both expanding the school system and taking care of the left-out through non-formal system for producing desired results. The formal school system, the non-formal system and the adult education system should be integrated both in terms of teacher utilisation and educational and administrative supervision.

2. The Conference recommended that school committees should be set up representing all sections of the local community so that they would not only be helpful in ensuring attendance of teachers, maintenance of school timings, adjustment of school hours and vacations to suit local needs but would also mobilise additional resources locally to provide for developmental needs of the school.

3. The Conference felt that school education should become progressively more socially relevant, and schools should be encouraged to actively participate in activities which would create permanent assets for the society such as social forestry involving plantation and care of trees.

(B) SIXTH REGIONAL CONFERENCE OF MINISTERS OF EDUCATION AND THOSE RESPONSIBLE FOR ECONOMIC PLANNING IN ASIA AND THE PACIFIC (1993)

The Sixth Conference of Ministers of Education and those responsibile for Economic Planning in Asia and the Pacific, meeting in Kuala Lumpur from 21 to 24 June, 1993, examined a broad range of educational challenges facing the countries of the region today. The size and complexity of this region, which accounts for nearly two-thirds of the world's people and is predicted soon to become the largest force in the global economy, would suggest that a consensus on educational priorities would be difficult to achieve.

The Conference agreed, however, that two overarching concerns stood apart from all others. The first was the importance of values, ethics and culture in education; the second, the need to improve the situation of women and girls within the education systems of the region. These two imperatives are integral parts of education as the foundation of socio-economic development.

The Conference expressed the profound conviction that the only path to the restoration of a balance in its value system in a world increasingly shaped by materialism was to assign a significant place for the teaching of ethics, values and culture in the school curriculum. On the subject of women and children, consistent with the Universal Declaration of Human Rights and in particular with the spirit and letter of paragraph 26 relating to the right to education, equity, that is the quality of fairness or justice, must lie at the centre of national and regional educational plans.

Since women and girls constitute half the population of the region and, in many parts of the region, are deprived of equity in education and employment, they must receive special emphasis in the preparation of national educational plans.

Bearing the foregoing in mind, the Conference called upon the countries of the region, on UNESCO and on international community to:

— review their existing education systems with a view to formulating appropriate values education within the curriculum at all levels of the education system;
— promote the use of effective pedagogical strategies and

Source : Progressive Educational Herald, 8(1), January, 1993.

curriculum to inculcate ethical, cultural and moral values;

— ensure their education systems play a positive interventionist role in the promotion of women's status by developing targeted action plans, removing both women's illiteracy and barriers inhibiting their access to, and retention in, education;
— emphasize women's participation in scientific, vocational, technical and professional education;
— foster development of new values through gender appropriate curricula, learning measures, and the enhanced awareness of gender issues amongst teachers, planners, and administrators;
— continuously monitor the progress of education for women and girls.

The Conference further called upon international agencies and non-governmental organizations to give top priority in their developmental programmes to the education of women and girls; and upon the United Nations to place on the agenda of the forthcoming World Conference on Women, the issue of women and girls' education, with emphasis on access and equity.

Asia and the Pacific: A Renewed Commitment to Education for All

Countries of the Asia-Pacific region renewed their commitment to Education. For All and the increased access of women and girls to education at all levels at the conclusion of the Sixth Regional Conference of Ministers of Education and those Responsible for Economic Planning in Asia and the Pacific (MINEDAP VI) organised by UNESCO in Kuala Lumpur, Malaysia, from 21 to 24 June.

Thirty-one Member States pledged to work out more effective programme monitoring and assessment in order to improve learning achievement, strengthen staff support for greater decentralization of Education For All Activities (EFA), improve the data-bases on which EFA-related decisions are made, reinforce parental and community support for basic education through a closer partnership with the media and non-governmental organizations and step up the involvement of women as experts and resource persons.

Addressing delegates at the closing of the Conference, UNESCO's Assistant Director General for Education, Colin Power, expressed satisfaction with the work that had been accomplished. "I like to think", he said, "that there is a near-complete identity of views between professional educators and policy-makers."

The Conference adopted most of the recommendations propsed by the Advisory Committee on Regional Co-operation, which met earlier in Kuala Lumpur from 14 to 17 June.

To UNESCO, the Conference recommended the strengthening of the Asia-Pacific Programme of Education For All (APPEAL), greater decentralization of funds to field offices, redoubled efforts to obtain extra-budgetary support, the reinforcement of education of women, minorities, refugees, the disabled and other disadvantaged groups, and a broader, more intensive media role.

Member States pledged to forge stronger links between general education and technical and vocational education, and between technical and vocational education and industry, agriculture and other fields.

The Asia-Pacific Programme of Educational Innovation for Development (APEID) was urged to give special attention to problems of the environment, population, health and nutrition, AIDS and drugs.

The Conference recommended that UNESCO help in upgrading teacher education, developing learning materials and providing opportunities for teacher educators to study abroad in order to enhance their knowledge, skills and understanding.

In their Declaration adopted at the end of the Conference, the ministers called upon the countries of the region, on UNESCO and on the international community to give top priority to the education of women and girls. The United Nations, they suggested, should place this issue on the agenda of the 1995 World Conference on Women, with emphasis on access and equity.

Finally, the Conference urged UNESCO to give special and urgent attention to populous countries with high illiteracy rates, to small island States and to the landlocked, newly independent Central Asian Republics. It recommended that the allocation in the 1994-95 Draft Programme and Budget for the Pacific Member States be increased and that UNESCO assess and analyse needs and policies in the context of national reform and reconstruction in response to requests from Member States.

Three round tables on matters crucial to the future shape of education were organised during MINEDAP VI. They dealt with funding, education and the world of work and values in education.

The question of resources is an acute one in nearly all countries. Donor agencies who spoke at the round tables stated that they acted only in an advisory capacity and had no prescriptive role to play. As such, priorities had to be set by the countries themselves, and the demand for assistance in education could, at times, be preceded by demands for nutrition or clean drinking water.

Delegates agreed that the importance of technical and vocational education could not be over-emphasized, given that education was meant to equip the learner with skills and training for life. They recommended that UNESCO encourage its Member States to promote the mutual recognition of qualifications in co-operation with industry. The Organisation, they said, should support the co-operative development of curricula which link science, humanities and cultural and traditional values to the world of work in each countries.

Values education emerged as a pervasive theme in MINEDAP VI. If poverty eradication and human resources development were pre-conditions of peace, then the inculcation of values was a necessary part of education, for it was through values that the individual and society find their worth.

Recommendations

1. Education for All

A. The Conference recommends that Member States renew their commitment to EFA goals and further strengthen EFA programmes and continue to make use of the Asia-Pacific Programme of Education For All (APPEAL), with an emphasis on:

1. More effective programme monitoring and assessment as a means of improving learning achievement with a view to reporting in 1995 on the progress towards EFA 2000 goals.
2. Strengthening staff support and professional development for decentralized planning and management of EFA programmes.
3. Improving the data base on which EFA-related decisions are made and its reliability.
4. Reinforced community and parental support for basic education by means of strengthened partnership with the media, NGOs, and other relevant Ministries.
5. Greater involvement of women as experts and resource persons in EFA programmes.

B. The Conference recommends to UNESCO that:

6. APPEAL be strengthened in order to better fulfil the objectives of the programmes, giving due consideration to the specific needs and expectations of the Member States and field offices of the region.
7. Further, decentralization of EFA funds to PROAP, APIA, and other field offices be foreseen in 27C/5 with particular references to target countries in the region (large countries, small island states and least developed countries).
8. Efforts to obtain multilateral and bilateral financial support for EFA programmes be strengthened for the forthcoming biennium and through the remainder of the decade.
9. Partnership with UNESCO National Commissions as well as national mechanisms and institutions of relevance to EFA's goals be promoted.
10. Programmes to support the involvement of the media and other social service sectors in parental and community support for basic education be foreseen in the approved work plan of the Organization for 1994-95.
11. Continued vigorous support be given to re-inforce national efforts on behalf of girls and women as well as to minorities, refugees, the disabled, children of the border areas where there is a mingling of cultures, languages and traditions, the urban poor and other disadvantaged groups.
12. APPEAL's efforts for the improvement of curriculum, learning materials and training of personnel of EFA including literacy and continuing education be strengthened.
13. Support be given to the priority efforts of the government of Bangladesh in the eradication of illiteracy and in their establishment of a Centre for Non-formal Education, which would promote exchange of experiences among countries of the region.

II. Education for Women and Girls

The Conference recommends that Member States commit themselves to the:

14. Development of targeted action plans to increase access of girls

and women to education at all levels.

15. Development of educational contents, materials, and methods in both formal and non-formal systems, that take into account the unique needs and problems of women and girl learners and introduce changes which will contribute to their equal participation in all aspects of learning.
16. Priority placement of education programmes for girls and women, as well as training on gender issues for those in education, within the framework of national development plans which reflect an adequate analysis of the social and educational situation on girls and women.
17. Establishment of monitoring systems to prepare a progress report on women's education to the International Forum of Education for All and the United Nations World Conference on Women in 1995.

(C) DELHI SUMMIT (1993)

C.1 UNICEF Background Paper—Education for All

Introduction

UNICEF prepared a background Paper for a Panel Discussion for the Summit of Nine High Population Countries, held at New Delhi in December 1993. The Paper entitled 'Education For All, All For Education' discusses various aspects of Popular Participation, Mobilization and Decentralization for Education for All.

Opportunity and Challenge

Because basic learning needs are complex and diverse, meeting them requires multisectoral strategies and action which are integral to overall development efforts. Many partners must join with the education authorities, teachers and other educational personnel in developing basic education if it is to be seen, once again, as the responsibility of the entire society. This implies the active involvement of a wide range of partners—families, teachers, communities, private enterprises (including those involved in information and communication), government and non-governmental organizations, institutions etc.—in planning, managing and

Source : Reported from *Progressive Educational Herald*, 8(2), January, 1994.

evaluating the many forms of basic education (World Declaration on Education for All, Framework of Action, Principles of Action No. 11).

The 1990s are likely to be characterised as the decade in which a new global ethic for children began to emerge. An unprecendented period of activism in the international community in support of human development is beginning to be seen as the landmark of the decade.

The World Conference on Education for All (Jomtien, Thailand, March 1990) was the global platform of proclaiming the urgent need for action to redress the denial of basic education to intolerably large numbers of the world's children and adults. Access to basic education for all and achievement of a functional and sustainable level of learning and life skills by a large majority—at least 80 per cent was the suggested target—were regarded as the criteria for universalisation.

The Convention on the Rights of the Child that made free and compulsory primary education an obligation of the state and the right of all children came into effect in Septembr 1990. Since then, over 150 countries have ratified the Convention, more than for any other human rights treaty.

The World Summit for Children, the first truly global summit meeting, established a range of social development goals including universal access to primary education and completion of the primary cycle by at least 80 per cent of those enrolled. Over a hundred countries have been re-examining their national priorities and strategies for basic education in the wake of the Jometien Conference and the Summit for Children; most have prepared national programmes of action to accelerate progress. Regional forums of governments, several at the level of heads of state and government, have endorsed the global goals and some have adopted regional decade and mid-decade targets.

The World Summit for Social Development scheduled for 1995 will be another major occasion for world leaders to take stock of progress and constraints, to intensify the efforts to reach landmark social targets by the year 2000 and to maintain the momentum into the 21st Century.

The Education For All Summit of nine high population countries, representing over half of the global population, (held in Delhi from December 13 to 16, 1993) is in keeping with the new consensus and activism at the international level by national leaders on social and human development priorities. The preparatory process had already helped to energize national efforts in EFA and to draw increased international attention to the need for accelerating the pace of progress. The Declaration of Principles and the Framework for Action expected to be adopted by the leaders of the nine countries will be a powerful instrument for advocacy and mobilization in the hands of national leaders and all activists in the cause of education for all in each country and internationally.

The increased worldwide attention now being paid to Education for All, presents a new opportunity and poses the challenge for broadening and deepening people's participation, mobilization of the whole society and bringing authority and decision-making closer to communities and families in each country in support of education goals.

Inter-related and Overlapping Concepts

The educational system should not be regarded as a branch of the bureaucracy. Instead, it should be a sub-system highly interactive with all other parts of the social whole. The point is to give pupils, parents and teacher's responsibility over their own affairs, to the point of enabling them to administer the educational system on their own within the context of natural or contractual communities. This assumption of responsibility must necessarily embrace three indispensable areas—participating in design and decision-making processes; regular, structured involvement in the processes of management and evaluation; and finally, financial accountability with ragard of both income and contributions (Ki-Zerbo, 1990, p. 86).

The terms *participation, mobilization* and *decentralization* have become common in current education and development parlance all over the world. They all refer to the same general category of needs. In the context of education, these needs are to define educational development in terms of people's real priorities and demands, to unleash the energies and resources of people and society to make education a concern and a task of the whole society and to create conditions and institutional environments for people to articulate their goals and priorities in education and to make their contribution to educational development. These three terms together constitute the key elements of a framework for promoting and assessing progress in educational development.

People's participation is a *sine qua non* in Education For All. By definition, education for all must engage people widely and actively as beneficiaries and contributors. But even more, participation, in its various dimensions, has come to be recognized as a basic *principle of action, an overall development strategy*, in national development efforts including educational development. It is both a means and an end of development. As a principle that guides action, participation derives its rationale from values and goals that are important in most societies, such as :

- Accepting democratic practices and values as a way of organizing society;
- giving a prominent role to institutions of civil society in the nation's governance;
- giving people the chance to participate in events and processes that shape their life;
- liberating people's energy, creativity and entrepreneurial spirit; and
- equitable access to opportunities of life including essential social services such as basic education.

In the context of basic education, therefore, participation is an expression of the overall development strategy of recognizing the critical role of people's collective action in the broad range of political, social and economic arenas.

Participation

To participate literally means being part of something. But there are various ways and degrees of "being part of" or "taking part in": (1) use of a particular service; (2) contribute resources, materials and/or labour; (3) attend; (4) be consulted on a particular issue; (5) get involved in the delivery of the service; (6) take part in the implementation of delegated powers; (7) take part in decision-making. On the other hand, it has been argued that "the participation issue is not so much a problem of degree or quantity but rather of the quality of such participation". It is also stressed that participation is "not only an agreement to follow but an active decision to assume responsibility in considering the rationale, implications and potential outcomes" of any particular process.

Participation, if understood as an empowering and formative experience, may enable people to : (a) gain knowledge, awareness and democratic experience, as well as self-confidence, self-reliance, pride and autonomy; (b) take action to solve their own problems; (c) gain control of their own lives; and (d) gain social and political power.

Social Mobilization

Social mobilization is a broad-scale movement to engage large number of people in action for achieving a specific development goal through self-reliant efforts. It is a planned process that seeks to facilitate change and development. It takes into account the felt needs of the people, embraces the critical principle of community involvement and seeks to empower individuals for action...

Mobilization in the context of basic education refers to active involvement of all relevant sectors of society in promoting and supporting education. Social mobilization, therefore, is a manifestation of the principle of participation through organized and systematic actions.

The martial overtone of the term social mobilization is not accidental. It reflects a sense of urgency about overcoming a common problem or achieving a common purpose through expression of collective commitment of society, formulation of strategies to achieve results and engagement of large numbers of people in coordinated and goal-oriented group actions. The spread of participatory democratic values and new forms of social organization such as popular organisations of women, youth and workers; cooperatives; religious and cultural organizations; professional associations; non-governmental and voluntary organizations; and elected bodies of local government, has created new opportunities for social mobilization. At the same time, advances in communication technology—electronic and print media as well as new and traditional forms of cultural expression reaching large audiences—have expanded the potential reach of social mobilization to a degree unthinkable in the past.

Decentralization refers to the organization and structure of governance that make it possible for the participatory principle and its manifestation in action through social mobilization to be practised. The dominant connotation is of a shift of authority and decision-making from the central government and capital city to regions, districts, towns and villages that would allow participation, facilitate mobilization and promote efficiency. Along with the vertical shift to remedy over-centralization of political and economic structures, a redefining of roles and functions of governance at different levels is also necessary. It is not a matter of divesting central authorities of their responsibilities and obligations, but assigning authorities and tasks at levels where they can be handled most effectively, conforming to the principles of participation and requirements for effective social mobilization. For decentralization to function effectively, national leaders and the administrative and legislative organs of central governments, for example, must continue to define the overall objectives and priorities for educational development, ensure that adequate national resources are mobilized for and directed to human priorities, determine broad allocations of national resources among competing categories of needs, promote principles of universality and equality for all the people and foster a political culture including adoption of legislative and administrative measures for decentralization.

Decentralization

Decentralization can take three forms: deconcentration (passing down adminstrative functions with authority to review and overule retained at the central level), delegation (passing down authority and decision-making powers with discretion to review and overrule retained at the central level) and devolution (granting decision-making powers to local authorities and allowing them to take full responsibility without reference back to central government with sharing of authority protected by legislative or statutory measures). In many developing countries, decentralization has not gone much beyond the deconcentration level. Decentralization also has a horizontal dimension, that is, the need to (re) distribute power among institutions at the same level.

Speaking of decentralization in education means an attempt to restructure the education system with three main objectives: (a) improving the finance, efficiency and quality of the system, (b) redistributing political power, and (c) promoting stability in the system.

Where We Are—Lessons from Experience

The Conventional Educational Model

The conventional education model has been characterized by highly centralized structures and decision-making in all spheres—legal, administrative, curricular, pedagogical, organizational. Typically, educational policies and reforms have been designed by political and technical elites, without systematic consultation with the larger society. A small group of individuals often decides what the learning needs are for all and now they are to be satisfied.

Although the rhetoric of participation has become commonplace, participation in education is still narrow in conception and limited in practice. Learners and communities are usually referred to as beneficiaries and teachers classified as inputs, together with textbooks and other instructional materials. Parents remain outsiders, requested to participate through "voluntary" contribution—cash or labour—to the (otherwise impossible to maintain) school system. Students are passive listeners in the classroom, teachers are passive executors of predetermined curricula, parents are passive receivers of complaints and results.

The tendency to consider education programmes as strictly sectoral Ministry of Education bureaucracy-controlled activity persists in most countries. Basic education does not figure high enough on political and development agendas and there is not enough opportunity for public debate and consensus-building around educational priorities, targets, strategies and performance. The extraordinary outreach capacity of mass media and communications technology to inform and involve people in burning social issues is not being exploited. The organizational and administrative structures that would allow people to participate effectively are still evolving in many countries.

Popular or community participation is to often understood in economic terms—participation viewed as "cheap labour" or "cost-sharing" and from a one-way perspective; what the community can do for the school rather than what the school can do for the community. Parents may even be allowed to have a say in organizational and administrative matters, but are not to "interfere with technical matters"—that is, with the nuts and bolts of their children's learning process—as attested to by restrictive private and public school regulations, and even some national education laws. Paradoxically enough, while school-related activities, especially at the pre-school and primary level, are considered a female domain in many countries (inasmuch as they are considered a simple extension of mothers' responsibilities and housework), the role of women in their children's education is not valued and women's education is grossly neglected.

Teachers have become increasingly alienated from their work, constrained by structures and practices that do not favour professional advancement, updating of skills, teamwork and experience-sharing. Teachers are increasingly held responsible for their students' learning achievements, but are not given the professional autonomy that goes together with such a responsibility. Over and over again they are required to accommodate to policy changes and to implement educational reforms without proper information, much less participation. Given this background—over and above the important issue of inadequate remuneration—it is not difficult to understand teachers' skepticism about "innovation" and even opposition to proposals for decentralization and community participation.

Students, meanwhile, have very limited, if any, participation in decision-making on educational matters, including the most elementary ones (*e.g.*, schedules, uniforms, etc.). It is taken for granted that children and youth have nothing pertinent to contribute to their own education. Even strong advocates of participation in education often ignore learners as legitimise educational partners.

Social mobilization for education has often taken the form of one-shot, short-term campaigns, around a particular action or goal. While social mobilization has been given greater attention in literacy, adult education and the non-formal education spheres, less common are social mobilization efforts in the context of the regular school system and the basic learning needs of children.

Decentralization in different forms is a subject of great interest in most developing countries at present. The prevailing mood in favour of "small government" and of divesting government of inefficient public services and enterprises has influenced ideas and action in the sphere of education. In some situations, central authorities have loosened control by allowing the private sector—including commercial profit-making enterprises—to play a greater role in the provision of services. This can be a positive development when society's needs are met effectively and equitably through harnessing the capacities and resources of the private sector. But it can also lead to a dereliction of public responsibility if the consequence is increased inequity in access and participation.

Shifting responsibilities for social services including basic education to local levels has been prompted in part by the resource crunch faced by central governments. To the extent that this is a major motivation and the resource base at the local level remains meagre, decentralization becomes a cover for governmental neglect of fundamental obligations to the public.

Country Experiences

If one takes a retrospective view of the past few decades, there is no doubt educational systems are moving in the direction of greater adherence to particular norms, more effective social mobilization and increased decentralization of authority and responsibility. However, much still needs to be done to bridge the gap between theory and practice, rhetoric and action and where we are and where we want to be. For too many children do not have access to schooling or non-formal education for too many enroll only to drop out soon thereafter due to the incapacity of educational systems to offer learning that is relevant to the conditions of poor rural and penurban communities.

Participation as a Political Norm

Most developing countries, including the meagre population countries, recognize the importance of participatory norms and values. However, participation as a democratic value and a principle of organizing the institutions of society, including basic education services, is difficult to practice. As UNDP's *Human Development Report 1993* put it, "Participation is a plant that does not grow easily in the human environment" (p. 28). The road is long and paved with difficulties, full of ups and downs and not without unexpected outcomes. Obstacles are numerous, including rigid legal systems, bureaucratic institutions and attitudes, outmoded social values and cultural norms, entrenched political interests and above all, inequity in the distribution of wealth and power. The starting point has to be the nurturing of a participatory culture and of participatory structures in a sustained participation-building process. Progress in developing the participatory culture, norms and practices, which cannot be applied in the sphere of education alone or in an isolated way, has been uneven among the nine countries. The urgent need to persist in this effort is clear in all of them.

Participation as Access

Participation in terms of access to educational opportunities (including continuation until completion of basic schooling) is more specific, quantifiable and easier to assess. Several of the nine countries have been successful enough in expanding access and continuation in primary education to come close to the universalization target. A political priority supportive of universal access to basic education and the development of participatory structures allowing communities to be actively involved in the education of children have been important factors in this success. The community's involvement takes different forms in different societies, but effective participation always implies both enhancing the resources for education and taking part in defining and guiding the programme at the community level.

How Communities may Participate in Basic Education

* Parents and family members working with teachers to help and guide children;
* Community organisations encouraging all potential learners to participate in learning activities;
* Community organisations looking after upkeep of educational facilities and their contribution to establishing or adding to such facilities;
* Community organisations ensuring that schools function, teachers attend to classes, students do not play truant and so on;
* Helping identify people in the community to take up part-time teaching assignments in non-formal centres and encouraging them to perform better;
* Helping define learning needs in relation to developmental needs and prospects of the locality and make learning activities connect better with other development activities; and
* Helping different learning activities work in a mutually supportive way, responding to total learning needs of the community.

(M. Ahmed *et al., Basic Education and National Development: Lessons from China and India*, pp. 127-28.)

Social Mobilization Lessons: Attention to social and human development goals in the 1980s in the developing countries, including the nine populous countries, has generated useful lessons for social mobilization. The importance of the underpinning of participatory culture and values and strengthening of participatory social organisations for effective social mobilization has already been noted.

Five conditions stand out as critical in successful, large-scale social mobilization efforts in such areas as universal child immunization, adoption of new farming practices and literacy campaigns:

* Objectives and targets reflect important needs of society, are defined in clear and precise terms and are widely understood and accepted;
* Political goals and ideology are supportive of social mobilization and the ideological and political priority is forcefully and

unambiguously expressed by national leaders;

* The programme supported by social mobilization is lifted out of the bureaucratic sectoral confines and implemented as a national endeavour with the contribution and involvement of all who are in a position to become involved;
* Emulation and competition within the country and among countries are encouraged with models and examples serving as the source of motivation for greater effort as well as useful practical lessons; and
* A systematic process of monitoring with a few well chosen indicators reported, reviewed and given wide publicity serves to keep public interest alive and maintain the momentum of the programme.

The Social Mobilizers: In the context of primary and basic education, of special significance are the roles of children, women, teachers and parents.

'The individual learners themselves constitute a vital human resource that needs to be mobilized'. Students are obviously the key actors and partners in the educational process. Experience all over the world in such fields as adult literacy, health and environment has shown that youth are a resource that is all too often neglected and underutilized. Young people are not only open to new ideas and change, but are also enthusiastic and committed innovators when provided the right conditions and support. Youth can help revitalize and renovate education and revitalize themselves by getting involved in a socially relevant task.

Given the opportunity, children have proven to be good communicators and social mobilizers. Children are not only able to teach their families and neighbours what they learn in school, but they can help change parental and community perceptions and attitudes towards education. "Child-to-child" projects in various countries are living examples of children's active involvement in promoting health, education and children's rights.

Empirical evidence and evaluation of programmes confirm that, despite cultural and economic barriers, girls and women all over the world are not only eager to learn but they do the most with what they learn. Women constitute the majority of learners in most adult literacy programmes, stay longer in the programmes and their learning results are often better than those of men. Women are the first and most important promoters of children's education. Mothers' expectations and attitudes towards their children's schooling are an important determinant of success or failure in children's performance. Women are effective programme organizers and implementers, are dominant in the ranks of primary teachers in many countries and have assumed key educational roles as both early childhood and adult educators. Employment of women teachers have been found to be a critical factor in overcoming gender disparity in primary and basic education programmes.

Despite all the remarkable progress that has been made in information and communication technology teachers obviously cannot be replaced as the main contact point of basic education programmes with their learners. Decentralization of authority and community ownership of primary education go hand-in-hand with teachers' and schools' responsiveness to the needs of learners and the community. This means, on the one hand, a less bureaucratic and hierachical administrative system with greater authority at the community level with the school made accountable to the community and on the other hand, a greater autonomy of individual institutions with teachers and headmasters being able to interact with the community. Teachers' unions and associations are legitimate partners and implementing educational reforms. The antipathy sometimes demonstrated by professional organisations of teachers to community control of education would soften if the teachers' professional leadership was perceived as being linked to community accountability.

It is only reasonable that parents should be the most interested party among all those who are concerned with the education of children. Parents' and teacher-parents' associations are beginning to be seen as important beyond the material and financial contribution they may make. Parental and community involvement in the development of curriculum, an important new initiative in the formal school tradition, has been incorporated into the educational laws of Indonesia and is evolving less formally in several other countries. Parents' schools for orienting and preparing parents for their role in the school's affairs and in guiding their children's education is a feature of Chinese primary education.

Not all Answers in Decentralization : Various forms of decentralization, deconcentration, delegation and devolution of authority and functions—have been introduced or are being debated in most developing countries. Greater success in universalization of primary education and expansion ofbasic education opportunities in the nine high-population countries correlate with a higher degree of effective decentralization in planning, management and control of resources in educational programmes. At the same time, these countries also illustrate the problems and dilemmas that decentralization often generates. These shortcomings can defeat the very educational principles and social objectives that decentralization is expected to serve unless the practice of decentralization is adapted to specific circumstances and complemented by necessary countervailing measures.

For example, decentralised elaboration of curricula and production of instructional materials do not necessarily lead to relevance, flexibility and adaptation to the learners' and communities' needs. Without the required technical capacity and social sensitivity, locally designed curricula and textbooks may be even more rigid and prescriptive than those produced centrally. They may also be weak pedagogically and lack creativity.

Often, "decentralization" in practice consists of giving local governing units new responsibilities but little real authority, as observed in a study conducted in three Sub-Saharan African countries—Ghana, Ivory Coast and Nigeria. Analysis of four Latin American countries—Argentina, Chile, Colombia and Mexico—conclude that decentralization did not increase resources for education, that it was not an important factor in enrolment and internal efficiency and that the quality of education did not improve. In the specific case of Chile, the quality of education even deteriorated during—and partly as a result of—decentralization.

There is general agreement that decentralization (and more so privatization) may result in greater social inequities and regional imbalances. Growing economic and financial constraints have reinforced the trend of depending on local communities for financial resources for education. However, while community financial or labour contribution may encourage parents' interest in their children's education, empirical evidence also shows that community finance may have negative effects on equity, quality and social cohesion. Community schools often serve as instruments of social stratification and community finance may exacerbate inter-regional and intraregional disparities. The cases of China and Zimbabwe, while generally presented as overall positive examples, are also illustrative of such contradictory results.

In summing up, it can be said that centralization is neither the sole culprit for all the problems that educational systems face today, nor is decentralization the panacea that will solve all of them. On balance, the trend of decentralization has to be supported and encouraged; it has to be carried to communities and villages from the provincial and district levels and has to include real transfer of authority and meaningful decision-making so that people can actively participate and be involved. However, decentralization has to be implemented with sensitivity and countervailing measures are needed to compensate for unintended negative consequences.

Some Lessons on Decentralization and Participation

— Major decentralization with greatly enhanced local responsibility and popular involvement is crucial for creating a conducive environment for solving key problems of basic education;
— A political choice has to be made to adopt decentralization and devolution of authority as a key strategy for giving national development efforts a human development focus;
— Legislative measures will help establish structures of effective decentralization and participation, such as village education committees with statutory functions;
— A multi-level system of technical support is needed for capacity-building at local and sub-national levels;
— A competent cadre of basic education planners and managers at the local and regional/sub-regional levels has to be built-up; the total neglect of this critical need has to be remedied urgently;
— Voluntary organizations, social activists and the higher levels of the government have to serve as countervailing forces to entrenched local structures of domination and exploitation; and
— A norm of partnership between local government, voluntary organizations and the private sector has to be developed to meet the diverse basic learning needs of the entire community.

(M. Ahmed, et al., *Basic Education and National Development: Lessons from China and India*, pp. 13-15.)

Fulfilling the Potential: What should be done

A substantial body of experience and knowledge has emerged on how the three related concepts of people's participation, social mobilization and decentralization of organizations and functions can be put to work to promote universal basic education. People, government and national leaders are readier than ever for decisive action. Fulfilling the potential that now exists requires building and acting on experience and major lessons that have accumulated, including :

1. *A clearly Articulated Goal and Vision* : A clear definition of goals with time-bound objectives and programmes that people can understand and relate to will facilitate effective participation and social mobilization. For countries in which a large proportion of children are deprived of primary education, primary education for all children within the shortest possible time has to be the rallying cry for participation and mobilization. The internationally adopted target of access to primary education in a formal or an equivalent programme for all children by the year 2000, with at least 80 per cent of them completing the primary stage, provides an easily and widely understood focus for advocacy, participation, mobilization, programme planning and monitoring. Major strategies or sub-goals such as reducing gender disparity and preventing large-scale drop-outs would then fit under the over-arching goals. The children who should complete primary education by the year 2000 must enroll in school in the next two to three years. The class of 2000, consisting of all current primary entry-age children, deserves everything their societies can give them to ensure a successful outcome for them by the year 2000. Providing them with the support they need to stay in school and learn what they need to learn should become the pivot of a nationwide mobilization effort in each country.

2. *High Profile and Frequent Monitoring* : An education programme of universal scope that aims to reach large numbers—all primary school age children in the case of primary education—within a specific time-table must develop an effective method of monitoring progress. A system of monitoring that includes a few clearly defined indicators; that reports results frequently, regularly and publicly; that is undertaken at national, regional and local levels; and that leads to quick remedial action when problems are detected, is an unmistakable signal of commitment and seriousness. Monitoring can be a powerful tool for promoting popular participation and social mobilization. National leaders at the highest level can use the monitoring system as an effective instrument for mobilization and action by personally leading public reviews of progress, deciding on necessary course-corrections and encouraging officials down the line to do the same.

3. *Visibility on the National Agenda*: If the whole of society is expected to participate in and mobilize around universal primary education, it must be brought to the centre of national attention. In order for this to happen, it must be shown how primary education provides benefits across the board in major areas of societal concern, such as better

health, labour productivity, greater democratic participation, enhanced competitiveness in the global market, protection of the environment and slowing of population growth. Obviously, the message is not that expansion of primary education will solve all these problems; it is that primary education is the linchpin of the nation's effort and of each individual's contribution to addressing these critical national concerns. National leaders have to take the lead in this nationwide dialogue and recruit opinion leaders in all sectors of society to the cause. The aim is to build public awareness and understanding leading to support and involvement of the whole society.

4. *Building a National Consensus*: Participation and mobilization on an enduring basis can be promoted only on the foundation of a national consensus on the major goals and priorities and the main strategies for achieving them. Reaching a consensus on as critical and sensitive subject as education is difficult and it is not reached once and forever. Consensus-building is an ongoing process that needs to be nurtured. The national leaders, especially the government leaders in the ruling political parties, have a special responsibility to initiate and support open dialogue on key issues of policies and strategies and to ensure that the consensus on basic goals and strategies are non-partisan enough to survive changes of government and personalities in high places.

5. *Identifying, Emulating and Creating Success Stories* : Nothing succeeds better than success. The problems and constraints of universal primary education are largely known; so are the elements of the solution. It is essential to identify promising examples of success, creative and innovative combinations of action that have helped to move the system out of a rut and accelerate progress. These models have to be used for emulation and motivation and as sources of useful practical lessons both within a country and among countries. All of the nine countries and others as well have many examples of success which need to be studied and adapted for wider application.

6. *Decentralization Based on Shared Responsibilities* : Decentralization of responsibility and functions must be introduced and implemented in such a way that it is not seen as an excuse for abdicating the State's responsibility for basic education or as a means of shifting the burden from the central authorities to the local level. Decentralization works when it is a means of redistributing functions and authority among different levels of government and of the civil society in order to make systems more efficient and democratic, allowing people to participate and contribute. The role of central organs of the state and national leadership

in defining national purposes and priorities, setting national standards, compensating for disparities, creating conditions for local levels to function and maintaining a national overview is and will continue to be vital for the success of decentralization efforts. At the same time, a system of planning, management, monitoring and community mobilization has to function effectively at each local administrative unit in order to achieve genuine participation in education in each community and household.

7. *Building on Existing Institutions and Practices* : The starting point for promoting popular participation, social mobilization and decentralization has to be the existing institutions, practices and norms in each society. Local government in one form or another has always existed. There are traditional structures for community efforts. Religious, cultural, labour, professional and other types of organizations and collective entities exist. It is important to identify the potential and weaknesses of these institutions and practices, build on the strengths and find ways of overcoming the weaknesses so that they all can contribute at the local and national levels.

8. *Effective Use of the Power of Modern Communication* : Recent advances in information and communication technology have brought virtually every citizen within the effective reach of modern communication. Yet the potential of the communication media for expanding people's access to educational opportunities and for mobilizing people's support for and involvement in education is far from being fully exploited. Mass media cannot substitute for effective organization and leadership; but the possibility now exists for use of the media for interactive communication so that the vision of the leaders is widely shared and people's voices are expressed leading to a collective sense of mission and direction.

The last decade of the 20th century offers a rare window of opportunity for accelerating social progress and Education For All occupies a critical place on the world's agenda for priority action. Let us not allow this opportunity to slip through our fingers.

C.2 Education For All: Delhi Summit Declaration

Introduction

Heads of State and Government of Nine High Population Countries, all

Source : Progressive Educational Herald, 8(2), January, 1994.

of which are developing countries accounting for more than half of the World's population, held a Summit in Delhi on December 13-16, 1993 to discuss the Goal of Education For All. (Only two heads, however, attended the Summit—President Sukarno of Indonesia and Prime Minister P.V. Narasimha Rao of India. The rest of the countries were represented by Ministers of their governments). Given below is the Text of the Declaration adopted on the concluding day of the Summit, December 16, 1993.

—Editorial Comments

Declaration

We, the leaders of nine high population developing nations of the world, hereby reaffirm our commitment to pursue with utmost zeal and determination the goals set in 1990 by the World Conference on Education For All and the World Summit on Children, to meet the basic learning needs of all our people by making primary education universal and expanding learning opportunities for children, youth and adults. We do so in full awareness that our countries contain more than half of the world's people and that the success of our efforts is crucial to the achievement of the global goal of Education For All.

We recognise that:

> The aspirations and development goals of our countries can be fulfilled only by assuring education to all our people, a right promised both in Universal Declaration of Human Rights and in the Constitution and law of each of our countries.

Education is the pre-eminent means for promoting universal human values, the quality of human resources, and respect for cultural diversity.

The education systems in our countries have made great strides in offering education to substantial numbers, and yet have not fully succeeded in providing quality education to all our people, indicating the need for developing creative approaches, both within and outside the formal system.

The content and methods of education must be developed to serve the basic learning needs of individuals and societies, to empower them to address their most pressing problem—combating poverty, raising productivity, improving living conditions, and protecting the environment—and to enable them to play their rightful role in building democratic societies and enriching cultural heritage.

Successful education programmes require complementary and convergent actions on adequate nutrition, effective health care and appropriate care and development of the young child, in the context of the role of the family and the community.

The education and empowerment of girls and women are important goals in themselves and are key factors in contributing to social development, well-being and education of present and future generations, and the expansion of the choices available to women for the development of the full potential.

The pressure of population growth has seriously strained the capacity of education systems and impeded needed reforms and improvements. Moreover, given the age structure of the population in our countries, it will continue to do so throughout the coming decade.

Education is and must be, a societal responsibility, encompassing governments, families, communities and non-governmental organisation alike, it requires the commitment and participation of all in a grand alliance that transcends diverse opinions and political positions.

Conscious of the vital role that education must play in the development of our societies, we hereby pledge that, by the year 2000 or at the earliest possible moment, we will ensure a place for every child in a school or appropriate education programme according to his or her capabilities, in order that no child be deprived of education for lack of a teacher, learning material or adequate space. We pledge this in fulfilment of our commitment under the Convention of the Rights of the Child which we have ratified.

We will consolidate efforts towards the basic education of youth and adults from public and private sources, improving and expanding our literacy and adult education programmes within the context of an integrated strategy of basic education for all our people.

We will eliminate disparities of access to basic education arising from gender, age, income, family, cultural, ethnic and linguistic differences and geographical remoteness. We will improve the quality and relevance of basic education programmes by intensifying efforts to improve the status, training and conditions of teachers, to improve learning contents and material and to carry out other necessary reforms of our education systems.

We will, in our actions, accord to human development the highest priority at national and other levels, ensuring that a growing share of national and community resources is dedicated to basic education and improving the management of existing resources for education.

We will rally all sectors of our society towards 'Education For All' as we hereby endorse the framework of action accompanying this declaration and undertake to review our progress at the national level and to share our experiences among ourselves and with the global community.

We hereby call upon:

International collaborators to raise substantially their support for our efforts to expand our national capacities for expanding and improving basic education services.

International financial institutions, in the context of structural adjustments to recognise education as a critical investment without imposing predetermined ceiling on such investments to promote an international environment to enable countries to sustain their socio-economic development.

(D) 45TH ALL-INDIA ADULT EDUCATION CONFERENCE (1994)

Introduction

The 45th All-India Adult Education Conference of the Indian Adult Education Association organised in collaboration with Rajasthan Vidyapeeth Kul began its 4-day session in Ajmer (Rajasthan) on June 15, 1994. The theme was "Total Literacy in the context of Education for All by 2000".

Over 250 delegates from 18 States and UTs attended the Conference. Most of the affiliated organisations of IAEA, State Governments, State Resource Centres, Shramik Vidyapeeths, TLC Districts and the universities of Aligarh Muslim, Amravati, Annamalai, A.P.S. (Rewa), Dr. Baba Saheb Ambedkar (Aurangabad), Bangalore, Barkatullah (Bhopal), Bharthidasan, Bhavnagar, Calicut, Gurukul Kangri (Hardwar), Jiwaji (Gwalior), Kurukshetra, Magadh, Manipur, M.S. University of Baroda, Nagpur, Rajasthan Vidyapeeth, Rani Durgabai (Jabalpur), Saurashtra, Sri Venkateswara (Tirupati), South Gujarat, Poona, Vikram (Ujjain) and Viswa Bharti deputed their representatives. Inaugurating the conference, Prof. Kanta Ahuja, Vice-Chancellor, Maharishi Dayanand Saraswati University, Ajmer said that

Source : Indian Journal of Adult Education 55(2) April-June, 1994.

girls were being kept out of school because their parents did not appreciate the importance and value of education. The condition of the school and the quality of education specially in the government schools in the rural areas were other bottlenecks in attracting children towards the school. She feared that unless the gender gap which was widening was reduced, the illiterates between age-group 15-35 would only be women.

Prof. Kanta Ahuja emphasised the need to provide education and awareness to the adult illiterates so that they send their children specially girls to schools. India, she said, was poised towards the phase of accelerated growth and progress and to continue with it, it was essential that there should be consensus on education and other national issues at the political level. Literacy, education, population and environment protection were areas that need to be kept free from politics along party lines, she emphasised.

Plenary Sessions

In the first plenary session, the working paper was presented by Prof. B.B. Mohanty, Resident Director, Indian Institute of Mass Communication, Dhenkanal, Orissa.

The delegates were divided into six groups to discuss the following sub-themes of the conference :

1. Resource Mobilization
2. Creation and Sustenance of Environment for Learning
3. Training of Functionaries
4. Media Support
5. Women's Literacy
6. Post Literacy and Continuing Education

The Chairmen of the groups were Dr. M.S. Talwar, Prof. R. Krishnamoorty, Dr. S.K. Kejariwal, Prof. Nanubhai Joshi, Smt. Kamala Rana and Dr. D.P. Mukherjee.

Zakir Husain Memorial Lecture

The Zakir Husain Memorial Lecture was delivered by Dr. Chitra Naik. She said that the goals of the literacy and Education For All need to be fixed in local context and in a disaggregated manner, for their effective pursuit.

Education For All, she said, was a comprehensive concept. It covers mass literacy, universal primary education and further education facilities. Learning to handle new information, analysing it and processing it for application to work, family life and social affairs, would henceforth require not only basic literacy skills, but skills involving a well-developed cognitive process at a much higher level, she said.

Stressing the need for continuing education, she said, that young and old men and women should be liberated and empowered not merely by literacy and basic education but by a clear realization of their cultural and intellectual potential.

Shri V.S. Mathur, President of the Labour Organisation of the Rural Poor presided.

Reports of Member Organisations and TLC Districts

The representatives of member organisations of IAEA and the TLC Districts presented their reports during the plenary sessions. Over 20 reports were presented.

Role of ASPBAE and ILSS

In another plenary session Dr. Om Shrivastava, Asian Regional Coordinator, ASPBAE spoke about the role of Asian South Pacific Bureau of Adult Education (ASPBAE) for promoting adult education in the Asian and Pacific region. He said that the ASPBAE was an organisation of NGOs. But in countries where there were no NOGs, the governmental agencies were enrolled as members.

Dr. Shrivastava said that ASPBAE was focusing on five issues:

1. Literacy, post-literacy and universalization of elementary education;
2. Education for empowerment of women;
3. Education for sustainable development;
4. Education for peace and human rights; and
5. Education for the workers.

He said that 120 organisations from the Asian pacific region are members of the ASPBAE. It is not a funding agency and now believes in partnership concept, he stressed. It provides learning opportunities through arranging exchange visits, workshops and training programmes. It is providing access to information through newsletters and ASPBAE Courier.

The International Literacy Support Service (ILSS) was established by the International Council for Adult Education (ICAE) during the International Literacy Year 1990. It is confining its activities at present for promotion of women's literacy.

Thematic Workshops

Three thematic workshops were also held during the conference. The following three themes were discussed :

1. Adult Education and Communal Harmony—Chairman—Prof. Yashvant Shukla;
2. Monitoring and Evaluation—Chairman—Prof. B.B. Mohanty;
3. Empowerment and Education of Women and Weaker Sections—Chairman—Prof. K.K. Vashisht.

Cultural Programmes

Two cultural programmes were organised on the 15th and 16th June. The folk dances and folk music of Rajasthan were presented.

Recommendations

1. The 45th All India Adult Education Conference on "Total Literacy in the context of Eucation for All by 2000" which met in Ajmer on June 15-18, 1994 welcomes the initiative and efforts made by the Government of India and the State Governments to achieve total literacy through campaign approach, but it feels that there are several issues on which greater quality is needed.
2. The Conference notes that lot of efforts are being made to create environment through the Jathas, Street Plays (Nukkad Nataks) etc., but feels that one time effort is not sufficient to sustain the interest of learners and volunteers. It recommends that with the help of local voluntary organisations environment building should be a continuous process so that the motivation of volunteers and of the learners should continue till the completion

of the six months programme. It further stresses that the local talent should be utilized to create need based environment.

3. The Conference recommends that each district in the country must be analysed in terms of its strengths and weaknesses. The strengths particularly should be higlighted so as to motivate others for this programme.
4. The Conference urges that school children must be involved by assigning them projects to make atleast two illiterates literate.
5. The Conference recommends that adult education functionaries should be trained not only in imparting 3 R's but also for mobilising the community support so that literacy really becomes people's own programme.
6. For promoting communal harmony through adult education, the Conference recommends that national integration should be invariably interwoven in the training programmes of all levels of functionaries. It further recommends that relevant materials on the subject should be produced which could go a long way in promoting communal harmony in the country.
7. The Conference recommends that there is an urgent need to prepare more and more success stories through the print and the audio-visual media so that both educated and uneducated get inspiration to participate in this national endeavour.
8. The Conference feels that for achieving total literacy by the year 2000 multi-pronged approach should be adopted and not restricted to the literacy campaigns only.
9. For JSNs, the Conference feels that no general prescribed criteria be fixed for the entire country. It should be designed according to the need of the area. It recommends that Prerak in the JSN should be given a minimum honorarium of Rs. 500 so that it commensurates with his/her duties and responsibilities.
10. The Conference feels that both print and electronic media have to play a meaningful role in making it a people's movement. For achieving this the electronic media should televise at the prime time success stories so that a learning environment is created. The traditional media has an equally important role and should be effectively utilized.
11. To make literacy programme a success, the Conference feels that it should be interwoven with the rural development programmes. This integration, it feels would be beneficial for both.
12. The Conference recommends that monitoring in the context of

Total Literacy Campaigns has to be a continuous on-going process so as to provide the necessary timely correctives; and evaluation has to be less mechanistic, participatory and more humane providing continuous feed-backs for overall improvement in the programme. The Conference further recommends that monitoring and evaluation should be built into the curriculum of the various training programmes organised in the context of Total Literacy Campaigns.

(E) 46TH ALL INDIA ADULT EDUCATION CONFERENCE (1996)

Indian Adult Education Association in collaboration with Centre for Continuing/Adult Education, M.S. University of Baroda organised 46th All-India Education Conference in Vadodara on March 9, 1996. The theme was Strategies for Post-Literacy in the Next Decade.

Recommendations

1. The 46th All India Education Conference organised by the Indian Adult Education Association and the Department of Continuing Adult Education and Community Services, MS University of Baroda notes with satisfaction that post-literacy programme has been expanded considerably during the last 3-4 years and about 140 districts at present are in the post-literacy phase.
2. The Conference notes that at many a time there is a wide gap between the literacy and post-literacy phase. This it feels results into relapse into illiteracy and wastage of efforts and resources. It, therefore, recommends that the gap between the TLC and PLC should be reduced. The functionaries both at the top level and at the grassroot level should adopt suitable strategies to achieve it.
3. The Conference notes with satisfaction that Continuing Education Centres in every village on experimental basis are to be started soon. But it feels that the part-time *Prerak* would not be in a position to deliver the goods. It urges that *Prerak* should be a full time person with an honorarium of not less than minimum wages prevalent in the State.
4. The Conference recommends that Jan Shikshan Nilayams/ Continuing Education Centres should be provided adequate

space and other infrastructural facilities to make them effective centres. There should be at least two rooms for the centre as recommended by Ghosh Expert Group.

5. The Conference notes that no concerted effort has been made to make adult literacy programme for women effectively linked with development plans. It urges that after completing the post-literacy phase the women should be provided competitive skills for employment or self-employment so that they forge ahead in the next decade as responsible agents for social change.
6. The Conference urges that post-literacy programme to be effective must be linked with economic development through active cooperation of other training institutions for vocational and technical skills. It should be closely linked with job oriented skills such as TRYSEM, IRDP, JRY and DWARCA.
7. The Conference recommends that village institutions particularly Panchayats should be entrusted with the responsibility for the conduct of the post-literacy programme. It feels that involvement of school teachers, extension workers, health workers and other important village leaders is also essential for its success.
8. The Conference recommends that the neo-literates should be encouraged to continue their education and undertake open school examination so that they could get gainful employment.
9. The Conference notes with satisfaction that some districts have started newsletter to stabilise the knowledge of reading and writing of neo-literates and to provide current information to them and to the members of the family. But, it feels that all PC/CE districts should bring out the newsletter so that neo-literates get opportunities for self-education. But, before bringing out the newsletter the persons involved with newsletter should be oriented in editing, production and distribution so that the right message reaches the people at the right time.
10. It feels that studies at grassroot level are necessary to identify the specific needs of the target group so that the teaching/learning process gets strengthened. For this the Conference feels that research institutions and universities could play a leading role in conducting such studies.
11. The Conference feels that Universities are playing an effective role in continuing education of the masses, but, uncertainty

regarding their continuation beyond March 1997 is considerably effecting their programmes. It urges upon the University Grants Commission (UGC) to announce its policy regarding continuation of the Department/Centres of Adult and Continuing Education beyond March 1997 so that adult and continuing education becomes a permanent system in the university structure.

6

Development of Adult Education Programme

Introduction

A Draft Policy Statement on Adult Education and an Outline of National Adult Education Programme were prepared by the Ministry of Education and Social Welfare on the basis of extensive consultations with the educationists and adult education field workers. These documents have been considered in a number of forums and some modifications have been made in the final version.

(A) NATIONAL ADULT EDUCATION PROGRAMME (1978)

(i) Adult Education: A Policy Statement

1. Exclusion of a vast majority of the people from the process of education is a most disturbing aspect of educational and social planning. This has been uppermost in the consideration of the present Government ever since it assumed office in March, 1977. While determined efforts must be made to universalise elementary education upto the age of 14 years, educational facilities must be extended to adult population to remedy their educational depriviation and to enable them to develop their potentiality. Indeed, universalisation of elementary education and of adult literacy are mutually inter-dependent.

2. The Government have resolved to wage a clearly-conceived, well-planned and relentless struggle against illiteracy to enable the masses to play an active role in social and cultural change. Literacy ought to be recognised as an integral part of an individual's personality. The present thinking on adult education is based on the assumptions : (a) that

illiteracy is a serious impediment to an individual's growth and to country's socio-economic progress; (b) that education is not co-terminus with schooling but takes place in most work and the life situations; (c) that learning, working and living are inseparable and each acquires a meaning only when correlated with others; (d) that the means by which people are involved in the process of development are at least as important as the ends; and (e) that the illiterate and the poor can rise to their own liberation through literacy, dialogue and action.

3. Adult Education should emphasise imparting of literacy skills to persons belonging to the economically and socially deprived sections of society. Many amongst them have grown up in a culturally rich environment where learning has been through the spoken word transmitted from generation to generation. The adult education programmes must respond to their cultural and intellectual level and build upon the innate artistic perceptions and skill in crafts. However, motivation for sustained participation in literacy and follow-up programmes is an issue which needs to be faced. In this context, stress should be laid on learning rather than teaching, on use of the spoken language in literacy programmes, on harnessing the mass-media and the cultural environment. Motivation also depends on an awareness among the participants that they can transform their destinies and that the adult education programmes will lead to advancement of their functional capability for the realisation of this objective. Moreover, a literacy programme unrelated to the working and living conditions of the learners, to the challenges of the environment and the developmental needs of the country cannot secure an active participation of the learners; nor can it be an instrument of development and progress. Adult Education, therefore, while emphasising acquisition of literacy skills should also be:

— *relevant* to the environment and learners' needs;
— *flexible* regarding duration, time, location, instructional arrangement etc.;
— *diversified* in regard to curriculum, teaching and learning materials and methods; and
— *systematic* in all aspects or organisation.

4. Highest priority in adult education needs to be given to the illiterate persons. In the post-independence period, the achievements in the field of literacy have been far from satisfactory. In 1947, the rate of literacy was 14 per cent, which rose to 34.45 per cent (excluding the age-group 0—4) in 1971. Yet, owing to population increase and half-heartedness of the past

effort, the number of illiterate persons has risen from 247 million in 1951 to 307 million in 1971. According to the Census of 1971 the total number of illiterate persons above 14 years of age is 209.5 million of which 97.1 million are in the age-group 15—35, which is likely to be about 100 million in present. A massive programme should be launched to cover this vast segment of population in 15—35 age-group as far as possible within five years of its launching. This implies organisation of special programmes for women and for persons belonging to Scheduled Castes and Scheduled Tribes. The regions which have a concentration of illiteracy will also require special attention.

5. While the conceptual position stated in paragraphs 2 and 3 needs emphasis, the need to view the programme as a mass movement must also be underlined. For the organisational point of view it is of utmost importance that elaborate preparations are made before launching this massive programme. Identification and motivation of the instructors, preparation of curriculum and teaching/learning materials and training have been the main areas of deficiency in adult education programmes in the past. A satisfactory level of preparedness in these areas must be reached before the programme is to be launched. Besides, adult education must cease to be a concern only of the educational authority. It should be an indispensable input in all sectors of development, particularly where participation of the beneficiaries is crucial to the fulfilment of development objectives. A pre-requisite of an adult education movement is that all agencies, governmental, voluntary, private and public sector industry, institutions of formal education etc. should lend strength to it. Voluntary agencies have a special role to play and necessary steps shall have to be taken to secure their full involvement. Instructional work shall have to be done by the teachers, students and unemployed men and women. It would be of great advantage if unemployed or under-employed youth having the potentiality to organise adult education programmes are provided necessary training and then entrusted with the responsibility for organising such programmes. To ensure effectiveness and systematic analysis of the problems, the programmes should have built-in mechanisms for monitoring and evaluation as well as for applied research.

6. All programmes of adult education and literacy must be followed up by effective arrangements for continuing education—which would include library services, group discussions and other forms of organised learning, reactivation of group cultural activities and

festivals, and community action.

7. Adequate financial and administrative support will be essential for organisation of the massive programme. Provision shall have to be made for a programme comprising literacy as well as environmental and social education, extending to approximately 300-350 hours or about 9 months, and also taking into account other costs. The required resources shall have to be provided by the Government, local bodies, voluntary agencies, trade and industry etc. A realistic assessment should be made of the size and capability of the administrative and professional apparatus which would be necessary for the programme and necessary steps taken to create it.

8. In addition to organising a massive programme for adult illiterates, it is necessary to provide special programmes for special groups based on their special needs. For example, programmes are needed for :

— the rural youth to train them in the scientific methods suited for small scale production, both in agriculture and industry, and in rural leadership;
— urban workers to improve their skills, to prepare them for securing their rightful claims and for participation in management;
— Government functionaries such as office clerks, field extension workers and police and armed forces personnel to upgrade their competence;
— employees of commercial establishments such as banks and insurance companies to improve their performance;
— housewives to inculcate a better understanding of family life problems and women's status in society.

Programmes for these and several other categories of persons could be organised through class-room participation, correspondence courses or mass media, or by a combination of all these.

9. It is of the greatest importance that implementation of adult education programmes is decentralised. It would also be necessary to establish agencies of coordination and catalisation. A National Board of Adult Education has been established for this purpose by the Central Government and similar Boards should be established at the State levels. Suitable agencies should also be created at the field level for coordination and for involvement of the various agencies in the programme.

(ii) National Adult Education Programme : An Outline

This paper aims at delineation of operational details for giving effect to the Policy Statement on Adult Education. This is not an attempt at laying down of rigid guidelines, but rather an exploration of alternatives. It may be recapitulated that the objective is to organise adult education programmes, with literacy as an indispensable component, for approximately 100 million illiterate persons mainly in the age-group 15—35 with a view to providing to them skills for self-directed learning leading to self-reliant and active role in their own development and in the development of their environment. The conceptual position and general strategy is spelt out in the Policy Statement on Adult Education, which should be read as a part of this document.

Phasing of the Programme

NAEP will be inaugurated on 2nd October, 1978. However, for all practical purposes the period until the end of March, 1979 will be treated as the period of intensive preparation. Preparatory action would include the following areas :

(1) Substantial stepping up of the programme from the existing level of approximately 0.5 million to at least 1.5 million in 1978-79.
(2) Creation of an environment favourable to the launching of NAEP.
(3) Preparation of case studies of some significant past experiences, particularly those where the failures or successes have a bearing on the planning and implementation of NAEP.
(4) Detailed planning of the various segments of the programme by appointment of expert groups—this would include preparation of detailed plans for each State and Union Territory.
(5) Establishment of necessary structures for Administration and Coordination and necessary modification of procedures and patterns.
(6) Identification of various agencies, official and non-official, to be involved in the programme and taking necessary measures to facilitate the needed level of their involvement.
(7) Undertaking of necessary exercises to clarify the required competencies, particularly in literacy and numeracy, which

would form part of all field programmes.

(8) Development of capability in all States by preparation of diversified and need-based teaching/learning materials as well as making available teaching/learning materials for starting the programme.

(9) Development of training methodologies, preparation of training manuals as well as actual training of personnel at various levels to launch the programmes.

(10) Creation of a satisfactory system of evaluation and monitoring as well as the required applied research base.

Preparatory action will, however, not conclude at the end of 1978-79. Action on almost all the items listed above would need to be taken for at least a year even after launching of NAEP. Indeed, in a series preparatory action for the following year, based on concurrent appraisal, shall have to continue right upto the conclusion of the Programme.

The annual phasing of coverage will have to be worked out on the basis of the level of achievement reached in a preceding year. The measure of preparation would include the probable achievement of target. The success of the Programme will depend on the manner in which the beginning is made in the first couple of years and every effort shall be made to extend the programme to approximately 100 million illiterate persons by the end of 1983-84. The present projections of targets are as follows :

Table 6.1: Projections of Targets

Year	Annual Coverage (in millions)	Cummulative Coverage (in millions)
1978-79 (year of preparation)	1.5	1.5
1979-80	4.5	6.0
1980-81	9.0	15.0
1981-82	18.0	33.0
1982-83	32.0	65.0
1983-84	35.0	100.0

It needs to be clarified that these are effective targets and even if a very efficient programme is organised, there could be about one-third wastage and the programme shall have to be organised keeping this in view.

What is aimed at that by 1983-84 a capability to organise adult education programmes for 35 million persons would be built up. At that stage it would be necessary to diversify the programmes—the aim then would be to strive for a learning society in which life-long education is a cherished goal.

Creation of Favourable Environment

The results of the Experimental World Literacy Programme as well as the experience of the countries where illiteracy eradication programmes have successfuly been implemented show that a systematic effort must be made for creation of an environment favourable for launching of such a massive programme. No country, however, perhaps with the exception of China, faced the problem of illiteracy of the magnitude we are facing. And hardly any country has had such a long tradition of respect for learning and knowledge or the vast resources which we have. What is necessary, it is indeed a pre-requisite for motivation of all persons to be involved in NAEP, is to engender a spirit of hope and confidence. The Prime Minister and the Education Minister have already declared that the highest priority needs to be given to adult education. Leaders of all political parties in Parliament have wholeheartedly endorsed the programme and have given assurance of support. This, it is hoped, would be followed up by leaders in various other walks of life such as trade unions, trade and industry, students and youth. A critical role can be played, in this context, by the mass-media—films, TV, radio, newspapers, publicity posters, etc. This would require an ingenious and co-ordinated efforts, in which official and non-official media shall have to converge to serve the objectives of the programme. In addition, a number of other methods could be explored, including holding of seminars and symposia, celebration of the World Literacy Day in schools and colleges, etc. The various ways in which an environment can be created shall have to be studied in detail and necessary measures taken as soon as possible.

The Approach

The two most basic problems faced by our country are poverty and illiteracy. One obliges a vast mass of our citizens to live under conditions of want and degradation, the other hinders opening of the doors of development and affects the ability of the poor to overcome their predicament. Indeed, the problem of poverty and illiteracy are two aspects of the same stupendous problem and the struggle to overcome one without at the same time waging a fight against the other is certain to result in aberrations and disappointments. For this reason, NAEP is visualised as a means to bring about a fundamental change in the process of socio-economic development; from a situation in which the poor remain passive spectators at the fringe of the development activity to being enabled to be at its centre, and as active participants. The learning process involves emphasis on literacy, but not that only; it also stresses the importance of functional upgradation and of raising the level of awareness regarding their predicament among the poor and the illiterate.

Our country has a distinctive value system with a tradition of learning—perpetuated through oral communication, fairs, festivals and informal skill training—which dates back to the earliest days of human civilization, enriched and harmonised over the centuries by the contact of diverse cultures and religions. The distinctive feature of our cultural pattern is that production, art and education are integral to each other. This must be recognised by the planners and organisers of all adult education programmes; and by the learners themselves and, at the same time, they must acquire a questioning faculty towards features which shelter narrowness and blind belief.

Traditionally, distinction is made between the selective and the mass approaches—distinction being based on the extent of coverage and quality of the programme. NAEP is a mass programme with the quality of planning and implementation of a selective programme. In fact, in relating the programme to the needs of the learners, NAEP is even more audacious than the conventional selective approach. At the same time it has to be recognised that a task of this size can be faced only if NAEP is viewed as a mass movement, to which all sections of people and all agencies must contribute.

One of the recurrent issues in adult education planning is motivation of the adult learners. Even when they can be stimulated to participate in adult education programmes initially, their interest is not sustained and they tend to drop-out. The problem is particularly grave in respect of women and persons belonging to the Scheduled Castes and Scheduled Tribes. It is true that if the programme has organisational flexibility and relevance of the content and methods with the felt needs and problems of the learners, it would fulfil the pre-conditions of sustained participation of the learners. Also, creation of an environment favourable to the organisation of mass programme can act as an effective motivation. However, these may not suffice and the matter needs to be examined in a much greater detail.

Exclusion of the vast majority of adult population from the organised system of education will not cease only by organisation of one-time adult education programme. The perspective of life-long learning, and provision of arrangements, therefore, shall have to be kept in view in planning and preparing for NAEP. From this point of view the NAEP will not conclude with the end of the quinquennium. Systematic follow up programmes shall have to be organised almost with the beginning of the NAEP—they would comprise a well organised system of mass production of books and their dissemination and inclusion in the communicational circuit of the neo-literates. It would be desirable to follow up adult education programmes with organised developmental action.

It is important that the adult education movement should be closely linked with the planning strategy, which emphasises elimination of destitution through intensive area planning and by giving employment orientation to development. For this purpose close co-operation should be created with the dominant development activity of the area, whether it goes under the rubric of Integrated Rural Development or Integrated Tribal Development or Employment Oriented Area Planning or DPAP, or whatever. The adult education programmes should strive to establish mutually supportive linkages with that developmental activity.

Each State will decide about the comparative priority to be given to various agencies. However, as a broad guideline, it may be mentioned that owing to the needs of careful local level planning, precedence ought to be given to voluntary agencies. In addition to voluntary agencies, a number of other agencies shall have to be identified for implementation, these could include Nehru Yuvak Kendras, educational institutions, employers of various categories etc. The role of Government would primarily be to co-ordinate the activities of these various agencies and to fill in the gaps. In several parts of the country the Government may have to take almost the entire responsibility. Wherever it becomes necessary to do so, a beginning would be made with a few selected districts and within a selected district with a few compact blocks. The objective would be to concentrate effort in well-defined geographical area and then to enlarge the activity.

In practice different agencies will organise programmes which would appear most relevant and feasible to them. In all cases, it needs to be underscored, the programmes would be expected to be drawn up within the framework of the Policy Statement. The range of the types of the programmes which may be organised are indicated below:

- Literacy with assured follow-up.
- Conventional functional literacy.
- Functional literacy supportive of a dominant development programme.
- Literacy with learning-cum-action groups.
- Literacy for conscientization and formation of organisations of the poor.

Resource Development

The conceptual position spelt out in the Policy Statement implies creation and development of a resource base for NAEP. The resource base should include creation of diversified and need-based learning materials, equipping the various categories of personnel for playing their role and infusion of a system of evaluation and research to impart dynamism to the programme. At the national level the Directorate of Adult Education as well as the various agencies of the Central Government and National level voluntary agencies would form the National Resource Group. The important level in resource development is the State Resource Centre (SRC) which, in co-operation with the National Resource Group and continuously interacting with the field, can become the focus for resource development. One of the important functions of the SRC is to strive for devolution of resource base at the district or project level. SRCs are not to be institutions working in isolation from other institutions, but rather as coordinating agency for involvement of various institutions and individuals having a contribution to make in resource development. The efficacy of SRCs will depend on the professional and technical capabilities developed by them, their capacity to secure and coordinate resource (of institutions and individuals) available in the region they purport to serve and on the support provided by the State Governments concerned. However, the primary responsibility for resource support to the programme shall have to be at the district/project level. Resource development being of critical importance the Central and State Governments as well as other agencies should be willing to provide all necessary financial and administrative support for this purpose.

Involvement of the people, *i.e.* the illiterate masses for whom this

Programme is primarily meant, with resource development will be crucial to the authenticity of the resource base. This is also inherent in the conceptual position as spelt out in the Policy Statement. A number of practical ways shall have to be tried for this involvement. This would include :

— Well-designed surveys to ascertain the learners' needs.
— Realistic testing and try-out of methods and materials by securing uninhibited reaction of the potential learners.
— Holding of frequent conferences and camps where workers in the State/District Resource Centre think and work with the rural people.
— Identification of a number of articulate village youth and orienting them in the Programme with a view to eliciting through them the latent as well as manifest problems of the potential learners groups.
— Systematic involvement of persons living and working among the rural people.

In addition to the potential learners it is necessary that the Resource Centre, whether at the State level or at district level, secures the contribution and criticism of their work by the supervisors and instructors. Appropriate arrangements shall have to be worked out to systematise this, without however letting it get into stereotypes. What is necessary is to always remember that NAEP should be dynamically linked with the existential needs of the learners and for this purpose it is necessary to organise a two-way traffic, from the experts and administrators to the learners and the other way round.

The various resource components may be identified as follows :

Teaching-learning Materials—The initial exercise in this connection shall have to be about identification of learners' needs. Detailed curriculum, indicating among other things the expected learning outcomes, shall have to be spelt out on the basis of the identified learning needs. On the basis of the curriculum and after necessary testing, teaching aids and learning materials shall have to be prepared with the greatest care. The Policy Statement makes reference to imparting of literacy skills in the spoken language. Without taking this to an absurd limit, it should be possible to organise learning in the spoken language, wherever necessary with bridges built for the learner to acquire facility in the regional language. Since it may not be possible to develop teaching-learning materials at the district/project level within the next one year, as an interim measure SRCs will prepare materials in standard regional or sub-regional languages/dialects. By the second or third year it should be possible to prepare materials at the district/project level.

Training—The categories for whom training shall have to be provided would include :

— Key functionaries at the national and state levels.
— Professionals and experts in specific areas such as curriculum construction, preparation of teaching/learning materials, training, evaluation etc.
— Functionaries at the district, project and block levels.
— Field level supervisors.
— Adult education centre instructors.

Training of key personnel at the national, state and district levels has to be the responsibility of the Central and State Governments. SRCs should be able to co-ordinate training programmes for project and block level functionaries as well as for supervisors and the responsibility for organisation of training programmes for the instructors of adult education centres shall have to rest with the agency responsible for implementation of the programme at the field level. Various alternatives shall have to be explored regarding duration, comparative emphasis on one-time and recurrent training, methods of training etc. Unless unavoidable, new training institutions should not be set up; the existing ones should be encouraged to develop capability for training of various categories of functionaries involved with NAEP. Universities and other institutions of higher education may have an important role to play in this behalf. Generally speaking, the agencies responsible for training should function as co-ordinators to secure the assistance of various institutions and individuals who can contribute in organisation of satisfactory training programmes.

Monitoring, Evaluation and Applied Research—A mass education programme, inevitably, faces the risk of considerable wastage and misreporting. In this connection the importance of systematic monitoring and evaluation cannot be exaggerated. It must permeate the entire programme and should provide feedback for introducing necessary correctives from time to time. It is also important to have inbuilt arrangments for applied and co-ordinated research so that the experience of NAEP is systematically analysed and provides guidelines for future action. The Central Government and State Governments are naturally interested in systematic monitoring. Universities and institutions of higher education as well as SRCs will have an important role to play in evaluation and applied research. Monitoring and evaluation mechanisms should get built at the district and project levels also, for it is mainly there that the feedback has to be used for introduction of correctives.

The 'Instructional' Agencies

The governing consideration in assigning responsibility for instructional arrangements should be the suitability of the persons concerned to organise programmes with a grasp of the conceptual standpoint and with a spirit of commitment. The various categories of persons who could be assigned instructional responsibility would include the following :

(a) *School Teachers:* In spite of several obvious limitations based on the experience of their performance, particularly authoritarianism and rigidities connected with the formal system, the teachers may have to be one of the main agencies for organisation of instructional arrangements in NAEP. Although, ultimately work in an adult education centre could be made an essential part of the duties of the teachers, for the present it would be desirable to keep this entirely voluntary. Even amongst persons who volunteer to take this responsibility, a selection may have to be made of persons who can be expected to be genuinely committed to this programme. It would also be fair to provide an honorarium of Rs. 50 per month for this work. Involvement of school teachers can be facilitated if the support of their professional organisations is secured.

(b) *Students:* Either as a part of the National Service Scheme, or in any other appropriate manner, students in institutions of higher education may provide a valuable agency for organisation of adult education centres. For this purpose it would be necessary to involve the teachers of these institutions also. It would be necessary to re-think regarding the present timing of academic sessions, the system of credits, certification etc. Student involvement in this programme should be voluntary, but the leaders in the university system shall have to create an atmosphere in which students find this work worthwhile and satisfying.

(c) *Village Youth:* There are a large number of unemployed or under-employed village youth with some education who could be entrusted this responsibility after they are given a carefully planned training for necessary upgradation of their academic level and an orientation for this responsibility. Besides, village youth who are not unemployed or under-employed but who have had some education could also be motivated to function as organisers of adult education centres. Work among women and tribal people can be greatly facilitated if persons drawn from their groups are re-introduced as peer leaders to organise the adult education centres. Such persons can continue to pursue their vocation and can be paid an appropriate monthly stipend. The unemployed or under-employed youth, who take up this programme on more or less full-time basis, could also take responsibility for organisation of non-formal education centres for pre-school children or for 6—14 age-group. Apart from providing a most suitable category of adult education instructors, this could also help generate a new class of rural leadership and may also contribute to the reduction of rural unemployment.

(d) *Ex-servicemen and other Retired Personnel:* This category of persons can play an important role in urban as well as rural areas. Retired personnel do need financial supplementation of their income; equally important, they need an occupation to keep themselves busy. Although there are certain obvious limitations regarding their capacity to organise programmes which would be in conformity with the conceptual position stated in the Policy Statement, they have the advantage of their experience and the respect in which they are generally held in the community.

(e) *Field Level Government and other Functionaries:* It might be possible to involve functionaries such as the village health worker, gram sevika, bal sevika, VLW, functionaries of Co-operative Societies and Village Panchayats etc.

(f) *Voluntary Social Workers:* Particularly among the urban areas, there are large number of persons who are willing to make their contribution to community development. The energies of such persons should be tapped and special arrangements made for their involvement.

The Implementation Agencies

The Government will naturally have to gear up to shoulder its responsibility in NAEP. On the basis of review, the existing programmes run by Government agencies shall have to be recast. It seems desirable that rather than spreading the programme thin in all parts of all the districts in the country, in the beginning effort should be concentrated in compact areas. The size and the programmes of the Ministry of Education shall be substantially enlarged with a view to widening the involvement of various agencies. However, a mass movement which would extend to such a large segment of population cannot be organised by one Ministry or department. Every effort must be made to involve other Ministries and departments with a view to sharing the responsibility for organisation of adult education programmes. The other Ministries/departments would be encouraged to organise such programmes, with a component of functional literacy, as well as to supplement the learning activity being undertaken through the educational authority. It would be necessary for those Ministries/departments to set apart within their sectoral budgets funds for such adult education programmes. Whether the programme forms part of a Central scheme, or is administered through any other agency, the State Government will have to play a most important role. For all practical purposes it can be said that the implementation responsibility will rest squarely with the State Governments. The State Governments will have to reappraise the adult education programmes they have been running in the past and steps will have to be taken to appropriately modify and strengthen them. While the primary responsibility of co-ordination and implementation will rest with the State Governments, the Central Government should be concerned not only with policy formulation and issue of general guidelines but should also oversee that the programmes are implemented by the State Governments in accordance with the Policy Statement.

The programme which gives importance to flexibility and diversity in organisation as well as its content can be best implemented through voluntary agencies. At present the involvement of voluntary agencies is somewhat limited and systematic attempts shall have to be made (a) to involve all voluntary agencies working at present in the field of adult education or having the potentiality to do so, and (b) to create circumstances for emergence of new agencies, particularly in areas where such agencies are few. It is also necessary to recognise the partnership role of voluntary agencies and it would be desirable to consult them in decision making at all levels, particularly in matters which might affect the work of those agencies, as well as the procedures for making grant shall have to be reviewed.

Whether or not NAEP becomes a mass movement will be determined by the extent to which youth and students can be motivated to commit themselves to this programme. It might be comparatively simple to review the functioning of the Nehru Yuvak Kendras and to concentrate their effort on adult education. Similarly, young men and women who have completed their formal education and who feel stirred to participate in this programme would be natural partners in this endeavour. The critical group is the students in universities and other institutions of higher education. For too long the universities have theoretically espoused about desirability of contact with the community. The NAEP provides a challenging situation for the universities and colleges to overcome their seclusion and to enter the mainstream of mass education. What is needed is that adult education should cease to be the concern of only one department, but should involve all members of faculty and of course, the students. Indications are already discernible that the university system is preparing itself for this massive involvement and to make necessary reorganisations in its priorities.

The employers, whether in private sector or public, must play an important role in the spread of adult education among their employees. It might be appropriate, in due course, to make organisation of adult education programmes obligatory for all employers. Meanwhile, through organisations of trade and industry and other employing agencies an effective beginning could be made. The Government should provide leadership by setting apart funds for this purpose in the public sector undertakings as well as in construction works. The resultant reduction in the hours of work and marginally higher expenditure would be adequately rewarded by improvement in the quality of performance of the workers and by their positive participation in the developmental activity. Education of the workers in the organised sector can be greatly facilitated if the trade unions are actively involved in this Programme.

The local bodies, such as municipalities and *panchayati raj* institutions, have been playing an important role in the field of formal education as well as social education. These agencies, which have civic and developmental functions, have the advantage of being in touch with the people—their everyday problems as well as their needs—and, therefore, they should be expected to participate in implementation of NAEP.

Planning, Administration and Supervision

This is the first time that the Government have decided to launch a well-planned programme of adult education for such a large segment of the illiterate population. Planning for such a programme and its implementation will require support by a large variety of persons including social workers, perspective planners, management experts, systems analysts, interdisciplinary teams of academics and, of course, adult educators. Exercise in planning have to take place not only in the Central and State Governments but also in local bodies, voluntary agencies, universities, professional organisations of teachers etc. The Government, however, have to play a leading role in involvement of the various individuals, institutions and organisations. It is also necessary to set up appropriate agencies for coordination and catalisation at the State and district levels. For this purpose State and District Boards of Adult Education should be set up as soon as possible.

The existing administrative structures at the Central, State and field levels are altogether insufficient for NAEP. A careful examination has already been initiated to suggest the type of administrative structures which would be most appropriate for the task. Only broad indications can be given for the present :

> *Central Government:* The set-up in the Ministry would be appropriately strengthened keeping in view the responsibility to be assigned to the Adult Education Division. The Directorate of Adult Education will have to substantially enlarge its activities and necessary wherewithal shall have to be provided for it to be able to play the expected role.
>
> *State level:* Immediate steps are necessary to set up State level administrative and planning machinery with an independent Director, or an Additional Director with the Director of

Education at the helm. Necessary supporting staff shall also have to be provided to the State level organisation. Each State Government would be advised to examine the need for a separate division to deal with adult education in the Education Department of the State Secretariat.

District and Block Level: The districts selected for the programmes may have to have Adult District Education Officer with necessary supporting staff. Emphasis shall have to be laid on adequacy of staff for each project, for administration and supervision, as well as for providing the necessary technical support.

Voluntary Agencies: Necessary support shall have to be provided to national and State level voluntary agencies, State Resource Centres etc. to set up necessary machinery to enable them to make their contribution to NAEP.

A programme of this magnitude must provide adequate arrangements for supervision and guidance. The supervisor should not be an Inspector in the traditional meaning of the word but a specially selected professional with an aptitude to facilitate the work of the incharge of the Adult Education Centre.

One of the major deficiencies being faced by Government as well as voluntary agencies is the absence of professional cadres of adult educators. Existing facilities in universities for preparation of such personnel are extremely limited and there is a case for their expansion. Training programmes of varying varieties for professional development shall also have to be organised by Government, universities and voluntary agencies. In addition to training, it would also be necessary to examine the pay structure of the professional workers involved in adult education programme. As far as possible, it would be desirable to ensure that persons coopted into adult education system continue to grow and progress within the system rather than being pushed out of it.

Financing the NAEP

The past experience has shown that owing to pressures of various types it becomes necessary for the State Governments to divert funds provided for adult education either to other programmes of education or to other sectors of development. It is, therefore, necessary to devise an arrangement under which funds earmarked for adult education cannot be so diverted. At the same time, it has to be fully appreciated that the responsibility for planning and implementation of the programme in a State must rest with the State Government, with the Central Government being assigned the responsibility for wider involvement of voluntary agencies, try-out of innovative programmes etc.

In addition to the mechanics of funding, it is necessary to emphasise adequacy. A Group of Experts drawn from the Planning Commission and the Ministry has come to the conclusion that the per learner cost would be Rs. 60, excluding the expenditure on Central and State level administrative structures, evaluation and monitoring and research and innovation. The Group has calculated this cost with reference to the number of persons enrolled and not those who will successfully complete the programme. The number of those who will do so may be about two-thirds the number of persons enrolled. However, the cost of some of the programmes may be somewhat less because of shorter duration of some of the urban programmes and voluntary contributions. It would be safe to assume that the per learner cost would not be less than Rs. 80. The expenditure on Central and State administrations, evaluation and research etc. would be approximately 10 per cent of the total arrived at on the basis of aggregate of per learner cost. Adequate funds on the basis of these calculations will have to be provided.

In addition to the expenditure involved in organisation of adult education programmes, provision shall have to be made, from the very beginning, for follow-up and continuing education of neo-literates and persons who have acquired literacy in the formal system of education. It would be reasonable to provide an amount of approximately 20 per cent of the total expenditure for this purpose.

International Cooperation

The frontiers of poverty and illiteracy extend far beyond national boundaries. The experiences and insights gained by one country ought to be shared with other countries by mutual exchange and continuing communication. Naturally, we cannot but be conscious of our own financial and human resources, which are not too limited when something so vital for the nation's destiny is at stake. In formulating NAEP and in its implementation cooperation should be pledged to UNESCO and other instrumentalities of international cooperation based on mutual respect and equality. However, audacious the objectives of NAEP be, we must begin humbly with a spirit to learn from those who have been harbingers in this field and from those who have developed special capabilities.

(B) DEVELOPMENT OF ADULT EDUCATION IN 1996-1997

Literacy is a major component of Human Resource Development and is basic to any programme of social and economic progress. Development can never become self-sustaining unless it is accompanied by corresponding changes in the attitude, value, knowledge, and skills of people as a whole. The only way this change can be accomplished is through education and literacy is the first step towards education. The National Literacy Mission was set up in 1988 with the goal of making 80 million people literate by 1995. The Total Literacy Campaigns is the dominant strategy for achieving the literacy goals of the nation. The Indian experience in literacy has aroused the interest of the international community and has become the role model for many Asian and South Asian countries. At the national level the aim is to consolidate the gains of literacy and to concentrate efforts in the four major Hindi-speaking States in the Hindi heartland where the bulk of the illiterate population resides.

The Mission which was set up with the objective of imparting literacy to 80 million non-literates in the age group of 15-35 by the year 1995 has now been set with the goal of covering 100 million non-literates by the year 1999. Children in the age group 9-14 are also included where there are no NFE Centres. The Total Literacy Campaigns have been extended to 417 districts in the country of which 178 have entered post-literacy phase. An estimated 90 million learners have been enrolled in the programme and 56 million are reported to have been made literate. A number of programmes were taken up under the NLM this year which include : (i) A national workshop to review the UNFPA funded Population Education Project and to decide on future perspectives, issues and strategies for the implementation of the project in the 3rd phase from 1997-2001 was organised on May 27-28, 1996 at Kodaikanal, Tamil Nadu; (ii) A regional workshop on the Scheme of Continuing Education for neo-literate was held from June 26-28, 1996 at Hyderabad; (iii) As part of the International Literacy Day celebrations, a Saksharta utsav was held in New Delhi on September 7, 1996; (iv) On the occasion of the 30th International Literacy Day on September 8, 1996 in New Delhi, two

---

Source : Annual Report 1996-97: Part I, Department of Education, Government of India, New Delhi, 1997.

books, *viz. Women and Literacy* and *Our Hopes and Our Dreams—In Our Words* were presented to the President of India; (v) A Conference of Chairpersons/Directors of State Resource Centres was held in New Delhi on September 24-25, 1996; (vi) A SAARC Conference of Voluntary Agencies working in the field of Literacy and Continuing Education was held from October 14-16, 1996 in New Delhi in which representatives from the countries of Nepal, Bangladesh, Pakistan and Sri Lanka participated; (vii) The second National Conference of State/UT Directors of Adult/Mass Education was held in New Delhi on October 17-18, 1996; (viii) A SAARC Conference of Voluntary Agencies working in the field of Literacy and Continuing Education was held from October 14-16, 1996 in New Delhi in which representatives from the countries of Nepal, Bangaladesh, Pakistan, Sri Lanka and India participated; (ix) In collaboration with State Resource Centre, Bhubaneshwar, ACCU-UNESCO held its 14th Regional Workshop on the preparation of literacy follow up materials for adults in rural areas in Asia and the Pacific in Bhubaneshwar, Orissa from November 12-23, 1996; (x) An orientation workshop for literacy consultants on Operation Restoration on TLC/PLC projects was held in New Delhi on November 29-30, 1996; (xi) In collaboration with the Government of Maharashtra and SAHAS (Saksharta Hak Samiti), Greater Bombay, National Literacy Mission organised a National Conference on Urban Literacy Campaign in Indian context on December 27-28, 1996 in Mumbai, Maharashtra.

Special Projects for Education of Illiteracy—TLC/PLC

National Literacy Mission Authority set a target of making 100 million citizens functionally literate in the age group of 9-35 by the end of 1999.

The Total Literacy Campaign (TLC) is the principal strategy of the NLM for eradication of illiteracy in the country. The literacy campaigns under the Scheme are area-specific, time-bound, delivered through voluntarism, cost-effective and outcome-oriented, and are implemented by Zilla Saksharta Samitis usually headed by District Collectors.

The campaigns are initiated with appropriate environment-building activity coupled with a door-to-door literacy survey during which potential learners and volunteers are identified. Suitable primers are developed and primer-specific training is provided to the required personnel. The environmental-building activity as well as monitoring and internal evaluation are continued through the teaching/learning activity which accounts for a total of 200 hours spread over a period of 6 months.

An external evaluation is made at the conclusion of the teaching.

After completion of the TLC, Post Literacy Campaign (PLC) is launched to mop up the left-over illiterates to consolidate the gains of literacy acquired during TLC, and to enable the neo-literates to develop abilities for self-learning.

The literacy campaigns are implemented through direct funding to the ZSS by the Central and State Governments in the ratio of 2:1. However, for districts under the Tribal Sub-Plan their ratio is 4:1.

Implementation of TLCs in various parts of the country has evoked an enthusiastic response from the weaker sections of the society, especially the Scheduled Castes and Scheduled Tribes. Experience has also shown that more than 60 per cent of the learners attending classes are women. The number of TLC/PLC projects have covered 417 and 178 districts either fully or partially in the States of Andhra Pradesh, Assam, Bihar, Delhi, Goa, Gujarat, Haryana, Himachal Pradesh, Jammu and Kashmir, Karnataka, Maharashtra, Madhya Pradesh, Manipur, Meghalaya, Orissa, Rajasthan, Tamil Nadu, Tripura, Uttar Pradesh, West Bengal and the U.T.s of Chandigarh, Daman and Diu, Dadra and Nagar Haveli and Pondicherry.

The focus of the TLC has now shifted to the Hindi speaking areas where bulk of the illiterate population resides. So far 172 districts under TLC and 32 districts under PLC have been sanctioned in the four major Hindi-speaking States of Bihar, Madhya Pradesh, Rajasthan and Uttar Pradesh. Besides, the special measures taken under NLM in these four states are : (i) Sensitization workshops for collectors and other officials and non-officials involved in literacy campaigns and similar workshops for writers and media personnel for sensitization on literacy issues are organised regularly; (ii) The State Governments have been reviewing the progress of literacy campaign, with a view to improving the implementation of projects; and (iii) The State Resource Centres of all the four States have been strengthened and their financial assistance augmented.

Rural Functional Literacy Project

The centre based Rural Functional Literacy Programme has been phased out with effect from April, 1991 except in States/UTs of Jammu and Kashmir, North Eastern States, Sikkim, border districts of Rajasthan under the Border Area Project and Dadra and Nagar Haveli. These areas have relatively low literacy rates as well as extremely difficult terrain, hindering communication and mobility. During 1995-96, no viable proposals were received. Most of the projects sactioned during 1994-95 have been carried over to 1995-96 for implementation.

Shramik Vidyapeeths (SVPs)

The *Shramik Vidyapeeths* represent an institutional framework for offering non-formal, adult and continuing educational and polyvalent training programme to industrial workers. *Shramik Vidyapeeths* are working under auspices of State Governments/Universities/Voluntary Agencies. During 1996-97, 53 *Shramik Vidyapeeths* are in operation, 44 in voluntary sector and remaining 9 are under State Governments/ Central Government.

Scheme of Continuing Education for Neo-literates

The National Literacy Mission (NLM) lays specific emphasis on Continuing Education for Neo-literates which is the modified form of the Scheme of Post-Literacy and Continuing Education, launched in March, 1988. The basic objectives of the scheme of Continuing Education are : (i) Provision of facilities for retention of literacy skills and continuing education to enable the learners to continue their learning beyond literacy stage; (ii) Creating scope for application of functional literacy for improvement of living conditions and quality of life; (iii) Dissemination of information on development programmes and widening and improving participation of traditionally deprived sections of the society; (iv) Creation of awareness about national concerns such as national integration, conservation and improvement of the environment, women's equality, observance of small family norms and sharing of common problems of the community; (v) Improvement of economic conditions and general well-bring through short duration training courses for providing vocational skills and linkages between continuing education and developmental activities; (vi) Provision of facilities for library and reading rooms for creating an environment conducive for literacy efforts.

Voluntary Agencies

The Scheme of financial assistance to Voluntary Agencies working in the field of Adult Education continued to encourage and provide financial assistance to the non-governmental organisations who are considered to be the partners in achieving the goals of the National Literacy Mission.

The main objective of the scheme is to provide financial assistance to voluntary agencies for their involvement in the following activities: (i) Implementation of time-bound, area specific, result oriented and voluntary based literacy projects; (ii) To take responsibility in well defined non-ZSS areas for eradication of illiteracy and running of post-literacy and continuing education programmes; and (iii) To take up innovative and experimental projects, environment building activities including organisation of seminars and conferences, etc.

The scheme is continuing with its endeavour to encourage greater participation of voluntary agencies in the adult education programmes.

Directorate of Adult Education

The Directorate of Adult Education (DAE), a subordinate office of the Department of Education, continued to function as the National Resource Centre in the field of Adult Education and Literacy campaigns. The Directorate has different units with identified professional and administrative functions. The main activities of the Directorate included preparation of materials and surveillance under which the Directorate organised: (i) 12 monthly meetings of the Improved Pace and Content of Learning (IPCL) Advisory Committee for review of the teaching learning materials developed by the SRCs/RRCs, TLC Districts and other related agencies concerned. Guidelines were laid down for preparation of material for Basic literacy, Post literacy and Continuing Education Programmes; (ii) Training and orientation workshops for writers and artists were organised at Bhubaneshwar, Itanagar, Dimapur, Leh and Imphal for orientation of writers in techniques of designing IPCL materials plus preparation of sample material in Assamese, English, Dogri, Urdu, Kashmiri, Bodhi and other tribal languages; (iii) Three regional workshops were organised at Mysore, Gangtok and Ahmedabad for assessment of Population Education Components integrated in the Basic Literacy, Post-Literacy and Continuing Education materials and preparation of supplementary materials on the messages not adequately covered in the serials so far, and (iv) One national workshop was organised at Udaipur in collaboration with the SRC, Jaipur as follow-up programme of the Nepal Workshop of Asian Cultural Centre for UNESCO (ACCU) Japan on Developing Basic Literacy Materials for Women and Girls in Asia and Pacific.

State Resource Centres (SRC)

SRCs had been providing academic and technical resource support to literacy campaigns in the country. With the increase in number of Literacy Campaigns upto 414 districts in the country, responsibilities of SRCs by way of development of materials, training of field functionaries, monitoring and evaluation of campaigns etc., have increased manifold.

Resource Centres extended resource support to voluntary agencies and other educational institutions. In this regard, several of the SRCs intensified collaborative action with Zilla Saksharta Samitis.

The National Literacy Mission (NLM) took several measures to strengthen the SRCs, upgrade their capability and involve them more vigorously and intimately in the literacy efforts. In view of this, a National Conference of Directors of State Resource Centres was organised by the National Literacy Mission/Central Directorate of Adult Education on September 23-25, 1996. Some Chairpersons and the State Directors of Adult/Mass Education also attended the conference.

The activities of SRCs were monitored regularly and the Annual Report on State Resource Centres for the year 1995-96 was brought out.

Shramik Vidyapeeths (SVPs)

The scheme of SVP is one of the prominent programmes of non-formal adult and continuing education for the urban community. 53 SVPs were set up by the year 1995-96 and likely to be expanded during Ninth Plan.

The basic idea behind the multi-dimensional or polyvalent approach to the education of urban working community in SVP is to meet the various inter-related needs of target groups with specifically tailored programmes. This provides knowledge and imparts skills simultaneously and in an integrated manner.

The prime concern of the SVP is to conduct courses of varying duration involving vocational/technical skills for skill development/ upgradation to participate in income generating activities. It is to improve socio-economic status of the poorest of the poor beneficiaries. The programmes of SVPs have been very widely recognised as very potential means of promoting continuing education and develop attitude for lifelong learning. The Directorate of Adult Education is extending Technical Resource Support Services for smooth functioning of the SVPs in the countries.

During the year 1995-96 the SVPs conducted 10119 programmes and benefited 376802 persons. The participation of women in programmes was to the extent of 63.21 per cent and that of males was 36.79 per cent only. 87.84 per cent persons were of the age group of 15-35 years. 83.55 per cent were of income group below Rs. 155 per month.

(C) DEVELOPMENT OF ADULT, CONTINUING AND NON-FORMAL EDUCATION BETWEEN 1990-2000

(i) Non-Formal Education

Non-formal education will have a very special place in the movement towards Education for All by the year 2000. Such a place has to be assigned to it because NFE can have the flexibilities required to provide educational facility to children who are out of school. These children, as we have noted in the Chapter on Access and Equity, are school dropouts, children in habitations without schools, working children and girls engaged in family chores. We have observed in the Chapter on Goals and Targets that the targets have been projected in terms of school education, with a clear understanding of the non-formal alternative also being available where schools are not within the reach of children, or are not otherwise accessible. While giving clear preferences to systematic schooling, the strategy of EFA recognises that the socio-economic situation in the country will make it impossible to enable all children to receive the banefit of schooling. Therefore, in the strategy of EFA, the Non-formal Education will have a central role and will be indispensable for providing education to children who would otherwise remain deprived of it. It is estimated that nearly one-third of the children in the 6-11 age group will be served by non-formal education programmes up to 1995.

It may be appropriate to begin by specifying what we mean by non-formal education. There are, of course, no universally accepted definitions. In the Indian context we can describe what we intend while referring to NFE, adding that this is not an attempt at definition, and that there are many ways of viewing NFE. Some of the characteristics we have accepted are as follows :

In terms of cognitive learning NFE is comparable with the

Source : Education for All by 2000: Indian Perspective, National Institute of Educational Planning and Administration, New Delhi, 1990.

corresponding stage in formal education. Attention is to be paid in NFE to non-cognitive aspects of learning, just as much as we propose in the school system.
It has flexibility to adjust curriculum and textual materials to the needs and interests of the learners.
Its total duration is generally shorter than in formal education.
The programme can be organised at the time convenient for the learners, generally in the afternoons for girls and in the evenings for working children.
It is not dependent on highly paid professional teachers but is organised by local persons who are specially trained for it.
There is the possibility of migration between the formal and non-formal systems.

Although the above characteristics hold good for most of the programmes we can expect to plan for, programmes of non-formal education can range from pursuit of a formal course to the acquisition of mere functional literacy. The programmes in the context of EFA would attempt to introduce elements of non-formal education in the formal system and incorporate the benefits of the formal system in NFE. This would be attempted by non-formalisation of formal education. We describe below, by way of illustration, some of the programmes/activities of NFE which would be taken up.

(a) The formal primary education system would be made more relevant and child-centred by the introduction of non-formal characteristics such as :

(i) adjustment of the school calendar and vacations according to the convenience of pupils;
(ii) giving environmental orientation and learners' need orientation to the content and process; and
(iii) making it possible for local women with lower qualifications to serve as teacher, etc.

(b) *Introduction of the Shiksha Karmi Pattern* : This pattern involves entrusted a primary school to 2-3 specially selected local persons who are imparted short duration pre-service training, for improvement of their scholastic competence and to enable them to serve as teachers. These *Shiksha Karmis* could replace teachers in remote rural schools where teachers are generally reluctant to be posted, or they may take responsibility for the organisation of primary education in habitations without schools. Generally, *Shiksha Karmis* would also organise non-formal education, and adult education programmes in the evenings. This is an amalgam of formal and non-formal education.

(c) *Night Schools for Primary Education* : Particularly in urban areas, there is a demand for night schools, which generally are of about two hours' duration, usually run in regular schools, following the regular syllabus and textbooks. As more and more jobs require education up to the middle level, children of migrant workers and slum dwellers who do some work in the day attempt to acquire the necessary educational qualification for regular employment. For all practical purposes, these are primary schools, but run for a shorter duration in the evenings.

(d) *Condensed Primary Education through NFE Centres* : These programmes, popularly known as the Madhya Pradesh Model, provide competence in language and maths of the same level as primary education. The programme is run for 1.5 to 2 hours in the evening for about two years. The responsibility for running the NFE centre rests on a locally selected instructor who is imparted short-duration training. This is the most widespread NFE programme in the country.

(e) *Pre-primary-cum-lower-primary Centres* : At several places in the country, voluntary agencies are running *balwadis* for children 3-4 to 8-9 years. These children get acclimatised for primary education and receive instruction up to Class II or III and then move on to a regular primary school. The instruction corresponds to the ungraded unit in a primary school, but it generally unstructured and completely non-formal.

This is an illustrative description of the range of NFE programmes possible in our country. In fact, the types of programme can be more numerous and several voluntary agencies have, indeed, taken up is innovative programmes which differ from place to place.

Deficiencies

The programme of NFE is at present confined mainly to the ten educationally backward states in which 240,000 NFE centres are run. In addition to government programmes, about 250 voluntary agencies run NFE programmes, almost all of them on the pattern of government projects. The existing programmes of NFE suffer from many deficiencies, the most glaring among which are the following :

(a) There is generally a lack of conviction. The state governments are not willing to commit resources for NFE, the administrative system gives it a step-motherly treatment, and there is generally a lack of faith among functionaries and the families of the children who are supposed to benefit from it.
(b) Although there is scope for adjusting the syllabus to the special needs of the learners, in fact hardly any attempt has been made in this direction.
(c) The quality of instructors and their training leave much to be desired. For all practical purposes, routinely selected persons serve as instructors and the training is so inadequate that the instructor follows the methods by which he/she was taught rather than a genuinely non-formal method.
(d) The management system is totally deficient for the needs. The attempt to group the NFE centres in compact projects has had limited success and there are unconscionable delays in remittance of funds to instructors for their honorarium and lighting arrangements. Sometimes learning materials reach weeks after the start of the centre.
(e) Funds provided for NFE are far short of the needs. The instructor is underpaid and enough learning materials are not available. Lighting arrangements and instructional equipment are below the acceptable level.

The New Strategy

Keeping in view the importance of the NFE, the entire programme will be reorganised from 1990-91. The main elements of the new strategy will be as follows :

(a) *Area Coverage* : All agencies taking up NFE programme would be assigned project responsibility for a specific area and they would be expected to ensure that, in co-operation with the formal school system, all children regularly attend and complete primary education, either through formal education or through non-formal centres.

(b) Comprehensive micro-planning exercises will be undertaken to determine the need for non-formal education centres. Special attention will be paid to areas where children work under exploitative conditions. NFE centres will also be opened in habitations without schools.

(c) The comparability between FE and NFE will be reiterated. This does not mean that the two educational programmes will be identical, but the competence, particularly in language and mathematics, at the end of the primary education level will be more or less the same and would correspond to the minimum levels of learning laid down for the region concerned.

(d) Adequate technical resource support would be provided. From the institutional point of view this would be done by revamping SCERTs and by setting up resource centres with voluntary agencies at the state, regional and district levels. Animational training will be organised for instructors.

(e) Just as the teacher is treated as the principal actor in the formal education system, so would the NFE instructor be. Her/his honorarium will be raised, the quality of training improved, and opportunities provided for continuing education. Wherever possible good instructors would be promoted as *Preraks*.

(f) The involvement of voluntary agencies will be enlarged and they would be encouraged to take up flexible programmes oriented to the needs and interests of the learners.

(g) The system of management will be improved. There will be a separate directorate for NFE at the state level and a district NFE officer will be appointed. These persons will be specially selected, exclusively on merit. All programmes will be run in the form of projects, which will have sufficient delegation of powers and cheque-drawing authority to ensure disbursement of honorarium and the necessary funds to instructors.

(h) A clear preference will be given to women in the management and running the NFE programmes. Women appointed in these programmes will be given special training of the kind referred to in the chapter on Women.

(i) So far, the NFE system has not begun to work at the upper primary level. Attention will be paid to it now and an opportunity will be provided to children either to enter the formal system, if they so desire, or to continue their education through the open school.

(j) A proper system of monitoring and evaluation will be established to ensure that necessary qualitative and quantitative data become available in time for improvement of the programme.

(ii) Adult Education

According to the 1981 census the literacy rate in India was 36%. Although no exact estimates regarding the likely literacy rate for the year 1990 are available, on the basis of trend-analysis and taking into account: (i) the efforts made in the sphere of adult literacy since 1981; and (ii) improvement in enrolment and retention in primary education; it is estimated that the literacy rate in 1990 would be about 44%. The census data regarding literacy, however, suffer from two major drawbacks: (a) For purposes of census operations, literacy has been defined as ability to read and write simple sentences with comprehension, which is below the level of functional literacy defined in the National Literacy Mission document; and moreover, there is not sufficient verification in the course of census operations. (b) The figures relate to the entire population, *i.e.*, from the birth of a baby onwards. We may take up the first, and expatiate on the point regarding the standards of literacy. An effort is being made in primary education to lay down minimum levels of learning and to insist that practically all children attain these levels in primary schools, or in non-formal education programmes. Likewise, levels of 3 Rs to be achieved in NLM have been spelt out quite clearly and efforts are being made to ensure that all persons who are declared literate achieve mastery level learning with reference to these norms. Therefore, while it may not be practicable to change the definition of literacy in census operations, it would be reasonable to assume that persons who would enter the category of literate persons in future would have significantly higher levels of literacy and numeracy. The Registrar General of Census has also been requested to give instructions to the State Superintendents of Census Operations and, through them, to field-level enumerators to ensure that due rigour is observed in the collection of data.

Strategy for the Reduction of Illiteracy

Between the years 1990 and 2000 we must move from being a

predominantly illiterate country to a literate and better educated nation. Part of this endeavour would be a simple reform in census tabulations, but much of it would require a well-planned stress on the spread of education at all levels. In concrete terms the multi-faceted effort at achievement of a higher level of literacy and education will comprise the following measures:

(a) There is, at present, a wide variation in the manner of calculation of the literacy rate. While some countries follow the pattern of India, namely, deriving the literacy percentage with reference to the entire population, a number of countries exclude the 0-6 age group, and several others exclude the age group up to 15 years. We propose to calculate the rate of literacy after the 0-6 age group. It is estimated that this alone will make a difference of about 88% in the literacy rate.

(b) The first priority in literacy planning has to be on the provision of education for the 6-14 age group. Much of this document describes how universalisation of education will be achieved in the 6-14 age group by the year 2000. The goals and targets for 1990-95 are also quite ambitious and should ensure that new illiterate entrants in the adult age group dwindle at a fast pace.

(c) The concentration in NLM will continue to be on the 15-35 age group. The importance of this age group is well recognised in educational planning. It arises from the fact that the decline in fertility rate and the bringing about of socio-economic change is dependent on the role of people in this age group.

(d) There is enough justification to encourage the spread of literacy in the 35+ age group also. Restrictions on the upper limit of age are seldom appreciated by the villagers, and older people in our country definitely influence the lives of the younger ones.

(e) Although it has been said several times elsewhere, the absolute priority to be accorded to female literacy cannot be stressed enough. That, indeed, is what would make out difference—to women's status, to child development, to the fertility rate, and to education and culture.

(f) The monitoring of who are illiterates, and who have become literate will have to be improved. Proper surveys, as a part of micro-level planning, will be undertaken of all illiterate persons, particularly in the 15-35 age group. For tabulation of figures regarding literacy, only those persons who have completed a literacy course and have achieved the prescribed levels of literacy would be counted as literate.

The concentration, as we have stated above, will be on the 15-35 age group. The population of illiterate persons in this age group is estimated to be about 100 million. The target up to 1995 is to make at least 80% persons literate among men and women, as well as each section of the society. Illustratively, we may say that if a CD block is taken up under a project, the achievement of targets would imply not only that 80% men but also 80% women of the block will become literate within the timeframe, and likewise, 80% men and women among the Scheduled Castes as well as the Scheduled Tribes would become literate. This would call for a thorough disaggregated and target group-oriented micro-level planning.

For achievement of a target of 80 million persons during 1990-95, it would be necessary to set a target of about 20 million per year. Perhaps, the achievement in 1990-91 would be 15 million or even less, but as the new programme picks up, it would be 20 million, and, perhaps, somewhat more during the close of the quinquennium. For the achievement of a target of this size, we would need to adopt three distinct approaches :

(1) Centre-based approach
(2) Volunteer-based approach
(3) Campaign approach

Centre-based Approach

If the centre-based approach could be reorganised, it would have the capacity to make a very substantial contribution to the eradication of illiteracy in the 15-35 age group. The present capacity under the Rural Functional Literacy Programmes and the State Adult Education Programmes is of about 3,00,000 operational AECs. The voluntary agencies are at present running about 30,000 AECs, and another 15,000 AECs are being run by the Nehru Yuvak Kendras. Between these, *viz.*, voluntary agencies and NYKs, it should be possible to increase the number of AECs to 1,00,000 in 1990-91. The third part of the strategy to increase the number of AECs would comprise reintroduction of the functional literacy programme for women as a part of the ICDS programme. There are at present over 2,00,000 ICDS centres, and it should be possible to start functional literacy programmes with the help of the *anganwadi* workers in 100,000 ICDS centres. This would take the total number of AECs to 500,000. With the introduction of IPCL, to which a reference has been made later in this chapter, nearly half of the AECs can be expected to run two courses in a year. The number of persons effectively covered at each AEC may, therefore, be calculated at the rate of 30 and at it is estimated that 15 million persons could be made literate each year through 500,000 AECs.

The existing centre-based programme, however, suffers from many deficiencies, as revealed by the various external evaluations undertaken by institutions of Social Science Research. Some of these deficiencies are as follows:

(a) The absence of an area specific and time specific approach resulting in the continuance of a project for a long period of time without achieving the desired objectives.
(b) The improper selection of staff, lack of commitment among them and the absence of proper accountability.
(c) The poor quality of training and a lack of capacity among instructors to impart literacy instruction.
(d) Faulty management, characterised by delay in the supply of teaching-learning materials, in the payment of honorarium and in the provision of lighting arrangements.
(e) An undependable management information system leading to a lack of credibility of the programme as a whole.

Although these deficiencies are of a serious nature, the suitability of the centre-based approach in our system remains undiminished. After an objective analysis of the deficiencies it would be possible for us to move on to a thorough recognition of the centre-based approach.

Reorganisation of the Centre-based Pattern

It is proposed to strengthen, consolidate, and make full use of the infrastructure created for the centre-based approach by adopting the following strategy of reorganisation :

(a) *Area Approach* : An essential requirement in the modified strategy has to be a insistence on the eradication of illiteracy through area specific and time specific action plans drawn up and implemented with rigour. Such a plan presupposes that a detailed survey of every household and person to be covered will be undertaken, the location of AECs decided with proper care, an insistence on the entire teaching-learning process to be on the achievement of pre-determined levels of learning, due attention to functionality and awareness, and a system of evaluation which will build confidence and motivate the learner. A project will continue without waiting for any further approval till the end of the planned time schedule.

(b) *Priority to Women's Literacy* : This has several implications for planning and management of the revised programme and would include :

(i) pre-literacy motivational programmes for illiterate women;
(ii) selection and training of women instructors, with facilities for continuing education for those who do not have the prescribed qualification;
(iii) location of AECs at places convenient to women and flexibility in timing to suit their convenience;
(iv) conduct of the programme in a manner which involves health, hygiene, vocational training etc.

(c) *Reorganisation of Management* : It needs to be reiterated that the project approach in the implementation of RFLP/SAEP needs to be retained and strengthened. Project-based management envisages taking up of the total eradication programme in a compact and continuous area with a strong project management which enjoys sufficient delegation of powers. Some of the essential aspects of reorganisation of the project management system are mentioned below :

(i) There will be a clear delineation of responsibility, and a system of reward for good work. For example, a *Prerak* or instructor who is able to eradicate illiteracy within the prescribed timeframe would be retained in the continuing education system and given higher honorarium.
(ii) The suitability of the existing personnel will be evaluated to decide whether they may be retained or dispensed with. All future selection of staff at all levels will be only on the basis of merit. While *Preraks* and instructors are part-time

workers, other project staff would be selected from a wide range of catchment. As far as possible, women will be appointed in all future vacancies.

(iii) There will be decentralisation and delegation of powers. The Project Coordinator will operate a bank account and will have the power to draw funds, particularly to pay remuneration to *Preraks* and instructors, to secure teaching/learning materials, to provide lighting arrangements, etc.

(iv) Wherever feasible, RFLP projects, which at present have 300 AECs, will be divided into smaller units. Smaller projects, as small as 30 AECs, may also be taken up.

(v) A proper record will be maintained of all illiterate and literate persons. Micro-level planning techniques, referred to in the chapter on Management, will be used for the involvement of the community surveying and securing participation of all persons regularly. A computerised management system will be introduced for monitoring progress.

(d) *Variable Methods of Field Activities :* The stereotyped centre-based programme would be replaced by programmes implemented with the help of the community. The selection and training of *Preraks* and instructors would be improved and AECs encouraged to take up community work. In addition to the traditional EECs, the following types of approach may also be encouraged :

(i) *Prerak*-centred approach, in which a *Prerak* is given complete freedom to organise his/her work for the complete eradication of illiteracy through paid or honorary workers;

(ii) Instructor-centred approach, which envisages an instructor being given a similar responsibility and a public recognition on successful completion of total eradication responsibility;

(iii) Outcome-oriented approach, as being tried out at present in West Bengal, in which a modest reward is given to a *panchayat* or some other local body or a voluntary agency after a thorough evaluation of complete eradication of illiteracy;

(iv) Open learning opportunity for women, under which women

workers would take responsibility for a variety of programmes of women's development, vocational training, as well as literacy, and would be remunerated accordingly.

(e) *Improved Pace and Content of Learning (IPCL):* The innovative technique of IPCL provides for a reduced duration of learning, an improved motivation of learners and fuctionaries, and an in-built mechanism for evaluation, including self-evaluation by learners. A three-graded primer is introduced under IPCL. This primer includes space for practice by the learner and a continuous evaluation in the primer itself. It is ensured that through a number os simple tests, the learner achieves the expected levels of learning within about six months. The new technique would introduce a process of self-directed learning and self-evaluation by the learner from the beginning. With heightened motivation, which will be the key issue in the new technique, the rate of drop-out should come down and with the possibility of almost two cycles of an AEC in a year, the programme should become cost-effective, while ensuring a larger coverage.

Volunteer-based Approach

We have noted above that the centre-based programme would have the potentiality of imparting functional literacy to about 15 million perons per annum. A good deal of the remaining 5 million persons would be covered under the volunteer-based programme. Such a programme is referred to as volunteer-based because no remuneration as such is payable to persons who take up literacy work. The various categories of persons who may take up such programmes would include the following :

(a) *Students :* As a part of the National Service Scheme, about 3,00,000 students are already engaged in literacy work. As a part of "socially useful literacy work" students at secondary and higher secondary levels are also beginning to take an interest in literacy activities. Proper record is not being maintained of the number of persons actually made literate by students and the programme so far has served more the interest of the education of students, than the actual spread of literacy among adults. In the coming years there will be an attempt to widen the students' involvement in literacy work. The motivation of students, their training learning materials provided to them, and the quality of monitoring will need to be greatly improved.

(b) *Teachers :* Although the NLM document had envisaged that teachers will take up literacy work on a voluntary basis on a large scale, and national organisations of teachers have also called upon their members to take up these programmes as a part of their duty to the nation, little headway has been made so far in this regard. A good deal more effort will have to be made to call upon the teachers to take the responsibility for at least a small number of illiterate persons. Even if 1,00,000 to 2,00,000 teachers actively involve themselves in voluntary work, they can make a significant impact.

(c) *Housewives and Elderly Persons :* As a part of NLM activity during the last couple of years persons who can volunteer to take up literacy work are being asked to do so through TV. The response so far has been most encouraging. What we have not been able to do is to follow up the initiatives taken by volunteer workers, or to organise orientation for them. Arrangements for involving service-oriented persons, in NLM will have to be reorganised.

Campaign Approach

On 4 February 1990 the Prime Minister declared Ernakulam as the first fully literate district and also launched a campaign for complete eradication of illiteracy in the State of Kerala by the beginning of 1991. What has been achieved in Ernakulam, and is being attempted in the rest of Kerala, is eradication of illiteracy in the 6-60 age-group. Similar campaigns have been started in Pondicherry and Goa, in several talukas of Karnataka and in 2-3 districts of Tamil Nadu. An effort is being made to launch campaigns for the eradication of illiteracy in large metropolitan towns, such as Bombay, Calcutta, Delhi, Madras etc.

The main characteristic of the campaign approach is a large-scale mobilisation of literate persons as well as illiterate persons and the creation of an atmosphere in which youth come forward to take responsibility for the eradication of illiteracy. So far most of these campaigns have started in areas which already have a high rate of literacy and the overall environment is favourable to the acquisition and retention of literacy. The crucial question is whether such campaigns can be launched in areas which are predominantly illiterate and where literacy programmes have not succeeded in the past. In the following paragraphs we refer to the importance of mobilisation for campaign in those areas.

Mass Mobilisation

Interest in mobilisation has been aroused mainly because of the leadership provided by persons like Dr. Ram Lal Parikh in Gujarat, Dr. M.P. Parmesvaran in Kerala, Dr. B.B. Parmesvara Rao in Andhra Pradesh, Shri Prembhai in UP, and several People's Science Groups throughout the country. It is obvious to any person who has been familiar with the problems of bringing about social change in our country that the government by itself can do little to secure mass mobilisation and people's participation. It is mainly the people who have not only a deep personal commitment to the cause of upliftment of the deprived sections of society, but also exceptional leadership and organisational qualities that can organise a mobilisation on a large scale. The experience of the last two to three years shows that mass mobilisation can be the vehicle for improvement in all aspects of the programme throughout the country. Special effort will be made in the next few years to intensify mass mobilisation. Some of the measures that may be taken for this would be as follows :

(a) *Paidal Jatha* (mobilisation teams on foot) : These are to be organised with the help of a large number of Gandhian and Sarvodaya voluntary agencies as well as youth activists, who will move from village to village, talking to people, writing and painting on walls, forming village committees and identifying volunteer literacy workers.
(b) *Gram Vigyan Jatha* (mobilisation through People's Science Movement Agencies): As in the case of Kerala, where Kerala Sastra Sahitya Parishad has involved hundreds and thousands of teachers, students, artists, government servants, unemployed youth, etc. to take up work relating to environmental conservation, science popularisation, and adult literacy, People's Science Groups would be asked to spread their network and create such organisations in all the states. KSSP will provide the

necessary support for this purpose.

(c) *Use of the Mass Media for Environment Building :* The role of the Press, Radio and TV in influencing people's minds and attitudes has come to be fully realised. A systematic effort will have to be made to harness these media for literacy.

(d) *Youth Training and Deployment and VECs :* A large programme of training village animators, *Shiksha Sathins*, members of VECs and of *Mahila Samooh*, etc. would be taken up. These people will come together to form VEC or *Mahila Samooh* to undertake micro-planning and mobilisation of the local community for active participation in mass education programmes.

Continuing Education

Education is a lifelong process. In India, we have an old tradition of *swadhyaya* (self-study or introspection). In the context, however, of a much wider access, participation, and achievement in primary education and adult education programmes, continuing education acquires a place of great importance. On the provision of appropriate facilities of continuing education would depend:

the retention and upgradation of levels of literacy and numeracy acquired through primary education or literacy courses;
further education and skill training to relate better the earlier learning to the needs and interests of the learners; and
the application and use of primary education and literacy for improvement of conditions of the learners themselves, their families, and the community.

The strategy for continuing lifelong education will comprise a number of measures aimed at reaching out to as large a literate population as possible. These would include the following :

(a) *Strengthening of Existing Institutional Structures :* Libraries were established at the district, block, and sometimes at village levels during the First and Second Five Year Plans. In addition, some state governments and voluntary organisations have created large networks of public libraries. A concerted effort needs to be made to revive and strengthen this library system.

(b) *Extension and Vocational Training Programmes :* Several government departments and other organisations have skill training and systematic extension programmes including :

Farmers' training;

Training of the youth and women and of SC, ST persons for self-employment;

Polytechnics and *Krishi Vigyan Kendras* running training programmes for securing access to new technologies and information;

The Central Social Welfare Board has a large vocational training scheme.

These programmes will have to be related with the skill development needs of youth who acquire primary education, and neo-literate adults.

(c) *Opening up of the Institutional Facilities :* Libraries and reading rooms in schools and colleges remain unutilised in the evenings. We need to start a movement for providing adult education literature in these institutions and to open them up in the evening for adults. The cost involved would be small, but we could have over 50,000 libraries/reading rooms, although mostly in urban and suburban areas.

(d) *Establishment of New Learning Facilities:* Under NLM a nationwide network of libraries and reading rooms is envisaged in the form of *Jana Shikshan Nilayams*. JSNs will also provide facilities for sports and cultural activities and are to serve as centres of information and communication. There is justification for providing a higher level library-cum-resource centre for approximately each 10 JSNs.

(e) *Mass Media and Distance Learning :* Radio and Television are used in our country, and in other parts of the world, to provide continuing education. In addition, open schools have been set up by the Central Government and some Boards of Secondary Education using mainly the correspondence mode.

(f) *Folk and Traditional Media :* The traditional forms of learning in our country have been puppetry, *katha*, folk theatre, singing of ballads, etc. It will be necessary to prevent a situation of dichotomy between literacy and traditional and folk media of learning. This would be one of the major challenges during the next few years.

As we approach the twenty-first century we have to ensure that India does not remain a country where people simultaneously live in several centuries—some people tucked away in hills, deserts and forests who can neither read nor write and have remained unaffected by the progress in science and technology, and others who are handling computers and new gadgets with ease. Unfortunately, this chasm also illustrates the economic disparities. The gender gap is exemplified by women remaining in *Purdah*, steeped in a culture of silence, and a very small number of women able to have the best education which our universities and professional and technical education institutions have to offer. The challenge of adult education is to reduce this gap, and to create a society in which the basic instrumentalities of learning are available to all, and these are supplemented by diverse traditional and modern modes of communication.

7

Adult, Continuing and Non-Formal Education in Universities and Colleges

Introduction

Involvement of the universities in the eradication of illiteracy has been very minimal. Their participation in the adult education programmes has not been very much encouraging. There is an urgent need that they should assume a much larger responsibility for educating the adults. There is also a need to energise the university adult education departments to engage themselves in innovative research, teaching and extension. None can disagree what S.Y. Shah has said that it cannot be denied "the fact in spite of tremendous expansion of university adult education during the 1980s and hundred per cent financial support from UGC, they could not make any significant dent in terms of developing innovative models of extension and research." Literacy campaigns require research support for a number of their problems. Only the universities which have experience and are adequately equipped to take up research studies on adult education problems can give proper guidelines to adult education educators, administrators and decision-makers in adult education programmes.

In terms of manpower, infrastructure, and finances they are in an advantageous position and can play a major role in dealing with some of the problems of the society and in contributing to social development and change. In doing so, they would have to go outside the four walls of the campus and address themselves to the needs of local communities and evolve ways and means of redressing their problems. While some of the agricultural universities and Gandhian institutions in India have been trying to actively associate themselves with the problems of local communities for quite sometime, the majority of Indian universities have delimited their activities to teaching and research until 1977 when the University Grants Commission recognised extension as the third dimension of the institution of higher education.

(A) UGC AND UNIVERSITY ADULT EDUCATION: AN APPROACH TO NINTH PLAN*

> *"There is not a single Department of Adult Education in any Indian university where atleast 3-4 members of faculty are engaged in innovative research, teaching and extension. Apart from the absence of team spirit, there is considerable academic inertia and pessimism among the faculty members. The only silver lining is the silent work of a handful of dedicated individuals in some universities. Otherwise Indian University Departments of Adult Education are merely implementing agencies of Government designed, monitored and funded programmes."*

These comments made by a renowned professor of adult education from an overseas university who visited India during the last winter with a view to developing collaborative academic programmes with Indian counterparts, may seem to be too harsh to Indian adult educators who may dismiss them as biased view of an outsider. However, on deeper probe and objective evaluation, it becomes evident that the ciriticims are not baseless. The fact that the overseas professor made comments after spending three months in visiting some of the universitiy departments of adult education and interacting with a number of academics and reviewing the researches carried out in India lend credence to his observation. There is no denying the fact that in spite of the tremendous expansion of university adult education during the 1980s and hundred per cent financial support from the UGC, they could not make any significant dent in terms of developing innovative models of extension and research. The plight of adult education departments becomes more clear when compared to the departments of Bio-technology which also emerged during 1980s and which succeeded in carving out a distinguished place for themselves in Indian university system. Till today majority of departments of adult education have not become permanent constituent

---

* *Development of Higher Education in India: A Policy Frame*, New Delhi: University Grants Commission, 1978.

S.Y. Shah, UGC and University Adult Education, In *Society, Education and Development*, Association of Indian Universities, 1998, pp. 74-84.

bodies of universities but continue as projects or remain as non-teaching departments with temporary staff. Uncertainties loom large in the horizon of the departments of adult education Why did adult education fail to strike strong roots in the university system? Is it due to the University Grants Commission (UGC) policy ? What should be the role of university adult education during Ninth Plan ? Should UGC formulate new guidelines or revise the existing ones and continue to support university adult education ?

UGC Policy

There has been a continuous debate about the role of universities in developing countries and it is now generally recognised that they should no longer remain confined to discharging the two traditional functions of teaching and research. It is argued that since education is a sub-system of society, the educational institutions cannot remain unconcerned with the problems of society. The universities which have vast resources launching of the National Adult Education Programme (NAEP) in 1978 by the Government of India provided an opportunity to them to actively involve themselves with the solution of one of the crucial problems of our society—eradication of illiteracy. With the exception of a few universities like Mysore, Poona, Rajasthan, Baroda, Gujarat Vidyapeeth, Madras and Sri Venkateswara, most of the universities took up adult education programme only after 1978 and that too mainly in response to UGC policy and persuasion.

The different guidelines, communications and review committee reports of UGC issued since 1978, consistently emphasized the great responsibility of universities to society as a whole and their role in transmitting culture and knowledge besides providing leadership to the whole nation. Identifying the ways in which universities could play their role, the former chairperson of UGC, late Dr. Madhuri R. Shah emphasised training, preparation of teaching learning materials, evaluation and action research as key areas.[1] The role of universities in teaching and research was highlighted by the UGC Review Committee (1985):

> "It is university that can tie adult education to action programmes through well designed and effectively conducted research programmes. The universities at the apex of the educational ladder can undertake more fundamental and applied researches rather than

action research... Since the non-formal adult, continuing education and extension programmes are growing very fast, it is urgent and imperative that systematic efforts are initiated to develop professional manpower suitable to conceive, plan, and implement these programmes effectively. The country is already experiencing acute shortage of professionally trained manpower resulting in adhoc recruitment of personnel with hardly any professional abilities and skills which slows down the pace and efficiency of the programme."[2]

After the proclamation of New Education Policy (1986) and the launching National Literacy Mission (1988), the focus of UGC guidelines changed. The thrust of new UGC guidelines (1988) was mainly on identifying an area around the universities and eradication of illiteracy through the organization of literacy centres.[3] The subsequent guidelines issued in 1991 & 1993 also focused on achieving total literacy and setting up *Jan Shikshan Nilayams* and organizing continuing education programmes. Far from developing innovative models of extension, the emphasis of adult education departments shifted to merely implementing UGC guidelines on adult and continuing education. The UGC funds were released mainly for the implementation of literacy, post literacy and continuing education programmes. No money was allocated for curriculum development or research. The interested universities were requested to apply separately to UGC under the scheme of research projects. The monitoring and evaluation criteria of UGC was based mainly on the number of literates made, number of training programmes organized and other extension activities. The research and publications, which are integral parts of university adult education were not considered to be the main work of the staff of adult education departments. Since a large number of staff of adult education departments did not have research degrees or interests (?) there were no protests. Those who were interested in research had a tough time in convincing their colleagues about the importance of research and publications. Hence total number of research projects and publications brought out by university departments were few during the last ten years.

While UGC did succeed in persuading 60% of Indian universities and a large number of colleges in implementing adult, continuing education and extension programmes, the coordinating cell at UGC has been too small to effectively liaison with different universities to monitor the progress of programmes. Due to these limitations of UGC in monitoring the progress of adult education programme, the idea of nodal universities was introduced during 1992. UGC identified fourteen universities and entrusted them with the task of monitoring the progress of the implementation of UGC programmes in their respective states. Accordingly each nodal university convened an annual meeting of the state level universities to discuss and prepare a consolidated report for submission to UGC. Since some of the universities have strong reservations about the choice of nodal universities, they do not extend full cooperation. In fact, they feel that by designating certain universities as nodal agencies, UGC has shown favouritism. If the UGC could consider the idea of entrusting the work to state-level research institutions, which are identified by the National Literacy Mission for evaluation work, or to the National Institute of Adult Education, the monitoring could be done in a more objective manner.

While UGC could legitimately take the credit for the tremendous expansion of university adult education and providing employment to nearly 500 members—300 faculty and 200 supporting staff—it cannot absolve itself of the problems that were generated. When this writer drew the attention of the former UGC Chairperson, the late Dr. Madhuri R. Shah who played a key role in the expansion of university adult education, she stated that had she not personally encouraged the universities (she wrote personal letters to all the Vice Chancellors), then perhaps only few would have introduced adult education programmes. To quote her,

> "I am a strong supporter of adult education. As a Chairperson of UGC if I succeed in sowing the seeds of adult education in Indian universities and be fortunate in witnessing the germination and growth, then I would be delighted. I am afraid that if I fail to push adult education during my tenure and if my successor does not show the same interest, then the progress of adult education will be slow. I am not bothered how the plant of university adult education grows, it depends on the soil of universities, the extent of irrigation and now the saplings are tended. This is clearly the role of universities and UGC can only be a sympathetic observer."[4]

The former UGC chairperson did succeed in sowing the seeds of adult education in Indian universities during her tenure, when nearly 60% of Indian universities took up adult education projects. Perhaps nowhere else in the world, as many as 90 Departments of Adult Education were set up within a short span of 3-5 years. The indiscriminate policy of UGC of encouraging all the Indian universities to set up Adult Education Departments during 1980s when there were not enough qualified manpower in the country paved the way for the appointment of less qualified and disinterested staff who due to their lack of expertise and probably ignorance failed to nurture university adult education. One of the reasons why the university adult education could not succeed in making a significant impact may be traced to the quality of staff.

Response of Universities

The majority of universities accepted the UGC package on Adult, Continuing Education and Extension as a plan project and tried to implement the programme as per UGC guidelines. For them, it was yet another fully funded project. However, some of the universities which had a vision and strong leadership, saw tremendous potential in developing adult education project as fulfledged departments of teaching, research and extension. With the policy and funding support from UGC, the task seemed to be simple. While about ten universities succeeded in starting post M.A. Diploma in Adult, Continuing Education, only one university developed Master's degree course in extension education during 1980s. With the exception of two universities, Madras and Sri Venkateswara, which had started M.A., M.Phil. and Ph.D. programme in adult education earlier, the rest continued as implementing agencies of UGC funded field programme. In some of the universities, where the staff of adult education projects tried to set up fulfledged departments there was vehement opposition from the departments of education. It was argued that provision for research and teaching in adult education could be made in the existing departments of education and other social sciences in a cost effective manner. The proposal to develop adult education project as an Extension Department was also vetoed by certain universites which felt that extension should become an integral part of all the departments and by setting up an exclusive department for extention, the impact would be very limited. Since the existing staff of adult education projects were initially recruited on temporary basis for developmental work, their credentials and competence in taking up teaching and research were also questioned by a section of university community.

The UGC has issued a number of circulars to universities during the last ten years to grant the status and privileges of teachers to the staff of adult education projects. With the exception of a few, the designations of the staff have not been changed in majority of universities. It is argued that since the staff of adult education projects were initially recruited by the selection committees of non-teachers, change of their designations could be legally challenged, unless universities made suitable amend-ments in the existing rules and regulations. This is not acceptable to certain universities due to a variety of reasons. It is feared that induction of adult education staff into teaching community might upset the seniority of the existing teachers for housing or other privileges. A section of teaching community feels that the granting of the privileges of teachers to those who were not recruited through proper advertisements and the selection committee of teachers would be a retrograde step and the regularisation of temporary project staff as permanent teachers of universities may even set an unhealthy precedence. Besides, some of the universities are also opposed to the idea of change of designations for fear that as teachers, the staff of adult education projects might not take up extension work and the real purpose of setting up adult education departments would suffer. Even among adult educators there is a group of directors who oppose the idea of change of designations since they feel that their hold over their colleagues might loosen once they become teachers. This fear is more evident in those universites which follow rotation of headships.

Because of these criticisms and practical difficulties many universities have been very cautious in granting the privileges of teachers to the staff of adult education projects or setting up regular teaching departments. Although some of the universities have absorbed the staff on permanent basis and given them the service benefits of non-teaching staff, merit promotion scheme has not yet been given to them. Thus, apart from the uncertainty of tenure, the staff of adult education projects continue to stagnate which seems to demoralise them and affect their performance.

Approach during the Ninth Plan

The development of university adult education in India has been mainly guided by the UGC since 1978. So far UGC has been taking initiative in formulating the guidelines and deciding the priority areas and funding support. The varied experiences of the past eighteen years of implementation of adult, continuing education and extension programmes through university system have provided valuable insights to the members of the staff of adult education departments. Today, majority of them are aware of the ethos and functioning of their respective universities, attitude of vice chancellors, administration and academic community. Hence university adult educators would be in a better position to decide their programme priorities, operational strategies and funding requirements. As a first step in enabling them to formulate university specific adult education programme during the Ninth Plan each university needs to undertake an internal evaluation of its performance (ever since the inception of their respective projects) focusing on significant achievements so that they may plan only such programmes for which they have the requisite expertise and cooperation of the university.

The approach towards university adult education during the Ninth Plan should be on the identification of strengths of the existing members of adult education departments (as no university terminate their services) and strengthening them through the formulation of university specific programme in any one selected area. For example, if a particular department of adult education has undertaken mainly extension work during the past and achieved some excellence, it may be assumed that the faculty may have developed some expertise in that area and hence it would be logical for them to select extension as a key area during the Ninth Plan. On the other hand, research and teaching may be opted by those departments which may have done substantial work on such areas. Instead of providing general guidelines for all the universities and expecting them to comply, if each university is encouraged to identify a particular area—extension or research or teaching—and develop university specific programme and budget them, it would not only enable them to develop as centres of excellence but also provide scope for diversification and specialisation. Keeping in view the 73rd amendment to the Constitution and the increasing emphasis on grassroot level planning, it would be desirable if UGC encourages a decentralised approach to university adult education.

Instead of the present practice of inviting annual plans and releasing yearly grants, which entails considerable delays, the UGC may consider the idea of giving approval for a five year programme and releasing 90% grants in one instalment so that universities may implement the programme in a steady and systematic manner. The UGC may also consider the possibility of making one time final grant to university adult education and make an exit. In such a case, the universities should have the freedom to use the grants as a revolving fund or in any other manner which they deem appropriate, otherwise, if UGC continues to support university adult education as a plan project, universities may not get an opportunity to make it an integral part of university system and adult education would continue to remain as a temporary project. Does UGC envisage such a scenario? Are universities prepared for such temporary status?

There is considerable apprehensions among the university adult educators about their role when UGC ceases funding. According to a survey conducted by this writer, all the three agencies involved in adult education programme, *viz.*, Government departments, non-governmental organizations (NGOs) and educational institutions consider the generation of knowledge and its dissemination to be the most important role of university adult education. With the tremendous expansion of NGOs and their active involvement in a number of developmental activities including adult education at grassroot levels, they do not welcome the participation of universities in developmental work which they consider their monopoly. They feel that as NGOs they have more flexibility in programme planning and are closer to people. Unlike universities, whose commitment to programme and people depends on the flow of funds from UGC, NGOs have multiple sources of funding and can effectively function as activists mobilising and conscientising masses on several crucial social issues. They do not like the entry of universities into their domain as competitors. On the contrary, they expect the universities to provide technical resource support to their programmes besides documenting their work and studying its impact on the society. Although a large number of university adult educators have participated in the total literacy campaigns launched in different parts of India, in some places like Delhi the involvement of schools are preferred to universities. Some of the government officials feel that unless universities continue to provide qualified manpower and generate knowledge through researches, there is no justification for supporting university adult education. It is argued that if universities conceive and confine their role as implementation agencies of UGC then the task can be more effectively and economically carried out by lesser qualified and paid staff. What is the need to appoint a Ph.D. to implement the tailor made guidelines of UGC? On the contrary, if universities aim at developing adult education projects as regular departments like Social Work, Community Medicine, Rural Development, which provide ample scope for teaching, research and extension, then it would be a welcome addition. There is no place for an academic department of adult education in universities which refrains from teaching and research, but carried out limited extension work of a stereotyped nature which could be assigned to NGOs or government departments. This assumes signficance as most of the universities find it difficult to involve students and teachers in extension programmes. Their limited participation in some universities and non-participation in the rest defeats the very purpose of university adult education. Unless a systematic study is undertaken to examine the different factors influencing the participation of students and teachers in extension, the university adult education cannot succeed in the objective of actively involving university community in the process of national development.

The opinion of the academic community on the role of university adult education reiterates the views of NGOs and government officials, majority of them view adult education as a populist or marginal programme and categorically state that unless university adult education focuses on developing some innovative models of extension, relevant courses, fundamental and applied researches and pursues an active publication programme, there is little need for adult education departments in universities. This implies the need for shifting the focus of adult education from being a field of practice to a discipline of study. Since active involvement of the staff with field programme hardly leaves any time for serious research or publication, there is practically no concern for the development of adult education as a district discipline of study at the university level. If university adult educators do not take up this challenge, then the character of university adult education would be distorted and its future would be in jeopardy. Hence the priority of university adult education during the Ninth Plan should be on its development as a discipline of study. This can be achieved by emphasising research and publications. As most of the university departments of adult education do not undertake these activities they fail to receive due recognition or cooperation from academic community. Today there is hardly any difference in the roles of the staff of adult education departments in a university, NGOs or government. There is no study which shows that the performance of highly paid and qualified university adult educators is better than the workers of NGOs or government departments. Unless university adult educators function differently from the NGOs and government departments and involve themselves in teaching research and publication they cannot become an integral part of university community. At best they may remain on the periphery as "service departments" or clubbed with non-teaching departments like physical education. Should university adult education become a marginal field? Should it be dubbed as an implementation agency of UGC? Can the departments of adult education in universities strive to carve out a niche for themselves?

REFERENCES

1. UGC Chairperson's letter to all Vice Chancellors, dated 13th Nov. 1984, file no.: 1-22/84/AC-UGC, see also letter dated 4th April 1985, file No. 1-3/85/AE-UGC.
2. *University System and Extension as the Third Dimension: Report of the Review Committee Appointed by the University Grants Commission*, New Delhi, University Grants Commission, 1986, p. 71kl.
3. *New Guidelines on Adult and Continuing Education and Extension Programmes in Universities and Colleges, 1988*, New Delhi, University Grants Commission, 1988, p. 5.
4. Interview with (late) Dr. Madhuri R. Shah conducted on 12th Aug. 1985.

(B) ROLE OF UNIVERSITIES IN TOTAL LITERACY CAMPAIGNS

Literacy is a basic human right and minimum need on the part of every individual. It is an essential tool to widen the mental horizon of the people and to make effective utilisation of their knowledge, skills and competencies in development process. It is essential for the emergence of a strong democratic society and to accelerate the pace and mangitude of economic development of the country. It is a boon for the half-clad, ill-fed and starving population suffering from poverty, disease and ignorance. The government has made several efforts to extend educational opportunities to those who were deprived of it during their childhood through various formal, non-formal and adult education programmes. As a result of it our literacy rate has increased from 16.67% in 1951 to 52.1% during 1991. Still half of the country is illiterate and the government is committed to wipe out illiteracy in a phased manner through total literacy campaigns by 2000 AD.

The success of the total literacy campaigns depends upon the effective involvement of the various government and non-government agencies. Among these agencies the universities, which are considered as institutions of higher learning have a major role to play. Universities have a social and moral obligation to serve the community through extension, apart from their regular activities of teaching and research. The universities through its good number of students and teachers can move to the community in a phased manner to wipe out illiteracy in the nearby areas. The students and staff members can disseminate knowledge of their respective disciplines through extension lectures for the qualitative

Source : Kumaraswamy, T. and Bhasah, S. Khadar, Role of Universities in Total Literacy Campaigns, In *Society, Education and Development*, Association of Indian Universities, New Delhi, 1998, pp. 85-90.

improvement of the community. As a matter of fact, participation of students in adult education activities provides them with an opportunity to improve their knowledge through interaction with the community. Involvement of women students would help to increase the attendance rate of women learners in the centres. Further, it is an opportunity for the students to serve the community during their study period. The universities can offer their infrastructure facilities like buildings, library, hardware equipment, etc. to facilitate effective instruction about modern methods and scientific advancements to the community.

Several universities and affiliated colleges have been participating in literacy programmes successfully since 1978 onwards under the direction and guidance of the Centres/Departments of Adult, Continuing Education and Extension at universities by organising adult education centres. The centre based approach was supplemented by 'Each One Teach One/Five' approach. 'Mass programme for functional literacy' was introduced in 1986 where maximum involvement of students was emphasised on voluntary basis. This programme could not achieve the expected results due to various deficiencies in training, supervision, monitoring, evaluation, post-literacy activities, etc. The universities have organised centres under Area Based Approach from 1988 onwards. Later, the government started to finance the district administrations for total literacy campaigns from 1989-90 onwards under National Literacy Mission. The campaign approach is now continuing and district administrations are not utilising the resource support of the universities due to lack of sufficient directions from UGC and government; and added to this the universities have their own rigid structures to extend their support. Whatever the reasons for this state of affairs the district authorities require the professional and technical support of the universities to effectively implement the total literacy campaigns. The following are the thrust areas where the universities can bestow their attention for the promotion of literacy.

Motivation and Mobilisation of Resources

Creation of a favourable environment is a precondition for the success of any literacy campaign. Motivation is the first step in literacy and without adequate motivation the adult learners, volunteers, students, teachers and local elite cannot participate in it. The universities and colleges can design strategies to motivate the public and mobilise the resources for launching the literacy programme. A few students can be trained to survey the illiterates in the selected area and a few students can be entrusted with the work of identifying the resources like school building, *panchayat* office, local organisations, resource persons, social workers, etc. to train the volunteers and to start literacy centres. A few students and staff members can be assigned the task of preparing slogans, posters, banners, drama skits, street plays, role plays, pamphlets, articles, newspaper advertisements etc. to develop favourable environment to enthuse the public and the illiterate learners to join the literacy centres. The organisation of padyatras, cycle rallys, meetings, door to door campaigns can be undertaken by the colleges in a planned manner. The Centres/Departments of Adult, Continuing Education and Extension at the university level may take the lead and work out the strategies with the principals, teachers and students to boost up the campaign and mobilise the resources for its successful implementation.

Material Preparation

Total literacy campaigns require a wide range of materials which include: (a) publicity materials, (b) teaching/learning materials like primers, volunteer's guide, stimulation pictures, numeracy charts, etc., (c) newsletters, magazines and graded materials for post literacy and continuing education, (d) training materials for various functionaries like key resource persons, master trainers, supervisors, student volunteers, *preraks*/monitors of post literacy phase, and (e) other materials like survey forms, monitoring forms, schedules, checklists, learner assessment sheets, progress reports and evaluation tools. The Centres/Departments of Adult, Continuing Education and Extension which have adequate experience in organising adult education programmes can undertake this work. Preparation of materials for literacy and post-literacy phases requires intellectual involvement and the universities are the right agencies to conduct workshops, seminars, field testing, etc. for material preparation taking into consideration the IPCL (Improved Pace and Content of Learning) norms and norms for preparation of post-literacy materials.

Training

The competency level of functionaries in discharging their duties in total literacy campaigns depends upon the quality of training that they have been exposed to. It is through training that a better understanding of the concepts, values and importance of the campaign, motivation of the learners, method of teaching primers and evaluation of the campaign is provided. The Departments/Centres of Adult, Continuing Education and Extension of the universities are the right agencies to train the various functionaries of total literacy campaigns in view of : (a) their expertise in employing various training techniques like lecture, dialogue, discussion, demonstration, debates, role play, brainstorming, simulation, etc., (b) the availability of infrastructure facilities, (c) their past experience in organising various training programmes for adult education functionaries representing state, district and local levels, and (d) their ability to make the training programmes specific, objective based, participatory and field oriented.

Monitoring and Evaluation

Monitoring and evaluation are essential to know whether the programme is making a headway, whether learners are attending the centres, whether the functionaries are attending to their works, whether the programme duration is sufficient, whether there is need for in-service training, etc. Mere utilisation of the forms of monitoring is not sufficient and what is needed is adequate and timely guidance to improve the field situation. The programme may face several natural hazards like floods, famine, disturbances like deaths of national leaders, crop seasons, festivals, terminal holidays for colleges, elections, etc., and there may arise the need for taking up several crucial steps. The University Departments/Centres for Adult, Continuing Education and Extension can periodically review the progress of the campaign through monitoring and evaluation so that the programme is successfully implemented.

Post-Literacy and Follow-up Activities

Post-literacy activities form an integral part of the total literacy campaigns and these activities are necessary to check the illiterate learners from relapsing into illiteracy and to enable them to apply the reading and writing skills acquired in their day to day life situations and to continue their education. The universities can train the students to work as monitors/*preraks* for post-literacy activities like organising literacy centres (for neo-literates, ex-learners, dropouts, etc.), library, reading room, *charcha mandal*, sports and recreational activities and skill development programmes. There is dearth of graded materials for post-literacy and the universities can develop suitable materials on various topics like income generating schemes, development programmes, immunisation, afforestation, mother and child care, nutrition, rights and duties, legal knowledge, scientific temper, etc., and provide the same to post-literacy centres. The universities can organise simple and short term training camps directly and also in collaboration with other agencies like banks, agricultural extension centres, cooperative societies, government departments of health, animal husbandry, etc. for the benefit of the neo-literates.

Research and Documentation

Total literacy campaigns require sufficient research support to obtain a more adequate solution of the problems and to answer urgent questions like content, method of instruction, training techniques, administration, supervision, duration of the campaign, teaching/learning process, community support, level of involvement of functionaries, cost effectiveness, impact of the campaign, type of post-literacy activities desired, retention and use of literacy skills, etc. The universities can provide research support to the total literacy campaigns as they have expertise in developing research tools, methods and treatment of data through improved statistical techniques. The universities can do research through quick appraisals, and short term projects so that results so obtained can be disseminated to the field functionaries to take corrective measures. Documentation of training materials, research reports, studies, etc. is highly warranted for total literacy campaigns and the universities can undertake this activity for reference and future guidance.

To conclude, universities possess professional and technical resources to support the total literacy campaigns in the thrust areas like motivation, training, material preparation, post-literacy activities, monitoring and evaluation, research and documentation, etc. What is needed is effective utilisation of the universities for total literacy campaigns and ensuring that the UGC/government issues guidelines to the universities and the district administrations before starting the campaigns. Further, universities should strengthen the extension dimension and develop the extension culture among the students and staff members through flexible approaches. The universities can adopt a few *mandals*/areas within their proximity to promote literacy among the community through total literacy campaigns. Let the universities offer their resource support to the total literacy campaigns and let the total literacy campaigns herald, symbolise and contribute to new development strategies.

8

Research, Evaluation and Monitoring

Introduction

One of the major factors for painfully slow progress of adult education is that the planners and the administrators of adult, continuing and non-formal education formulated the programmes on the parameters most of which were not based on researches and experiments. They were not to blame as they were not provided with the contents that should have been the outcome of the intensive research studies. The role of university adult education departments has been very much disappointing in this regard. They were provided with the adequate funds by University Grants Commission for this purpose, but they showed lackadaisical attitude towards it. It would be appropriate to quote the UGC Committee Review (1985):

> "It is university that can tie adult education to action programmes. The universities at the apex of the educational ladder can undertake more fundamental and applied researches rather than action research... Since the non-formal adult, continuing education and extension programmes are growing very fast, it is urgent and imperative that systematic efforts are initiated to develop professional manpower suitable to conceive, plan and implement these programmes effectively. The country is already experiencing acute shortage of professionally trained manpower resulting in *ad hoc* recruitment of personnel with hardly any professional abilities and skills which slows down the pace and efficiency of the programmes."

Source : N.K. Ambasht, *Fifth Survey of Educational Research: Trend Reports*, National Council of Educational Research and Training, New Delhi, 1997, pp. 545-58.

(A) REVIEW OF STUDIES (ADULT, CONTINUING AND NON-FORMAL EDUCATION)

Adult Education

Bhagria, R. (1992) studied the impact of the polyvalent centres of Shramik Vidyapeeths on industrial workers and found that the Shramik Vidyapeeths (SVs) have played a major role in raising the quality of life, improving the thinking process and life-pattern of the industrial workers. She also found that the vocational and technical education through the SVs had benefited both the workers and the management as well and that the workers became more disciplined and wastage was also minimised. Only marginal benefits were noticed in bringing about political awareness. The SVs did a good job in the field of population education, preserving cultural heritage, civic responsibility, socio-economic growth and trade union orientation. It was also noticed that the workers and their families felt motivated to participate in SV programmes; sufficient opportunities for vertical and horizontal mobility existed; and that the SVs are making efforts to make workers self-reliant. The employers were reported to be happy with these programmes as these were found to be useful in terms of cost benefit, production, quality, resource expertise, formulation and implementation of programmes as per their requirements. The SVs sponsored by Voluntary Agencies showed better performance and were recognised by the state, and loan facilities were available to the beneficiaries for establishing small industrial units.

Bhat, S.S. (1990) studied the growth and development of adult education programmes in India. It is a study that traces the history of adult education from the very ancient period to the contemporary period and goes on to justify the need for establishing a National Council of Adult Education.

Chandel, N.P.S. (1992) made a cost-effectiveness analysis of National Adult Education Programme (NAEP) with special reference to the Seventh Five Year Plan. He found that in 1989-90, the per-learner cost of State Adult Education Programme (SAEP) and Rural Functional Literacy Project (RFLP) were Rs. 168.36 and Rs. 166.87 respectively; the office records showed a wastage of 8.38% and 9.71%, respectively. Under the effectiveness analysis it found that among the input indicators, 22.25% RFLP and 38.05% SAEP instructors were matriculates; the caste-wise distribution of instructors and learners did not match; 52% SAEP and 46% RFLP learners indicated the adequacy of the seating place; 80% SAEP and 70% RFLP instructors got supply of materials in time and in sufficiant quantity. The process indicators revealed that there were poor supervision practices; 40% village leaders were consulted at the time of opening of the centres; 30% village leaders reported that their AE centres were running; and 25% reported an increase in enrolment, etc. The output indicators reveal that the majority of the beneficiaries belong to the SC, ST, OBC and the minorities in both the programmes; 60% of them are female. According to the office records, 91.31% RFLP and 92.24% SAEP were declared successful; SAEP learners achieved significantly higher than RFLP learners and there was no significant difference between the achievements of male and female learners. The value of CI was highest for SAEP male learners (162), followed by SAEP female (154.10), RFLP male (145.50) and RFLP female (138.10); SAEP was more cost-effective than the RFLP.

Gupta, P.L. (1988) undertook an evaluation study of adult literacy centres in relation to their programme objectives in Himachal Pradesh and found that the majority of the people attending the adult literacy centres were in the age-group 15-35. The interesting thing discovered was that most of them stayed in the centres for about a month to learn to write their names (their signatures) only. The main causes for the drop-out from the centres were many, such as lack of physical and infrasturctural facilities, lack of occupational training courses, inadequate training and supervision of the instructors, etc. The centres ran for ten months only, they did not have post-literacy programmes, and followed the alphabet approach to learning language. At the state level there was no system of monitoring and evaluation of the adult education (AE) programme. There was significant difference between the six districts in literacy, functionality and overall performance as measured by the achievement tests. There was no significant difference found in the performance of learners on the component of awareness. Sex did not play any significant role in the performance in the component of literacy, functionality and awareness.

Chugani, R. (1987) made a study of rural functional literacy project in North Arcot district of Tamil Nadu and found that the reading and writing achievement of Class III students were higher than the Rural Functional Literacy Project (RFLP) participants, but in arithmetic there was no significant difference between the two. Age, caste, and family income of the participants were significantly correlated with their literacy achievement. The age and occupation were not related to the functionality level but cast, marital status, family income were correlated signficantly with the functionality level.

Das, M. (1990) studied the socio-economic problems in the implementation of AE programmes in Assam. He found that besides the poverty, illiteracy, ignorance and unwillingness of the illiterate adults, social customs, religious fanaticism, conservatism and traditionalism and also natural calamities like floods were playing a detrimental role in the expansion of adult education. The attendance in the combined adult education centres was low because males and females hesitate to learn together. But in the case of tea-garden labourers, both male and female, work together freely and therefore, they do not hesitate to learn together. There were two noticeable sections of adult illiterates who were not participating in the AE programmes—those who were well off but lacking motivation and those who were very poor and who would not come to AE centres unless there were some income generating activities. There were defects in instructional strategies and selection of learning activities which were responsible for the slow expansion of the AE programmes. Therefore, a need-based AE programme for the socially and economically deprived would necessitate identification of homogeneous groups, assessment of educational needs in the light of their economic needs and aspirations, formulation of suitable and relevant curricula, etc.

Dhanbal, K.R. (1991) assessed the impact of rural development functional components on adult literates of Sakkotai Block and came to the conclusion that the adult education centres could be effectively used for inducting the problem-solving approach, and the adult education instructor will have to assume the role of the problem-solver for both the learner and for the community problems.

Desai, D.B. *et al.* (1982) (not documented in earlier surveys) evaluated the National Adult Education Programme in seven districts of Gujarat and found that there were several discrepancies in establishment of the centres. The distribution of the villages with Adult Education Centres (AECs) in terms of concentration of SC and ST population and literacy levels as indicators of local need for adult education showed that there had not been any deliberate attempt to reach areas with greater needs. They also found that the total number of those made literate in three years was abysmally low, with 56,430 literates as compared to the target of 14,17,772. It was also revealed that the programme beneficiaries were almost all (96%) SC, ST and OBCs. The timings of the centres were suitable to the needs of the learners. The community supported the programme but there was no indication of the active participation of the community in the functioning of the AECs. This study is now dated and is overtaken by the establishment of the NLM and the launching of the TLCs.

Jacob, P.J. (1990) identified certain curricular areas in functional science and constructed certain select models for adult education. He found that the functional science areas are neither adequately covered in the primers of adult learners nor are they relevant to their needs. The emphasis on science subjects was also inadequate. The learners did not have adequate awareness of the health science, home science, agricultural science and veterinary science aspects. The models that he tested were found to result in greater awareness and practical knowledge among the learners. He established that there was a need for revising the adult education curricula with more components of functional science. For this he emphasized the need assessment of the learners and orientation of the learners and he further established that the models he tested were effective.

Kaur, M. (1992) developed three learning packages for the illiterate adults of Punjab: (a) one consisting of two units (i) of alphabets, and (ii) of *matras*; (b) numeracy package consisting of seven units of numbers, place value, simple addition, etc.; and (c) a social science package consisting of three units of social, health and economic problems. The effectiveness of these packages was tested on male and female learners. She found that the packages of literacy, numeracy and social awareness were equally effective on both the groups of learners.

Khatun, S.A. (1991) studied the problems of adult learners of the RFLP centres in the district of Cuttack (Jagatsinghpur Block) and found that 50% drop-out was a regular phenomenon; that the reading and learning materials supplied were inadequate; that the various authorities from different development departments visited the centres from time to time; that the learners were irregular and, therefore, the teaching was not effective; that the centres opened in the evening; that the learners were in the age-group of 15-35 years, that there was a hesitation among the grown-ups to learn with 15-year-olds; that the pressure of economic earning was so great that there was no energy and urge left for attending the centres; and that there was no provision for mass media, like TV or Radio in the centres. There was also no provision of any vocational training in most of the centres; the attendance of the learners was not recorded in these centres; and there was no useful books in the libraries of the centres. She also found that the illiterate women do not get equal status with literate women in the society; that in slum areas there was no provision of a dispensary; that the examinations were not held at the proper time; that most of the classes were held in the club, in the school or some such other places, including the houses of the instructors; and that the majority of learners are SC and ST.

Pushpakumari, B. (1992) studied the role of income-generating activities in motivating the women learners of the AECs of Kerala. She reached the conclusion that income-generating activities, if provided, did not play a decisive role in motivating the women learners of the AECs of Kerala. She further pointed out that there were certain psychological, sociological, economic and religio-cultural factors related to motivation of women learners; the women learners of the urban areas were better motivated than the rural women, irrespective of whether income-generating activities were provided, at the centre or not.

Malhotra, K. (1991) made a study of the learning needs for adult education among rural and tribal youth in Bihar and proposed a programme of response. She found that literacy, numeracy, social awareness and vocational skills were the needs of the rural and tribal youths alike. Irrespective of the SES, age and sex, literacy and numeracy learning were common to all but social awareness and vocational skill were patterned by age and sex. One significant finding that stood out was that the tribal youth felt the need of the medium of instruction being the mother tongue whereas the rural youth had accepted the existing medium of instruction. The need perceptions of females were identical, irrespective of the fact whether they were tribal or rural.

Manavalane, R. (1990) evaluated the adult education programme implemented by the Annamalai University in the Keerapalayan Panchayat Union of Chidambaram Taluk and concluded that the participation of the SC learners was more in AE programmes than others; those in the age-group of 15-24 years were participating more, and their reading skills were better than their writing skills.

Mohanty, N. (1988) evaluated the functional literacy programme in the Puri district of Orissa. She found that more emphasis was laid on literacy than on functionality; actual skill development in functionality was observed in only 40%; local people did not cooperate in management of the centres; infrastructural inadequacies were the main bottlenecks; irregular classes were also reported to be the reason for its tardy success; the motivating reasons were reported to be learning to sign one's name, maintaining accounts, and writing letters.

Mohan, S.N. and Usha, M.N. (1992) undertook an evaluation of the TLCs in Bijapur and Dakshina Kannada districts of Karnataka. The study revealed that there were ideological differences and personal rivalries among the members of different committees that were hindering the progress though the organisational set-up was conducive to the programme. The content of the primers was found to be comprehensive and gender issues were given priority and yet the latter lacked perspective. The motivating strategies like Jathas and street plays, etc., are effective though their impact waned if not sustained throughout. The multiplier-effect strategy was diluted due to the percolation effect. The teaching-learning process was well planned and there were very few drop-outs. The achievement of literacy skill at levels I and II were very high, but at level III it was around 89% in Dakshina Kannada and 56% in Bijapur. Monitoring and supervision needed further phasing and meticulous planning to make the programme more effective. The study concluded that there was a need for relaxing the time-frame of such campaigns in view of the varying literacy levels and the socio-economic and cultural demands of the situation. It recommended strengthening the post-literacy programmes.

Murthy, D.S. (1988) studied the factors responsible for the effective implementation of NAEP in Andhra Pradesh. He found that the door-to-door contact by the instructors helped to increase the enrolment; learners favoured the instructors who were regular; the discussion—followed-by-demonstration method found favour with the learners; the content, though satisfactory, needed more information about culture, business, commerce, marketing and small scale and cottage industries; instructors with matriculation qualification were more successful; instructors who joined for earning livelihood were more committed; the programmes were more successful where DRDA, Banks and elders, etc., showed interest; mass campaigning helped in creating literacy awareness.

Padmini, N. (1992) studied the 'Arivoli Iyakkam' (Mass Literacy Programme) in selected areas of the Pondicherry region and found that 68% were illiterates; 32% were drop-outs from primary schools; 80% adult learners were reported to gain appreciable literacy level; only 14.67% participants put the items learned into practice; literacy ranked first, followed by awareness and functionality in that order; the attitude of learners towards the 'Arivoli Iyakkam' was positive. It was suggested that the thrust now should be on post-literacy campaign since total literacy has been achieved.

Pathak, S.N. (1991) made a study entitled, 'Adult Education and Socio-economic Development in Azamgarh district', and came to the conclusion that the NAEP lost its effectiveness due to non-supply of learning materials in time, lack of proper publicity, facility, motivation, supervision, lack of sound knowledge of NAEP among the trainers, inadequate infrastructure, lack of departmental coordination, little honorarium, low achievement in functionality and awareness. He also found that 81.4% participants could not learn copying language or writing of letters or applications.

Rajan, R. (1992) critically studied the mass programme of functional literacy in Tamil Nadu, and found that the volunteers were inspired by MPFL—the motivation, the encouragement, special meetings, guest lectures, special certificates, etc.—and most of them joined because of their interest in the programme. The majority of the programme officers and programme coordinators were trained; 69.8% programme officers held a positive opinion about the literacy kit. The learners' expectations from the programme were that it would enable them to read the bus numbers, posters, name boards and the newspapers as also enable them to write letters and applications. 96.13% volunteers were satisfied with the MPFL, and 68.50% said that their studies were not hampered with this programme. The strengths of the programme were the interest and commitment of the principals, volunteers and the programme officers.

Rao, G. (1992) studied the impact of the adult education programme on the social uplift of women in the rural areas of Madhya Pradesh and noticed an overall improvement in all the fields, *viz.*, social, economic, hygiene, etc., in women in the experimental group due to the adult education programme. Changes were noticed in the maintenance of the kitchen, in general cleanliness and in the development of civic sense. The experimental-group women became aware of the legal rights of women and the social welfare programmes initiated by the government and also realised the importance of education and started educating their children. Attitudinal changes towards living conditions were also noticed. The experimental group had developed a positive attitude towards the adult education programme, developed self-confidence and started solving social problems of the community.

Reddy, D.J. (1991) studied certain factors related to persisters and drop-outs of adult education centres and found, among many other things, that marriage had a negative effect on persistency.

Reddy, M.C.R. (1988) studied spatial variations of literacy in Andhra Pradesh and found that there was a wide disparity in the literacy rates of different districts of Andhra Pradesh. Out of 41 predictor variables used in the study, 29 that accounted for the variation in literacy rates were identified. He grouped these different variables under 10 categories to build different predictor models of literacy, out of which nine explained the variance in the literacy rate after having been subjected to multiple regression analysis.

Reddy, S.P.V. (1991) studied the job satisfaction of adult education supervisors in Andhra Pradesh. He found that the variables of age, sex, qualifications, marital status, salary, experience, deputation/direct recruitment did not make any significant difference among teachers. The difference was significant when classified on the basis of forward castes, backward castes and SC/ST. There was also signficant difference between backward castes and the SC/ST. The attitude of the supervisors towards adult education differed significantly on the basis of above classification. Among many other findings which were important, regression analysis showed that when all the independent variables were considered together they explained 15.23% variance in the job satisfaction of the adult education supervisors.

Reddy, P.A. (1990) studied the socio-psychological factors relating to adult education instructor effectiveness and found that women function more effectively than men as instructors of adult education; age did not come in their way; there was a direct correlation between achievement motivation and the effectiveness; same was true with higher educational achievements among the instructors; older instructors with positive attitude towards adult education were more effective; exposure to mass media leads to greater effectiveness.

Reddy, P.A. (1992) made a study of the determinants of adult education instructor effectiveness and came to conclusion that men and women instructors did not differ; younger instructors were more effective on learner rating; the other castes, backward castes and SC/ST had significant difference in terms of effectiveness, again on learner rating; similarly, the effectiveness of instructors had a direct relationship to their education according to the learner rating, etc.

Ramadevi, B. (1990) made a comparative study of the organisation and conduct of various agencies involved in the adult education programmes in Kerala and found that the majority of instructors were females and in the age-range of 21-25 years with less than a year to two year's experience. The Centre of Adult and Continuing Education was working better in terms of teaching methods and bringing back the drop-outs. In the Centre for Adult Education and Extension, all the instructors had Master's degree while 14.7% had Ph.D. The agencies were found not to be very different as far as the organisation of the programmes was concerned. CAEE and KANFED have published materials which are used by others, while CAEE has conducted some evaluation studies also. The four agencies studied have some common characteristics in terms of learning materials and choice of centres, but the CAEE was found to be more effective than the rest.

Sachchidanada *et al.* (1991) evaluated the Project on Radio Education for Adult Literacy (PREAL) in Hiropatti of Madhubani District and found that the women learners came from the backward and Scheduled Castes families; they liked learning through radio; the average attendence on usual days varied between 9 to 12, but on the PREAL days it increased to 12-15; some trends of change initiated through PREAL was observed, such as the emergence of self-confidence and assertiveness among the women; the appreciation for education was more; there was a more positive orientation towards personal hygiene and cleanliness of the household than before. The conclusions of this study were only one-third of the beneficiaries continued till the end and thus got full benefit of the programme; the learners got attracted to the PREAL due to its novelty factor which wore off in a couple of months time; the programme's shortcomings were also revealed in this study, *e.g.*, short duration and less frequent broadcasts; the radio lessons were in Hindi and the content had unfamiliar Hindi words in the primer, which made it incomprehensible to the Maithili-speaking learners. This confusion in the minds of the learners made them stay away from the programme. There were also the logistical problems like delay in repairs, shortage of lighting arrangements, etc., which hampered the programme. It was, therefore, suggested that corrective steps on in the light of above findings should be taken and close supervision ensured.

Sachchidananda (1992) evaluated SAMU (Saksharata Muzaffarpur). He found that the school-teachers and the students had played a crucial role in the environment building survey, and monitoring and coordination of the SAMU programme. Students had run a large number of centres themselves. The concept of earning while learning did not prove effective, because income-generating activities could not be provided in all literacy classes; the Monitoring Information System (MIS) did not work effectively; there was no means of knowing if the MLLs were achieved; it was suggested that it might be worthwhile to have a uniform test to assess the learners achievement in 3 R's, awareness and skills. SAMU's progress was adversely affected by administrative red-tapism and it was necessary to give it a support to enable it to emerge as a really good voluntary agency. It was also noted that the programme lacked support from the government, and the political will needed to be demonstrated more conspicuously. The functionality and awareness components of the programme had suffered at the cost of the 3 R's. On the positive side it was noted that SAMU had successfully involved the women, particularly from the backward communities, for teaching, learning and participation in cultural programmes. The researcher saw the possibility of greater cooperation from the people if its management was toned up and the loopholes were plugged. There was need of more dedicated and wholetime workers and trainers to tighten the programme. He suggested that in the light of shortage of trained manpower it was advisable to take up areas in smaller segments like blocks and consolidate rather than spread to larger areas.

Saldhana, D. *et al.* (1991) conducted a study entitled, "Institutions of higher education and extension: the case of adult education", and found that the extension programmes have not been integrated with higher education adequately, and it remains as a secondary function; the extension programmes had very limited impact on adult literacy. However, the community-oriented extension programmes linked to the curriculum were found to be more successful.

Saldhana, D. (1992a) studied the literacy campaign in Wardha district and found that the men performed marginally better than women in literacy; workers of the urban sectors performed better; women with no jobs performed better than women with jobs; instructors of the same sex influenced learning, especially of men learners; school students, teachers and unemployed youth got more involved in the teaching process; and the campaign created a pro-literacy atmosphere that was favourable to formal primary education.

Saldhana, D. (1992b) presented a consolidated report on the TLC in Sindhudurg District and came to the conclusion that learner variables, *e.g.*, female sex, higher age and the Buddhist community influenced literacy rates negatively; female instructors have negative influence on male learners; school-teachers and young enthusiastic people make good teachers; the Village Literacy Committee plays a major role in TLC and that it made a positive impact on the literacy rate.

Seetharamu, A.S. *et al.* (1991) studied the adult education programme in Karnataka State. They found that the performance of the AECs in terms of clientele attendance was: in SAEP, 80%; and in RFLP, 55%; the lack in motivation was found to be responsible for gaps in performance and the learners were forcibly enrolled; lack of effective monitoring was found to be the major reason for many dysfunctionalities like enrolment of the learners, appointment of instructors, supply of learning materials, training of functionaries, provision of physical facilities, etc. There were certain bright spots in the functioning of the AECs and the JSNs. To name a few: the class affinity between the personnel and the clientele; consideration shown to sex and caste in opening the centres, the practice of holding periodical tests and giving home assignments (?); remedial programme for slow learners; etc. In comparison to the districts having multi-political-party panchayats, the district having a single-party panchayat was found to work more efficiently in this particular programme. The MPFL run by the UGC was also found to be full of promise and potential.

Sharma, B. (1990) studied the role of adult education in the socio-economic development of the weaker sections in the rural areas of Uttar Pradesh (a case study of rural areas of Allahabad District). He found that the adults did not attend classes for the full duration; there was no proper motivation and everything was left to the instructor; lack of involvement of development departments in the programme was conspicuously absent; learning materials were not available; women were not attracted to learning literacy skills because their domestic responsibilities came in the way of sustained interest; and the number of drop-outs at the centres was fairly large.

Sharma, R.D. (1989) published a paper on the theoretical approach to adult learning. He has attempted to present the major contribution of various psychological theories of learning to the study of human learning.

Tantray, G.N. (1990) undertook an appraisal of adult education in Jammu & Kashmir and found that there was no survey undertaken for deciding the location of the AECs, and mostly they were opened on public pressure; instructors were identified from the local community but from amongst respectable(!) families who had some kind of clout with the Project Officers. These instructors were mostly youngsters having studied up to high school and took this work as employment rather than voluntary work. Although most of the instructors were trained, yet the quality of their training in terms of content, method and duration left much to be desired. The centres were in the houses of the instructors with little arrangement for lighting, etc. The learners came to learn the 3 R's and were in the age-group of 15-20 years, instead of 15-35 years. The teaching-learning materials were not provided in time. The role of the development department, though extremely important, was totally absent. The supervision was very poor and monitoring had been reduced to filling the proformae. Most of the learners could read the alphabets hesitatingly and could write them, though not correctly, and some could scribble their names, again incorrectly. Awareness had been found to exist but functionality was totally absent.

Thakre, P.G. (1991) studied the adult education programme launched by Nagpur University and assessed its impact on the target group. His conclusions were that the colleges in rural areas responded well and were involved with active participation in the programme but the momentum was gradually decreasing; the rise in the adult education programme was due to euphoria generated by the liberalism in releasing grants in the beginning and timely response given by the principals, professors-in-charge and the students; the decline of the programmes was due to the decline in the availability of financial resources, absence of the incharges and bifurcation of Nagpur University into two—Nagpur and Amravati Universities; the whole programme was considered as an appendix to the main functioning of the colleges and it did not attract the common masses; the programme was considered as an economic activity by the functionaries; absence of proper evaluation and non-existent accountability of individual and institutions were conspicuous. The impact assessment revealed that there was no significant impact; the criteria for selection of supervisors and instructors were disregarded; no valid evaluation of learners achievement was adopted; the remuneration to functionaries was too meagre to sustain interest; the learners maintained a distance from the instructors and did not share their learning problems, and there was a scarcity of learning materials, etc.

Sivapalan, U.T.R. (1991) enquired into the workers' education programme in Kerala with a view to suggesting improvements. He found that 'trade unionism' was closely linked to the workers' education programme and influenced the scheme very much; facilities for the unit-level classes in industries were not up to the mark; reading materials and related literature were not sufficient; rural workers and rural industries took the scheme more seriously; topics dealt within the unit-level class were generally limited to trade unionism, industry and labour legislations; the 'worker-teachers' were dissatisfied with lack of rewards, incentives recognition, etc., and modern methods and techniques were not used in the programme.

Upasani, N.K. (1988) studied rural enrichment/education project featuring development of alternating models and strategies for self-learning for the rural youths on topics relevant to their life. He found that all the students who were involved in bookbinding and making exercise books were confident of making the exercisebooks on their own; all of them (who were from Classes VII, VIII and IX) showed significant improvement in English vocabulary, pronunciation and spelling. He also developed a model for self-study for rural youths based on the experience of the study, which was found successful.

Verma, K.K. *et al.* (1992) evaluated PREAL through holistic study in the village Gomti in Vaishali district of Bihar and found that the PREAL had not significantly contributed to creating social awareness among the learners. There were many adverse factors for such a poor impact of PREAL, such as: faulty procedure of selection of instructors; selection of learners(?) without proper survey of illiterate persons in the village; inadequate training of the instructors; lack of proper supervision; delayed and inadequate supply of teaching-learning materials and other logistic support; lack of motivation among learners; and failure of other government programmes in the area. Based on these findings they have offered suggestions to remedy the situation.

Verghese, U.S. (1989) evaluated the teaching-learning materials in Malayalam used in the adult education centres in Kerala and concluded that different agencies working in the area are producing and using different primers for the adult education programme. There were 24 primers, four workbooks, three guides and two handbooks, out of which 'janabodhana sahayi' was the most used, and only four workbooks and two handbooks could pass the test of the criteria laid down for teaching-learning materials. These teaching-learning materials were not evaluated periodically and the workbooks and guide books were not prepared in relation to the contents in any particular primer.

Continuing Education

The researches in the area of continuing education are too small in number to give any indication of the trend. In fact, there are only three studies, and those too lie partly in the area of adult education.

Muthuchamy, I. (1991) studied the role performance of adult-continuing education *preraks* in RFLP of Tamil Nadu. This study could be in the grey area of both adult education and continuing education as *preraks* are not classified as adult learners though they are working for adult education. He found that the *prerak's* role performance was high as organiser of cultural and recreational programmes, recorder of educational activities and as supervisor. Their performance was low on the roles of organisation of literacy and post-literacy activities, teaching of literacy, dissemination of functional information, generation of awareness, mobilisation of resources, professional devotion and guidance.

Passi, B.K. *et al.* (1983) had developed a proposal for the creation of a department/centre of adult/continuing education and extension work but it hardly merits any analysis as it concerns itself with establishing a department, and that perhaps could perhaps give some indication of the growing trend in the field of adult and continuing education.

Rani, R. (1992) studied the involvement of the Avinashlingam deemed university in adult/continuing eduction programmes and found that the animators were able to make an impact on the adult learners specifically in the area of the 3 R's. This, however, has little to do with continuing education on the parameters laid down in the beginning of this chapter.

Non-Formal Education

The efforts in the area of Non-formal Education largely emanate from the scheme of Non-formal Education as implemented by the Government of India through the state governments and the voluntary agencies and autonomous institutions. The researches carried out in the universities and elsewhere revolve round the scheme, or development of materials for the implementation of the scheme. Very few works, independent of the governmental concerns, have emanated.

Arora, S.R. (1989) studied the administrative structure of the Non-formal Education Scheme and its supervision and monitoring. She makes an appraisal of the administrative aspects in the backdrop of the Programme of Action for the Implementation of the National Policy of Education (1986).

Das, T. (1989) while studying the effectiveness of the Non-formal Education in the district of Puri in Orissa, found that there was overcrowding in the çentres; in the same breath he says that only few students are coming to the centres regularly! He also laments that there was no uniformity in teaching hours in the different centres! (should there be uniformity?).

Dasgupta, P. (1990) again rests her study of the NFE Curriculum and Instructional Materials—their implications for instructional programmes—on the NFE Scheme being implemented by the state governments. She concludes that the different state governments have either adopted or developed NFE curricula based on the formal schools' curricula although there is an evidence of efforts being made to evolve problem-based integrated or partially integrated NFE curricula in different states. The approaches in development of instructional materials are divergent though not exactly innovative in the sense that these were earlier tried out under various experiments carried out under the formal primary education. Dasgupta found that there was need for more systematisation of the evaluation of the NFE children.

Grewal, J.K. (1991) while studying both adult education and non-formal education programmes in females, came to the conclusion that in the matters of non-formal education the motivating factors were related to age, marital status, caste and income; almost every participant was satisfied with the content and timings of the programme; about three-fourths of the participants were regular; age did not affect the rate of attendance but caste did, and it was significantly and directly related to income; non-attendance in the centres was attributed to the role of the learners in improving the family income. (Compare this with the satisfaction with the timings of the centre, and the genesis of NFE in the fact that the learner would be free to follow his/her economic activity and education would be so adjusted that the centres function according to the needs of the learners.)

Jha, M.K. (1992) evaluated the Non-formal Education Programme in Bihar which is a study of fifty primary-level centres and ten middle-level centres. He came to the conclusion that the honorarium of the instructors was highly unsatisfactory; the training was poor; and learning materials were inadequate and irregular, and thus the programme was ineffective in the State.

Mishra, R. and Mishra, S. (1990) studied the training inputs for non-formal education instructors whereby they tested a module and came to a conclusion that there was considerable transformation in the attitude and capabilities of the instructors after training. This may sound a paradox as this as well as the previous study of Jha, M.K. (1992) both were done in Bihar. But the latter restricts itself to the Nav Bharat Jagriti Kendra—a voluntary agency in the district of Hazaribagh—the agency which sponsored this study. They also indicate in this case that the instructors' performance in the field was encouraging and that they were making use of the training inputs to a large extent. Also, they found that the success of the trainees seemed to depend on the organisational climate, their personality dispositions and societal forces. They suggested that the instructors selected should have proper(!) aptitude and capabilities; training should be on the residential-camp approach(?) and should be conducted in a rural setting; it should be based on 'active and constructive participation of the trainers and the trainees alike'. They also suggested that constant monitoring should be an essential component of the training.

Mohanty, A. (1991) studied the reactions of the facilitators to the learning materials developed for non-formal education developed in Orissa. He found that while the format of the instructional materials was satisfactory, the time indicated in each capsule for the average learner was not appropriate, (Mohanty is considering the materials developed under Comprehensive Access to Primary Education Project). The capsules do not contain all the relevant information regarding the authors, publishers, etc., (Is it necessary at the primary stage?) He found that the content of these materials was very effective for urban, rural and tribal learners, although a few urban facilitators have pointed out the inadequacy of specific instructional objectives while still others have found it a little too difficult for the learners. The specific instructions to facilitators have been conspicuously missing. The language used was not within the understanding level of these learners and the presentation of vocabulary items had not been done properly with illustrations; the contents of the capsules were not found to be properly graded according to the difficulty level; also, the contents had not been hierarchically arranged from known to unknown. Mohanty's study brings out the inadequacies of the materials from the point of language textbook writing techniques and it should be a reminder to those who write these materials that these aspects need to be considered, except of course, that in the case of the modular approach each module is independent of the other yet is sequential in nature as in programmed learning approach. Mohanty was, however, convinced by his study that the only way to eradicate illiteracy was non-formal education. It may however be pointed out that Mohanty had seen NFE as a tool of eradicating illiteracy rather than as an alternative approach to primary education.

Natarajan, P. (1990) studied the role of non-formal programmes of education in promotion of literacy. It may be noticed that in the topic itself there was conceptual confusion as non-formal programmes (not education programmes!) as means of promoting literacy only. The objectives of the study were to assess the contribution of primary education to the enhancement of literacy and also of the non-formal programmes to the same end. It is matter of concern that Natarajan sees the entire primary stage as a literacy programme! Conceptual clarity is totally lacking in this kind of research and it throws a very poor light on the seriousness of the research. However—with whatever limitations—he came out with findings like there was increase in enrolment in some areas while in some other there was no increase. He concluded that drop-out and stagnation are the major problems of primary education and adult education. (Compare with the objectives!) In spite of this, the achievement is said to be encouraging.

Nayak, A. (1990) studied the entry-level characteristics, learning needs and occupational interests of non-formal learners and found that the non-formal learners in the age-group of 9-14 years generally came from the weaker sections of the society. On the basis of culture-free intelligence test scales and achievement tests prepared by the NCERT, with slight modification made by him, he came to the conclusion that their level of intelligence and achievement was not equal, but varied. He also concluded that the learning needs and occupational interests were also not equal(?). The factors affecting learning needs were habitation, family background, achievement, intelligence level, hereditary/parental occupation, socio-economic condition, etc. Nayak found the sex of the learner played a certain role in determining the learning needs and occupation. The reasons for drop-out were related to many factors, such as lack of parental interest, poor economic condition, behaviour of the teacher, etc. Among the reasons for not attending schools were found to be poor economic condition, lack of schooling facilities in nearby places, physical handicap of the learners, etc. He also identified eight learning needs: social recognition, economic development, better citizenship, vocational efficiency, cultural development, utilisation of leisure, successful family life, and understanding and manipulating environment. (I think Nayak means the motivational factors rather than learning needs). He goes on to identify 15 occupational areas for the non-formal learners: service, agriculture, business, technical and industrial worker, animal farming, weaving, pottery, clay modelling and sculpture, blacksmithy, fishery, goldsmithy, laundering, daily-wage earning, and household work. One can see that almost all the conventional occupations have been listed. There are many questions that remain either vague or unanswered.

Shakuntala, S.N. (1987) made a critical study of NFE for drop-outs and non-enrolled children of Karnataka State in the age-group 9-14 years. Although it was done previously to the period under report, her work was not included in the Fourth Survey. She found that the NFE centres were not located in a manner so as to be accessible to the majority of out of school-children; the community participation was minimum; the centres lacked several infrastructural facilities. It was not clear what the expectations of desirable infrastructure were? If it was the same as the primary school, then the NFE has no provision for that. The NFE scheme envisages a certain infrastructure and that has to be the yardstick for

measuring the sufficiency or otherwise. She attributed the non-participation of the girls in the NFE programme to the fact that the lady instructors were not there. She found that only 5.8% children from the NFE joined formal schools to continue their studies. She concluded that there was a need for expansion of the NFE centres in the immediate vicinity of the out of school-children.

Sharma, H.L. (1988) identified various approaches/practices of NFE in voluntary organisations. He found that all voluntary agencies laid down that the objective of NFE, as they understood it, was to provide primary education to the children who were not attending formal schools; the teaching-learning materials used by them in the NFE programmes were the same as developed by the SCERTs of their respective states; the training programmes for NFE instructors and supervisors are organised by SCERTs of the respective states; these training programmes were of a general nature and needed in-depth study; and, finally, the voluntary agencies had their own procedure for pupil evaluation. One can hardly come out with any specific inference for programme improvement from this study!

Shukla, N.N. (1988) studied the role of NFE in social change in Gwalior District. He concluded that: (a) the students in non-formal education developed socially with a little difference in the Scheduled Castes and higher castes students; (b) they developed democratic values and scientific attitudes; and (c) they had a desire to join the mainstream, specially the girls and the Scheduled Caste students. This study based its conclusions on a number hypotheses tested for significance by relevant statistical methods.

Shukla, N. (1992) undertook the preparation of tools and techniques for evaluating NFE children's achievement and reached the conclusion that instruction in the NFE centres had largely been based on developing the academic and national aspects of a child's personality; the vocational and social aspects had not been duly emphasised. There was a need for development of tools for evaluation of achievements in every field.

Sood, N. (1987) undertook an evaluation of the non-formal pre-school education component in the Mangolpuri ICDS block and concluded that although no definite picture could be drawn about the directionality of the better performing *anganwadi* within the ICDS groups, yet there was sufficient evidence to say that the ICDS group as a whole performed better than the non-ICDS group on all aspects of a development included in the study. Exposure of ICDS enhanced the overall developmental status of the pre-schoolers; children graduating from *anganwadis* perform better in schools; and exposure to ICDS raised the level of mothers' awareness about the value of pre-school education and the health/nutrition needs of their children.

Kumari, V.P. (1991) made a critical analysis of the difficulty levels of writing Telugu alphabets as perceived by teachers and learners in the formal, the non-formal and the adult education institutions. She categorised the alphabets into three groups as 'very difficult', 'difficult' and 'easy', based on the difficulty level of writing them (presumably the lexical difficulty) and she tested the siginificance of difference for each of the letters for each pair of subgroups.

Venkataiah, N. and Naidu, J.K. (1990) compared the drop-outs and non-starters on achievements and found that there was significant difference in academic achievements of the drop-outs and non-starters at the NFE centres, with the former having better achievement; there was significant difference between the academic achievements of drop-outs divided on the basis of the length of their primary schooling. No significant difference was found in the academic achievement scores between (a) drop-outs with three years and two years of formal schooling, and (b) drop-outs with two years and one year of formal primary schooling, but there was significant difference between the drop-outs with three years and one year of formal schooling in their academic achievement. It is not clear whether the gap between dropping out and restarting was kept in view.

Yadav, M.S. *et al.* (1990) made a rapid appraisal of the NFE-CAPE Programme in Rajasthan. They found that with over 10,000 centres working in the state with about 3 lakh learners, the attempt to decentralise the administration was a significant step. The involvement of the voluntary agencies was praiseworthy but their potential was not fully exploited for the cause. The State Institute of Educational Research and Training had the necessary expertise for training NFE personnel but it was found that they had insufficient resources in comparison to the enormity of task. They also found that training was crucial to the entire effort of NFE, CAPE material was found to be effective. At the same time it was found that the NFE curriculum fell short of the Minimum Learning Outcomes (at the time). Girls were found to prefer NFE to formal schooling. NFE was found to have a potential to cater to the needs of out-of-school children, and serious efforts were required in planning and execution to maintain the quality of education.

Future Research Needs

An analysis of the researches carried out in the area of Adult Education shows that out of 41 researches reported, as many as 16 are either evaluative in nature or are impact studies; 23 are applied researches; and one is developmental, and one, fundamental in nature. In the area of Continuing Education, there are only three studies of which two are applied researches, and one, a developmental study. It may, however, be stated here that even these three studies are overlapping with Adult Education and do not strictly fall in the area of Continuing Education according to our theoretical perspective set forth earlier in this chapter. Of the 20 studies in the area of Non-formal Education covered in this chapter, 13 are applied, five evaluation/impact studies, and two, developmental studies.

The one research in adult education classified as fundamental research may give us some kind of wrong notion of the attempt in this direction. In fact, this is a research article and not a full study and has some inclination towards fundamental thoughts, not exactly clarifying any theoretical concept or making any conceptual contribution. It would be seen from the foregoing review of the researches done in the period under review that applied and evaluation aspects have been rather more researched areas in the field of adult, continuing and non-formal education. Our first section has amply brought out that there is still scope for concept stabilisation in the three fields. To reiterate, it should be once again pointed out that the Continuing Education and Adult Education have overlapping fields, and there is a need for theory building so that a clear line of demarcation between the two is established. A similar situation exists on the international scene when adult and non-formal education are considered. However, with Ambasht's working definition in the Indian context referred above in this chapter, some concretisation has taken place in concept clarification.

Whereas, it is a welcome sign that the abundance of applied and impact/evaluation studies are undertaken in a developing society, it is also necessary that fundamental researches do find place in the scheme of researches in order to build up the body-politic of the knowledge. At least in these areas there is an emerging need to carry out researches of fundamental nature, and our future researches should give a certain amount of attention to this field. It is not denied that there is need for applied and evaluation studies. They are absolutely necessary for any developing society. For instance, there is an urgent need for more researches on the impact of the National Literacy Mission (NLM) on the literacy rate, awareness build-up and functionality components of the programme by researchers so that programme improvement may be undertaken if necessary.

The area of Continuing Education is still a very green area. The impact of institutions like open universities, open schools, directorates of correspondence education, are some of the fields in which one could take up researches. Studies of achievement through these institutions and through the traditional system could throw light on the relative efficacies!

In the area of Non-formal education too, developmental as well as impact studies are of prime importance because the field is growing and the massive programme is chasing the elusive target of universal elementary education.

(B) NATIONAL ADULT EDUCATION PROGRAMME: THE FIRST YEAR (1979)

Introduction

The present report is an appraisal of the working of the National Adult Education Programme (NAEP) during 1979. The programme was formally launched on 2nd October, 1978.

The most significant aspects of NAEP, perhaps are the flexibility of the approach built in it and the conceptual position which visualised as indispensable to the country's development. Naturally, there is a considerable variety in the type of programmes being organised and it has induced a fresh look at issues in education and development.

The appraisal could have been better and unequivocal if the data had been more complete, particularly about coverage of women and of persons belonging to the Scheduled Castes and Scheduled Tribes, and if some kind of verification could have been undertaken of the information furnished by the various agencies. However, this report contains enough information to justify the assertion that the Programme has indeed got off to a start.

Looking Back

"For the poor, education means food and clothing", Gandhiji said way

---

Source : Ministry of Education and Culture, New Delhi, 1979.

Note : Table numbers have been provided to confirm to Chapter numbers.

back in 1943. By putting it thus, he taught us that for education to be meaningful it must be correlated with the living and working conditions of the people. For Gandhiji education was the primary method of development.

Mahatma Gandhi's vision of people's education was built into the assumptions on which the Policy Statement on Adult Education was based. The publication of this Statement and the Outline of NAEP in January, 1978, was preceded by extensive consultations with political leaders, representatives of trade unionists, teachers, youth and of voluntary agencies. The University Grants Commission and the Association of Indian Universities also accepted this programme and made recommendations regarding the manner in which universities and colleges might contribute to it. The Parliament's Consultative Committee on Eduction and the National Board of Adult Education also lent their support to these documents.

The operational details of the NAEP were examined by a Working Group which comprised official and non-official experts. The recommendations of this Working Group were examined by representatives of the State Governments. The Policy Statement, Outline of the NAEP and the recommendations of the Working Group were considered and approved in a Conference of Education Ministers of all States in July, 1978.

When the NAEP was launched on the 2nd October, 1978 there was already a national consensus behind it. The launching of the Programme was marked by celebrations at the national, state, district and village levels. Practically every university and nearly 3000 colleges organised seminars of discussion sessions on the NAEP. There was an awareness among all that a momentous new programme was being launched.

The experience of the last one year reinforces the conviction that education can be a means of involvement of the poor and illiterate masses in the process of development. Also, during this period it has become increasingly evident that it would be wrong to assume that all agencies responsible for the planning and implementation of this Programme necessarily have a commitment to it. The mechanism of vigilance must remain active to deepen commitment and to warn against the persistent danger of the Programme becoming a mere literacy campaign, rather than a part of the country's strategy of economic development and redistributive justice.

Implementation Agencies

NAEP can be implemented only through a determined effort of all sections of society. It is not the sole responsibility of one department in the Central or the State Governments, not even of Government alone; nor is it only a partnership of educational institutions and Government, or of voluntary agencies and Government. A pre-condition for the success of the Programme is active participation of all sections at all levels, particularly in the field where the adult education centres are to be organised. From the very beginning, therefore, it was envisaged that a variety of agencies would share implementation responsibility. While the strengths and weaknesses of the various agencies would surface over a period of time, the size of the programme being implemented by them and certain perceptible trends are being described here.

The State Governments

While the State Governments have responsibility for implementation of all aspects of the programme through all the agencies in the State, they have a specific role to play as the largest implementation agency in most of the States.

Every State and Union Territory has taken steps for implementation of the programme. All of them have accepted the recommendation of the Working Group to implement the programme in the form of compact projects to be taken up in one or more blocks through specially chosen staff. They have also adopted the financial norms set out by the Working Group. The NAEP is mainly a programme for the rural areas, and even there the emphasis is on coverage of women and of persons belonging to the Scheduled Castes and the Scheduled Tribes. These priorities have also been fully accepted by all the States. They also accept that NAEP is not a mere literacy programme, but is an indispensable part of a development plan aimed at signficant amelioration of the condition of the poor through provision of a package of minimum needs.

While the will exists in the State for implementation of the NAEP, the progress of projects taken up by them has been uneven. While in some States—such as Bihar, Gujarat, Nagaland, Arunachal Pradesh and Jammu & Kashmir—not only the Centrally-funded Rural Functional Literacy Projects, but the projects funded by the State Government have also got off to a good start, the progress in most other States has been slow. Delays in laying down of new procedures for selection of personnel have necessitated deferment of the new programme in UP, Rajasthan, Maharashtra, Karnataka, Andhra Pradesh, Haryana, Manipur and

Sikkim. In most of the remaining States concrete steps for the start of the new projects are yet to be taken. They are continuing to run the earlier Centrally-funded or States' own projects. In UP and Tamil Nadu, owing to drastic reduction of funds, the programme being run in the earlier years with the States' funds has also been drastically reduced.

Voluntary Agencies

From the beginning of the Programme it was visualised that in addition to the State Governments, the voluntary agencies would play the most important part in the implementation of the NAEP. The Scheme of Assistance to Voluntary Agencies was, therefore, reviewed and the pattern of financial assistance liberalised. The voluntary agencies can now receive as grant from the Ministry 100 per cent of the programme cost and 75 per cent of the administrative cost. In accordance with the recommendation of the Working Group, it was decided that the organisations of the following categories, while they have an important role to play in the motivation of the learners as well as the various categories of functionaries, should not be eligible to receive financial assistance under the Scheme:

> The political parties and their mass organisations of women, youth, workers and peasants;
> All-India cultural, religious and youth organisations; and
> Federations/associations of teachers, employees and of trade and industry.

Concern was expressed in the National Board of Adult Education and in Parliament's Consultative Committee regarding mushrooming of voluntary agencies. It was, therefore, decided that only those voluntary agencies which have been registered for a year and have given some evidence of voluntary involvement in adult education activities, would be eligible for financial assistance. With the help of a number of all-India organisations—such as Indian Adult Education Association, Adimjati Sevak Sangh and Gandhi Peace Foundation—steps were taken to mobilise voluntary agencies for the NAEP. The voluntary agencies themselves have shown an enormous vitality and have come forward in large numbers to participate in the NAEP. There is now a visible resurgence of voluntary effort—and that is the most hopeful sign for the future of the NAEP. A remarkable feature of the last couple of years has been the participation in adult education of institutions of khadi and village industries of rural development and those which had so far been concerned exclusively with formal education. At present 603 voluntary agencies have been sanctioned funds for running 27,956 adult education centres extending in 17 States and 4 UTs. While the mobilisation of voluntary agencies in Maharashtra, Gujarat, Bihar, Rajasthan and Manipur is impressive, and it is picking up in UP and Karnataka, it is yet to take place in a number of other States like West Bengal, Assam, Orissa, Madhya Pradesh, Tamil Nadu, Kerala, among others.

Table 8.1: Statewise break up of Voluntary Agencies approved for financial assistance as on 1st September 1979

State/Union Territories	No. of Agencies approved	Amount of grant approved (Rs. in 00,000)	No. of Centres approved
Andhra Pradesh	8	7.43	440
Assam	8	4.94	300
Bihar	71	44.21	2750
Gujarat	112	123.39	7480
Haryana	4	3.28	200
Himachal Pradesh	1	0.77	60
Karnataka	25	18.48	1040
Kerala	12	9.56	460
Madhya Pradesh	24	14.40	905
Maharashtra	139	76.10	4430
Manipur	7	5.92	444
Orissa	18	11.69	620
Punjab	2	1.75	120
Rajasthan	66	50.48	2870
Tamil Nadu	23	24.30	1377
Uttar Pradesh	48	32.26	1590
West Bengal	11	8.81	570
Delhi	11	6.66	390
Goa, Daman & Diu	1	0.50	30
Mizoram	1	1.18	60
Pondicherry	1	0.49	30
All India Organisation	10	26.58	1790
Total	603	473.18	27956

A large number of voluntary agencies have the advantage of having served the community for which they now organise adult education centres. Besides, experienced and committed social workers generally guide the work of these agencies. However, it has been observed that most of the agencies are not able to visualise the developmental promise of adult education, and their management is in need of reorientation. There has also been criticism about the administration of the Scheme by the Central and the State Governments. Dissatisfaction has mainly been regarding the delays in processing of the cases of the voluntary agencies in State Governments and in release of funds by the Central Government.

Universities and Colleges

The University Grants Commission and the Association of Indian Universities have called upon all universities and colleges to actively participate in the NAEP. The Commission has issued Guidelines on Adult Education and Extension Programmes. The Indian Council of Agricultural Research has adopted these Guidelines for agricultural universities and other institutions of higher education being supported by it. These Guidelines commend running of adult education centres through university and college students and assure financial assistance for such activities.

It has also been decided to give much greater importance to adult education activities in NSS. The NSS and adult education personnel are working closely together in universities and colleges. A large number of seminars for involvement of teachers and students have been organised throughout the country. Detailed curricula for training of students and part-time supervisors have been developed and several institutions of higher education have shown interest in producing teaching and learning materials and in organisation of research and evaluation connected with the NAEP.

While involvement of universities and colleges is a nation-wide phenomenon, in the States of Maharashtra, Bihar and Tamil Nadu the enthusiasm evinced by them is most impressive. At the end of August, 1979, 49 universities and 515 colleges had been sactioned funds by UGC for running of adult education centres. In all nearly 80 universities and over 2000 colleges have decided to participate in the NAEP. Most of them are conducting surveys and organising discussions to determine the manner of their involvement and the size of the programme to be taken up by them.

The extent of involvement of universities and colleges has been a significant advance. Students and teachers of institutions of higher education can impart to the NAEP a dynamic and critical vitality. It is also probable that the involvement in this programme would bring the institutions of higher education closer to the community and would give to the students and teachers a challenging opportunity for giving practical shape to their idealism.

Nehru Yuvak Kendras

As a part of preparatory action for the NAEP it was decided to examine the manner in which the NYK programme might be dovetailed to the NAEP. The National Service Volunteer Scheme was also launched in 1977-78. It was decided to provide 2-6 National Service Volunteers for each NYK and to organise 15-20 youth centres (called *Chetna Sanghs*) through each NS Volunteer. A *Chetna Sangh* is an adult education centre with arrangements for sports and recreation, social service activities, cultural programmes and discussion groups. These *Chetna Sanghs* are also organised in compact and contiguous areas with special emphasis on organisation of rural youth. It has been laid down that 50 per cent of NS Volunteers should be women and 50 per cent of the *Chetna Sanghs* established should also be for women.

Only those NYKs where the incharge has had a one-month training in youth organisation and adult education, have been entrusted the responsibility of organisation of *Chetna Sanghs* through the NS Volunteers. There are 138 such NYKs, and the number of *Chetna Sanghs* being organised by each NYK varies from 30 to 100. The NYKs function with considerable autonomy and take their own decisions regarding the teaching and learning materials to be used and the details of the programme. In the past one year, the NYK method of organisation of adult education activities has developed as a feasible model of organisation of Government programme.

Employers

A consensus is now emerging among the Ministries of the Central Government regarding the role of public sector undertakings in organisation of adult education programmes. The arrangement which is acquiring acceptability is that as soon as a decision is taken to set up a large industrial (or mineral or power generating) plant, steps should be taken for education and training of the population which is displaced as a result. This is intended to be done by establishment of *Shramik Vidyapeeths* (Workers' Polyvalent Adult Education Institutes). The objective would be to prepare the displaced families for employment which would be offered as a result of setting up of the plant or opening up of mines.

This point can be best illustrated by citing examples. (1) Coal India Ltd., a public sector undertaking with operations mainly in four States, might organise programmes for all the illiterate and unskilled miners in 15-35 age group as well as their families within the next 3 or 4 years. For doing so, they will set up a separate organisation in each of their subsidiaries. (2) The Ministry of Energy is setting up a 2000 MW power generating plant at the cost of Rs. 7000 million at Singrauli. This is a tribal area and the setting up of a power plant would force a large number of tribal families to retreat into the interior villages. Massive investments of this size could mean considerable hardship for the local people. The Ministry of Energy plans to set up a *Shramik Vidyapeeth* from the very beginning of the project to train practically all the displaced tribal families. The expenditure will form a part of the cost of the project. (3) Steel Authority of India Ltd., a giant public sector undertaking, has asked all its steel plants to take up adult education programmes for all unskilled and illiterate employees and for the families of all workers. They have also asked the plants to organise adult education and literacy programmes, with skill training suited for the employment needs in the plants, for the illiterate and poor population of the district where the plant is situated.

Discussions have been held with the FICCI to create a similar interest in private sector. A number of private sector industries are already organising welfare and adult education programmes for their employees. Efforts are now being made to enlarge these activities.

Table 8.2: Statement indicating the number of Adult Education Centres running on 30-6-1979

States/ Union Territories	R F L P	State Govt. Projects	Voluntary Agencies		NYKs	Univer-sities	ICDS
			With GOI	Without Assist.			
1	2	3	4	5	6	7	8
Andhra Pradesh	584	330	288	214	1066	199	232

(Contd.)

Table 8.2 *(Contd.)*

1	2	3	4	5	6	7	8
Assam	2400	4200	270	—	238	66	127
Bihar	1490	1945	1936	—	399	64	309
Gujarat	2000	711	5342	1426	226	443	43
Haryana	2089	820	190	—	81	—	100
Himachal Pradesh	715	—	60	—	410		48
J&K	1143	231	—	—	68	—	94
Karnataka	880	—	458	6834	324	105	90
Kerala	1200	—	374	3490	378	—	122
Madhya Pradesh	3000	1300	778	170	620	88	180
Maharashtra	3314	530	3090	1224	—	465	142
Manipur	183	300	374	—	140	—	73
Meghalaya	165	178	—	—	—	—	50
Nagaland	340	200	—	—	3	—	20
Orissa	1020	1110	439	40	521	224	56
Punjab	—	—	120	—	236	38	100
Rajasthan	1369	1064	2600	—	414	—	85
Sikkim	170	254	—	2	4	—	64
Tamil Nadu	3600	—	1124	137	364	720	296
Tripura	608	1421	—	43	102	—	100
Uttar Pradesh	—	2457	1176	35	984	341	352
West Bengal	880	1825	380	—	296	845	255
Arunachal Pradesh	191	216	—	30	23	—	—
A&N Islands	60	34	—	3	4	—	—
Chandigarh	54	84	—	—	38	—	—
Dadra & Nagar Haveli	41	30	—	—	—	—	11
Delhi	241	270	—	2	109	70	100
Lakshadweep	30	—	—	—	—	—	—
Goa, Daman & Diu	—	—	—	—	22	—	—
Mizoram	160	70	—	—	—	—	—
Pondicherry	67	64	30	—	59	16	—
Total	27996	19644	19029	13650	7129	3684	3049

Source: Col. 2, 3 & 5—State Governments/Union Territories Administration concerned, Col. 4—The Voluntary Agencies, Col. 6—The NYKs, Col. 7—The University Grants Commission; and Col. 8—The Ministry of Social Welfare.

Resource Development

All educational programmes need a variety of technical services, such as development of curriculum, appropriate instructional and learning materials, training, evaluation, etc. In the NAEP these services have been described as resource support, and are expected to be relevant to the needs of the learners and to have sufficient flexibility for use in different kinds of programmes organised by different agencies. The importance of resource development in the NAEP is not only that it affects the quality of the programme, but, what is more important, effectiveness of the adult education functionaries and the motivation of the learners are related to maintenance of satisfactory standards in resource support. While considering the Outline of the NAEP, Parliament's Consultative Committee had desired that in implementation of the NAEP special importance should be given to resource development and that no effort should be spared for creating a satisfactory system for this purpose.

Curriculum Development

The Directorate of Adult Education had been undertaking extensive study of the subject of curriculum construction since 1976. Since the decision to launch the NAEP the Directorate has (a) prepared survey schedules for determining the interests and learning needs separately of rural and urban groups; (b) published a book on curriculum development; (c) worked out the norms in reading, writing and arithmetic which should be attained in the expected programme of 300-350 hours; (d) developed illustrative curricula for certain specific learner groups, such as small and marginal farmers of western UP, small farmers in the Mahendergarh district of Haryana and agriculturists participating in the Drought Prone Area Programme in Anantpur district of Andhra Pradesh. Some of the State Resource Centres—*e.g.*, the Indian Institute of Education, Pune, Tamil Nadu Board of Continuing Education, Madras, and Bengal Social Service League, Calcutta—have done a number of exercises in identification of interests of learners and in preparation of teaching and learning materials on that basis.

While some significant advance has been made in developing methodologies of curriculum construction, and most agencies producing intructional and learning materials have based their materials on some curricular objectives, yet systematic curricula have seldom formed the bases of teaching and learning materials in most cases. Development of competence in curriculum construction, based on systematically identified interests and needs of the learners, would be a challenging task in the coming year for all agencies concerned with resource development.

Materials

In the context of resource development materials include teaching aids, learning materials as well as post-literacy and follow-up materials. Materials are not confined to the printed word, but include a wide variety of media. When the decision was taken to launch the NAEP there were practically no materials in several important regional languages. It was, therefore, decided that priority should be given to production of satisfactory materials in all regional languages. As of now reasonably satisfactory materials are available in all regional languages, as well as in several important dialects. A beginning has been made in production of materials in the tribal languages, particularly of the North-Eastern region and the tribal tracts in the regions which border West Bengal, Orissa and Bihar. Materials are now available in more than 16 major tribal languages, in each of which the script of the regional language is used. Special attention has been paid to the need for creation of materials in Urdu, which enjoys a unique status as a minority language in practically all the states of the country. A large number of agencies administering projects have developed capability to prepare their own learning materials related to the development programme of the region and the problems of the learners.

The fact that considerable headway has been made in the production of teaching and learning materials must not blur the limitations in this sphere. Firstly, because the materials are, by and large, not based on scientifically developed curricula, they may not seem relevant to the learners. Secondly, it has not yet been possible to build a system of evaluation in materials development. Therefore, the process is still one-sided—from the professionals to the learners and not the other way round. Thirdly, there is excessive reliance on the printed word, to an almost complete disregard of the other media. Only minimal use is made of radio, TV, films, slides, etc., as supportive learning aids. Fourthly, well planned production of materials for post-literacy and follow-up programmes is yet to get organised. This is another sphere in which no further time should be lost.

Training

An appraisal of the past programmes had shown that the common weakness among them was the absence of satisfactory training. Therefore, considerable attention was paid to training from the very beginning. While planning for the NAEP it was envisaged that the Directorate of Adult Education and the State Resource Centres would develop training materials and would assist the other training agencies in developing training capability. The training of senior level personnel in administration, as well as among implementation agencies, was envisaged to be the responsibility of the Directorate of Adult Education. The responsibility for training of project officers and supervisors was to rest with SRCs, and other specially designated training institutes. The agencies responsible for implementation of the projects were to take care of the training of the instructors.

In early 1978, a four-week workshop of experts and field workers was organised in two parts, at Udaipur and Pune, to prepare a Handbook on Training of Adult Education Functionaries. The workshop was very successful and the Handbook was published by the Directorate of Adult Education in March 1978. It has provided the much needed practical guidance to the various agencies undertaking training activities. The Directorate of Adult Education has also published a number of other books to assist in organisation of training programmes. It also intends to get a number of films made for the training of the instructors.

Training of key personnel of various types has proceeded satisfactorily. These training programmes have included the following:

(a) Two reorientation seminars of District Collectors and senior officials of State Development Departments—organised at the National Institute of Educational Planning and Administration, Delhi (NIEPA) and the National Institute of Rural Development, Hyderabad.

(b) Two 2-day seminars, organised on regional basis, for State Education Secretaries, Directors of Education, State Adult Education Officers, etc.—sponsored by the Ministry of Education.

(c) One 15-day field operational training programme and three 6-day reorientation seminars for senior level administrative personnel, leaders of voluntary agencies and selected teachers from universities, one organised by NIRD and two by NIEPA.

(d) Eight seminars for university adult educators and National Service Scheme Coordinators—organised by University Grants Commission, Indian Universities Association for Continuing Education, NIRD and NIEPA.

(e) Three 1-week reorientation programmes for Youth Coordinators of Nehru Yuvak Kendras.

In addition, a large number of orientation and training seminars have been organised for key personnel in voluntary agencies. In organisation of these seminars the State Governments, Indian Adult Education Association, and the State Resource centres, and a number of voluntary agencies have played a leading part.

Training of project officers and supervisors has mostly been organised through the State Resource Centres. Governments of UP, Bihar and Maharashtra have decided to designate, in addition to SRCs, other institutions also for organisation of training programmes for project officers and supervisors. Most SRCs secure cooperation of some other agencies for organisation of these training programmes. With the exception of the North-Eastern region, satisfactory training capability has been developed for the personnel of these categories in all parts of the country and every agency which selects project officers and supervisors can expect to send them for training within a few weeks after their selection. While many of the training programmes lay emphasis on field orientation and use participatory and experiential training methods, some of the training programmes tend to be excessively lecture and classroom oriented. The duration of training is expected to be 21 days, but there is a tendency to reduce the duration on the ground that a second round of training is necessary after these persons have had some field experience.

There is a great variation in the manner in which training is organised for instructors. On the one hand, there are some agencies with considerable experience in organisation of training programmes and they organise intensive programmes for a duration of 3-4 weeks. A fair number of agencies organise the expected 3-week training programme, but there is much to be desired in the quality of their training. Most of the training progrmmes for instructors are for duration substantially less than the recommended 21 days. These training programmes are, moreover, organised in a routine and unimaginative manner. The number of trainees is generally so large that effective programmes are difficult to organise.

One of the significant gains of the last couple of years has been the growing awareness regarding the importance of training. While training arrangements for senior level personnel and for project officers and supervisors seem satisfactory, the expectation that each project agency would be able to organise satisfactory training programmes for the instructors has proved to be unrealistic. It has now been decided to create a District Resource Unit, mainly to improve the training of instructors. The District Adult Education officers, as the coordinator of the District Resource Unit, would assist, through specially trained resource persons, in the training programmes for instructors. In the coming year it would be necessry to strengthen the District Resource Units and to closely appraise the effectiveness of this training arrangement.

The Resource Structure

At the stage of planning of the NAEP considerable thought was given to resource structure—the type of institutional base needed, expectations from it and inter-institutional linkages. A decision was taken not to create new institutions at the national, State and district levels. The idea of developing existing institutions was preferred. The selection of existing institutions was to be determined by their capacity for nonformal and flexible approaches to technical matters. Even these institutions were not expected to become huge and unwieldy organisations—rather, it was felt, they should be able to coordinate the existing resources in the Government, universities, voluntary agencies, retired personnel, etc. They were to be guided by the proposition that while professional competence is essential for good performance, rigid and sterile professionalism, which builds a wall to exclude the so-called "uneducated" or lay persons as contributors to resource development, is to be shunned.

The Directorate of Adult Education

At the apex of the resource structure is the Directorate of Adult Education (DAE), a wing of the Ministry, which serves as the national resource agency. It advises the Ministry as well as the State Governments in all technical matters and also oversees the work of the various State Resource Centres and other agencies involved in resource development at the national and state levels. Since the launching of the NAEP some expansion of staff has taken place in the Directorate, but the emphasis has been on establishing mutually supportive working arrangements with a large number of international and national institutions and organisations. A special mention may be made in this context of the support that has been secured by DAE from the following :

UNESCO for organisation of population education and training programmes.

International Institute of Educational Planning, Paris, for improvement of evaluation and monitoring system.

Central Institute of Indian Languages and Taraqqi-e-Urdu Board for development of teaching and learning materials.

NCERT, including its various departments and Regional Colleges of Education, for development of teaching and learning materials, instructional aids, training and educational technology.

Family Planning Association of India and National Institute of Health and Family Planning for health education, population education and family planning input in the programme.

National Labour Institute and the Central Board of Workers Education for serving as resource agencies for various employers in the organised sector.

National Institute of Educational Planning & Administration and National Institute of Rural Development for training of senior level key personnel.

National Book Trust and the Directorate of Extension of the Ministry of Agriculture for development of suitable post-literacy and follow-up materials.

Indian Adult Education Association and some other voluntary agencies for dissemination of the concept and the Outline of NAEP and for training.

In addition the DAE has been able to establish cooperative arrangements with a number of university departments and institutions of social science research for resource support. While the existing support from these institutions relates mainly to evaluation and monitoring, it is intended to extend it to other areas, particularly research. Besides, to harness sophisticated new technology the DAE secures the assistance of expert agencies on an ad hoc basis.

The Directorate recognises that no single agency can provide expertise and resource support for the entire country. It has, therefore, encouraged all implementing agencies to develop their own capability in the areas of training, materials production, monitoring and evaluation, publication and dissemination, and research. To this end, the Directorate has lent its support through its technical personnel and funding. There is hardly any training programme, materials production workshop or training seminar held in any part of the country where the assistance of the Directorate is not sought. The Directorate deputes its technical staff to participate in these activities whenever possible. The Directorate publishes from time to time books and information materials. Among its publications are reference books, collections of articles on adult education, training manuals, seminar reports, research findings, prototype materials and publicity materials.

The Directorate has a unit which is concerned with the planning of the follow-up and post-literacy programme under the NAEP. As a part of this, it administers the scheme for holding a competition for books for the use of neo-literates. This unit is compiling lists of materials available for neo-literates. The Directorate also plans to organise regional workshops for the production of material for the neo-literates.

The Directorate has also provision for developing resource bases throughout the country in the area of population education. Technical staff in this area is available in the Directorate and collaborative progammes with the Ministry of Health and Family Welfare, Family Planning Association of India, and university departments of population education have been part of the regular functions of the Directorate. Plans for integrating population education with NAEP are being worked out.

State Resource Centres

It was considered necessary to identify in every State an institution which would be able to provide technical support to the State's programme. This is how the SRCs came into being. The idea of the SRCs has developed a good deal in the last couple of years as a result of the experiences gained and on the basis of the three Conferences on SRCs, organised in August, 1997, August, 1978 and May, 1979. The Ministry as well as the DAE have also been closely following the development of the SRCs and, in consultation with the State Government concerned, several measures were taken to strengthen them.

The functions of the SRCs are related to the specific needs of a particular State. There are, however, some functions which are expected to be performed by all SRCs. These are :

(a) Curriculum development and preparation of teaching and learning materials—publication of methodological guidelines as well as prototypes.

(b) Training of project officers and supervisors as well as of resource persons which would assist the District Resource Units, also publication of training handbooks and other aids.

(c) Post-literacy and follow-up materials—including review of existing literature, publication of new materials, issue of organisational guidelines.

(d) Evaluation, research and innovation—including formative evaluation of the activities of the SRC itself as well as other institutions and agencies cooperating in development of curriculum and materials as well as training, action research and publication of case studies on innovations.

(e) Assistance in environment building—through mass media, publication of posters and other material, exhibitions, etc.

(f) Other publications—including translations of the publications of DAE and other SRCs, knowledge building, books on adult and nonformal education, bulletins and periodicals in regional languages.

In practice all SRCs are not able to discharge all these functions. Special priority is given by all to production of teaching and learning materials and to training. In addition to the functions mentioned above, SRCs take up programmes and activities as they may consider appropriate. Many of them have also taken up small field programmes to serve as a laboratory for try-out of their activities.

In its working the SRC is advised by an Advisory Committee on which representation is given to the State Government, the agency under the auspices of which the SRC has been established, and some persons drawn from amongst implementation agencies. Although the staff of the SRCs has been increased on the basis of recommendations made by the Conferences on SRCs, it is still small. Like the DAE, the SRCs function in close cooperation with other agencies and individuals having interest and capability to support the work of the SRCs. It is also expected that rather than doing all the work themselves, the SRCs should "farm out" activities to other suitable agencies. Emphasis is also laid on taking of concrete steps by the SRCs for resource devolution, *i.e.*, training and guidance to the personnel of the District Resource Units and other local agencies which can provide locally relevant resource support to the implementation agencies.

At present there are 15 SRCs, providing technical support to 19

States. Four of the SRCs have been set up under the auspices of universities, and the rest with voluntary agencies. All large States, with the exception of Madhya Pradesh and Assam, are covered by SRCs. These two States are being provided resource support, to the extent possible, by the DAE, the NCERT and the Central Institute of Indian Languages. Some States which do not have suitable voluntary agencies or institutions of higher education—such as Sikkim, Nagaland, Andaman and Nicobar Islands and Mizoram—are either setting up State Institutes of Adult Education or are creating a separate wing for adult education resource development in their State Councils of Educational Research and Training.

District Resource Unit (DRU)

At the time of the planning of the NAEP it was envisaged that the project agencies would have considerable self-reliance in resource support, in particular it was expected that they would be able to take responsibility for training of their instructors. This expectation was based on the assumption that in each district there are a number of institutions and individuals who could cooperate with the implementation agencies in provision of resource support. This expectation proved to be unrealistic, mainly because effective arrangements for securing the contribution of the various agencies and individuals in the district was not worked out. A need was, therefore, felt to improvise an alternate arrangement for decentralised resource support, particularly in regard to training of instructors.

Meanwhile, reports were being received from a number of districts—such as Ranchi and Monghyr in Bihar, Bikaner and Udaipur in Rajasthan, and Baroda in Gujarat—of the various voluntary agencies having formed themselves into a consortium for mutual assistance. A large number of District Adult Education Officers have also been appointed and discussions with them revealed that they can play an effective role in coordinating resources support for the various implementation agencies, but some kind of formal structure would be needed for them to play this role. It has, therefore, been decided to create a DRU in each district. A DRU is a committee, with the District Adult Education Officer functioning as its coordinator, which can ascertain the resource needs of all project agencies and has the capability to provide essential resource support to them.

The main function of the DRU is in the area of training. It should be able to identify the training needs of the various project agencies. It should also be able to locate appropriate institutional arrangements and persons who could function as resource persons for the training programmes. Besides training, a DRU could assist the project agencies in project planning survey methods, introduction of locally relevant components in the curriculum and in selection of teaching and learning materials. As the project grows, the DRUs could also play an important role in planning and implementation of post-literacy and follow-up programmes.

It should be noted that the State Governments and SRCs have only recently been advised regarding the formation of DRUs. Keeping in view the importance of decentralisation in resource development, the idea of DRUs holds immense promise.

Resource Consciousness at the Project and AE Centre Levels

The objectives of resource development would not be fulfilled unless resource consciousness permeates at the project and the adult education centre levels. In concrete terms this means that the project agency should be able to secure the essential resource support, including the arrangements needed for organisation of satisfactory training programmes for its personnel. The monthly meeting of the instructors with the supervisors could become a means of programme evaluation and continuing education. The project agency should be able to circulate a bulletin to facilitate the instructor's work. They should have the freedom, as well as the capability, to introduce locally relevant issues in the curricular structure.

Similarly the adult education instructor should be able to depart from the curricular guidelines handed down to him. He should also be able to use locally available resources for improvising learning materials. Learning in an adult education centre should not be confined to a classroom, but should extend to the village-pond, fields, grazing grounds and forests.

Programme Management

The NAEP was started as a result of initiatives taken by the Central Government. From the very beginning, however, it was clear that the administration of the Programme shall have to be based on the principles of decentralisation and autonomy to the field functionaries. It was also emphasised that non-officials, and other persons with field experience must be involved in the decision making process at all levels. In designing the administrative structures, stress was laid not only on adequacy of structures, but also on proper selection of personnel and their training. It was hoped that women and persons belonging to the Scheduled Castes and Scheduled Tribes, who are to be given priority in the coverage would receive similar priority in manning the administrative structures.

The National Level

The National Board of Adult Education was established in August 1977. Its membership includes Ministers of Central Government, a Minister dealing with adult education from each of the regions of the country, heads of organisations such as the University Grants Commission, Central Social Welfare Board, Khadi & Village Industries Commission, Federation of Indian Chambers of Commerce & Industry, Indian Adult Education Association, and a number of other non-officials and field workers. Four meetings of the Board have been held since its establishment. The Board has set up the following committees to attend to specific tasks:

(a) Committee on Preparatory Action (since wound up)
(b) Committee on Motivation
(c) Committee on Voluntary Agencies
(d) Committee on Post-Literacy & Follow-Up Programmes
(e) Committee on Evaluation

These committees have met from time to time and have made recommendations to the Board, which the Board has generally endorsed. The Board has given serious consideration to the various aspects of the NAEP. Practically all the important decisions since the establishment of the Board have been taken in consultation with it. The Board has, by and large, appreciated the conceptual position and the operational outline of the NAEP. The Board has also welcomed the involvement of a variety of agencies such as the voluntary organisations, universities and colleges, employers, etc. The Board has, however, expressed concern about insufficient commitment to the Programme, particularly about involvement of voluntary agencies, in a number of States. It has also cautioned that unless vigilance is maintained, the NAEP could become a literacy drive, and the components of functional development and awareness building could get comparatively neglected.

The overall responsibility for administration of the NAEP rests with the Ministry of Education. It provides secretariat to the NBAE. The Ministry also deals with various inter-ministerial matters and generally oversees the implementation of the Programme in the States. The schemes of Assistance to Voluntary Agencies and of *Shramik Vidyapeeths* are directly administered by the Ministry. The Rural Functional Literacy Projects, under which a project with Central assistance is intended to be established in each district of all the States, as well as the schemes of Strengthening of Administrative Set-up are implemented through the State Governments. Under these schemes, funds are placed at the disposal of the State Governments and the latter implement the programmes in accordance with guidelines provided by the Ministry.

Apart from the Ministry of Education, other Ministries and Departments of Government of India have also taken positive steps for linkage of their programmes and activities with the NAEP. The Ministry of Social Welfare has expanded the programme of Functional Literacy of Adult Women as a part of Integrated Child Development Services Programme taken up in 150 Blocks. In view of the fact that there may be as many as 5 million blind and other physically handicapped illiterate persons in 15-35 age group, the Ministry of Social Welfare has set up a Planning Group to design an accelerated adult education and vocational training programme for those persons. The Ministry of Health & Family Welfare has decided to closely link health-care and family planning with the NAEP. This would be achieved through utilisation of Community Health Volunteers as adult education instructors wherever possible, and by utilising an adult education centre for discussion regarding problems of health-care and family planning. Practically all Ministries and Departments dealing with large public sector undertakings, as well as private sector industries, mines and plantations have issued instructions asking for organisation of adult education and skill development programmes for the personnel of the establishements. The Ministry of Labour has decided to enlarge the work of the Central Board of Workers Education to extend support to the NAEP. This would be done directly by organisation of adult education centres through worker-teachers and by reorientation of the staff of the 40 Regional Directorates so that they may by able to provide technical support to industries, mines and plantations. The various programmes of the Ministries of Agriculture and Rural Reconstruction are intended to be linked with the NAEP. Particular mention should be made of linkage with the NAEP of programmes of

agricultural extension, including Farm Information Unit and Farmers' Training, as well as the Ministry of Rural Reconstruction's Scheme of Training of Rural Youth in Self-Employment.

The State Level

During the First and Second Five Year Plans (1951-1961) administrative structures at the State, district and block levels were created with considerable care and imagination. Over the years, however, those structures got disintegrated in practically all States except Orissa, West Bengal, Assam and Meghalaya. Even in these States the structures lack vitality. The programme of the size of the NAEP cannot be implemented without adequate administrative machinery. It was, therefore, decided to set up in each State, as well as in every district, an office of adult education. In six States full-fledged Directorates of Adult Education have been set up, in the remaining of them the State Adult Education officer forms a part of the Directorate of Education (of the Directorate of Social Welfare in Madhya Pradesh). In most of these States senior officials have been put in charge of adult education, with necessary supporting staff.

In all States and Union Territories, State Boards of Adult Education, as well as Steering Committees have been set up. The State Boards are headed by the Chief Minister or the Education Minister, and include Ministers or Secretaries of the various development departments and a number of non-officials. While in some States, notably Bihar, Gujarat, Maharashtra and Rajasthan, the State Boards of Adult Education have met frequently and have influenced the State's programme, the meetings in other States have been infrequent and the State Boards have had little influence on the programme. Comparatively speaking, the Steering Committees, which are headed by the Chief Secretaries and include Secretaries of the concerned departments, Director of the States Resource Centre, and generally also a couple of non-officials, have been more effective. The Steering Committees have been providing means to overcome problems of coordination and have attempted to ensure that bottlenecks do not occur.

The District Level

At the district level the Collector (CEO in States like Maharashtra and Gujarat) is responsble for the steering of the programme. He is to function on the advice of the District Adult Education Board, the membership of which includes district-level development officials, educationists, teachers' representatives, persons connected with voluntary agencies, etc. The District Adult Education Officer is the Member-Secretary of the District Adult Education Board.

In view of the importance of coordination of the various development programmes with the NAEP and the significance of the district level in our administrative system, it was decided that a small administrative unit should be set up in all the districts. These units are, however, to be established as the programme grows, not mechanically in all the districts of all the States. By the end of August, 1979, sanction had been accorded for establishment of district administrative units for 163 districts in 13 States.

The District Adult Education Officer who is the head of the district administrative unit, has three types of functions. He assists the District Collector in arranging coordination and in the various promotional activities. Secondly, he is expected to generally oversee and monitor the programme implemented by the various agencies. Thirdly, he is the coordinator of the District Resource Unit. In this capacity he has to arrange necessary technical support, particularly in regard to training for the various project agencies of the district.

The district set-up is still in the process of being established in most States. While advice has been issued by the State Governments regarding establishment of a District Adult Education Board, they have not really become functional in practically all the States, Gujarat and Rajasthan being conspicuous exceptions. A number of States have appointed District Adult Education Officers. In some of them *e.g.*, Tamil Nadu, Kerala, Andhra Pradesh, Maharashtra and Gujarat—they have started to discharge their responsibilities. The reports from the districts show that several departemental functionaries are enthusiastic about the use of an adult education centre for extension of information and facilities.

The Project Level

One of the most important innovations introduced in the NAEP was the project approach—a more or less autonomous administrative unit responsible for implementation of a programme in a compact and contiguous area. During the last one year or so, the project approach has been fully accepted by the State Governments and the various other implementation agencies. Although it has not been possible to keep the boundaries of a project coterminous with a CD block, most NYKs and voluntary agencies have confined their activities to one CD block, the aim being to cover the entire illiterate population within the next 4-5 years. The Government projects are often somewhat larger and extend to two blocks.

Each project has a project officer, and a supervisor for a number of centres. The part-time supervisors in universities and colleges (they get Rs. 150 per month) oversee 10 centres and in most voluntary agencies and in NYKs a supervisor is responsible for about 20 centres. In projects administered by State Governments, a supervisor's responsibility extends to 30 centres. Since the projects are expected to be in compact and contiguous areas, and wherever feasible two or more centres are established in a village, the area to be covered by a supervisor is reasonably small and manageable. It is expected that a supervisor should be able to visit each adult education centre for which he is responsible at least twice a month.

The critical unit in the whole programme is the adult education centre, which is under the charge of an instructor or an adult education organiser. The instructor is paid an honorarium of Rs. 50 per month, and although initially there was considerable doubt whether persons would become available at this small honorarium, experience has shown that it is possible to find volunteers to take up this work. For these volunteers the amount of money is not the main consideration, rather they are governed by a spirit of service. Reports, however, continue to be received that the honorarium is too low to attract good workers. While practically all voluntary agencies and NYKs, as well as several State Governments, have preferred local village youth as adult education instructors, availability of a large number of unemployed trained "teachers" has made some State Governments give them a preference in appointment. Utilisation of the various development functionaries *e.g.*, community health volunteer, secretary of local cooperative society, milk collector, etc., as adult education instructors has been accepted as desirable by all implementation agencies. However, in practice, only rarely are these persons so engaged.

Similarly, retired personnel, particularly ex-servicemen, have not found favour with most implementation agencies. Experience has shown that an attempt to set up a large number of adult education centres without necessary preparation and without involving the community is counter-productive. The arrangement under which there is emphasis on thorough preparation and which envisages gradualness of expansion has been found to be much more effective.

From the very beginning of the programme, in accordance with the recommendations of the Working Group on Adult Education, all State Governments as well as other implementation agencies were requested (a) to ensure that at least 50 per cent of all adult education functionaries are women; (b) to give due representation in appointment to persons belonging to Scheduled Castes and Scheduled Tribes; and (c) to recruit personnel not only from the Education Department but from other development departments as well. While all State Governments, as well as other implementation agencies have made strenuous effort to appoint as many women as possible, their numbers are far below the recommended norm. Several reasons are given for this. Some point out that women supervisors are likely to find it difficult to travel alone in the rural areas. In regard to selection of women instructors they say that educated women are not available in the rural areas, and where they are, they seldom volunteer to work as instructors. It seems reasonable to say that while there are difficulties in appointment of women to the various posts, the implementation agencies do not fully share the commitment regarding the need to appoint women. Similarly, according to available reports, due representation is not being given to persons belonging to Scheduled Castes and Scheduled Tribes. As far as the source of recruitment of staff is concerned, while a number of State Governments have succeeded in attracting agricultural and animal scientists, social welfare officials, etc., the Education Department continues to dominate the source of recruitment.

Financial Arrangements

The estimated coverage under the NAEP during the Sixth Five Year Plan (1978-83) is 65 million. The requirement of funds for this is Rs. 6,860 million. Against this requirement the draft Plan document makes a provision of Rs. 2,000 million. This is mentioned as only one source of funds for the NAEP and it is suggested that funds for this purpose would also become available in other developmental sectors. The Commission has also stated that the present outlay will be stepped up if necessary on the basis of the experiences gained. The provision of Rs. 2,000 million is equally divided between the Central Plan and the State Plans. Besides, two of the Schemes for which funds are provided in the Central budget, namely Rural Functional Literacy Projects and Strengthening of Administrative Structures, are to be implemented through the State Governments and funds are to be transferred to them.

Apart from making recommendations regarding requirement of funds, the Working Group on Adult Education also made detailed calculations regarding per learner costs, administrative and evaluation expenditure, and expenditure on post-literacy and follow-up programmes. Per learner cost was taken at Rs. 80 per learner to which was added 10 per cent, being the administrative and evaluation costs, and 20 per cent of the total so arrived at (per learner costs plus administrative and evaluation costs) was taken as expenditure involved in post-literacy and follow-up programmes. The working group also recommended that all State Governments should accept this cost structure. It did, of course, add that this uniformity should be tempered by flexibility to accommodate special situations. The Working Group also emphasised the need for decentralisation in financial management. In making this recommendation it was guided by the past experiences in which funds provided, insufficient through they were, could not be used with effect due to excessive centralisation of financial powers.

Preparatory Year

During the preparatory year (1978-79) the costing pattern, as well as the desirability of flexible administration and decentralisation of financial powers, were accepted by all State Governments. Although the expected target of 1.5 million was achieved in that year, not all projects to be administered by the State Governments were regrouped and revitalised. Instead of starting with the Rural Functional Literacy Projects, as well as similar projects with State Governments funds, adult education centres continued to be run as before in most States. A number of States have, however, undertaken a review of their earlier Schemes and have taken steps to revamp them.

In the Ministry of Education the old schemes of non-formal Education for 15-35 age-group and Farmers' Functional Literacy Projects were merged into the modified Rural Functional Literacy Programme.The Scheme of Assistance to Voluntary Agencies and *Shramik Vidyapeeths* were revised on the basis of appraisals. The pattern of financial assistance to voluntary agencies was revised from 75 per cent to 100 per cent on programme costs and 75 per cent in administrative costs. In the new schemes of *Shramik Vidyapeeths*, the earlier schemes of Workers' Social Education Institutes and Polyvalent Adult Education centres have been merged. The *Shramik Vidyapeeths* are autonomous organisations the objective of which is to organise adult education and skill development programmes for workers and their families in the organised as well as unorganised sectors.

The Year 1979-80

Meetings of Working Groups, for each State separately, were convened in the Ministry of Education (October-November, 1978) before the exercises for preparation of Annual Plan 1979-80 were undertaken by the various State Governments. Keeping in view the importance of adult education, the existing size of the programme, and the capability of a particular State Government to consolidate and expand the programme, recommendations were made by the Working Group regarding the size of the programme to be taken up in 1979-80 and the financial allocation needed for it. The Planning Commission advised the State Governments that, keeping in view the fact that adult education formed part of the Revised Minimum Needs Programme, the allocation recommended by the Working Groups should not be altered while finalising the budget estimates for 1979-80. In the event, the recommendations of the Working Group were indeed kept in view by the State Governments in making provision in the budget for 1979-80. There was, however, a feeling in some States that adult education was a Central programme and that funds for it will be, or ought to be, provided in the Central Plan. Although an effort was made to clear this misunderstanding, it persisted in a few cases. This was one of the reasons why the financial allocations by some States such as Andhra Pradesh, Punjab, Tamil Nadu, U.P., etc., were substantially reduced. In the case of U.P., the reductions made were most glaring because practically no provision has been made in the Plan of the current financial year. These State Governments have been requested, even now, to reconsider the matter and made appropriate provisions.

The anticipation that the State Governments could provide approximately the same amount as the Central Government has not been borne out. Nor has the hope, that provision for adult education would be made in the various development sectors, been fulfilled. Although several Ministries of the Central Government have programmes which can be covered under the broad rubric of adult education, their provision rarely goes towards total anticipated outlay for coverage of a population of 65 million. The manner in which the commitment of the State Governments is to be retained, and extended to those States where it does not exist in the same measure, and how it is to be ensured that appropriate financial provision is made by them, will have to engage the attention of those responsible for planning and implementation of the NAEP.

Table 8.3: Allocation for Adult Education in States/Union Territories for 1979-80

States/ Union Territories	Plan (Rs. in lakhs)	Non-Plan (Rs. in lakhs)	States/ Union Territories	Plan (Rs. in lakhs)	Non-Plan (Rs. in lakhs)
Andhra Pradesh	30.00	16.76	Rajasthan	70.00	3.16
Assam	70.00	15.64	Sikkim	2.00	3.48
Bihar	80.00	13.86	Tamil Nadu	20.00	1.72
Gujarat	93.00	97.17	Tripura	15.00	77.41
Haryana	44.00	24.53	Uttar Pradesh	0.15	127.00
Himachal Pradesh	5.20	5.25	West Bengal	100.00	6.47
Jammu & Kashmir	25.00	20.74	A&N Islands	2.00	Nil
Karnataka	39.27	38.63	Arunachal Pradesh	5.00	Nil
Kerala	25.00	1.14	Chandigarh	2.80	0.02
Madhya Pradesh	100.00	48.62	Dadra & Nagar Haveli	0.50	Nil
Maharashtra	85.44	14.25	Delhi	25.00	30.30
Manipur	6.00	3.98	Goa, Daman & Diu	7.85	3.75
Meghalaya	3.00	11.99	Lakshadweep	7.74	1.28
Nagaland	7.00	4.51	Mizoram	2.01	3.41
Orissa	81.75	6.58	Pondicherry	3.00	1.09
Punjab	19.97	55.81	Total	987.68	627.62

Monitoring and Evaluation

In the context of the NAEP, monitoring and evaluation are regarded as complementary processes their aim being not to 'prove' but to 'improve' programmes. Monitoring is regarded as a process which helps in finding out the shortcomings or weaknesses of programme implementation and provides appropriate direction for applying corrective action. Evaluation is regarded as a more comprehensive, dynamic and development-oriented term and is regarded as a process for checking and improving all the stages of programme planning and implementation.

As recommended by the Working Group on Adult Education, the main responsibility for monitoring and evaluation of the NAEP rests with the Central Government, particularly the Directorate of Adult Education. Responsibilities, however, are being shared with the State Governments that are mainly responsible for implementing the adult education programme in the States.

Monitoring System

The monitoring and evaluation plan for the NAEP has evolved as a result of a national seminar held in New Delhi in August, 1978 and thereafter a series of 4 zonal seminars which were organised in February, 1979 in collaboration with the International Institute for Educational Planning, Paris. As a result of the consensus reached at these seminars and meetings, the following four critical areas have been identified for which monitoring is considered necessary for periodic attention and timely action.

1. *Financial aspects*—information relating to timely release of funds from the highest to the lowest levels, payment of honoraria to the instructors, etc.
2. *Administrative aspects*—information pertaining to the administrative structure for implementing the NAEP, appointment of personnel, creation of boards/committees at various levels, arrangements for coordination between different departments, etc.
3. *Academic or technical aspects*—information on programme content, availability and suitability of instructional and learning materials, training of personnel including provision for in-service training, etc.
4. *Physical aspects*—information relating to the number of centres in operation, location of centres, adequacy of seating and lighting arrangements, supply of equipment, attendance, coverage of women and of persons belonging to Scheduled Castes and Scheduled Tribes, etc.

A set of forms seeking the crucial information on each of the above-mentioned areas has been sent to the State Governments. With regard to levels of reporting, it was decided to restrict the levels to the minimum to ensure speedy flow of information. The data will now flow from the Instructor to the Project Officer and from the latter to the State Government. The State Government, in turn, will send a consolidated statement to the Directorate of Adult Education. At each level, however, quick feedback is visualised to ensure correction and improvement in the programme.

From this it is clear that there is now a shift, in emphasis from the earlier quantitative, target-oriented reporting, which tended to pay little attention to the content, quality and process of programmes. The new emphasis is on learning rather than on mere organization of classes and on making sincere efforts to improve the functioning of the centres rather than on mere reporting of numbers. Unfortunately, the ethos that has prevailed, and still continues to prevail, demands that the organizer of the adult education centre should report regular attendance of the prescribed 30 learners, or the Project Officer to report that all the sanctioned centres are running according to the prescribed enrolment, and for the State Governments to merely multiply the number of projects by the number of centres and the number of centres by 30. A new orientation has now to permeate the entire system of monitoring and evaluation. All the implementation agencies as well as the various types of functionaries have to know, and must be reassured, that correct and frank reporting would not be penalized; rather the purpose of monitoring would be lost if inaccurate reports are sent. Unless a new ethos develops that allows the functionaries to examine their own work and to make a constant endeavour to improve their efforts, the monitoring system will not be effective.

Evaluation

Evaluation can be internal or external. State Governments have been asked to prepare their own State plans for evaluation and some States have already taken the lead in initiating action on the preparation of such plans. Likewise, every project can work out mechanisms for self-evaluation or participatory evaluation. Thus instructors and supervisors could get together once a month and take stock of the problems faced, and consider how these problems could be solved. The advantage of the participatory process is that inter-learning can take place and, if carried out successfully, it could become a learning experience in itself.

One area that needs particular attention is formative evaluation. The importance of assessing the learners' needs, designing appropriate teaching and learning materials and providing feedback information so as to improve the effectiveness of the materials, needs to be better understood by the programme implementers. Likewise, evaluation has to become a part of the training programmes so that a constant effort is made to improve the training contents and training methodology. Efforts will now be made to strengthen the formative aspects of evaluation to ensure that better and more effective teaching and learning materials and better training strategies and programmes are evolved.

External evaluation has also been made an indispensable part of the NAEP. The objective of external evaluation is to secure veracity of the data furnished by the various implementation agencies and to involve institutions of higher education and of social science research in evaluation and research at all stages. It is also expected that external evaluation of this kind would caution the implementation agencies and would be an additional motivation for their sending correct reports. Besides, the informed public, who have been accustomed to questioning the accuracy of field data, would have access to reports from agencies whose credibility cannot be doubted.

In consultation with the State Governments concerned, it has been decided to assign responsibility for external evaluation to the following institutions of Social Science Research:

(1)	Sardar Patel Institute of Economic & Social Research, Ahmedabad	Gujarat
(2)	Indian Institute of Management, Ahmedabad	Rajasthan
(3)	Tata Institute of Social Sciences, Bombay	Maharashtra
(4)	Madras Institute of Development Studies, Madras	Tamil Nadu
(5)	Indian Institute of Economic Growth, New Delhi	Delhi
(6)	A.N. Sinha Institute of Social Sciences, Patna	Bihar

Negotiations are on for deciding the agencies which could take on this responsibility for U.P., Karnataka, West Bengal, Andhra Pradesh and Kerala.

The Sardar Patel Institute of Economic and Social Research undertook an appraisal of 47 voluntary agencies of Gujarat and published its report in January, 1979. (NAEP in Gujarat—An Appraisal). The appraisal revealed that 94 per cent of the centres included in the sample were actually functioning and the rate of drop-outs was only 2 per cent. It also showed that 43 per cent of the enrolment comprised women and the percentage of enrolment of Scheduled Castes, Scheduled Tribes and other backward classes was 75 per cent. Another finding of the Appraisal Report was that the element of functional development and creation of awareness had tended to be somewhat neglected in comparison to literacy and the quality of supervision and training was not quite satisfactory.

The Directorate of Adult Education convened at Ahmedabad a

meeting to which respresentatives of the State Government, Sardar Patel Institute, State Resource Centre and some representative persons from the voluntary agencies appraised, were invited. The meeting examined ways and means to reinforce the strengths of the programme and to find remedies for the weaknesses.

In the coming few months, it is proposed to make concerted effort to build up the monitoring system and an evaluation consciousness among the administrative, technical and field personnel.

Looking Ahead to the Second Year

The first year after the formal launching of the NAEP gives hope that the Programme can, indeed, be implemented if the flexibility is maintained regarding implementation agencies and programme content and if the commitment of the Central and State Governments not only continues but gets further deepened.

From the point of view of social and economic planning the main justification for NAEP is that it can involve in the process of development the vast masses of illiterate and poor people who have remained deprived. That this is possible has been shown by the performance of several projects. It has also been shown that if a proper environment is created, if the organisers of the programme are serious, and linkage with development programmes is visible, the inert and illiterate masses respond to the call with simplicity and enthusiasm. The task for 1979-80 is to intensify environment building activities and to create a conviction among the organisers of the programme, various development agencies and among the illiterate and poor learners themselves that real development is possible only by the involvement of the latter through a process of education.

Obviously, there are several areas of limited success, and some which may be considered as failures. In the latter category must be listed the absence of satisfactory training of instructors and the fact that, generally speaking, official and non-official functionaries are still preoccupied with achievement of targets rather than creation of a dynamic and development-oriented learning system. To these areas, and several other areas where success has been manifestly limited, a good deal more attention shall have to be paid in the coming year.

It would be only too easy to either rest on the limited laurels of success in the NAEP or be cynical because of the weaknesses revealed during the first year. Neither of these would be justified. What is needed is determination and a high degree of both commitment and optimism, for without these no programme of adult education can succeed in this vast country, where for generations people have learned to suffer and accept a fate which is imposed upon them by man-made conditions and circumstances. Education and organisation of the poor are that catalytic element which stimulates the process of development aimed at amelioration of the condition of the deprived masses.

Therefore, we step into the Second Year with greater confidence and stronger determination.

The thinking on adult education is based on the assumptions : (a) that illiteracy is a serious impediment to an individual's growth and to the country's socio-economic progress; (b) that education is not coterminus with schooling but takes place in most work and life situations; (c) that learning, working and living are inseparable and each acquires a meaning only when correlated with others; (d) that the means by which people are involved in the process of development are at least as important as the ends; and (e) that the illiterate and the poor can rise to their own liberation through literacy, dialogue and action.

(C) EXPERT GROUP ON STATUS-CUM-IMPACT: EVALUATION OF LITERACY CAMPAIGNS IN INDIA (1993)

Introduction

An Expert Group was constituted in April 1993 under the Chairmanship of Professor Arun Ghosh to undertake the Status-*cum*-Impact Evaluation of Literacy Campaigns launched in different parts of the country since 1991. The objectives proposed were as under :

(a) (i) To measure the outcome of literacy campaigns among learners/participants with respect to prescribed levels of literacy as per National Literacy Mission Norms.

(ii) To analyse the estimated number of persons made literate by gender, age group and social group (SC/ST and others).

(b) The process and effectiveness of environment building/mass mobilisation through mass literacy campaigns.

(c) Involvement and partnership between Government bodies and

Source : Ministry of Human Resource Development, Department of Education, New Delhi, 1994.

voluntary groups in literacy campaigns.

(d) Duration of implementation of the campaign with special emphasis on the duration of teaching/learning.

(e) Resources available and mobilised for mass literacy campaigns including the cost effectiveness of the campaign.

(f) To study and assess the fall-out impact of the literacy campaign on related socio-economic development programmes, such as primary education, health, nutrition, family welfare, gender sensitivity, women and child development programmes, national integration, etc.

The Expert Group held 19 meetings, interacted with a number of social science institutions and evaluation agencies, held extensive discussions with field functionaries, programme implementors, policy-makers, educationists, academicians and social activists, visited several States like Maharashtra, Goa, Gujarat, Rajasthan, Madhya Pradesh, Karnataka, West Bengal, Orissa, Bihar and Uttar Pradesh for on-the-spot study and submitted its findings on the evaluation of the Literacy Mission.

Recommendations

(a) Literacy Campaigns

1. Adoption of an appropriate approach for mass support from various quarters including a strong political commitment, constitution of a strong core group committed to Literacy.
2. Integration of TLC with NFE, improvements in the teaching learning materials, training and the monitoring and evaluation system.
3. Carrying out accurate initial survey of the non-literates.
4. Adequate facilities and provisions in the learning centres.
5. Constitution of a core group at State and district level to guide and support the programme.
6. Emphasis on voluntary character of this programme which was deemed essential for its success.
7. Concentration on Hindi belt where there are about half of the non-literates in India.

(b) Post-literacy Measures

1. Bringing internal evaluation procedure close to the external evaluation procedure and continuing interaction between internal and external evaluation agencies.
2. Adoption of adequate representative sample for reliable evaluation of TLCs, assessing at least 10 per cent of the learning centres.
3. Adoption of appropriate design for external evaluation based on stratified random sampling design including blocks, panchayats and villages.
4. Validity of target population and absenteeism.
5. Assessing at least 80 per cent of the learners.
6. Assessing the impact of the TLC and adopting proper procedure for storage of TLC data.
7. Conducting impact evaluation studies.

9

Adult Education and Women's Equality and Empowerment

(A) ADULT EDUCATION PROGRAMME FOR WOMEN

1.1 Women's Educational Deprivation

It has long been accepted that exclusion of vast masses of people from educational opportunity affects women much more adversely than men. This point admits of reiteration and elaboration. From the quantitative point of view the following tables bring out the size of the problems:

Table 9.1: Adult illiteracy in the age-group of 15+

Year	Total Population	Illiterate Population		
		Total	Men	Women
1951	2150.17	1735.73 (80.74%)	784.93 (70.6%)	950.80 (91.6%)
1961	2588.54	1870.02 (72.24%)	782.28 (58.55%)	1087.74 (86.85%)
1971	3178.25	2095.11 (65.92%)	863.80 (52.31%)	1231.31 (80.64%)

Source : Report of the Committee Appointed by the Ministry of Education and Social Welfare, New Delhi.

Notes : (i) Figures in brackets indicate the percentage of illiterate population to total population.

(ii) Table numbers have been provided to conform to Chapter number.

(iii) Para number refer to the para numbers of the document.

Table 9.2: Illiteracy among Scheduled Castes in all age-groups

Year	Total Population	Illiterate Population		
		Total	Men	Women
1961	644.17	578.01 (80.73%)	273.36 (83.04%)	304.65 (96.71%)
1971	800.05	683.71 (85.33%)	320.99 (77.64%)	361.72 (93.56%)

Table 9.3: Illiteracy among Scheduled Tribes in all age-groups

Year	Total Population	Illiterate Population		
		Total	Men	Women
1961	298.79	273.31 (91.47%)	129.59 (86.17%)	143.72 (96.84%)
1971	380.15	337.19 (88.70%)	157.99 (82.37%)	179.20 (95.15%)

The gravity of the problem is not uniform in all parts of the country, nor would any explanations be valid for all States. The basic problem is that the community, including the planners and the administrators do not accord to women's education the same importance as they do to the education of men. This arises from the visualisation of the role of women in family and society. In other words, women's educational disadvantage is both a symptom and a cause of their social oppression.

1.2 It has to be recognised that illiteracy creates the barrier to the realisation of the constitutional goals of social justice and equality of status and opportunity between men and women. The Report of the Committee on the Status of Women in India (1974) drew pointed attention to the failure of constitutional and legal guarantees in changing the lives of the vast masses of our women—because they do not have access to even knowledge about the status and rights that are guaranteed to them, or to the various programmes for social welfare and development that aim to improve their status. Policies to extend educational opportunities—both formal and non-formal—to women have failed to bridge the knowledge gap between the sexes which was emphasised as the main task by the National Committee on Women's Education (1958-

59) two decades ago.

Need for a New Approach

2.1 The reasons for this failure lie partly in the community's discriminatory attitude towards women and partly in the inadequate realisation among planners and administrators of women's multiple role in society. Viewing them primarily as home-makers, education for women was visualised mainly as an input to strengthen their roles as mothers and housewives. Both formal and non-formal systems emphasised the importance of household arts in women's education, ignoring the other reality that women formed a substantial and integral segment of the labour force in agriculture, industry and services. Failure to strengthen their productive and economic roles—particularly in the case of rural women—has also contributed to the gradual erosion of their economic opportunities, increased unemployment, mass poverty, and burdened them with exacting labour for inadequate returns, in addition to their housework and childcares. The lack of leisure for either education or entertainment is the one common reality in the lives of poor women in both rural and urban areas. Educational programmes for women should at least partially be out of the hours of work. An educational programme that includes improvement of productive skills and opportunities for alternative or supplementary employment is more likely to be acceptable to women.

2.2 This is not to say that women do not need, or want, other forms of knowledge. Health, nutrition, childcare and family planning, which feature in most adult education programmes for women, are vital because they help to strengthen some of their natural roles. What is missing is the understanding of equality of rights and responsibilities between the sexes, the view of women as individuals with basic rights to dignity and autonomy, not merely as instruments of production and reproduction. Mahatma Gandhi believed that a just social order would become possible when women recognised their historic social role, rejected their unequal position and actively involved themselves in working for social transformation.

2.3 The NAEP should therefore aim at :

(a) making women and men more conscious of their rights and responsibilities, the implications of the laws governing women's status in society and developing an understanding about the various, manifest and concealed ways which cause women's oppression;

(b) assisting women to achieve economic viability, through acquisition of literacy and other necessary skills and resources;

(c) providing women access to knowledge in other areas, particularly in health, childcare, nutrition, family planning etc.;

(d) assisting women to form their own groups for learning and productive activity, and to strengthen their participation and voice in the developmental process.

Operational Structure

3.1 The Policy Statement on Adult Education has stated clearly that the adult education programmes have to be relevant, flexible and diversified. In planning adult education programmes for women the following broad categories can be identified as they have reasonably well defined characteristics and problems which offer a base or an entry point for the programmes.

3.2 The most well defined and easily reachable category is that of women in the organised sector, which includes factories, mines, plantations, public undertakings like Railways etc. Their organised status and grouping and the fact that their employers are exposed to several forms of Government regulations suggest that it may be worthwhile to make a beginning with this category. Women industrial workers are normally relegated to jobs requiring minimum skills with lower remunerations and are denied training and consequent promotional opportunities. Their participation in trade union activities is low and with a few exceptions they are seldom able to organise themselves into pressure groups. Other characteristics of this group are mechanical relationship between employers and workers, low wages, insanitary and crowded housing, inadequate amenities and continuous drudgery—both in the home and at work. In addition to their double burden of house work and earning, majority of them have to face ill treatment, including physical violence from men in their families, particularly when the latter are under the influence of alcohol or drugs. These women are not always able to control even their own earnings.

3.3 The second category consists of workers in semi-organised industries, *e.g.*, construction, bidi, match, agarbati etc., and contract or casual labourers in various organised or semi-organised establishments. They suffer from all the problems mentioned for the first group but in more acute forms. In addition, women in this group are victims of various forms of exploitation—by employers and intermediaries as well as insecurity and stagnation at low levels of skill and wages. Unlike their counterparts in organised occupations, they enjoy no protection, either by law or by trade unions, and are not provided with essential services like maternity benefits, childcare or basic health care arrangements.

3.4 Generally speaking organisation of adult education programmes for both these groups would be facilitated if the employers could also be involved in the process. An illustration of their involvement would be by relieving women workers from duty for the duration of the adult education class, provision of facilities for organisation of classes on work premises and by expansion of the scope of the Workers Education programmes. The employers could also be persuaded not to discriminate against employment of married women and to provide facilities for childcare. It would not, however, be realistic to expect all employers in the organised or semi-organised sector to provide facilities without some motivation, such as tax incentives or rebate for loss of work, public awards etc. In the case of the semi-organised industries this may prove far more difficult as these establishments generally evade the long arm of public regulation by a variety of disingenuous ways. The greatest need of women in this category is unionisation, to strengthen their powers of collective bargaining, and the best strategy could be to make this the core of the adult education programme.

3.5 The largest category consists of rural women, whose characteristics and problems vary across groups. Since traditions play a more important role in rural society, it is important to understand these differences to be able to design appropriate strategies for education of adult women in the rural areas.

3.6 Traditionally most rural women have been integrally involved in the production and distribution of goods and services in agriculture, live-stock rearing, dairying, fishing, etc., in the primary sector, in cottage or household industry of all types, and in the traditional services *e.g.*, washing, retail distribution of various agricultural and industrial products in local markets etc. This, of course, is invariably in addition to servicing their individual families through cooking, clothing, childcare, nursing etc.

3.7 Traditional constraints on these multiple roles of rural women are primarily sociological. Women of high caste or aristocratic families are not permitted to engage in any economic activity outside their houses, so their roles are limited to processing/storage of agricultural products. Their responsibilities included feeding and health care of the labourers (and their families) as well as looking after the members of their own families. For women in the non-aristocratic groups, the only constraints were imposed by (a) the traditional division of labour between the sexes and consequent stratification of skills; (b) the position of their families in the rural hierarchy with its consequent taboos, privileges and pressures; and (c) levels of poverty and ill-health aggravated by frequent pregnancies and malnutrition.

3.8 For the women in this group, the landless agricultural labourer the small farmers, the artisan and the service castes, poverty manifests itself in over extended work days, scrounging for a living with low returns, minimum time and resources for family care and household activities, malnutrition and perpetual insecurity of life and living for themselves and their families. The introduction of a new crop, a new method, a new tool, of chemical weed killers, a drought, a flood can take away their precarious living, leaving them to join the ever-increasing group of perpetually moving migrant women—in search of some employment somewhere. If their traditional skills are no longer wanted by the society, they have no time to acquire new ones. They can become unskilled manual labourers in construction gangs, coolies or domestic workers in urban areas, or get recruited into anti-social, illegal, degrading or criminal activities.*

3.9 The contemporary scene, however, is in many ways different, and poses a challenge to the planners. The spread of modernization—in agriculture, industries and services—has resulted in a displacement of many rural women from their traditional occupations. Increasing complexity and commercialisation of all economic activities, the entry of science, technology and professionals, and of planned development by government have precipitated on gap between rural men and rural women, in access to information, skills and services. Inequalities have widened, and the impact of increasing differentiation between prosperous and improverished rural families have affected women even more adversely than men.

3.10 By and large this group is also afflicted by rigid caste formulations, and it would require an ingenious and enlightened educational programme for the women to overcome the barriers created by the caste system. Another characteristic of rural life is the absence of differences between girls and adult women and separate programmes for

* This may appear to be an impossibly bleak picture—but there is enough data, from both macro and micro studies to substantiate it as a generally prevalent pattern.

them may not be necessary.

3.11 Keeping in view the above mentioned characteristics it would be worthwhile to avoid organising the programmes for women in rural areas during harvesting or sowing seasons, and to give importance to some recreation to relieve them from day-long drudgery. The meeting time for adult education class for women who are engaged in wage earning activities may have to be late in the evening or at a time appropriate to their housework. At the initial stages, there may be no escape from organising programmes separately for different communities with provision for inter-communal participation. The class strength of 30 need not be insisted upon for women's classes.

3.12 In addition to agriculturists a fair number of rural women are artisans of one category or another. These include weavers, leather-workers, potters etc. Women trained and engaged in Khadi and Village Industries and on handlooms are often attached to an institution or cooperative society. Adult education programmes for these women can be generally facilitated if Khadi & Village Industries institutions, cooperative societies of handloom weavers or other sponsoring/marketing agencies could be involved in the programme.

Some General Suggestions

4.1 All adult education programmes for working women will need an understanding of the special problems which affect their participation. Some arrangements for childcare would be helpful to enable mothers to participate in these programmes. In some areas school students of the neighbourhood, or university and college students have provided these services as a part of NSS activity. This needs to be encouraged. Volunteers can also organise services to relieve women learners of some other chores, such as drawing water from the well, assistance in cooking etc. These activities, particularly systematic care of children of women participating in adult education classes should be a preferred activity under NSS.

4.2 Organising skill training—both to upgrade existing skills and to promote new ones—which may include productive, managerial, organisational and participatory skills tend to be somewhat expensive. It may become necessary to link them with other skill training programmes being organised by various development agencies that aim to promote supplementary or alternative sources of wage-earning. These would include artisan training by SFDA, programmes of the Khadi and Village

Industries Commission, programmes for promotion of handlooms, Rural Industrialisation Projects, Krishi Vigyan Kendras, etc. For this purpose it would be necessary to establish appropriate coordination—both at the Project and at the Centre levels.

4.3 Although the NAEP emphasises the 15-35 age-group as its main target, keeping in view the uninhibited participation of girls in all family-activities, the age criteria should not be enforced to exclude girls below 15 and women over 35.

Methodology

5.1 A good deal of thinking and innovation is necessary on the content and methods of adult education programmes for women. Whereas, literacy must form an indispensable component of such programmes, it would normally have to be preceded by several days of promotion of active participation by and consciousness building among the learners. Health programmes, particularly for their children, are known to interest women. They also have keen interest in affairs affecting their community and region. Learners can be helped to overcome shyness by organised discussions. In some cases it might be necessary to divide the class into smaller groups to help the participants' initial diffidence.

5.2 It would be desirable to organise seminars or discussion groups on local and regional basis to evolve suitable methods and materials with reference to the problems and conditions obtaining in different regions.

5.3 Discussion of their present predicament, leading to increasing awareness regarding women's status in society and the various instrumentalities for overcoming social, economic and civic oppression should form part of adult education programmes. It may be hoped such awareness would logically lead to formation of women's organisations—such organisations could be simple Mahila Mandals or Trade Unions or Cooperatives—to strengthen the women in asserting their voice more effectively in all decision makings.

5.4 Another aspect of programmes content and methodology which cannot be overemphasised is recreation and cultural activities to aid the learning process, without destroying their intrinsic value. This can take many forms such as :

— folks theatre
— community singing and dancing

— group games
— excursion to places of historical, religious and developmental importance
— film-shows, including feature films
— radio and T.V Sessions.

Instructional and Organisational Agencies

6.1 A crucial issue in organising a mass educational programme for women is the difficulty in obtaining women instructors. Although it is not essential that all the instructors must be women, (*e.g.*, farm women do not object to agricultural instruction from male instructors), the rationale and the strategy of the programme outlined above make it imperative that the major responsibility must be borne by women. In most earlier attempts almost total reliance was placed on women teachers or village schools. Although women teachers, who are interested and reside in the area where a programme is to be organised may become a suitable instructional agency, exclusive reliance on this category will not do, because the previous training and work experience of this group has not encouraged flexibility, innovativeness and dynamism. Owing to several reasons, women workers in rural areas are insufficiently paid and supplementation of their income can motivate them for adult education work provided they display the qualities needed for the approach outlined above. Such categories would include balwari and anganwari workers, gram kakis, grihalakshmis etc. In view of the massive nature of the programme visualised under the NAEP, other possible instructional agencies must also be explored. It is self-evident that the.majority will have to be women of the community for whom the programme is to be organised. There is likely to be a fair number of women who have had some education either in the formal system of education or under the Condensed Course Programme of the CSWB who might be motivated to take up this work.

6.2 Women's Colleges, particularly, Home Science Colleges, which already have some extension training component should also be invited to participate in this endeavour. Even, if these institutions are not able to undertake full responsibility for a complete project area, their involvement would be valuable for training of instructors and project staff, preparation of materials and experiments in programme organisation. Women workers need to be identified, suitably trained, supervised and guided, and enabled to develop a sense of confidence to shoulder this responsibility. Student groups can, if properly guided, play a catalytic role in the development of this programme and may even take field jobs during vacations.

6.3 The NAEP envisages that voluntary agencies, Government, universities, colleges and other educational institutions, employers, municipalities and panchayati raj institutions etc. all have a role to play in the implementation of the programme. There is a large variety of institutions which cater to one or other aspect of women's welfare. These agencies include Mahila Mandals, employment oriented training institutions, Nariniketans etc., as well as women's organisations like YWCA, AIWC, NFIW, BGMS etc. All these institutions should be advised to take up adult education programme for their illiterate beneficiaries.

6.4 The CSWB's earliest programme for Women's Welfare included adult literacy as an essential component. With increasing diversification of its activities and growing dependence on voluntary organisations, this earlier emphasis has been withdrawn. It is imperative to reintroduce it—particularly within the Board's currently expanding programme of socio-economic projects—so that they become models of integrated projects for women's development. The suggestion has already been made by the Working Group appointed by the Department of Social Welfare to formulate its 6th Five Year Plan. The same group also suggests that women's projects be developed around the ongoing and future ICDS projects initiated by the Department of Social Welfare. Another Working Group appointed by the Department of Rural Development, has recommended organisation of composite projects, including income generation, adult education and health and child care services through village-level organisations of rural women. The NAEP must establish coordinating channels with all these agencies, to maximise the effort and resources—both human and material—that would be needed to make this programme successful.

Adminsitrative Arrangements

7.1 For too long have men attempted to administer women's programmes and one of the tests of seriousness regarding extension of educational facilities to illetrate women would be the extent to which administrative responsibility is placed on women. This would include :

— adequate involvement of women at the advisory state, at the national, state, district and block levels;

— appointment of women in key administrative positions, again at the national, state and district levels;
— entrusting the operational responsibility of the programmes at the project level to women, particularly by appointing the majority of project officers and supervisiors from amongst women;
— involving women in resource development, particularly in preparation of teaching/learning materials and in training.

Only when the decision makers are convinced that in all such appointments preference should be given to women, who can empathy for the problems experienced by adult women, and may be expected to have a personal commitment to the cause of women's equality, would it be possible to develop the NAEP into a living and dynamic programme.

LIST OF MEMBERS WHO PARTICIPATED IN THE MEETING OF SUB-GROUP TO CONSIDER ADULT EDUCATION PROGRAMMES FOR WOMEN

EXPERTS

1. Dr. (Mrs.) Chitra Naik
   Director
   Indian Institute of Education
   "Prashant"
   49/A/23 Erandvena
   Pune-411004.

2. Smt. Anuthi Limaya
   Samajvadi Mahala Sabha
   250, K.Narayana Peth
   Pune-411030.

3. Smt. Ratna Kambla
   C/o Dr. Arole
   Janjhed
   Distt. Ahmednagar.

4. Smt. Elaben Bhatt
   Secretary
   Self-Employed Workers
   Association
   Majoor Mahajan Bhadra
   Ahmedabad.

5. Dr. (Smt.) R. Devadas
   Shri Avinashlingam Home
   Science College,
   Coimbatore.

6. Mrs. Veena Majumdar
   Indian Council for Social
   Science Research,
   Indraprastha Estate
   New Delhi.

7. Miss. Shanti Chakraverty
   Joint Director (Women's
   Programme)
   Directorate of Extension

Ministry of Agriculture
New Delhi.

8. Smt. P. Ramachandran
Joint Secretary
Department of Social Welfare
Minitry of Education & Social Welfare
New Delhi.

9. Smt. Shiela Trivedi
Principal
Family Life Education Centre, Literacy House
P.O.Alambagh
Kanpur Road
Lucknow-226005.

10. Kumari S. Anandalakshmy
Lady Irwin College
New Delhi.

OFFICERS OF THE MINISTRY AND DIRECTORATE OF ADULT EDUCATION

11. Shri Anil Bordia
Joint Secretary (N)
Ministry of Education & Social Welfare
New Delhi.

12. Shri J.A. Kalyanakrishnan
Financial Adviser
Ministry of Education & Social Welfare
New Delhi.

13. Miss. H.K. Singh
Deputy Educational Adviser
Ministry of Education & Social Welfare
New Delhi.

14. Shri M.C. Dubey
Assistant Educational Adviser
Minisrty of Education & Social Welfare
New Delhi.

15. Shri H.R. Gugnani
Assistant Educational Adviser
Minisrty of Education & Socail Welfare
New Delhi.

16. Mrs. B. Bhatnagar
Deputy Director
Directorate of Adult Education
J-17 Hauz Khas Enclave
New Delhi.

17. Shri B.C. Rokadiya
Director (PVC)
Directorate of Adult Education
J-17 Hauz Khas Enclave
New Delhi-110 016.

(B) REPORT OF THE TASK FORCE ON ADULT EDUCATION AND WOMEN'S EQUALITY

The Task Force on Adult Education and Women's Equality held nine meetings and consisted of the following members :

Ms. C.P. Sujaya, Department of Women and Child Development, New Delhi
Dr. Sarojini Bisaria, National Council of Educational Research and Training, New Delhi
Dr. Kumud Sharma, Centre for Women's Development Studies, New Delhi
Ms. Ranjana Roy, Balika Foundation
Ms. Jyotsana Roy, SRC, Bihar
Mrs. Bhatnagar, Directorate of Adult Education, Delhi.
Mr. A.K. Sinha, Director, Adult Education also attended two meetings and gave us the benefit of his views.

The Task Force Report is a self-contained one and dealt with several issues which are also being considered by the other Task Forces *i.e.* NIAE, Media, SRC, National Authority, MIS and Evaluation, Training of Instructors and Preraks and JSN and Supervision. It strongly recommended that these Task Forces should incorporate these recommendations in their reports and these should also reflect in the final report at the appropriate places. This Task Force requests the coordinators of the final report that this integration takes place so that they get implemented.

The National Policy on Education (NPE) envisages education as a powerful instrument for achieving basic changes in the status of women by (i) playing a positive interventionist role in the empowerment of women, (ii) contributing towards development of new values through redesigned curricula and text books, and (iii) promoting women's studies as part of various courses. It also envisages creating dynamic managerial, structures' to meet the targets and widen women's access to programmes of vocational, technical and professional education. Some of the basic parameters of empowerment are building a positive self-image and cohesion and group action for changing the social environment. In the following pages we have tried to operationalise the process of incorporating values at different levels of the learning process so that AEC is able to contribute it the empowerment of women through group dynamics.

(i) Curriculum Development

The curriculum development should reflect the values stated above, along with the contents of 10 core curricular areas as given in page 144 of the Programme of Action.There should be a continuous process of review and evaluation of all teaching/learning materials used for women's adult education centres and preparation of new material incorporating the values and ten core curricular areas mentioned above. The process of preparation of learning materials should be based on feed back from the evaluations, keeping targets and time-framers in mind. Organisations committed to women's development should be involved in this process of continuous evaluation. Instructors, supervisors, and SRC's, DIET's and DUR's with women's groups should be associated in the preparations of new materials. The values and 10 core curriculum areas should also be incorporated in the training modules of the instructors/ supervisors/adult education functionaries, at all levels.

Whereas the curriculum development and review have to be kept as on going activities, the post literacy curriculum would re-inforce and upgrade the literacy, numeracy already acquired. Post literacy programme has envisaged culling out elements for contents; the working groups to develop curriculum materials and packages will take into account all post literacy components (See Appendix 1).

(ii) Creating Favourable Learning Environment

Since any curriculum necessitates creating a favourable environment to achieve the goals and objectives of the curriculum conditions the adult education programme should ensure:

- creation of positive atmosphere in the general public where awareness of the AEP is highlighted;
- sensitisation of all senior officials, district level officers and officers involved in other development activities to adult education programmes;
- the development functionaries to be introduced to AEP to sensitise their departments as well;
- District Magistrates should get personally involved in the implementation of the AEP so that appropriate messages of

Table 9.4: Process of Empowerment of Women through Adult Education

	Objective	Type of Activity	Outcome	Time Frame	Remarks	By whom ?
1	2	3	4	5	6	7
Step One	Sensitisation awareness generation preceded by a survey on following : 1. Illiteracy-education-skill development-health benefits —increased income 2. Child rearing, health, control over body 3. Control over resources and income-decision making 4. Legal issues—abandonment, desertion, dowry, atrocities, property rights 5. Single, old, windowed women, Family Household 6. Alchoholism and drugs 7. Indebtedness exhorbitant expenses on marriage and death 8. Drudgery, hazards, technology support, Government's role	Meetings Home visits Cultural Events	Articulation on Women's issues—vocal section to emerge Identify Potential Learners	3 weeks	(Inclusive of survey)	Instructor helped by Prerak to be supported by local development functionaries.

(Contd.)

Table 9.4 : *(Contd.)*

1	2	3	4	5	6	7
Step Two	Engineer group solidarity on the basis of ideology as reflected in the values	Meetings Home visits etc. to be continued contact the development functionaries such as - Health - ICDS - RD - Non-conventional Energy - Contact women panchyat members	Emergence of (a) Learner's group (b) a group of articulate women (c) classes start	3 weeks	(Inclusive of survey) Location of Centre to be decided in consultation with learners	— AEC staff — Development functionaries — Panchyat Members (Women)
Step Three	Relate illiteracy to problems and issues identified	Selection of one issues and related to local context	Voluntary acceptance of legal programmes	First week of the life of the Adult Education Centre		Instructor
Step Four	Strengthen motivation and value orientation	Judicious selection and use of teaching material and other communication aids locally developed	The learners link lessons through words and symbols			Instructor

(Contd.)

Table 9.4: *(Contd.)*

1	2	3	4	5	6	7
		to strengthen the positive values through information such as responsibility for the sex of the unborn child is not that of mother. Learners to be involved in the preparation of communication material such as wall papers etc. during the classes.				
Step Five	Critical analysis of situational constraints and using collective strength as counter-vailing power	- Relating, learning exercises with everyday reality - Discussion methods of problem so long	An activated group for exercising their rights and changing their environment			Instructor

linkages are assimilated by development agencies in the district; Bi-annual meetings on AEP will be called by the District Magistrates in which all development functionaries of the District will be invited.

While the above steps would improve the general taking capacity of the district to adult education programme to create an appropriate climate, it is suggested that an Adult Education Centre should fulfil the following minimum environmental conditions:

— the AEC should be preferably run in a common place—community centre, primary school etc. However, if the community places are not available the AEC could function in the Instructor's house. The location of the AEC should be decided upon in consultation with the learners;
— the AEC should not be cramped, there should be enough space for the women to sit comfortably and write; mats should be provided for comfort;
— the time of the programme and the time of the day for running the Centre should be carefully decided keeping the nature and cycle of work in view;
— if the Centres run in the evenings the positioning of the sources of light should be such that each learners gets adequate light and the blackboard is also well lit;
— the learners should be seated in a way which facilitates interaction and which does not in any way reflect social distinction;
— the AEC should be done up attractively with posters, charts, slogans etc. which would attract learners and also help in reinforcing the skills in literacy and awareness they have already acquired;
— the surroundings of the AEC should be clean;
— model toilet facilities should be provided at a suitable distance;
— availability of drinking water, toilet, seating arrangements, space for creche etc. can also be facilitated if the AECs run in school premises or in an ICDS centre;
— a creche should be provided at the AEC to enable the women to attend and to concentrate in the class. The women could take turns at looking after the children or the sahayika of the ICDS Centre could be paid a token amount for looking after the

children out of the AEC budget.

The Adult Education curriculum in the final analysis must create a literacy milieu by pooling all its resources. The instructors with the help of the PRERAK should bring out a small wall paper, take help of the learners to post information on happenings in the village about the events like births, marriages, festivals, fairs, visit to health functionaries and any other available technological devices. Putting up sign boards where village events such as Panchayat meetings, visits of ANM's and other development functionaries from outside take place will help in creating literacy milieu in the location.

(iii) Training

Policy debates over the years have increasingly emphasised women's role as active participants and equal partners in the process of development and change. Only policy directives and suggested instrumentalities are not adequate to reach the objectives of women's development. A task force was set-up by the Department of Rural Development to suggest training modules for development planners and administrators to make them more responsive to women's development issues, as it was felt that new policy thrusts and approaches to women's development are not interpreted and communicated effectively within the existing institutionalised training programmes and understanding of key elements in women's development is necessary to work out appropriate strategies for training and orientation of key personal in development programmes.

Training is a complex but an integral function of the Adult Education Programme. Institutionalised and conventional training begins with the training of the trainers and then going down the ladder where each level of functionaries are trained separately *and there is no vertical integration in the training process*. The learning process, where trainers are expected to teach and trainees are expected to learn, needs to be reversed. TMEI recognises the need for revamping the training system by introducing participatory training process, increasing the number of days of initial training, provision of in-service and orientation through refresher courses. The TMEI also visualises increasing the number of women instructors by adjusting minimum qualifications and making arrangements for their continuing education.

Though training has been included as an inbuilt component of several schemes, competence in imparting training in a participatory way has always been rather limited. The need for new approaches and training strategies has been widely acknolwledged. Participatory training means something more than merely transfusion of information and skills and implies a definite role and participation as learners. Theoretical training in basic principles or objectives of the programmes can become infructuous unless it is concretised to show feasible and alternative ways of doing things. Structural training modules and capsules are alone the basis of the training programmes. Most of the training programmes lack practical learning situations. Instead of the 'process' the emphasis is more on content in most of the training programmes. The existing training programmes also lack an effective system of evaluation and monitoring regarding the effectiveness of training programme in communication ideas and skills.

(1) The common core curriculum for trainers and functionaries at different levels particularly for Preraks/instructors who are the key personnel in the programme, should incorporate values commensurate with positive changes in the self-image and status of women.

(2) Sensitisation of not only instructors and Preraks but also administrators and trainers by appropriate agencies at different levels through initial and in-service training and orientation and interaction through seminars/workshops should be taken up. An active involvement of concerned and committed agencies/persons involved in women's studies may help in developing training programmes.

(3) Training and communication is a continuous process. Unless trainers transform their attitude into one of respecting the dignity, intelligence and learning capacity of women and draw out their experience in searching solutions, it would be difficult to design training programmes according to specific situational needs, where people play a key role in identifying their problems and needs.

(4) Training should be need and information based and as such cannot be packaged in one short-term course. While Centre/State /District institutions will take the responsibilities for preparing materials and organising training programmes, it is also necessary to collaborate with institutions/organisations/resource centres specialising in women and development issues.

(5) For providing a better learner involvement, a learner centred approach is necessary where instructor acts as a facilitator by organising activities in such a way that enables learners to progress at their pace. For training of the key personnel, participatory training based on their

experience is recognised, however, actualisation of such training calls for considerable planning and innovativeness and flexibility regarding application. Proper orientation in concept methods/techniques and values is essential for field functionaries. NPE envisages that all NFE/AE instructors should be trained as agents of women's empowerment. This calls for considerable resourcefulness and imagination to train women instructors so that they can play an activist's role.

(6) Training of trainers—built in components on issues relating to women's equality.

(7) Seminars/workshops/orientation courses and training programmes organised by Institutions.

(iv) Monitoring and Evaluation

TMEI acknowledges that the monitoring system lacked credibility as there was considerable misreporting. It also envisages:

(A) A computerised Management Information system.

(B) Mission Management system for collection, flow and utilisation of information, systematic monitoring and mid-course corrections and impact evaluation.

(i) The village women's committee visualised in the report should be involved in evaluation, exercises.

(ii) Learners' participation in evaluation is important for an effective accountability system.

(iii) More emphasis on qualitative evaluation rather than quantitative assessment of physical targets achieved. The parameters for evaluation should be:

(a) values promoted through AEC,

(b) attendance and achievement of literacy levels,

(c) general awareness among women about women's problems and issues; awareness about their legal rights within the family at work and in the community and responsibilities. One of the objectives of TMEI is to make people aware of their deprivation and more towards amelioration of their condition through organisation and participation in development,

(d) improvement in access to health care (MCH, Family Planning, immunisation etc.) and other development programmes and inputs,

(e) co-ordination and linkage with other development programmes, ICDS, DWCRA, IRDP, Health and Family Planning),

(f) sending daughters to school,

(g) visibility in Community activities,

(h) acceptance of small family norms.

(iv) Concurrent evaluation of the programme on a larger number of indicators than on quantitative aspects. Centres/Institutes/Local women's organisations with commitment and competence should be involved in evaluation of programme. A list of such institutions must be maintained. Concurrent evaluation should be done by external agencies with the participation of learners functionaries.

(v) Evaluation of content of curriculum for both learners and trainers including techno-pedagogic inputs and information management and dissemination machanisms. It is expected that by 1990 facilities for literacy, learning, continuing education and vocational training will be extended to all parts of the country.

(v) Support Structures Participatory Development of Women

Women's participation in the Adult Education Programmes should improve their participation in other programmes of women's development. The convergence of all these programmes at the village level should be made possible by formalised and continuous interactions of the development functionaries in the village which can be facilitated by the Adult Education programme staff. The programmes benefiting women are illustratively listed below :

1. Development of Women and Children in Rural Areas (DWCRA)
2. Integrated Child Development Services (ICDS)
3. Maternity and Child Health (MCH) programmes and Family Welfare programmes.
4. Bio-gas, smokeless chullha and other new energy devices.

These programmes are implemented with the help of functionaries who are mostly women, such as:

— the DWCRA group organiser
— the Gram Sewak
— the Anganwadi worker
— the Community health guide
— the trained dai
— the Auxiliary Nursing Midwife
— the Chullha Mistry etc.

These development functionaries should form part of a women's Committee at the village level. The other members should be drawn from amongst the following:

— Vocal and articulate women from the target group in the village community,
— Women members of the Panchayat and Mahila Mandals,
— Women teachers,
— NFE instructors (Women).

The PRERAK / SUPERVISOR (AE) should be the convenor or the facilitator of the Committee. The frequency of the meetings of this Committee should be determined at each JSN level, but it should not be less than once a month. Since functionaries of many departments are involved the nodal responsibility of facilitating these meetings should rest with the Project authorities of adult education.

The village Education Committee will oversee Adult Education Programme in addition to NFE and Primary Education. In order to maintain functional co-ordination at this level between the two committees, women Instructor/ Prerak, Health and Rural Development functionary and few articulate women from the village Women's Committee should be represented as VECs.

The objective of the Committee will be as follows :

To cover the various programmes in an integrated and mutually reinforcing manner, on the target group of women, so that they are able to :

— create a demand for literacy as a right and to see it as a tool for development.
— maintain better health for themselves and their children.
— increase their earnings and at the same time improve their control over the increased income.

— improve both skills and knowledge.
— improve their physical environment.
— enhance their status *vis-a-vis* the other members of the community and their own family.

To achieve this desired convergence, the following steps will have to be taken :

I. Information Sharing

Complete information about the different programmes will be gathered and pooled for common use. This will consist, illustratively, of the following :

— A list of Anganwadi Centres.
— A list of DWCRA groups.
— A list of activities (economic, skill development) taken up by the DWCRA groups.
— The name of the ANM, and her schedule of visits to the village/ anganwadi centre.
— A list of Creches/day care centres/ balwadis functioning in the area.
— The name of the chullha mistry and her programme/schedule of work in the village.
— Information about family planning material availability.

II. Shared Use of Infrastructure/Resources

The different programmes mentioned above have built up various types of infrastructure over the years, such as buildings, sheds, teaching-learning material, toys, charts, kits, training equipment etc. Very often, the Adult Education Centres function in private houses/premises. The sheds built under DWCRA, the Anganwadi Centre, the Panchayat Ghar, Schools, the Village Cooperative Society etc. could be alternative locations. Schools have a built-in advantage because of their human and physical resources. The NPE emphasizes the role of educational institutions in programmes of women's development.

III. Use of Development Functionaries as Resource Persons

The development functionaries mentioned above should be used as resource persons for the adult literacy classes. The inputs provided by these functionaries should relate to the services delivered by the programmes in health, skill development, sanitation, maternal and child health and reduction of drudgery. The adult education instructor should, in turn, act as one of the resource persons, for the DWCRA women's groups, as well as other programme target groups. The Women's Committee with the guidance of the different authorities such as, CDPO, the Project Officer (Adult Education), the BDO etc. should work out these convergences.

IV. Formalised Interactions through Monthly Meetings

Each of these programmes involves a monthly meeting of different functionaries at the village/supervisory level. The adult education instructor should participate in the meetings held by the DWCRA and other programme functionaries. This schedule should be worked out at the JSN level.

(vi) Building of Group Solidarity

The Women's Committee should try to establish solidarity, through a process of coming together, of the target groups of women of the Adult Education Centre, the DWCRA group, the Anganwadi Centre, the Mahila Mandal or other women's development programmes. The coming together of the target group women, should be turned into a systematic process, which involves women in the analysis of their own situation. This systematic process should give women the skills and the confidence necessary to understand their own situation. It should then give rise to a collective effort to solve any problem arising from the situation. The collective effort should then lead to concrete action to change the situation.

In order to facilitate these processes, group discussions, data collection through surveys, or through discussions are necessary. These can be arranged by the Women's Committee in consultation with JSN and other development departments from time to time. However, a camp, or a workshop or a training programme at a place other than the village, preferably at the JSN level, can be used intensively as an educational as well as a reflective event. The camp should be organised over one or two days (at the maximum) with boarding and lodging arrangements. Women from nearby villages can all come together in an informal and free atmosphere , free from everyday burdens of work and pressures. This can take place once a quarter and can become an event the women will look forward to. The methodology should be entirely participatory. The Women's Committee and the target group women should consider these camps as a platform to exchange and share their work experiences, rather than as an event built upon a trainer-trainee relationship. These camps should offer opportunities for women to release their creative energies through songs, dance, role-plays and dramas. The camps should, therefore, be planned adequately in advance.

(vii) NGO's Involvement—Lessons

NGOs have a distinct advantage in being able to perceive the totality of women's situation and needs.This results in multi-dimensional and multi-directional approach which enchances the value of literacy since it links literacy to women's development in a more functional way. The valuable experience of NGOs should be used as learning and training material for functionaries of the government programme.

In view of the magnitude of the problem a fruitful and equitable partnership between the NGOs and the Government at all levels of the planning and implementation of the programme is necessary. Even while designing the programme, NGOs experience should be taken note off. NGO's experiences which have a potential for replicability should be made use of from redesigning and programmes. However, to facilitate greater involvement of NGOs and to motivate a larger number of NGOs committed to women's development, certain operational constraints need to be identified and removed.

Administrative procedures used to be streamlined and bottle-necks removed by (a) timely release of funds for more effective working, (b) more flexibility may also be allowed in the use of fund, (c) bureaucratic red tape should be done away with.

While it is strongly recommended that discrimination in selection of projects and VAs be exercised, unnecessary delays by the State Government in forwarding of scheme already identified results in their near collapse.

Instructors denied even of their pitifully meagre allowance, and lack of teaching material lose interest and learners enrolled after careful survey and motivation drop-out.

State authorities should call periodic meetings of VAs where project areas are demarcated after discussion according to the standing and evaluation of the organisations in their areas for more effective results.

(viii) JSN's Outreach Programme

The National Literacy Mission Report speaks of making arrangements for the continuing education of the women instructors. The design of the Jana Shikshan Nilayam envisaged in the Report, covering as it does, a cluster of 4-5 villages and a population of 5000, needs to be supplemented with a strong outreach programme for the women neo-literates. The double and triple roles performed by the women, inside and outside their homes, place constraints both on their free time as well as their mobility, making it difficult for them to attend the JSN evening classes, libraries, reading rooms, communication programmes etc. The presence of a strong JSN outreach in the village can be ensured by using the Women Adult Education Instructor as the Continuing Education Instructor. The human and physical resources of schools can be used for JSN outreach programme. Resources should be provided to the schools to provide support to Continuing Education Instructor. She should be given adequate technical, physical and financial supports to enable her to continue to discharge her duties in the village. Where there are more than one women AE instructor in a village, the village women's Committee will have to select a Continuing Education Instructor from among them, based on their previous performance, their rapport with the villagers and with the other development functionaries. The Continuing Education Instructor should continue to receive monthly remuneration on the same scale as the Adult Education Instructor. The village Women's Committee should continue to meet and provide overall supervision and guidance to the Prerak and the Continuing Education Instructor in facilitating and operationalising the convergences of various women's development programmes as well as maintaining group solidarity and cohesion in the village.

The Continuing Education Instructor should also maintain a continuous interaction with the Jana Shikshan Nilayam by frequent visits and close coordination with the Prerak. The National Literacy Mission speaks of evening classes, libraries, charcha mandals, training programmes, sports, adventure activities, cultural events etc. being planned and implemented as a phased programme by the JSN. The Prerak and the Continuing Education Instructor should ensure that as many of these programmes should be held at the village level for women, so that their full participation and involvement is ensured. A roster of these events to be held as part of the outreach programme should be drawn up for each JSN by the Continuing Education Instructor and the Prerak in consultation with the village Women's Committee. The CEI should regularly report to the village women and the neo-literates the programmes being run by the JSN.

The physical mobility of the CEI should be ensured, as this is one of the crucial factors leading to her playing an effective animator's role in the village. Subject to local conditions, a cycle could be thought of. In any case, financial support for her travel should be provided for by the JSN when budgetting the Women's outreach Programme.

The roles of the CEI and the Prerak are crucial to the success of the Continuing Education and Post-Literacy Programme. The need for unorthodox and innovative approaches has to be underscored by the JSN. A new understanding of women's problems and realities should be central to the approach of the JSN.

The right balance has to be struck between awareness and campaigning on issues and the battle to combat illiteracy. For this, no precise formula can be found to fit all situations. Every situation, every group, has its own dynamics. What is needed is sensitivity to these dynamics and flexibility and openness to changes in set patterns, whether of syllabus or other inputs.

The JSN should, therefore, internalise the premise that it is meaningless to run a literacy class in isolation of any other ongoing activity in a given area. The concept of intensive work in specific locations should, therefore, be adopted by the JSN. The strengths of different organisations, agencies and departments should be combined in order to strengthen programmes at the village level. The convergences and group awareness should be the objectives for JSN to work towards.

To attract more trained social workers who bring a greater expertise to the project it is suggested that at least the allowance of the P.O. of VAs should be at par with that given to government functionaries in similar positions.

NGOs may, however, be selected with care and their working evaluated and monitored periodically. Preference should be given in selecting NGOs in the field of women's development who are providing additional input of health, employment generation and linkages with other government development agencies such as DWCRA, CSWB, CAPART, STEP etc.

Appendix I

Post Literacy Components (P.L.C.)

— The P.L.C. would reinforce and upgrade the literacy, numeracy skills already acquired;
— the P.L.C. would provide a place for the activised group of women, formed during the literacy phase, to meet and discuss problem;
— solutions of problems which are local and effect their lives could be sought through solidarity and group action which is agreed upon in the P.L.C.;
— the P.L.C. which is to be called the J.S.N. would also be the venue where vocational training/information could be imparted by functionaries of various departments especially health and family welfare, rural technology-chulhas, latrines, biogas-nutrition, DWCRA, Dairy Cooperatives;
— some days should be fixed at the P.L.C./J.S.N. on which both men and women meet and discuss common problems;
— students of the local secondary schools or nearby colleges should be approached to help the various programmes of the P.L.C./ J.S.N.

(i) Family

— should be presented in a way that it is functioning as a unit in which responsibilities are shared;
— the role of the family as an institution should not be underplayed in respect of the changing role of women;
— all rituals which degrade women should be discussed and then rejected or a positive change and outlook be adopted—rituals like dowry, bride price, kanyadaan.

(ii) Political

— awareness of citizenship rights and duties
— encouragement to participate in public affairs and political processes
— women's role in the freedom movement to be highlighted with stories of famous women, stories of local heroines, if any.

(iii) Economics

- Dignity of labour of women to be projected, equal wages for equal work
- domestic work to be projected as productive economic activity
- equal participation in gainful employment.

(iv) Demography

- keeping in view the decline of females in the sex ratio in the country's population which reflects neglect of the female population, it needs adequate projection that women are as important as men for the good of the society.

(v) Geography

- to understand the interdependence of various geographical regions
- to understand special situation of the local area in the context of the country and world
- the role and division of labour to be understood in the light of geo-ecological conditions.

(vi) Science

- environment based-pollution, deforestation, soil erosion etc., cleaning of water sources, afforestation, soil conservation methods
- the sex of the child is not determined by the mother but by the father
- genetically and ability-wise women are equal to men, science and technology treat both equally and benefit both equally; they need higher levels of health care and nutrition because of child bearing and child rearing
- scientific knowledge of human physiology, especially reproductory systems
- age of marriage scientifically planned and suggested
- obscurantism and taboos with regard to sex, food etc. to be discussed and removed
- women who are trained in any vocation, skill, crafts should not

let their talent go a waste

— health of the family and child is the joint responsibility of the family, hygiene and adequate nourishment from local resources, hygiene etc. to be discussed, and also the affects health and nourishment have on the women as mothers, workers and as individuals.

(vii) Mathematics

— Work at the domestic level is equally productive and should be projected as a responsibility to be shared by all members of the family.
— Dignity of work in any walk of life should be reflected through exercises projecting computation of time, labour and energy consumed at each job.
— Growing participatory role of women in all walks of life must be reinforced and failure in participation must reflect on loss of labour force.
— Indicator of social, economic and cultural changes to be knit in mathematical exercises so as to imprint change indicators for raising aspiration level.
— Statistics on falling rate of female population should be used to indicate low status of the female child and women so that the learners conclude that equality in population size is a pre-requisite of equal status.
— Mathematics teaching must emphasise logical thinking so as to unveil evils of dowry system and bride price and bring out the importance of small family norm from the point of view of family welfare.
— Decision-making competence developed through mathematics teaching.
— In the context of equality of opportunities, to highlight through mathematical data that women can shoulder responsibilities equally.
— To help in the eradication of social evils such as dowry, death ceremonies, etc. by highlighting their arithmetical aspects.
— To minimise the allurement for gold, silver and other valuables and to increase the national resources by depositing in the saving banks.

— The biographies of women mathematicians and their contributions should be highlighted.

General

— stories of outstanding women in the freedom movement, sports, statesmen, philosophers, scientists and ordinary women around them who have been successful should be included;
— women should be viewed as part of the total situation;
— there should be equal participation of men and women in cultural-folk and tribal activities;
— women should be encouraged to make need-based expenditures and not to end up being considered as a 'symbol of the prosperity of men'.

This enumeration of contents is not exhaustive, keeping local practices and situations in view more could definitely be added.

APPENDIX II

State Resource Centres/DRUs

— to have a cell for women;
— to have exchange visits of functionaries to discuss and share their work experiences on various aspects of AEP for women;
— to have orientation courses for all their functionaries on the subject of Women & Equity in order to enhance their understanding, their empathy and their concern for the question on women;
— to share findings of special and experimental projects for women;
— to exchange teaching and learning materials which are produced by SRCs/DRUs;
— SRCs to have a strong research component to back up the work of material production, training, audio-visual materials and so on; and
— new and emerging technology should be visualised, analysed and utilised for input into the programme of JSN by SRCs and DRUs, especially in areas such as leather based, handloom weaving and spinning, collection of forest produce etc.

Table 9.5: System

Elements of Structure	Functions accorded	Women's question	Additional input	How to be organised	Watchdog functions
(1)	(2)	(3)	(4)	(5)	(6)
NATIONAL LEVEL					
(a) National Authority	Overseeing and planning	Ensure perspective on women's development throughout AEP	Integration of women's issues	Specialised Sub-Committee on Women	Department of Women and Child Development
(b) National Institute of Adult Education	Technical resource support	Facilitate and implementation of programmes ensure linkages in women's development	Budgetting, programming, resources for women's AE	A strong cell under a Joint Director	Women's bureau in the Deptt. of Education
STATE LEVEL					
(a) Commission Authority		Same as at National Level			Joint Director (Women's Development) in the Directorate of Education
(b) SRC	Training, technical resource support	Participatory training of women functionaries of AE	Involvement of women in preparation of programmes	A women's cell for functions (*see* appendix 2)	Same as above

(Contd.)

Table 9.5 *(Contd.)*

(1)	(2)	(3)	(4)	(5)	(6)
DISTRICT LEVEL					
(a) DBE DIET DRU	District level planning and administration programming	Identification and prioritisation of pockets of women's illiteracy	Micro planning skills	Specialised arrangements	Women's Education Institutes
PROJECT LEVEL					
Prerak/JSN	Organise AECs according to design organise continuing education, training	Participatory learning and programming, ensure women's participation, ensure support to CEI	Coordination with development departments and functionaries. Strengthen JSN outreach to women	Training, sensitisation and reorientation of Preraks	Educational Institutions for Women
VILLAGE LEVEL					
	Organise AEC and continuing education	Linkages, enhanced participation, value orientation, group solidarity	Investment of animator and catalyst roles links functionaries	Reaching common services to benefit groups of women	Village Women's Committee*

* VEC's have been organised in the TMEI to overcome AE, NFE and primary education programmes. The participation for having a separate women's committee and the need for representation of women AE functionary and other articulate women members on the VEC's has been given in the body of the Task Force Report.

(viii) Making the System Work

Educational infrastructure is riddled with multiple and parallel system and lack of co-ordination between them. It is important that the critical human and material resources should be geared to meet the challenge of attaining 100% literacy among women. In the Mission document it is visualised to build an infrastructure from National level to state, district and at JSN level. There is a need to invest more resources at the AEC level for both literacy and post-literacy programmes. Adult education programme could be linked with Operation Blackboard and both the schools and Village Education Committee involved. Mass literacy campaign should go along with mass mobilisation.

The POA visualises a management system of planning, co-ordination, monitoring and evaluation at each level through a network of cells within existing management infrastructure. The Task Force reiterates the urgent need to create and strengthen women's cells at every level of management system in Adult Education as indicated in the enclosed chart.

To attract more trained social workers who bring a greater expertise to the project it is suggested that at least the allowance of the P.O. of VAs should be at par with that given to government functionaries in similar positions.

NGOs may, however, be selected with care and their working evaluated and monitored periodically. Preference should be given in selecting NGOs in the field of women's development who are providing additional input of health, employment generation and linkages with other government development agencies such as DWCRA, CSWB, CAPART, STEP, etc.

(C) MAHILA SAMAKHYA PROGRAMME

The Mahila Samakhya Programme is a direct outcome of the commitment of affirmative action in support of women's education mandated in the National Policy on Education. A programme for women's education and empowerment, Mahila Samakhya endeavours to create a learning environment where women can collectively affirm their potential, gain the strength to demand information and knowledge, and move forward to change and take charge of their lives.

Education is understood as an ongoing process of learning and empowerment which transcends mere literacy. The programme, which is not constrained by present agenda or predetermined targets, responds and designs interventions to meet the articulated needs of rural poor women. The *sangria* (village level women's collective) is the nodal point around which the programme revolves.

The process of mobilising and organising women is facilitated by a *sahayogini* (a cluster co-ordinator in-charge of 10 villages). She is crucial link between the village Sangha and the district implementation unit of the programme. The latter provides resource support and inputs to meet the needs of the women. The district units in turn are supported by a State Office which ensures a facilitative environment and brings in necessary resource inputs for the programme. At the State level, an autonomous registered society as an empowered body has been set up to oversee the programme. At the national level the programme is coordinated by a Project Director. A National Resources Group, an advisory body of eminent women activists, academics, development workers and bureaucrats, supports the programme, bringing in new concepts, ideas and experiences and guides and advises on the programme, policies and strategies.

Mahila Samakhya has expanded its coverage to 31 districts in the country, while its approach has influenced several other educational proposals. Under Dutch funding the programme is being implemented in 2574 villages of 15 districts in the States of Uttar Pradesh, Karnataka, Gujarat and Andhra Pradesh. The effectiveness of the MS strategy in mobilising women for education has resulted in it being adopted by other basic education projects. Through the IDA assisted UP Basic Education Project, 6 districts have been additionally covered in UP. The programme is being implemented in 7 districts of Bihar as part of the Bihar Education Project and in 3 districts of Madhya Pradesh the programme is supported by the District Primary Education Programme.

Over the past several years the MS strategy has been validated in different regional contexts in the country. Womens' capacities and their information base are continually being enhanced, setting in motion a process of collective questioning and action. Vibrant and strong "Mahila Sanghs" or women's collective have evolved at the village level, thereby laying a foundation for women's empowerment at the grassroots.

The effectiveness of the MS strategy and its impact can be seen both in the rich texture of women's mobilisation and action as well as the various alternatives that the programme has thrown up. "Mahila Samakhya" in all States have engaged with a remarkable range of issues. The spheres of Sangha activity and action are ever expanding, ranging from accessing basic civic amenities; learning to deal with health issues; committing themselves to ensuring learning opportunities for their children, especially girls; doggedly trying to make themselves literate; breaking gender stereotypes in acquiring new skills like even becoming mechanics; learning to manage credit, effectively participating in Panchayati Raj processes; learning legal procedures and understanding how administrative and social structures work; gaining in strength to demand accountability and effective delivery of services; to confidently addressing issues like violence against women, child marriage and the devadasi system.

Women's Sanghas have taken an active lead in the area of children's/girl child education. The needs from pre-school education to adult literacy are being addressed.

In Gujarat, Early Child Care Centres are being run and managed by committees of *sakhis, sahayoginis* and *anganwadis*. These committees monitor the centres and mobilise local resources in cash and kind. In UP, the centres picturesquely called Udan Khatola, Hindola or Buransh cater to children who have dropped out, never gone to school and to pre-schoolers. Bal Melas and Bal Sabhas are periodically organised to enable children from various villages to meet and share their excitement. The teacher's (anudeshikas) skills are continually upgraded through a planned training programme. In Karnataka, some Sanghas are running balwadis with no financial assistance from MS except the initial setting up and training to the workers. These Sanghas are playing an active role in enrolling children into primary school.

Significant interventions have evolved specially in the area of girls/women's education. Bal Mitra Kendras (Non-formal education) for girls have been started in Andhra Pradesh to cater to the needs of girls. An important feature of these Kendras is the focus on establishing and creating a sense of partnership and ownership in this activity among the Sangha women, parents and the community. Sanghas and parents play a proactive role in selection of teachers, monitoring the centres and most importantly contribute financially to the teacher's fee.

The Mahila Shikshana Kendra (MSK) is a unique learning opportunity for adolescent girls and young women. This institution has evolved through the Mahila Samakhya programme and there is a major demand for setting up these centres in all MS districts and blocks. A residential programme, it varies in its focus and curriculum as it is designed to meet the specific local needs. There are 8 kendras being run in Uttar Pradesh, Andhra Pradesh, Karnataka and Gujarat. In Bihar 5 MSKs are being run by MS-BEP for school drop-outs and never enrolled adolescent girls. In Karnataka, the MSK helps and prepares school drop-outs to take school leaving examinations. In Andhra Pradesh, a one-year curriculum has been evolved to include basic literacy skills, health and environment awareness, mobilisation and vocational skills. In UP, an innovative and gender focused curriculum has been evolved along with the learners, whose ages range from 15 to 35. The duration of the condensed course is about 6 months. It is anticipated that the MSK would facilitate the learning and training of aware young women who will play a decisive role in the development of their communities.

Interventions for literacy have been propelled by the demand and desire of Sangha women to learn to read and write. In almost all instances this demand has emerged when women want to deal with issues like wages, savings, accessing government schemes, skills upgradation, interacting with socio-political structures. MS has responded to this demand by producing gender sensitive and learner friendly materials and through efforts to sustain the literacy efforts through camps/centres. In some cases linking up with on-going. Total Literacy Campaigns has also been done. In Karnataka, the Sanghas have awarded the title of "gnana gelathiyaru" or guiding light to women who have learnt to read and write and are now teaching others. The most significant achievement has been the training of neo-literate women in screen printing and production of broadsheets in Banda district of UP. The Mahila Dakhiya which is regularly published by Banda women, received the Chameli Devi National Media Award in March 1996.

To enable women to improve their health status, health awareness and trainings are systematically being imparted particularly in the States of Karnataka and Andhra Pradesh. As part of this training, herbal medicine, which traditionally was in the hands of women is being retrieved, documented and its usage validated. This has resulted in the emergence of Sangha women as health healers. Sanghas themselves are engaged in growing herbariums and keeping alive this indigenous knowledge system. In addition, Sanghas have also in many instances managed to enforce greater accountability from the health system and ensured that ANMs visit villages regularly. A health curriculum for adolescent girls is also being evolved in the States.

Learning to access and control resources has been an important objective of the learning process in Mahila Samakhya. To learn what resources are available, how to develop them to access fresh ones, the procedures involved therein, the bottlenecks likely to be encountered etc. are all part of the education that rural women find exciting and informative.

In Rajkot district of Gujarat, MS in collaboration with the District Panchayat and the UNICEF is involved in a major venture for handpump repair and maintenance through women's participation. This has meant training women as mechanics and the constitution of water committees. Discussions on health and environment have led to a variety of activities. In Banda district in UP Sangha women have been active in the Van Panchayat and afforestation programmes. In Andhra Pradesh's Medak district, as a result of health training, 830 women applied for and were sanctioned funds and materials for setting up toilets. An offshoot of this has been the initiation of training in masonry.

Savings and access to credit has been the focus of Sanghas in Bijapur district of Karnataka. With a savings pool of over Rs.7 lakhs, the Sanghas are now considering starting a rural women's bank. They have been able to negotiate with NABARD for income generation activities of their choice. The savings activities in all the States have led to training in accounts and record keeping and most importantly given a spurt to literacy activity. In all the States, strong Sanghas have now begun to consciously access schemes like DWCRA.

In UP, Sangha women and *sahayoginis* in Banda have formed a women's co-operative VANANGNA, which handles screen printing, handpump maintenance and contract jobs for masonry, as women in the co-operative are well trained to carry out these tasks.

Women across the MS supreme have confidently addressed issues of violence, child marriage and the devadasi system. In Karnataka and Andhra Pradesh the Sanghas have been effective in the prevention of initiation of young girls as devadasis. Legal awareness and education inputs are being run in all States. In UP the Saharanpur district unit provides legal support for registering cases of violence and assists in regular follow-up.

One of the most interesting alternative structures developed to deal with legal tangles issues, has been the setting up of a Nari Adalat in

Vaghodia block of Baroda district. Women have received para legal training and are handling cases relating to *stridhan*, maintenance, child custody and property disputes in community counts.

Taking conscious decisions and making informed choices have underlined the participation of Sangha women in all the States. This has logically brought women into the area of political processes especially at the local levels. Extensive dissemination of information on the provisions of the Panchayati Raj Act resulted in many Sanghas putting up women candidates and deciding upon strategies for election. 231 women from the MS programme in Gujarat, 135 in Karnataka, 120 in UP and 51 in Andhra Pradesh have been elected to various Panchayat bodies. Reports, particularly from Karnataka indicate that the participation of Sangha women in the working of the Panchayat is of a qualitively higher as they have shown themselves to be more aware, informed and articulate with gender-conscious agendas.

Empowering Women through Education

A corner-stone of the National Policy on Education is the removal of disparities in the field of education and to bring this about a well conceived edge in favour of women is posited.

Gender awareness, gender sensitisation and gender weightage are, therefore, ingredients in all educational interventions.

— One of the most successful efforts to link women's empowerment with education has been Mahila Samakhya. The programme is operational in 17 districts spread over the four States of Andhra Pradesh, Gujarat, Karnataka and Uttar Pradesh. The Samakhya approach begins with the understanding that women must identify their problems and evolve solutions at their own pace.

A critical factor in the process of empowerment has been the Sangha or women's collective. The Sangha is a forum where women can collectively analyse their problems and share their experiences. The Samakhya approach has been successfully adopted by several basic education programmes, including the Bihar Education Project, District Primary Education Programme in Madhya Pradesh and in Assam.

— The Total Literacy Campaign (TLC) has been successful in

raising the demand for education especially among women. In most of 417 districts, women made up over 60 per cent of adults enrolled in the programme. The classes have motivated women to fight for minimum wages and launch a crusade against prohibition.

In campaign mode, the programme actively seeks to attract women and girls to participate in the educational process. In 178 TLC districts, post-literacy campaigns have begun and these address the needs of neo-literate learners. TLC is gradually being extended in the educationally backward stages.

10

Statistics on Adult, Continuing and Non-Formal Education

Table 10.1 : Basic Indicators of Human Development

Year	Life Expectancy at birth+ (Years)	Literacy Rate @ (per cent)	Birth rate*	Death rate* (Per Thousand)	Infant Mortality rate*	Per Capita NNP at 1980-81 prices** (Rs.)
(1)	(2)	(3)	(4)	(5)	(6)	(7)
1951	32.1	18.3	39.9	27.4	146	1127
1961	41.3	28.3	41.7	22.8	146	1350
1971	45.6	34.5	36.9	14.9	129	1520
1981	50.4	43.6	33.9	12.5	110	1630
1982	NA	NA	33.8	11.9	105	1693
1983	55.4	NA	33.7	11.9	105	1691
1984	NA	NA	33.9	12.6	104	1790
1985	NA	NA	32.9	11.8	97	1811
1986	NA	NA	32.6	11.1	96	1841
1987	NA	NA	32.2	10.9	95	1870
1988	57.7	NA	31.5	11.0	94	1901
1989	58.3	NA	30.6	10.3	91	2059
1990	58.7	NA	30.2	9.7	80	2157
1991	59.4	52.2	29.5	9.8	80	2222
1992	60.8	NA	29.2	10.1	79	2175
1993	NA	NA	28.7	9.3	74	2243

(Contd.)

Table 10.1: *(Contd.)*

(1)	(2)	(3)	(4)	(5)	(6)	(7)
1994	NA	NA	28.7	9.3	74	2334
1995P	NA	NA	28.3	9.0	74	2449

NA = Not Available

P = Provisional

\+ Data for 1951,1961,1971,1981 relate to the decades 1941-50, 1951-60, 1961-70, 1971-80 respectively, centred at mid-point of the decade *i.e.* 1946, 1956, 1966, 1976. For 1983, data relate to 1981-85 centred at 1983. The estimates centred at 1988, 1989, 1990 and 1991 refer to the periods 1986-90, 1987-91, 1988 -92 and 1989-93. For 1992, it is based on the extrapolated values of the Standing Committee of Experts on Population Projection, centred at June, 1992.

@ Data for 1951, 1961 and 1971 relate to population aged 5 years and above and those for 1981 and 1991 relate to population aged 7 years and above . Data exclude Assam for 1981 and Jammu and Kashmir for 1991.

* Data for 1951, 1961 relate to the decades 1941-50, 1951-60 respectively and the estimates for 1971 and 1981 onwards are based on the Sample Registrations System (SRS).

** Relate to financial years 1950-51, 1960-61 and so on.

Source : *Economic Survey 1996-1997*, Ministry of Finance, Economic Division, Government of India, New Delhi.

Table 10.2 : Selected Indicators of Human Development for Major States*

States	Life expectancy at birth (Years) @ (1989-93)	Literacy rate** 1991			I.M.R. + Death rate + Birth rate (Prov. estimates of SRS-1995)		
		Total	Male	Female	(Per Thousand)		
		(per cent)					
(1)	(2)	(3)	(4)	(5)	(6)	(7)	(8)
1. Andhra Pradesh	60.6	44.9	55.13	33.72	66	8.3	24.0
2. Assam	54.9	52.89	61.87	43.03	77	9.6	29.3
3. Bihar	58.5	38.48	52.49	22.89	73	10.5	32.1
4. Gujarat	60.1	61.29	73.13	48.64	62	7.6	26.7
5. Haryana	62.9	55.85	69.10	40.47	68	8.0	30.0
6. Karnataka	61.9	56.04	67.26	44.34	62	7.6	24.2
7. Kerala	72.0	89.81	93.62	86.17	16	6.0	17.7
8. Madhya Pradesh	54.0	44.20	58.42	28.85	99	11.1	33.0

(Contd.)

Table 10.1: *(Contd.)*

(1)	(2)	(3)	(4)	(5)	(6)	(7)	(8)
9. Maharashtra	64.2	64.87	76.56	52.32	55	7.4	24.5
10. Orissa	55.5	49.09	63.09	34.68	103	10.8	27.7
11. Punjab	66.4	58.51	65.66	50.41	54	7.3	24.7
12. Rajasthan	58.0	38.55	54.99	20.44	85	9.1	33.2
13. Tamil Nadu	62.4	62.66	73.75	51.33	56	7.9	20.2
14. Uttar Pradesh	55.9	41.60	55.73	25.31	86	10.4	34.7
15. West Bengal	61.5	57.70	67.81	46.56	59	7.7	23.6
All India	59.4	52.21	64.13	39.29	74	9.0	28.3

* Major States include States with population of 10 million and above as per 1991 Census.

@ Data relate to average over 1989-93 as estimated by the SRS and centred at 1991.

** Relate to population aged 7 years and above for 1991 and excludes Jammu and Kashmir for All India.

\+ Infant Mortality Rate.

Source : *Economic Survey 1996-97*, Ministry of Finance, Economic Division, Government of India.

Table 10.3: Population Profile : India

(In lakhs)

1991 Census	Total	Male	Female
Population	84.63	43,92.3	40,70.7
Literacy Rate (%)	52.21	64.13	39.29
Non-Literate (7+)	32,88.8	12,83.6	20,05.2
Non-Literate (9-14)	3,55.5	1,38.7	2,16.8
Non-Literate (15-35)	12,12.9	4,38.9	7,74

Table 10.4 : Population Profile : World

(In lakhs)

	Total	Male	Female
Population* (1995)	5,71,50	2,87,90	2,83,60
Literacy Rate (15+) (%) (1995)	77.4	83.6	71.2
Non-Literates (15+) (1995)	88,47	32,00	56,47

**Source* : *Demographic Yearbook 1995*, United Nations, New York.

Table 10.5: Literacy Status in Some Asian Countries

Country	Total Non-Literate Population 15+ age (in millions)	Literacy Rate 15+ (%) (1995)		
		Total	Male	Female
1. South Korea	0.69	98.0	99.3	96.7
2. Philippines	2.23	94.6	95.0	94.3
3. Thailand	2.61	93.8	96.0	91.6
4. Vietnam	2.91	93.7	96.5	91.2
5. Sri Lanka	1.24	90.2	93.4	87.2
6. Indonesia	21.50	83.8	89.6	78.0
7. Malaysia	2.05	83.5	89.1	78.1
8. Myanmar	4.91	83.1	88.7	77.7
9. China	166.17	81.5	89.9	72.7
10. Iran	11.92	68.6	77.7	59.3
11. Iraq	4.84	58.0	70.7	45.0
12. Laos	1.17	56.6	69.4	44.4
13. Bhutan	0.55	42.2	56.2	28.1
14. Bangladesh	45.08	38.1	49.4	26.1
15. Pakistan	48.69	37.8	50.0	24.4
16. Afghanistan	8.16	31.5	47.2	15.0
17. Nepal	9.15	27.5	40.9	14.0

Source : *World Education Report 1995.*

Table 10.6: Highlights of 1991 Census : Literacy Rate State/UT-wise

A. High Literacy Rate (70 % and above)

(In percentage)

State/UT	Total	Male	Female
(1)	(2)	(3)	(4)
1. Kerala	89.81	93.62	86.17
2. Mizoram	82.27	85.61	78.60
3. Lakshadweep	81.78	90.18	72.89
4. Chandigarh	77.81	82.04	72.34

(Contd.)

Table 10.6 : *(Contd.)*

(1)	(2)	(3)	(4)
5. Goa	75.51	83.64	67.09
6. Delhi	75.29	82.01	66.99
7. Pondicherry	74.74	83.68	65.63
8. A & Nicobar Islands	73.02	78.99	65.46
9. Daman & Diu	71.20	82.66	59.40
B. Literacy Rate above national average and below 70 %			
State/UT	Total	Male	Female
1. Maharashtra	64.87	76.56	52.32
2. Himachal Pradesh	63.86	75.36	52.13
3. Tamil Nadu	62.66	73.75	51.33
4. Nagaland	61.65	67.62	54.75
5. Gujarat	61.29	73.13	48.64
6. Tripura	60.44	70.58	49.65
7. Manipur	59.89	71.63	47.60
8. Punjab	58.51	65.66	50.41
9. West Bengal	57.70	67.81	46.56
10. Sikkim	56.94	65.74	46.69
11. Karnataka	56.04	67.26	44.34
12. Haryana	55.85	69.10	40.47
13. Assam	52.89	61.87	43.03
C. Literacy rate below national avarage (52.2%)			
State/UT	Total	Male	Female
1. Meghalaya	49.10	53.12	44.85
2. Orissa	49.9	63.09	34.68
3. Madhya Pradesh	44.20	58.42	28.85
4. Andhra Pradesh	44.09	55.13	32.72
5. Uttar Pradesh	41.60	55.73	25.31
6. Arunachal Pradesh	41.59	51.45	29.69
7. Dadra & Nagar Haveli	40.71	53.56	26.98
8. Rajasthan	38.55	54.99	20.44
9. Bihar	38.48	52.49	22.89

Table 10.7: Distribution of Literates and Non-Literates (Among Population aged 7+)

(In million)

	Literates		
	Persons	Males	Females
All Areas	359.28	229.53	129.75
	(52.21%)	(64.13%)	(39.29%)
Rural Areas	226.14	151.21	74.93
	(44.69%)	(57.87%)	(30.62%)
Urban Areas	133.14	78.32	54.82
	(73.08%)	(81.09%)	(64.05%)
	Non - Literates		
	Persons	Males	Females
All Areas	328.88	128.36	200.52
	(47.79%)	(35.87%)	(60.71%)
Rural Areas	279.84	110.10	169.74
	(55.31%)	(42.13%)	(69.38%)
Urban Areas	49.04	18.26	30.78
	(26.92%)	(18.91%)	(35.95%)

Source : *Census 1991* (excludes J & K).

Table 10.8: State-wise Statement Showing Number of Districts Covered under Total/ Post-Literacy Campaigns and Continuing Education

State /UT	Total No. of Districts	Distts.covered under TLC (Fully/Partly)	Distts. Covered under PLC	Distts. covered under Continuing Education
(1)	(2)	(3)	(4)	(5)
Andhra Pradesh	23	23	22	8
Arunachal Pradesh	13	—	—	—
Assam	23	21	6	—
Bihar	55	32	8	—
Goa	2	2	—	—

(Contd.)

Table 10.8: *(Contd.)*

(1)	(2)	(3)	(4)	(5)
Gujarat	19	19	18	—
Haryana	17	16	2	—
Himachal Pradesh	12	12	11	—
Jammu & Kashmir	14	5	—	—
Karnataka	20	20	16	—
Kerala	14	14	14	14
Madhya Pradesh	45	45	12	—
Maharashtra	30	30	12	—
Manipur	8	1	—	—
Meghalaya	7	6	—	—
Mizoram	3	—	—	—
Nagaland	7	—	—	—
Orissa	30	20	11	—
Punjab	17	13	3	—
Rajasthan	31	31	12	—
Sikkim	4	—	—	—
Tamil Nadu	29	23	18	8
Tripura	4	3	2	—
Uttar Pradesh	68	68	8	—
West Bengal	18	17	13	2
A & N Islands	2	—	—	—
Chandigarh	1	1	1	—
Dadra & Nagar Haveli	1	1	—	—
Daman & Diu	2	1	—	—
Delhi	1	1	—	—
Lakshadweep	1	—	—	—
Pondicherry	4	4	4	4
Total	525	429	193	36

Table 10.9: Statement of Grants Released in respect of Total/Post-Literacy Campaigns 1992-93 to 1996-97

(In lakhs)

State /UT	1992-93	1993-94	1994-95	1995-96	1996-97
Andhra Pradesh	7,01.66	17,19.74	11.06.93	6,11.50	1,28.41
Assam	65.00	25.00	10,14.67	2,48.70	1,06.55
Bihar	1,25.00	8,74.08	13,11.00	16,76.73	7,43.45
Chandigarh	15.00	18.00	—	—	11.50
Daman & Diu	—	1.40	—	—	—
Dadra & N Haveli	—	—	17.00	—	—
Delhi	18.35	55.43	56.53	2,98.44	—
Goa	—	—	—	—	—
Gujarat	4,95.00	8,35.55	5,83.30	35.00	3,59.91
Haryana	2,95.00	1,81.05	2,32.42	1,41.43	35.44
Himachal Pradesh	2,11.00	64.67	92.87	11.14	35.79
Jammu & Kashmir	—	—	25.00	1,00.00	30.00
Karnataka	6,27.90	14,94.83	8,16.45	1,40.83	1,91.49
Kerala	—	1,00.00	—	—	—
Madhya Pradesh	1,40.00	11,60.99	25,11.99	6,90.20	3,43.84
Maharashtra	6,30.00	6,77.27	5,58.03	71,7.77	2,77.54
Manipur	—	—	—	—	—
Meghalaya	—	—	—	94.65	1,01.00
Orissa	4,68.00	4,32.38	4,22.95	6,27.05	1,93.42
Pondicherry	—	—	—	—	—
Punjab	—	25.00	2,61.34	3,44.47	1,35.00
Rajasthan	2,20.00	5,01.97	13.37.24	14,23.36	11,15.86
Tamil Nadu	11,46.00	9,26.00	11,51.53	9,64.82	1,01.22
Tripura	—	222.45	—	—	—
Uttar Pradesh	6,85.00	22,12.88	23,44.43	15,04.44	6,28.38
West Bengal	10,69.00	5,83.65	13,53.12	2,38.00	1,75.25
Total	69,11.91	1,21,12.34	1,51,96.80	98,68.53	47,14.05

Table 10.10: Number of School Level Teachers by Sex, India—1950-51 to 1995-96

(In 000)

	Number of Teachers								
	Primary Schools			Middle Schools			High/Higher Secondary Schools		
Year	Total	Male	Female	Total	Male	Female	Total	Male	Female
(1)	(2)	(3)	(4)	(5)	(6)	(7)	(8)	(9)	(10)
1950-51	538	82	456	86	73	13	127	107	20
1955-56	691	574	117	151	132	19	190	155	35
1960-61	742	615	127	345	262	83	296	234	62
1965-66	944	764	180	528	389	139	479	368	111
1970-71	1060	835	225	638	463	175	629	474	155
1975-76	1248	955	342	778	554	224	759	559	200
1980-81	1363	1021	342	851	598	253	926	669	257
1985-86	1496	1094	402	968	663	305	1132	793	339
1990-91	1616	1143	473	1073	717	356	1334	917	417
1991-92	1636	1144	492	1079	714	365	1381	931	450
1992-93*	1682	1189	493	1082	736	346	1353	908	445
1993-94*	1703	1196	507	1080	710	370	1405	938	467
1994-95*	1714	1181	533	1122	732	390	1446	956	490
1995-96*	1740	1187	553	1165	756	409	1493	982	511

* Provisional

Source : *Selected Eductional Statistics, 1995-96*, Department of Education, Ministry of Human Resource Development, New Delhi.

Table 10.11: Percentage of Girls in School Enrolment by Stages, India—1950-51 to 1995-96

Year	Primary I-V	Middle VI-VIII	Sec/Hr. Sec. 10+2/Inter	Hr.Education (Degree & above)
(1)	(2)	(3)	(4)	(5)
1950-51	28.1	16.1	13.3	10.0
1955-56	30.5	20.8	15.4	14.6
1960-61	32.6	23.9	20.5	16.0

(Contd.)

Table 10.11: *(Contd.)*

(1)	(2)	(3)	(4)	(5)
1965-66	36.2	26.7	22.0	20.4
1970-71	37.4	29.3	25.0	20.0
1975-76	38.1	31.3	26.9	26.7
1980-81	38.6	32.9	29.6	26.7
1985-86	40.3	35.6	30.3	33.0
1990-91	41.5	36.7	32.9	33.3
1991-92*	42.6	38.8	33.9	33.2
1993-94*	42.7	39.1	34.3	33.5
1994-95*	42.8	38.9	34.4	34.0
1995-96*	43.2	39.0	35.3	35.8

*Provisional

Source : *Selected Educational Statistics, 1995-96*, Department of Education, Ministry of Human Resource Development, New Delhi.

Table 10.12: Dropout Rates in Schools for General Education by Stages and Sex, India—1980-81 to 1994-95

		Primary Stage Classes (I-V)			Middle Stage Classes (I-VIII)			High School Stage Classes (I-X)		
No.	Year	Boys	Girls	Total	Boys	Girls	Total	Boys	Girls	Total
(1)	(2)	(3)	(4)	(5)	(6)	(7)	(8)	(9)	(10)	(11)
1.	1980-81	56.20	62.50	58.70	68.00	79.40	72.70	79.80	86.63	82.46
2.	1981-82	51.10	57.30	53.50	68.50	77.70	72.10	79.44	86.81	82.33
3.	1982-83	49.40	56.30	52.10	66.04	74.96	69.57	78.21	86.24	81.37
4.	1983-84	47.83	53.96	50.26	66.10	75.27	69.26	76.41	84.79	79.71
5.	1984-85	45.62	51.41	47.93	61.83	70.87	65.39	74.71	83.34	78.13
6.	1985-86	45.84	50.27	47.61	60.70	70.04	64.42	73.97	83.16	77.62
7.	1986-87	46.87	51.17	48.60	61.44	70.16	64.90	73.27	81.31	76.44
8.	1987-88	43.28	49.42	46.97	58.80	67.55	62.29	72.14	80.06	75.30
9.	1988-89	46.74	49.69	47.93	59.38	68.31	65.40	72.68	79.46	75.36
10.	1989-90	46.50	50.35	48.08	61.00	68.75	64.09	70.99	77.72	73.66
11.	1990-91	40.10	45.97	42.60	59.12	65.13	60.91	67.50	76.96	71.34

(Contd.)

Table 10.12: *(Contd.)*

(1)	(2)	(3)	(4)	(5)	(6)	(7)	(8)	(9)	(10)	(11)
12.	1991-92*	41.03	45.17	42.78	54.30	62.04	57.48	68.55	75.87	71.51
13.	1992-93*	40.07	43.02	41.30	53.99	60.06	56.48	68.15	74.69	70.80
14.	1993-94*	36.07	39.05	37.32	49.55	56.78	52.80	68.41	74.54	70.90
15.	1994-95*	35.18	37.79	36.27	50.02	56.53	52.74	67.15	73.78	69.89

*Provisional

Source : *Selected Educational Statistics, 1995-96*, Department of Education, Ministry of Human Resource Development, New Delhi.

Table 10.13: Total and Percentage of Women Employees in Central Government, 1971 to 1991

Years	No. of Employees		Percentage of Women to total employees
	Total (in lakhs)	Women	
(1)	(2)	(3)	(4)
1971	26.99	67369	2.51
1972	27.51	70874	2.58
1973	28.58	72879	2.55
1974	29.12	80371	2.76
1975	29.70	84051	2.83
1976	30.45	99272	3.26
1978	31.01	102321	3.30
1979	31.71	107172	3.38
1980	33.21	117139	3.53
1981	34.07	124032	3.64
1982	34.78	132010	3.80
1983	35.42	136598	3.86
1984	36.14	142011	3.93
1988	36.99	238984	6.46
1989	37.48	247158	6.60
1990	37.74	283380	7.52
1991	38.13	288999	7.58

Source : *Census of Central Government Employees,* Directotate General of Employment and Training, Ministry of Labour, New Delhi.

Table 10.14: Estimated Annual Expenditure: Sargent Plan

(Rs. in lakhs)

Branches of Education	Estimated Gross Annual Expenditure	Estimated Income from Source other than Public Funds	Estimated Net Expenditure to be met from Public Funds
(1)	(2)	(3)	(4)
Basic Education (Primary and Middle)	200.00	—	200.00
Pre-Primary Education	3.20	—	3.20
High School Education	79.80	29.00	50.00
University Education	9.60	2.90	6.70
Technical, Commercial and Art Education	10.00	2.00	8.00
Adult Education	3.00	—	3.00
Training of Teachers	6.20	1.70	4.50
School Medical	—	—	—
Services	(10 % of the gross expenditure of the stage on school medical service and education of the handicapped)		
Education of the Handicapped	—	—	—
Recreative and Social Activities	1.00	—	1.00
Employment	0.60	—	0.60
Administration	—	—	—
	(Including at every stage estimate of 5% of gross expenditure)		
Total	312.60	35.60	277.00

Source : *Report of the Post-war Educational Development in India, 1944*, Ministry of Education, 1964, p. 138. Quoted in *Landmarks in the History of Modern Indian Education* by J.C. Aggarwal, 1984, p.72.

Table 10.15: Distribution of Expenditure

(Rs. in lakhs)

State/ Ministry	Admi-nistration	Primary Education	Secondary Education	University Education	Technical and Voca-tional Education	Social Education	Other Schemes	Total
1	2	3	4	5	6	7	8	9
States	75.7	7,452.8 ***	830.4	925.1 ***	990.4	760.0	584.1	11,618.5**
Central Government	—	1,250.0	***	247.0	1,155.0	750.0	100.0	3,502.0
Total (1951-56)	75.7 (05%)	8,702.8 (57.6%)	830.4 (5.5%)	1,172.1 (7.8%)	2,145.4 (14.2%)	1,510.0 (10.0%)	684.1 (4.5%)	15,120.5** (100%)
Development Expenditure in 1950-51	9.5 (0.5%)	1,324.2 (67.7%)	88.9 (4.5%)	120.1 (6.2%)	265.6 (13.6%)	76.9 (3.9%)	71.1 (3.6%)	1,955.3 (100%)

** Figures do not include Rs. 46 lakh, earmarked for Jammu & Kashmir State, as break-up of this amount into sub-heads is not available.

*** Some expenditure is visualised on secondary education, promotion of federal and Indian languages, etc. out of Rs. 20 crore shown under basic & social education. Detailed break-up is not available.

Source : *First Five Year Plan, 1951-56*, Planning Commission, New Delhi, p. 562.

Table 10.16: Expenditure on Different Branches of Education

(Rs. in crore)

Sub-heads	1951-52 Actual	1952-53 Actual	1953-54 Actual	1954-55 Actual	1955-56 Revised	1951-56 Total
1	2	3	4	5	6	7
Primary Basic Education	12.3	13.3	16.6	20.4	22.2	84.8
Secondary Education	0.8	1.4	1.7	6.3	10.0	20.0
University Education	2.0	2.2	2.3	3.1	4.1	13.7
Technical Education	3.7	3.9	4.3	3.9	4.4	20.2
Social Education	0.2	0.8	0.8	1.0	1.9	4.7
Other Schemes	19.8	24.6	26.6	37.3	46.8	152.9**

** The distribution of outlay under different heads was broadly in accordance with that proposed when the plan was drawn up.

Source : *First Five Year Plan : Review, 1951-56*, Planning Commision, New Delhi, 1956, p. 250.

Table 10.17: Distribution of Funds on the Different Fields of Education

(Rs. in crores)

Sub-heads	First Plan	Second Plan
1	2	3
Elementary Education	93	89
Secondary Education	22	51
University Education	15	57
Technical & Vocational Education	23	48
Social Education	5	5
Administation and Miscellaneous Education	11	57
Total	169	307

Source : *Second Five Year Plan 1956-61*, Planning Commission, New Delhi, 1956, pp. 500-501.

Table 10.18: Expenditure during the First Four Years of the Second Plan

(Rs. in crores)

Sub-heads	Second Plan Provision	1956-57 Actual	1957-58 Actual	1958-59 Actual	1959-60 Budget	Likely expenditure	1956-60 Cols (344 547)	Col. 8 as percentage Col. 2
1	2	3	4	5	6	7	8	9
Elementary Education	93.01	6.14	12.65	17.01	23.68	26.25	62.05	66.7
Secondary Education	49.09	4.16	6.44	8.74	12.35	13.50	32.84	66.9
University Education	46.48	4.90	5.08	10.12	12.38	13.10	33.20	71.4
Technical Education	51.23	5.36	6.83	8.33	16.10	13.20	33.72	65.8
Social Education	5.00	0.56	0.73	0.70	1.13	1.00	2.99	59.8
Other Programmes	32.12	2.82	3.83	4.60	7.45	6.45	17.70	55.1
Total	276.94**	23.94	35.56	49.50	72.99	73.50	182.50	65.90

** Includes provision of Rs. 1.94 crore for schemes transferred from the Ministry of Rehabilitation to the Ministry of Education.

Source : *Second Five Year Plan : Progress Report, 1959-60*, Planning Commission, New Delhi, 1960, pp. 130-131.

Table 10.19: Distribution of Outlay

(Rs. in crores)

Sub-heads	First Plan	Second Plan	Third Plan	First Plan (%)	Seocnd Plan (%)	Third Plan (%)
1	2	3	4	5	6	7
Elementary Education	85	87	209	63.9	41.9	50.0
Secondary Education	20	48	88	15.1	23.1	21.1
University Education	14	45	82	10.5	21.6	19.6
Other Programmes	N.A.	4	6	N.A.	1.9	1.4

(Contd.)

Table 10.19 : *(Contd.)*

1	2	3	4	5	6	7
Social Education, Physical Education and Youth Welfare	14	10	12	10.5	4.8	2.9
Others	N.A.	10	11	N.A.	4.8	2.6
Total	133	204	408	100.0	98.1	97.6
Cultural Programmes	**	4	10	**	1.9	2.4
Grand Total	133	208	418	100.0	100.0	100.0

** The Outlay on Cultural Programmes in the First Plan was included under 'Other Programmes'.

Source : Third Five Year Plan, 1961-66, Planning Commision, New Delhi, 1981, p. 577.

Table 10.20: Progress of Expenditure under Education Centre, States/Union Territories 1961-65

(Rs. in crores)

Sub-heads	Third Plan Outlay 1961-66	1961-62 Actual	1962-63 Actual	1963-64 Actual Expen-diture	1964-65 Likely Expen-diture	1961-65 total of Col. 2	Col. 7 as per-centage
1	2	3	4	5	6	7	8
Elementary Education	207.00	26.88	28.62	38.40	48.59	135.89	65.6
Secondary Education	81.00	10.92	16.39	15.65	26.34	73.30	90.5
University Education	77.90	16.50	13.90	15.03	18.99	68.82	80.6
Social Education	6.00	9.46	0.46	0.45	0.60	1.97	32.8
Miscellaneous	23.90	4.81	5.86	9.66	15.48	35.65	154.6
Cultural Programmes	10.00	1.18	1.24	1.26	1.42	5.00	50.0
Scholarship (Centre)	4.10	0.13	9.80	4.00	3.08	4.56	111.7
N.C.E.R.T.	8.00	0.29	8.28	1.19	1.52	4.18	45.4

(Contd.)

Table 10.20: *(Contd.)*

1	2	3	4	5	6	7	8
Total General Education	418.00	62.17	68.54	86.59	115.95	423.29	78.3
Technical Education	142.00	18.57	21.91	24.46	30.32	95.06	64.9
Grand Total	560.00	70.74	98.25	411.02	143.25	418.35	74.7

Source : *Third Five Year Plan: Primary Report 1961-65*, Planning Commission, New Delhi, 1996, pp. 147-48.

Table 10.21: Sub-headwise Distribution of Outlay+ for Education : Centre, States and Union Territories

(Rs. in crore)

Sub-heads	Central and Cent-rally Spon-sored	States	Union Terri-tories	Total	Cent-ral and Cent-rally Spon-sored (%)	States (%)	Union Terri-tories (%)	Total (%)
1	2	3	4	5	6	7	8	9
Elementary Education	5.56	214.84	14.34	234.74	2.0	43.0	27.0	28.5
Secondary Education	0.27	104.25	13.80	118.32	20.1	20.8	26.6	14.4
University Education	103.99	76.06	3.47	183.52	38.4	15.2	6.7	22.3
Teacher Training	8.00**	12.20	0.97	21.17	3.0	2.4	1.9	2.6
Social Education	3.57	3.91	0.82	8.30	1.3	0.8	1.6	1.0
Other Programmes	75.36***	30.88	12.51	118.75	27.8	6.2	24.2	14.5
Cultural Programmes	7.26	4.87	0.36	12.49	2.7	1.0	0.7	1.5
Total General Education	204.01	447.01	46.27	697.27	75.3	89.4	89.4	84.8

(Contd.)

Table 10.21: *(Contd.)*

1	2	3	4	5	6	7	8	9
Technical Education	66.99	52.88	5.50	125.37	24.7	10.6	10.6	15.2
Total	271.00****	499.89	51.77	822.66	100.0	100.0	100.0	100.0

** Rs. 8 crore allocated for teacher training ; Rs.0.5 crore for adult education and Rs. 10.6 crore for technical education were to be administered by the UGC.

*** Includes Rs.8.30 crore for NCERT which, besides other programmes, had departments of Teacher Education and Adult Education.

**** Includes Rs. 32.4 crore (Rs. 19.4 crore in General Education and Rs. 13 crore in Technical Education) in the centrally sponsored sector as adjusted recently.

+ The Plan outlay was to be in addition to an average annual non-Plan expenditure of Rs. 550 crore.

Source: Fourth Five Year Plan: Summary, 1969-74, Publication Division, New Delhi, p. 119.

Table 10.22: Sixth Plan Outlay for Education and Culture

(Rs. in crore)

Sub-heads	States and Union Territories	Centre	Total
1	2	3	4
Early Childhood and Elementary Education	851.07	54.30	905.37
Secondary Education	370.00	28.01	308.01
Teacher Education	22.00	**	22.00
University and Higher Education	197.00	288.75	485.75
Adult Education	68.00	60.00	128.00
Physical Education Sports, Games and Youth Welfare	69.00	24.54	93.54
Other Programmes	69.41	60.15	129.56
Sub-total General Education	1646.48	515.75	2162.23
Art and Culture	32.90	51.00	83.90
Technical Education	109.61	168.00	277.61
Total	1788.99	734.75	2523.74

** Included under Secondary Education.

Source: Sixth Five Year Plan, 1980-85, Planning Commission, New Delhi, 1980, p. 361.

Table 10.23 : Progress of General Education During 7th Plan (1985-90)

Institutions = Numbers
Enrolment = Thousands

Sl. No.		1984-85 (6th Plan ending)		1989-90 (7th Plan ending)	
		Insti-tutions	Enrol-ment	Insti-tutions	Enrol-ment
1	2	3	4	5	6
1.	Primary Edn. (Classes I-V, age 6-10)	519701	83933	550700	97318
2.	Middle (Classes VI-VIII age 11-14)	129879	26153	143747	32188
3.	Elementary Edn. (Classes I-VIII age 6-14)	649580	110086	694447	129506
4.	Non-Formal Edn. (Classes I-VIII age 6-14)	NIL	NIL	27087 (Centres)	6400
5.	Grand Total—Elementary (Items 3+4)	649580	110086	694447 +27087	135906
6.	High/Hr. Secondary Edn. Classes (X-XII)	58834	13828	76119	19970
7.	Colleges (Art, Science, Commerce)	4005	2577	4755	3814
8.	Universities (Including deemed universities)	135	347	174	388
9.	Engineering Colleges	198	145	278	733
10.	Polytechnics	389	148	840	284

Source : *Selected Educational Statistics, 1984-85 and 1989-90*, Department of Education, Ministry of Human Resource Development, Government of India.

Table 10.24 : Achievement of Additional Enrolment at Elementary Stage (Classes I-VIII) and Adult Education in the Seventh Plan

(Fig. in lakhs)

Sl. No.	States/UT's	Primary Classes I-V		Upper Primary Classes I-VIII		Elementary Classes I-VIII		Adult Educa-tion
		Girls	Total	Girls	Total	Girls	Total	
1	2	3	4	5	6	7	8	9
1.	Andhra Pradesh	4.12	9.09	1.47	3.78	5.59	12.87	11.12
2.	Arunachal Pradesh	0.15	0.29	0.05	0.09	0.20	0.38	0.92

(Contd.)

Table 10.24: *(Contd.)*

1	2	3	4	5	6	7	8	9
3.	Assam	1.80	11.42	0.96	3.74	2.76	15.16	5.99
4.	Bihar	2.40	5.66	0.72	1.52	3.12	7.18	39.99
5.	Goa	0.04*	0.06*	(-)0.01	(-)0.04	0.03	0.02	0.017
6.	Gujarat	3.71	6.60	1.69	3.90	5.40	10.50	19.32
7.	Haryana	1.43	1.63	0.89	1.28	2.32	2.91	5.21
8.	Himachal Pradesh	0.40	0.70	0.47	0.71	0.87	1.41	1.43
9.	Jammu & Kashmir	0.48	0.99	0.31	0.72	0.79	1.71	2.88
10.	Karnataka	6.72	13.69	1.19	2.79	7.91	16.48	11.88
11.	Kerala	0.27	0.53	0.50	0.95	0.77	1.48	5.08
12.	Madhya Pradesh	7.39	16.35	3.26	8.65	10.65	25.00	26.02
13.	Maharashtra	5.07	7.66	4.30	8.70	9.37	16.36	20.90
14.	Manipur	0.15	0.23	0.04	0.04	0.19	0.27	1.17
15.	Meghalaya	0.20	0.39	0.06	0.10	0.26	0.49	0.89
16.	Mizoram	0.12	0.27	0.04	0.35	0.16	0.62	0.21
17.	Nagaland	0.07	0.13	(-)0.08	(-)0.18	(-)0.01	(-)0.05	0.65
18.	Orissa	2.55	5.83	2.03	2.87	4.58	8.70	8.22
19.	Punjab	0.64	1.07	0.58	1.05	1.22	2.12	4.86
20.	Rajasthan	3.19	7.20	0.83	3.34	4.02	10.54	14.46
21.	Sikkim	0.07	0.10	0.02	0.02	0.09	0.12	0.41
22.	Tamil Nadu	3.05	6.34	3.52	7.14	6.57	13.48	26.76
23.	Tripura	0.19	0.38	0.14	0.32	0.33	0.70	0.63
24.	Uttar Pradesh	10.32	17.89	2.25	4.26	12.57	22.15	39.72
25.	West Bengal	8.44	17.24	1.59	3.10	10.03	20.34	12.42
	Total (States)	62.97	131.74	26.82	59.20	89.79	190.94	261.157
26.	A & N Islands	0.02	0.05	0.03	0.05	0.05	0.10	0.13
27.	Chandigarh	0.07	0.15	0.04	0.07	0.11	0.22	0.17
28.	D & N Haveli	0.02	0.02	0.01	0.01	0.03	0.03	0.11
29.	Daman & Diu	0.05	0.10	0.04	0.08	0.09	0.18	0.001
30.	Delhi	0.72	1.63	0.56	1.16	1.28	2.79	3.60
31.	Lakshadweep	0.00	0.00	0.00	0.00	0.00	0.00	0.011
32.	Pondicherry	0.08	0.15	0.06	0.10	0.14	0.25	0.45
	Total (UTs)	0.96	2.10	0.74	1.47	1.70	3.57	4.472
	Total (States & UTs)	63.93	133.84	27.56	60.67	91.49	194.51	265.629

* Including Daman & Diu

Source : 1. Elementry Education : *Selected Educational Statistics of 1984-85 and 1989-90*, Department of Education Ministry of Human Resource Development, Government of India.

2. Adult Education: Directorate of Adult Education.

Table 10.25: Outlay and Expenditure on Education: Seventh Plan and Annual Plans: 1990-91 and 1991-92 Central and State Sector

(Rs. in crores)

Sl. No.	Sub-head	7th Plan 1985-90 Approved Outlay	Actual Expdr.	Annual Plan 1990-91 Actual Expdr.	Annual Plan 1991-92 Antic. Expdr.
1	2	3	4	5	6
1.	Elementary Education	1963.70	2854.69	805.77	937.50
2.	Adult Education	360.00	469.57	173.84	195.08
3.	General Education	4775.30	6549.51	1797.82	2120.21
4.	Technical Education	681.79	1083.34	314.63	537.45
5.	Art and Culture	482.13	450.89	103.90	132.41
6.	Sports & Youth Affairs	443.43	484.51	113.01	170.78
	(Total Col. 3 to 6)	6382.65	8568.31	2329.36	2960.85

Table 10.26: Outlay and Expenditure on Education : Seventh Plan and Annual Plans: 1990-91 and 1991-92 : Central Sector

(Rs. in Crores)

S.No.	Sub-head	7th Plan Approved Outlay	1985-90 Actual Expdr.	Annual Plan 1990-91 Actual Expdr.	Annual Plan 1991-92 Anticipated Expdr.
1	2	3	4	5	6
1.	Elementary Education	233.25	658.49	218.75	283.50
2.	Adult Education	130.00	313.04	131.15	129.19
3.	Secondary Education	667.75	596.01	195.21	209.90
4.	University & Higher Education	420.00	659.96	131.55	171.592
5.	Languauge Development	38.64	43.58	10.78	14.00
6.	Planning and Admn.	29.00	23.49	3.46	6.78
7.	Other Educational Programmes	NA	NA	NA	NA
8.	Total General Education	1518.64	2294.57	690.90	814.96
9.	Technical Education	220.00	610.96	157.60	188.25
10.	Art and Culture	350.00	268.73	60.41	74.20
11.	Sports and Youth Affairs	300.00	248.67	47.56	76.16
12.	Total Education (Col. 8-11)	2388.64	3422.93	956.47	1153.57

Table 10.27: Outlay and Expenditure on Education: Seventh Plan and Annual Plans: 1990-91 and 1991-92: State Sector

(Rs. in crores)

S.No.	Sub-head	7th Plan 1985-90 Approved Outlay	7th Plan 1985-90 Actual Expdr.	Annual Plan 1990-91 Actual Expdr.	Annual Plan 1991-92 Anticipated Expdr.
1	2	3	4	5	6
1.	Elementary Education	1730.45	2190.92	588.41	644.12
2.	Adult Education	230.00	156.53	43.52	71.44
3.	Secondary Education	N.A.	1235.50	326.16	315.99
4.	University & Higher Education	N.A.	541.17	159.37	154.93
5.	Languauge Development	N.A.	13.48	6.71	10.10
6.	Planning and Admn.	N.A.	10.05	7.15	9.72
7.	Other Educational Programmes	N.A.	107.35	26.89	29.88
8.	Total General Education	3256.66	4255.00	1158.21	1296.18
9.	Technical Education	461.79	472.38	157.03	349.20
10.	Art and Culture	132.13	182.16	43.49	58.21
11.	Sports and Youth Affairs	143.43	235.84	65.45	94.62
12.	Total Education (Col. 8-11)	3994.01	5145.38	1424.18	1798.21

Table 10.28: Eighth Plan (1992-97) Targets : Additional Enrolment: Elementary and Adult Education

(Figures in 000's)

Sl. No.	States/UTs	Primary (I-V Classes) Girls	Primary (I-V Classes) Total	Upper Primary (VI-VIII Classes) Girls	Upper Primary (VI-VIII Classes) Total	Elementary (I-VIII Classes) Girls	Elementary (I-VIII Classes) Total	Adult Education age 15-35 year
1	2	3	4	5	6	7	8	9
1.	Andhra Pradesh	1475	2588	840	1400	2315	3988	7778
2.	Arunachal Pradesh	12	27	14	36	26	63	175
3.	Assam	244	500	384	800	628	1300	4500
4.	Bihar	4032	8400	1008	2100	5040	10500	9400
5.	Goa	3	6	5	9	8	15	100

(Contd.)

Table 10.28: *(Contd.)*

1	2	3	4	5	6	7	8	9
6.	Gujarat	72	108	475	1100	547	1208	4300
7.	Haryana	173	275	180	300	353	575	5711
8.	Himachal Pradesh	58	125	29	66	87	191	800
9.	Jammu & Kashmir	62	150	185	227	147	377	600
10.	Karnataka	215	434	98	197	313	631	6000
11.	Kerala	129	252	42	80	171	332	980
12.	Madhya Pradesh	2310	3460	1796	2396	4106	5856	5500
13.	Maharashtra	600	1400	300	750	900	2150	9200
14.	Manipur	12	29	36.70	68.20	48.70	97.20	23
15.	Meghalaya	15	30	22	51	37	81	262
16.	Mizoram	12	25	12	29	24	54	32
17.	Nagaland	16	32	17.50	34	33.50	66	23
18.	Orissa	247	600	142	416	389	1016	130
19.	Punjab	80	190	54	127	134	317	5000
20.	Rajasthan	2180	2647	621	1565	2729	4212	11000
21.	Sikkim	5	11	7	16	12	27	4
22.	Tamil Nadu	215	425	491	1142	706	1567	7800
23.	Tripura	13	25	36	89	49	114	400
24.	Uttar Pradesh	866	2480	530	1930	1396	4410	16700
25.	West Bengal	801	1638	1359	2788	2160	4426	8559
	Total (States)	13775	25857	8584.20	17716.20	22359.20	43573.20	104977
26.	A & N Islands	4.00	9.00	2.00	6.00	6.00	15.00	10
27.	Chandigarh	4.80	10.10	3.80	8.10	8.60	18.20	26
28.	D & N Haveli	0.05	0.11	0.03	0.13	0.08	0.24	15
29.	Daman & Diu	0.50	1.00	0.50	1.00	1.00	2.00	20
30.	Delhi	38.00	96.00	24.00	85.00	62.00	181.00	750
31.	Lakshadweep	0.05	0.20	0.05	0.10	0.10	0.30	12
32.	Pondicherry	3.00	6.00	1.80	4.00	4.80	10.00	30
	Total (UTs)	50.40	122.41	32.18	104.33	82.58	226.74	863
	Total (States & UTs)	13825.40	25979.41	8616.38	17820.53	22441.78	43799.94	105840

Source : Plan Document of States/UT's and summary records of Working Groups as Education.

Table 10.29 : Percentage of Sector-wise and State-wise Approved Outlays to Total Outlays on Education: Eighth Five Year Plan, 1992-97

(Rs. in crores)

S.No.	States/UTs	Elementary	Adults	General	Technical
1	2	3	4	5	6
1.	Andhra Pradesh	63.03	6.13	79.78	20.22
2.	Arunachal Pradesh	75	1.84	100.0	0
3.	Assam	61.8	2.00	95.07	4.93
4.	Bihar	64.55	6.61	79.69	20.31
5.	Goa	35	1.42	83.33	16.67
6.	Gujarat	47.26	7.09	71.61	28.39
7.	Haryana	39.44	1.25	79.29	20.71
8.	Himachal Pradesh	36.36	0.65	84.56	15.44
9.	Jammu & Kashmir	47.16	2.14	94.32	5.68
10.	Karnataka	42.85	1.96	94.77	5.23
11.	Kerala	12.6	0.44	46.67	53.33
12.	Madhya Pradesh	61.5	2.82	87.86	12.14
13.	Maharashtra	36.64	2.3	76.43	23.57
14.	Manipur	55.51	2.79	92.52	7.48
15.	Meghalaya	69.95	3.66	98.51	1.49
16.	Mizoram	50.76	2.76	92.28	7.72
17.	Nagaland	38.93	1.52	90.52	9.48
18.	Orissa	39.76	7.36	86.42	13.58
19.	Punjab	11.42	2.62	52.52	47.48
20.	Rajasthan	59.12	3.18	89.57	10.43
21.	Sikkim	62.98	1.18	95.16	4.84
22.	Tamil Nadu	52.91	8.38	92.22	7.78
23.	Tripura	57.28	1.93	98.77	1.23
24.	Uttar Pradesh	49.33	1.80	80.86	19.14
25.	West Bengal	58.33	4.45	83.33	16.67
Union Territories					
26.	A & N Islands	37.42	0.61	76.18	23.82
27.	Chandigarh	24.01	1.20	79.11	20.89
28.	D & N Haveli	54.77	0.47	84.35	15.65
29.	Daman & Diu	31.26	1.76	59.02	40.98

(Contd.)

Table 10.29: *(Contd.)*

1	2	3	4	5	6
30.	Delhi	57.46	1.14	80.36	19.64
31.	Lakshadweep	29.93	2.28	100	0
32.	Pondicherry	31.72	0.7	65.23	34.77
	All States/UTs	49.82	3.24	83.86	16.14
	Centre	38.69	18.81	88.93	11.07
	Total (Centre and States)	45.59	9.16	85.78	14.22

Table 10.30: Outlays and Expenditure of Seventh and Eighth Plans and Annual Plans, 1992-93 to 1996-97

(Rs. in crore)

Sector/Major Scheme	Seventh Plan Exp.	Eighth Plan Outlay	Annual Plan 1992-93	
			Outlay	Exp.
1	2	3	4	5
1. Elementary Education				
i) Other than Ext. Aided	655.15	2350.0	261.10	293.84
a) NFE (State+VAs)	126.28	704.0	90.10	55.36
b) Others	528.89	1646.0	171.0	238.48
c) Mid-day-meal	—	—	—	—
ii) Externally Aided	8.62	530.0	22.90	13.65
Total:	663.77	2880.0	284.0	307.49
2. Secondary Education				
a) Navodaya Vidyalayas		650.0	75.0	92.09
b) Vocational Education		410.0	79.0	77.52
c) Others		459.0	55.0	54.52
Total :	596.01	1519.0	209.0	224.13
3. University and Hr. Edn.*	659.96	701.55	150.01	151.99
4. Adult Education	313.04	1400.0	120.0	97.58
5. Language Development				
i) Hindi		29.40	5.18	4.94

(Contd.

Table 10.30: *(Contd.)*

1	2	3	4	5
ii) MIL		14.25	3.05	1.44
iii) English		3.80	0.72	0.68
iv) Sanskrit		21.00	3.74	8.11
Total :	43.58	68.45	12.69	15.17
6. Scholarships	9.13	10.0	2.50	1.52
7. Book Promotion	5.74	8.0	2.0	1.49
8. Planning and Admn.	3.34	32.0	1.8	1.15
9. Technical Education				
i) Schemes under AICTE		365.4	79.48	73.97
ii) Schemes of Dep. of Edn.		458.6	90.52	88.87
Total :	610.96	824.0	170.0	162.84
BADP	120.50			
TOTAL	3026.03	7443.0	952.0	963.36

* The schemes of Hindi University and Urdu University have been transferred from Language Development to University and Higher Education.

Table 10.30 : *(Contd.)*

Annual Plan 1993-94		Annual Plan 1994-95		Annual Plan 1995-96			1996-97
Outlay	Exp.	Outlay	Exp.	Outlay	RE	Exp.	Outlay
6	7	8	9	10	11	12	13
358.77	356.81	439.57	425.52	559.00	1145.05	974.64	1959.00
108.67	106.69	131.32	131.27	158.50	153.50	153.50	158.25
250.10	250.12	301.25	294.25	400.50	379.76	379.76	400.75
—	—	—	—	—	611.79	441.38	1400.00
83.43	29.76	83.43	122.33	92.04	297.98	228.27	299.70
442.20	386.97	523.00	547.85	651.04	1443.03	1202.91	2258.70
131.71	132.00	152.63	152.63	200.00	177.00	177.00	186.00
85.00	85.00	33.46	75.26	82.00	82.00	69.07	82.00
89.16	86.54	93.91	92.83	127.11	105.10	93.85	113.11

(Contd.)

Table 10.30: *(Contd.)*

6	7	8	9	10	11	12	13
305.87	303.54	335.0	320.72	409.11	364.10	339.92	381.11
161.31	157.91	220.0	264.35	244.50	245.41	246.84	238.04
177.97	166.39	214.0	206.90	234.00	170.35	144.13	224.50
5.93	8.77	6.79	6.79	8.53	8.54	8.43	6.79
3.74	1.56	4.22	2.04	4.94	2.47	1.89	4.22
0.75	0.69	0.75	0.75	0.83	0.83	0.66	0.75
4.24	3.95	5.19	5.10	7.65	6.72	6.20	5.19
14.66	14.97	16.95	14.68	21.95	18.56	17.18	16.95
2.65	0.91	2.15	0.92	2.15	1.37	1.10	2.15
1.98	1.87	1.98	1.96	2.98	2.59	2.42	1.98
5.36	6.32	5.36	3.80	5.36	4.45	4.11	5.36
58.65	59.64	58.65	62.92	71.89	71.89	71.36	71.89
139.35	133.92	164.35	175.74	182.02	181.32	169.62	182.02
198.0	193.56	223.00	238.66	253.91	253.21	240.98	253.91
1310.00	1232.04	1541.46	1599.84	1825.00	2503.07	2199.59	3382.70

Source: *Annual Financial Statistics of Education Sector 1996-97,* Ministry of Human Resource Development, Department of Education, Planning and Monitoring, New Delhi.

Table 10.31 : Statewise Approved Outlays for Eighth Five Year Plan, 1992-97

(Rs. in crores)

S. No.	States/UTs	Elementary Education	Adult Education	General Education		Technical Education
	1	2	3	4	5	6
1.	Andhra Pradesh	176.13	17.12	222.95	56.50	279.45
2.	Arunachal Pradesh	113.92	2.79	151.90	0.00	151.90
3.	Assam	568.35	18.36	874.38	45.33	919.71
4.	Bihar	588.83	60.34	726.95	185.22	912.17
5.	Goa	27.30	1.11	65.00	13.00	78.00

(Contd.)

Table 10.31: *(Contd.)*

1	2	3	4	5	6
6. Gujarat	149.82	22.47	227.00	90.00	317.00
7. Haryana	202.44	6.40	407.04	106.30	513.34
8. Himachal Pradesh	98.90	1.77	230.00	42.00	272.00
9. Jammu & Kashmir	157.65	7.16	315.30	19.00	334.30
10. Karnataka	409.50	18.70	905.55	50.00	955.55
11. Kerala	22.21	0.77	82.25	94.00	176.25
12. Madhya Pradesh	432.68	19.84	618.12	85.38	703.50
13. Maharashtra	350.00	22.00	730.07	225.18	955.25
14. Manipur	40.80	2.05	68.00	5.50	73.50
15. Meghalaya	64.33	3.37	90.60	1.37	91.97
16. Mizoram	23.02	1.25	41.85	3.50	45.35
17. Nagaland	18.47	0.72	42.95	4.50	47.45
18. Orissa	242.66	44.91	527.52	82.86	610.38
19. Punjab	47.15	10.80	216.78	196.00	412.78
20. Rajasthan	567.75	30.50	860.23	100.18	960.41
21. Sikkim	36.40	0.68	55.00	2.80	57.80
22. Tamil Nadu	252.47	40.00	440.00	37.14	477.14
23. Tripura	69.60	2.34	120.00	1.50	121.50
24. Uttar Pradesh	663.53	24.26	1087.75	257.40	1345.15
25. West Bengal	350.00	26.72	500.00	100.00	600.00
Union Territories					
26. A & N Islands	20.74	0.34	42.22	13.20	55.42
27. Chandigarh	10.62	0.53	35.00	9.24	44.24
28. D & N Haveli	7.00	0.06	10.78	2.00	12.78
29. Daman & Diu	2.67	0.15	5.04	3.50	8.54
30. Delhi	321.80	6.37	450.00	110.00	560.00
31. Lakshadweep	1.68	0.16	7.02	0.00	7.02
32. Pondicherry	18.04	0.40	37.10	19.78	56.88
All States/UTs	6054.44	394.44	10194.35	1962.38	12156.73
Centre	2880.00	1400.00	6619.00	824.00	7443.00
Total (Centre & States)	8936.44	1794.44	16813.35	2786.38	19599.73

Source: *Analysis of Annual Plan 1992-93 (Education Sector)*, Planning Commission, New Delhi.

Table 10 .32: Sectorwise and Statewise Approved Plan Outlays, 1995-96

(Rs. in crores)

S.No.	States/UTs	Elementary	Adult	General	Technical	Total
1	2	3	4	5	6	7
1.	Andhra Pradesh	62.30	11.00	100.00	12.00	112.00
2.	Arunachal Pradesh	33.00	1.05	48.05	0.00	48.05
3.	Assam	166.00	0.00	298.05	14.73	312.78
4.	Bihar	93.00	9.99	118.99	61.92	180.91
5.	Goa	4.45	0.38	14.35	15.38	29.73
6.	Gujarat	14.51	3.95	33.90	30.00	63.90
7.	Haryana	38.34	1.00	86.02	38.54	124.56
8.	Himachal Pradesh	36.44	0.50	86.30	12.00	98.30
9.	Jammu & Kashmir	42.05	0.92	89.00	4.40	93.40
10.	Karnataka	176.15	7.19	287.95	19.00	306.95
11.	Kerala	6.05	0.00	32.70	30.50	63.20
12.	Madhya Pradesh	100.28	5.83	203.58	53.70	257.28
13.	Maharashtra	99.18	6.31	224.00	72.69	296.69
14.	Manipur	5.96	0.61	17.36	1.20	18.56
15.	Meghalaya	19.50	1.00	28.83	0.60	29.53
16.	Mizoram	5.00	0.00	10.70	0.80	11.50
17.	Nagaland	5.58	0.07	9.78	1.10	10.88
18.	Orissa	26.98	4.34	126.52	25.57	152.09
19.	Punjab	14.71	1.43	57.13	53.00	110.13
20.	Rajasthan	156.92	4.50	282.96	22.43	305.39
21.	Sikkim	7.85	0.15	18.73	0.59	19.32
22.	Tamil Nadu	54.13	19.43	98.17	10.64	108.81
23.	Tripura	24.00	0.00	40.55	0.38	40.93
24.	Uttar Pradesh	69.45	11.04	320.25	62.74	382.99
25.	West Bengal	31.90	5.26	80.40	25.24	105.64
Union Territories						
26.	A & N Islands	10.28	0.09	20.69	1.82	22.51
27.	Chandigarh	3.47	0.00	11.45	2.20	13.65
28.	D & N Haveli	2.50	0.05	4.06	1.80	5.86
29.	Daman & Diu	1.79	0.04	2.25	1.50	3.75
30.	Delhi	82.14	0.50	139.40	34.17	173.57

(Contd.)

Table 10.32: *(Contd.)*

1	2	3	4	5	6	7
31.	Lakshadweep	0.77	0.03	1.62	0.00	1.62
32.	Pondicherry	5.12	0.01	13.89	3.51	17.40
	All States/UTs	1399.80	96.67	2907.73	614.15	3531.88
	Centre	651.04	234.00	1571.09	253.91	1825.00
	Total (Centre & States)	2050.84	330.67	4478.82	868.06	5346.88

Table 10.33 : Eighth Plan Yearwise Approved Allocation for Schemes of Adult Education, 1992-93 to 1996-97

(Rs. in crores)

S.No.	Name of the Scheme	Approved Allocation (1992-93)	Approved Allocation (1993-94)	Approved Allocation (1994-95)	Approved Allocation (1995-96)	Approved Allocation (1996-97)
1.	Special Projects for Eradication of Illiteracy (TLS/PLC)	58.65	120.00	154.75	120.00	100.00
2.	Voluntary Agencies (VAs)	18.00	15.00	10.00	10.00	10.00
3.	Directorate of Adult Education (DAE)	2.50	5.70	6.00	12.00	12.00
4.	Shramik Vidyapeeths (SVP)	1.30	1.75	2.00	4.35	4.95
5.	Strengthening of Administrative Structure (SAS)	7.00	10.00	14.00	14.00	18.00
6.	Rural Functional Literacy Project (RFLP)	15.00	6.00	6.00	6.00	0.90
7.	Post-Literacy & Continuing Education (PL&CE)	10.00	13.50	18.00	66.00	75.50
8.	Mass Programme of Functional Literacy (MPFL)	3.75	2.50	0.75	0.00	0.10
9.	Technology Demonstration	0.50	0.47	0.30	0.15	0.05
10.	Cultural Exchange Programme	0.05	0.05	0.25	0.25	0.25
11.	National Literacy Mission (NLM)	0.25	0.50	0.75	0.75	2.00
12.	National Institute of Adult Education (NIAE)	1.50	2.00	1.20	0.50	0.75
13.	Nehru Yuvak Kendras (NYK)	1.50	0.50	0.00	0.00	0.00
	Total	120.00	177.97	214.00	234.00	224.50

Table 10.34 : Eighth Plan Approved Outlay, Actual Allocation and Expenditure for Adult Education, 1992-97

(Rs. in crores)

	Name of the Scheme	Approved Outlay (1992-97)	Actual Allocation (1992-97)	Actual Expenditure (1992-97)
1.	Special Projects for Eradication of Illiteracy (TLS/PLC)	1000.00	553.40	496.09
2.	Voluntary Agencies (VAs)	115.00	63.00	35.04
3.	Directorate of Adult Education (DAE)	14.50	38.20	42.91
4.	Shramik Vidyapeeths (SVP)	17.00	14.35	13.95
5.	Strengthening of Administrative Structure (SAS)	28.00	63.00	53.84
6.	Rural Functional Literacy Project (RFLP)	25.00	33.90	15.26
7.	Post-Literacy and Continuing Education (PL & CE)	132.00	183.00	53.31
8.	Mass Programme of Functional Literacy (MPFL)	25.00	7.10	3.83
9.	Technology Demonstration	8.00	1.47	0.38
10.	Cultural Exchange Programme	0.50	0.85	0.156
11.	National Literacy Mission (NLM)	2.50	4.25	1.81
12.	National Institute of Adult Education (NIAE)	17.50	5.95	1.35
13.	Nehru Yuvak Kendras (NYK)	15.00	2.00	0.00
	Total	1400.00	970.47	717.926

Table 10.35 : Eighth Plan Yearwise Actual Expenditure for Schemes of Adult Education, 1992-93 to 1996-97

(Rs. in crores)

S. No.	Name of the Scheme	Actual Expenditure (1992-93)	Actual Expenditure (1993-94)	Actual Expenditure (1994-95)	Actual Expenditure (1995-96)	Actual Expenditure (1996-97)
1.	Special Projects for Eradication of Illiteracy (TLS/PLC)	71.40	120.92	155.26	100.00	48.51
2.	Voluntary Agencies (VAs)	3.50	6.51	11.00	6.43	7.60
3.	Directorate of Adult Education (DAE)	3.26	9.61	5.87	11.86	12.31
4.	Shramik Vidyapeeths (SVP)	1.24	1.72	2.80	4.15	4.04
5.	Strengthening of Administrative Structure (SAS)	8.54	10.00	12.40	11.00	11.90
6.	Rural Functional Literacy Project (RFLP)	1.37	6.00	7.30	0.27	0.32
7.	Post-Literacy & Continuing Education (PL & CE)	6.20	9.02	11.05	9.33	17.71
8.	Mass Programme of Functional Literacy (MPFL)	1.44	1.40	0.75	0.19	0.05
9.	Technology Demonstration	0.02	0.30	0.06	0.00	0.00
10.	Cultural Exchange Programme	0.00	0.07	0.04	0.06	0.04
11.	National Literacy Mission (NLM)	0.16	0.34	0.37	0.50	0.44
12.	National Institute of Adult Education (NIAE)	0.45	0.50	0.00	0.20	0.20
13.	Nehru Yuvak Kendras (NYK)	0.00	0.00	0.00	0.00	0.00
	Total	97.58	166.47	206.90	143.936	103.12

Table 10.35 : Eighth Plan Funds Released to States for Adult Education, 1992-93 to 1996-97

(Rs. in lakhs)

States/UTs	1992-93	1993-94	1994-95	1995-96	1996-97	Grand Total
1	2	3	4	5	6	7
Andhra Pradesh	839.64	1846.70	1370.68	884.21	1081.06	6022.29
Arunachal Pradesh	8.59	28.73	71.56	25.63	20.72	155.23
Assam	111.50	125.21	1159.04	361.09	194.29	1951.13
Bihar	299.67	1109.93	1628.87	1997.84	1062.52	6078.83
Goa	5.29	15.37	11.59	5.95	3.32	41.52
Gujarat	659.44	1079.70	884.50	262.98	458.78	3345.40
Haryana	426.79	181.05	243.01	175.31	57.12	1083.28
Himachal Pradesh	214.69	80.07	109.15	26.43	49.18	479.52
Jammu & Kashmir	—	84.47	190.40	132.70	50.47	458.04
Karnataka	698.32	1683.64	1041.84	319.58	350.16	4093.54
Kerala	21.46	122.71	57.32	7.00	537.97	746.46
Madhya Pradesh	289.45	1455.12	2821.22	977.67	548.58	6092.34
Maharashtra	838.71	1453.16	1024.55	1153.63	432.83	4902.88
Manipur	7.55	28.18	72.67	17.62	20.63	146.65
Meghalaya	14.16	19.47	29.08	127.74	112.45	302.90
Mizoram	1.66	2.66	16.42	2.29	0.57	23.60
Nagaland	16.37	26.31	39.73	47.81	56.90	187.1
Orissa	589.51	614.12	606.36	801.36	310.13	2921.48
Punjab	5.29	25.00	277.61	370.34	135.00	813.24
Rajasthan	501.90	784.58	1745.0	1681.76	1304.62	6017.86
Sikkim	—	5.25	11.22	—	11.22	27.69
Tamil Nadu	1232.01	1200.00	1594.58	1212.48	261.21	5500.28
Tripura	—	224.18	6.77	0.10	4.73	235.78
Uttar Pradesh	897.09	2555.48	2805.58	1888.01	943.27	9089.43
West Bengal	1094.58	719.86	1583.69	308.40	728.11	4434.64
Union Territories						
Chandigarh	28.11	28.66	25.62	20.12	41.37	143.88
Delhi	50.42	117.17	120.77	322.58	158.57	769.51

(Contd.)

Table 10.35: *(Contd.)*

1	2	3	4	5	6	7
Pondicherry	—	—	—	—	—	—
Daman & Diu	—	1.96	0.56	0.50	—	3.02
Andaman & Nicober	5.82	9.81	12.15	8.12	12.56	48.46
Dadra & Nagar Haveli	0.58	0.84	0.83	—	—	2.25
Lakshadweep	2.57	1.57	7.41	1.62	4.32	17.49
Total	8,861.17	15,630.96	19,570.08	13,120.87	8,952.66	66,135.74

Bibliography

Abdul Gafoor, P.K. and Ayishabi, T.C., Role of Diels in the Adult Education Programme—An evaluation, *Indian Journal of Adult Education* 60(3) Jul-Sep. 1999, pp. 50-54.

Adult Education Programme for Women : Report of a Committee appointed by Ministry of Education and Social Welfare, New Delhi, Ministry of Education and Social Welfare, p. 11.

Agrawal, S.P. and Aggarwal, J.C., Development of Education in India : Select Documents 1993-94, New Delhi, Concept, 1997, Vol. 4, p. 447.

Agrawal, S.P. and Aggarwal, J.C., Second Historical Survey of Educational Development in India : Select Documents 1985-1990, New Delhi, Concept, 1991, p. 460.

Ali Ahmad, National Literacy Mission and Economic Development, *Educational Review* 104 (4) Mar. 1998, pp. 66-69.

Adalene, M., From Theory to Practice Grihini Schools: An Experiment in Adult Education. *Social Action* 18(1) Jan.-Feb 1968, pp. 57-64.

Adiseshiah, Malcom, Adult Education and Inequality, *Indian Journal of Adult Education* 52(3) July-Sep. 1991, pp. 12-21.

Adiseshiah, S. Malcolm, Illiteracy and Poverty, *Social Welfare*, 37(2) May, 1990, pp. 4-5.

Adult Education, *Indian Journal of Social Work*, 3(4) Mar. 1943, pp. 452-54; 4(3) Dec. 1943, pp. 283-86.

Adult Education : Can Indian Universities Undertake it (editorial *Education and Psychology Review* 8(4) Oct. 1968, pp. 241-43.

Adult education for the Educated. *Journal of Education and Psychology*. 2(4) Jan. 1945, pp. 145+.

Aikara, A., Adult Education Programme in Maharashtra—An Appraisal Bombay, Tata Institute of Social Sciences, 1984.

Akhtar, Naseem, A Case for Integration of Population Education with Adult Education, *Indian Journal of Adult Education* 52(3) Jul-Sep. 1991, pp. 49-52.

A.N. Sihna, Institute for Social Studies. Adult Education Programme in Bihar—An Appraisal, Patna, The Institute, 1980.

Ansari, N.A. and Rege, K.B., Per Capita Cost of Adult Literacy in India, *Indian Journal of Adult Education*, 25(a), Sep., 1964.

Apte, D.G., The Problem of Rural Adult Education in India, *Journal of Education and Psychology*, 7(3) Oct. 1949. pp. 133-36.

Association of Indian Universities. Society, Education and Development, New Delhi, The Association, 1998. p. 378.

Athreya, Venkatesh B. and Chunkalh, Sheefer Rani, Literacy and Empowerment Sage, New Delhi, 1996.

Banerjee, Sumanta, Flowers for the Literate, *Economic and Political Weekly* 29(48), 26 Nov. 1994, pp. 3013-3016.

Banerjee, Sumanta, Revisiting the National Literacy Mission, *Economic and Political Weekly,* 28(25) 19 Jun. 1993, pp. 1274-1278.

Bara, Dominic, *et al.* Tribal Female Literacy Factors in Differentiation among Munda Religion Communities, *Social Action* 41(4) Oct-Dec. 1991, pp. 399-415.

Bhargava, P.K., Population Dynamics and Health : Research Issues in Adult Literacy Programmes, *Indian Journal of Adult Education* 54 (3) Jul-Sep. 1993, pp. 41-51.

Bombay's Ten Year Plan: For the Liquidation of Illiteracy from the Adult Population of Bombay City, *Social Service Quarterly* 33(3) Jan. 1947, pp. 79-88.

Bordia, Anil, Adult Education in India, Bombay, Nachiketa, 1973.

Centre for Advance Studies in Education, Adult Education Programme in Gujarat—A Study, Bombay, The Centre, 1981.

Chakraborti, Vandana, Curriculum Development for Refresher Courses in Adult and Continuing Education, Extension and Fieldout Reach, *Indian Journal of Adult Education* 60 (2) Apr.-June 1999, pp. 28-32.

Chakravorty, M., New trends in adult education for women (special reference to weaker section of the society), National Seminar on New Trends in Adult Education for Women with special reference to literacy, Feb., 19-22, 1980.

Challenge of Educational Policy Perspective, New Delhi, Ministry of Human Resource and Development, Govt. of India, 1985. p. 119.

Charters, Alexander N., Comparative adult education, *Indian Journal of Adult Education* 52(1-2) Jan.-Jun. 1991, pp. 28-38.

Chatterjee, Bishwa Bandhu, Role of adult education in the Green Revolution, *Indian Journal of Adult Education* 31 (2) Nov. 1970.

Chelikari, Krishna Mohan Rao, A study of factors influencing adult education programme at project level; their different impact in tribal and non-tribal areas, (Theses) Gorakhpur, Gorakhpur University, p. 1991.

Chaudhuri, Indra Nath, Inter-disciplinary research and practice in literacy, *Indian Horizons* 40 (3-4) 1991, pp. 53-62.

Committee on the Adult Education Programme for Women, Report, New Delhi, Ministry of Education and Social Welfare, Govt. of India, 1976, p. 15.

Das, K.C., Towards total literacy by 1995, *Sarvodaya* 38 (6) Aug. 1993, pp. 4-8.

Das, Mamota, The learning process of illiteracy eradication, *Progress of Education* 64(9) Apr. 1990, pp. 220-223.

Das, Mamota, Teaching strategies for illiteracy eradication, *University News* 28(8), 19 Feb. 1990, pp. 7-10.

Dasgupta, Sugata, Social work and social education, *Indian Journal of Social Work,* 17(4) Mar. 1957. pp. 289-293.

Deroanji, Malay, Ande on the role of adult education in rural development. *Religion and Society*. 36(3) Sep. 1989, pp. 32-36.

Dhoundiyal, N.C., Training of total literacy campaign functionaries : Some considerations, *Indian Journal of Adult Education* 55(1) Jan.-Mar. 1994, pp. 60-66.

Dighe, Anita, The role of adult education in reducing class and gender disparities, *Journal of Educational Planning and Administration*. 6(2) Apr. 1992. pp. 133-40.

Dighe, Anita, Women and Literacy—Some policy considerations, *Indian Journal of Adult Education* 52 (1-2) Jan.-Jun. 1991, pp. 34-59.

Discussion on the philosophy of democratic adult education, *Journal of Community Guidance Research*. 11(2) May 1994, pp. 167-172.

Doraiswami, S., Curriculum preparation for adult education programme, New Delhi, Directorate of Adult Education, 1974.

Draft National Policy on Education 1986. New Delhi, Department of Education, Ministry of Human Resource and Development, Govt. of India, 1986. p. 30.

Draper, J.A., The Changing face of adult education : Personal reflections on India. *Indian Journal of Adult Education.* 52(1-2) Jan-Jun. 1991, pp. 5-14.

Draper, James A., Adult education a focus for the social science, IAEA, New Delhi, 1989.

Duke, Chris, Adult education and development : Some important issues, *Indian Journal of Adult Education* 52(3) July-Sep. 1991, pp. 22-34.

Dutta, S.C., New trends in adult education in India, Delhi, Indian Adult Education Association, 1962.

Dutta, S.C., Role of voluntary organisation in non-formal adult education, *Indian Journal of Adult Education* 39(7) Jul, 1978.

Dutta, S.C., Social education in community development, *Indian Journal of Social Work.* 17(4) Mar. 1957, pp. 286-289.

Ediger, Marlow, Adult education and the curriculum, *Progress of Education.* 69(1) Aug. 1994. pp. 2-5.

Ediger, Marlow, Lifelong education and learning, *Progress of Education.* 64(7) Feb. 1990 pp. 154-156.

Education for all 2000 : Indian Perspective. New Delhi, National Institute of Educational Planning and Administration, 1990, p. 107, Working paper.

Fisher, Welthy H., Each one teach one, *Indian Journal of Adult Education* 16(2) Jun. 1955.

Fraser, A.G. (*et al.*) Village education in India, New Delhi, Mittal, 1989.

47th All India Adult Education Conference : A report, *Indian Journal of Adult Education.* 58(4) Oct.-Dec. 1997, pp. 5-10.

Gajanayake, Jaya, People's participation in rural development : The rationale and significance, *Indian Journal of Adult Education* 45(3) Mar. 1984, pp. 13-16+.

Gakhar, S.C., Certain needs adult education programme, *Progress of Education.* 67(10-11) May-Jun. 1995. pp. 218-221.

Garg, B.S., Towards a learning society, *Indian Journal of Adult Education* 58(4) Oct.-Dec., 1997, pp. 11-16.

Gayatonde, S.N., Participatory approach to total literacy, *Indian Journal of Adult Education.* 52(4) Oct.-Dec. 1991, pp. 22-24.

Ghosh, A.K., Growth of female literacy in India, *University News* 31(45) 8 Nov. 1993, p. 1042.

Ghosh, Anjan, Practice of pedagogy in non-formal education, *Economic and Political Weekly,* 30(34) 16 Sep. 1995, p. 2303.

Govindappa, K. and Muralidharudu, Creating social awareness through adult education, *Kurukshetra.* 41 (8) May 1993, pp. 30-34.

Gugnani, Hansraj, Literacy liberation and empowerment of women, *University News.* 32 (28) 11 Jul. 1994, p. 1678.

Gupta, J.L. (*et al.*), Impact of literacy on socio-economic conditions of rural poors, *Indian Journal of Adult Education* 55(1) Jan.-Mar. 1994, pp. 67-73.

Gupta, H.R., Organisation of adult literacy programme, *Indian Journal of Adult Education*, 29(4) Apr. 1968.

Habib, Nasira, Community development through adult education among women, *Adult Education and Development* No. 53, 1999, pp. 149-164.

Harichandan, Dhaneswar, Adult education : Some basic issues, *University News.* 30(23) 8 Jun, 1992, pp. 11-13.

Harmesh Lal, Developing learning material for literacy and continuing education, *Indian Journal of Education.* 22(4) Feb. 1997, pp. 30-34.

Hirlekar, Yamunabai, Social service and adult education, *Social Service Quarterly* 33(1) Jul. 1946, p. 741.

Hooja, G.B.K., Approaches to total literacy, *Prasar* 18(3) Oct.-Dec., 1991, pp. 46-52.

Hooja, G.B.K., A literate world—New initiatives, *University News.* 30(37) 14 Sep. 1992, pp. 5-7.

Hooja, G.B.K., Mobilization for literacy, *University News.* 31(3) 18 Jan. 1993, pp. 14-16.

Hussain, Hamid and Muhammad Ayyub, Evaluation of academic programmes in continuing education in terms of their usefulness for the students. *Progress of Education.* 64 (12) Jul. 1990 pp. 265-269.

Increasing literacy and declining sex ratio, *Link.* 34(20) 29 Dec. 1991, pp. 16-18.

India, Ministry of Education, National Policy on Education, New Delhi, The Ministry, 1968.

India, Ministry of Education and Social Change, Report of a Committee on Adult Education Programme for Women, New Delhi, The Ministry, p. 11.

India, Ministry of Education and Social Welfare, National Adult Education programme—An outline (with modification upto July 15, 1978), New Delhi, The Ministry, 1978, p. 24.

India, Ministry of Human Resource and Development, Department of Education, National Policy on Education 1986, Programme of Action 1992. p. 249.

India, Ministry of Human Resource Development. Deparment of Education, Directorate of Adult Education, Crusade against illiteracy, A collection of success stories on adult education. New Delhi, The Ministry, nd. p. 44.

India, Ministry of Human Research Development, National Institute of Adult Education, Report of working groups on National Institute of Adult Education, New Delhi, The Ministry, nd. p. 16.

Jabbi, M.K. and Rajyalakshmi, C., Impact of population education in adult literacy programmes, *Social change* 22(3) Sep. 1992, p. 348.

Jain, S.P. (*et al.*), Research in Adult Education in India : A select Bibliography, New Delhi, Directorate of Adult Education, Ministry of Education and Culture, Govt. of India, 1984, p. 33.

Jejeebhoy, Shiree, J., Female Literacy in India: The situation in 1991, *Journal of Family Welfare* 37(3) Sep. 1991. pp. 23-34.

Joshi, Uma, Adult education is more than literacy, *Social Welfare* 36(8), Nov. 1989. pp. 11-12.

Kak, K.K., Adult Education and Communal Harmony : A Caveat, *Indian Journal of Adult Education* 54(3) Jul.-Sep., 1993, p. 573.

Kak, K.K., Planning and the non-literate Indian, *Indian Journal of Adult Education* 55 (4) Oct-Dec., 1994, pp. 5-15.

Kakadi, Kunja Jusum, Adult Education and Human Rights for Women, *Indian Journal of Adult Education*, 60(3) Jul.-Sep. 1999, pp. 5-13.

Kasinath, H.M., Literacy in India: An analysis of progress during 1981 to 1991, *Indian Journal of Adult Education* 56(2) Apr.-Jun. 1995, pp. 5-12.

Kassam, Yusuf, Who benefits from illiteracy? Literacy and empowerment, *Teacher Today* 34(4) Apr.-Jun. 1992, pp. 41-49.

Kaul, Lokesh, Priorities in adult education, *Worker's Educaiton*, Jan. 1979.

Khan, Azmat Hussain, Illiteracy : An Impediment for Development, *Indian Journal of Adult Education* 52(4) Oct.-Dec., 1991, pp. 17-21.

Kini, K.H., New problems of adult education, *Rural India* 12(11) Dec., 1949, pp. 469-71.

rishnammall, P., The Impact of adult education on the life styles of rural women. *Journal of Community Guidance Research* 9(3) Sep. 1992, pp. 195-211.

rishna Reddy, B. and Subba Reddy, P.V., A study on reading interests of neo-literates. *Indian Journal of Adult Education* 52(1-2) Jan.-Jun., 1991, pp. 79-83.

uldip Kaur, Education in India (1781-1985) : Policies, Planning and Implementation, Chandigarh, Centre for Research in Rural and Industrial Development, 1985, p. 545.

ulkarni, P.M. and Krishnamoorthy, S., Gender inequality in literacy, measurement and pattern. *Social Change* 22(3) Sep. 1992, pp. 19-30.

umarna Swamy, T. and Bashai, S., Kadhar, Role of Universities in total literacy campaigns. *University News*, 31 (46) 15 Nov. 1993. pp. 18-20.

umat, R.S., Critical issues in eradication of illiteracy, *Teacher Today,* 34 (4) Jul.-Sep. 1992, pp. 1-6.

ahiry, Subratar, Banishing illiteracy in present set-up : Some reflections. *Mainstream*, 32 (43) 10 Sep. 1994, pp. 32-34.

akshmi Reddy, M.V., Crapshooting with adult education organisations *University News* 32 (41), 10 Oct. 1994, pp. 4-6.

akshmi Reddy, M.V., Gender inequity in literacy: An analysis. *Indian Journal of Adult Education*. 55(3) Jul.-Sep. 1994, pp. 5-22.

akshmi Reddy, M.V.L., Conceptual proliferations in adult education : An overview. *Indian Journal of Adult Education* 54(4) Oct.-Dec. 1993, pp. 5-15.

iberation through literacy Ernakulam shows the way. *Social Welfare*. 34(1) Apr. 1990, pp. 11-12.

ieten, G.K., Literacy in post-land reform village. *Economic and Political Weekly* 27(3) 18 Jan 1992, pp. 103-109.

iteracy programme in eighth five year plan. *Prasar* 20(1-2) Apr.-Sep. 1993, pp. 37-50.

Maitra, Satyan, Training in TLC : A few observations. *Prasar* 20(1-2) Apr.-Sep. 1993, pp. 31-36.

Mali, M.G., Education of Masses in India, New Delhi, Mittal, 1989.

Malia Reddy, M., Instructional System in distance education. *Progressive Education Herald*, 5(4) Jul. 1991, pp. 45-48.

Mathew, A. and Rao, C. Krishna Mohan, Development perceptions of literacy campaigns : Towards a balanced view. *Mainstream*

32 (10) 22 Jan. 1994, pp. 15-24.

Mathur, J.S., Concept of Social Education. *Social Work Forum* 3(2 Apr. 1965, pp. 32-35.

Mathur, R.S., Utilisation of feedback from evaluation studies of adul education programme. *Indian Journal of Adult Education* 4: (3) Mar. 1984, pp. 17-22.

Mathur, V.S., Adult education : Our immediate need. *Education* 8(1 Apr. 1950, pp. 23-28.

Mehta, M.L., Adult education and total development. *Social chang* 19(2) Jun. 1989, pp. 24-36.

Mehta, M.S., Adult education the meaning and growth. *Maya Shiksha* 8(2) Oct. 1965.

Meueler, Erhard, Adult education : Learning involves fun and work *Indian Journal of Community Guidance Service*. 7(2) Ma 1990 pp. 61-72.

Meueler, Erhard, The art of going along with people : a study in adul education. *Indian Journal of Community Guidance Service*. 6(2 May 1989, pp. 1-20.

Mishra, Lakshmidhar, Adult Education and National Integration *Mainstream*. 28 (13) 20, Jan. 1990, pp. 17-18.

Mishra, Lakshmidhar, Can we create a learning society ? *Mainstrean* 27 (50), 9 Sep. 1989, pp. 19-21.

Mishra, Lakshmidhar, National Literacy Mission : Problems an Prospects. *Mainstream* 28(17), 17 Feb. 1990, pp. 14-16.

Mishra, Lakshmidhar, Total literacy campaign : Still an unwritte chapter in Indian history. *Mainstream* 30(46), 5 Sep. 1992, pp 11-16; 30 (47) 12 Sep. 1992, pp. 20-28.

Mohanty, B.B., Role of distance education in Promoting literacy, adul education and non-formal basic education for rural and socia development. *Indian Journal of Adult Education* 60 (4) Oct. Dec. 1999, pp. 9-21.

Mohanty, B.B., Total literacy in the confest of education for all b 2000. *Indian Journal of Adult Education* 55 (2) Apr.-Jun 1994. pp. 18-26.

Mohanty, Sunil Behari, Lifelong and Adult education, Ashish, Nev Delhi, 1988, p. 205.

Mohsini, S.R., History of adult education in India. Anmol, New Delhi 1993, p. 271.

Mukherjee, D.P., Cybernetic and ragogy : Educating, homoerectus t be homo-politicus. *Indian Journal of Adult Education* 55(1

Jan. 1994, pp. 20-25.

Mukherji, Girijapati, Adult Education, *Rural India* 3(3) Mar. 1940, pp. 154-156.

Mukhopadhyay, Ashim, Broken earth : Literacy and population control. *Frontier* 26 (43), 4 Jun, 1994; pp. 7-10; 26 (44) 11 Jun. 1994, pp. 7-11.

Murgesan, K.P. and Nanjaiyan, K., Constraints of adult learners in adult education centres. *Yojana* 36 (20), 15 Nov. 1992, pp. 19-20.

Mysore State Adult Education Council. Adult Education in Mysore. Mysore, The Council, 1949.

Naik, J.P., The Education Commission and After. New Delhi, Allied, 1982.

Nanavatty, Meher C., Job requirements for social education. *Faculty of Social Work Magazine*. 2 Apr. 1955, pp. 18-22.

Nanda, B.K., A critical study of the development of adult education in the Punjab during the period of from 1947 to 1972. Chandigarh, Punjabi University, 1978.

National Adult Education Programme : The first year. New Delhi, Ministry of Education and Culture, Govt of India, 1979. p. 40.

National Policy on Education 1986, National Policy on Education : Programme of Action 1992. New Delhi, Deptt. of Education Ministry, HRD, Govt. of India, p. 250.

National Seminar on Adult Education in the context of National Policy on Education (1985 : New Delhi), organised by India, Ministry of Human Resource Development. Department of Education. Directorate of Adult Education. Oct. 10-12, 1985.

National Seminar on New Trends in Adult Education for Women with Special Reference to Literacy (1980, New Delhi) Organised by Indian Adult Education Association, Feb. 19-22, 1980.

Nautiyal, K.C., Mass literacy programmes in India : Retrospects and prospect. *Journal of Indian Education* 19(1) May 1993. pp. 9-15.

Nanyak, R.C., Dynamic Concept and prospect of social education in India. *Indian Journal of Social Work*. 22(2) Sep. 1961, pp. 103-105.

Nayar, D.P., Towards a National system of education, New Delhi, Mittal, 1989.

Nimbalkar, M.R., Adult education and its evaluation system, New Delhi, Mittal, 1984.

Nuna, Sheel C., Literacy scenario in India during 1991 : A march towards development of underdevelopment. *Social Action,* 41(4) Oct.-Dec. 1991, pp. 454-63.

Omoruyi, FEO, Effective Communication with adult learners. *Indian Journal of Adult Education.* 60(3) Jul.-Sep. 1999, pp. 55-63.

Onane, A. (*et al.*), Handbook on training for post-literacy and basic education. UNESCO Institute for Education, Hamburg, 1990, p. 206.

Pakem, B., Adult Education in North East India: Evaluation of Adult Education programme in the states of Assam and Meghalaya. Shillong, ICSSR, 1992, p. 90.

Paliwal, M.R., Social Change and Education : Present and Future, New Delhi, Uppal, 1984. p. 357.

Pande, Manisha, Can satellite talk back facility overcome the limitations of distance education? *University News* 30(23) 8 Jun. 1992, pp. 2-8.

Pandya, Rameshwari, Adult education for women—Some observations. *Indian Journal of Adult Education* 61(1) Jan.-Mar. 2000, pp. 29-33.

Pandya, Rameshwari, Role of media in adult education. *New Frontiers in Education* 30(1) 2000. pp. 88-91.

Parameswaran, M.P., Experience of mass literacy campaigns in India : 1988-96. *Indian Journal of Social Work* (Part 2) 59(i) Jan. 1998, pp. 407-421.

Paraswaran, M.P., An experiment in literacy. *Seminar* 391, Mar. 1992. pp. 30-33.

Parikh, Ramlal, Renewing the adult education movement. *Indian Journal of Adult Education.* 45 (4) Apr. 1984, pp. 3-4.

Pati, S.P., Adult Education Ashish, New Delhi, 1989, p. 327.

Pati, S.P. and Sinha Debarati, Views of adult literate and illiterate women towards adult literacy programme. *Educational Review.* 104 (4) Apr. 1998, pp. 64-65.

Pati, Sura Prasad, Adult education, Ashish, New Delhi, p. 332.

Pillai, P. Gopinadhan, Universities and the total literacy campaigns. *University News.* 31(28) 12 Jul. 1993, pp. 8-10.

Pillai, P. Gopinadhan, UGC guidelines for university adult continuing education and extension in the IX Plan, a view point. *Journal of Higher Education.* 21(1) Sep. 1998, pp. 135-140.

Pillai, P. Gopinadhan, University adult continuing education and extension in the IX Plan, suggestions for review of UGC guidelines. *University News* 36(15) 13 Apr. 1998, pp. 5-8.

Pimpal Khare, M.H., International literacy year. *Progress of Education*, 64 (7) Feb. 1990, pp. 171-172+.

Pooja, G.B.K., National literacy mission and the universities. *University News,* 27(38), 18 Sep. 1989, pp. 5-7.

Prem Chand, Literacy scenario in India. *Prasar* 20 (1-2) Apr.-Sep. 1993, pp. 12-16.

Raghu, V., Continuing education and neo-literate literature. *Indian Journal of Adult Education* 56 (2) Apr.-Jun. 1995, pp. 37-41.

Rahi, A.L., Literacy campaign in India. *Indian Journal of Adult Education* 55 (1) Jan.-Mar. 1994, pp. 41-45.

Rahi, A.L., Literacy of the oppressed. *Indian Journal of Adult Education* 55(4) Oct.-Dec. 1994, pp. 16-23.

Rahi, A.L., Some thoughts on literacy in India. *Sarvodaya* 37 (12) Mar. 1994, pp. 16-19.

Rahi, A.L., Some thoughts on literacy in India. *University News* 32(2) 10 Jan. 1994, pp. 14-15.

Raina, B.L., The curriculum development and continuing education. *Prasar* 18 (4) Jan.- Mar. 1992, pp. 25-31.

Rajamani, R.C., Illiteracy : A daunting challenge. *Social Welfare* 37 (1) Apr. 1990, pp. 10+.

Rajan, K.R., Towards total literacy. *Social Welfare*. 36 (8) Nov. 1989, p. 940.

Ramabrahman, I., Literacy promotion: A chimeric exercise. *Mainstream* 33(13), 18 Feb. 1995, pp. 24-25.

Ramachandra, C., Literacy campaign needs mass support. *New Age* 38 (15) 15 Apr. 1990, p. 2.

Rama Devy, M. and Venkata Ramaiah, P., Impact of national literacy mission (NIM) on rural women learners. *Indian Psychological Review* 38 (2-3) Feb.-Mar. 1992, pp. 29-32.

Ramakrishnaiah, D. and Kumaraswamy, T., Distance education and student support services. *University News* 32 (32) 8 Aug., 1994. pp. 9-10.

Ramesh, G. and Ramesh Babu, B., The role of national adult education programme in developing political consciousness among rural adult learners—A study. *Progress of Education* 66(3) Oct. 1991, pp. 65-70.

Rao, Nitya, Total literacy campaigns : A field report. *Economic and Political Weekly,* 28(19), 8 May 1993, pp. 914-918.

Rao, T.V. *et al.*, Adult education for social change, New Delhi, Manohar, 1982.

Rao, V.K.R.V., Adult education and National development, New Delhi, Ministry of Education and Youth Services, Govt. of India, 1970.

Rao, V.S. Rama Krishna, Children activated literacy programme. *Primary Teacher* 16(4) Oct. 1991, pp. 33-37.

Rao, Vasuudeva and Subba Rao, D., Adult education and continuing education and national development. *Educational Review*, 90 (1) Jan. 1984, pp. 7-9.

Readdy, P.A. and Reddeppa, G., Determinants of prerak effectiveness. *Indian Journal of Adult Education* 56 (2) Apr.-Jun 1995. pp. 13-23.

Redeppa Reddy, M.C., Mobilization of resources for total literacy campaigns. *Progressive Educational Herald* 8(2) Jan 1994, pp. 23-28.

Reddy, G. Lokanadha *et al.*, Learning disabilities (difficulties) in adults —Need for intervention strategies. *Indian Journal of Adult Education* 61(1) Jan.-Mar. 2000, pp. 45-53.

Richardson, M.D. (*et al.*), Adult learning theory, implications for teachers of adults. *Indian Journal of Adult Education*. 52 (1-2) Jan.-Jun. 1991, pp. 22-27.

Rogers, Alan, Teaching adults, Sterling, New Delhi, 1989, p. 197.

Ross, Kidd and Krishna Kumar, Co-opting freire : A critical analysis of psendo-freirea adult education. *Economic and Political Weekly* 16(1-2) 1981, p. 27.

Sachdeva, J.L., Adult education : Challenges for the twenty-first century. *Indian Journal of Adult Education*. 58 (4) Oct.-Dec. 1997. pp. 17-23.

Sachdeva, J.L., Adult education in the central zone. *Indian Journal of Adult Education*. 54 (3) Jul.-Sep. 1993, pp. 67-80.

Sachdeva, J.L., Approaches of total literacy. *Indian Journal of Adult Education*. 52 (4) Oct.-Dec. 1991, pp. 43-48.

Sachdeva, J.L., Education of better life. *University News* 32 (34) 22 Aug. 1994, pp. 16-18.

Sachdeva, Rajesh, Inquest of parsa digni quo vadis adult education. *Indian Journal of Adult Education*, 54 (3) Jul.- Sep. 1993, pp. 23-40.

Sahoo, P.K., Evaluation of national adult education programme. *Indian Education*, 13 (8-9) Nov.-Dec., 1983, pp. 8-11.

Saiyidain, K.G., Problem of illiteracy and social education. *Indian Journal of Social Work.* 13(1) Jun. 1952, pp. 22-27.

Saldanha, Denzil, Literacy campaigns and basic education : Status and issues. *Indian Journal of Social Work* (Part II) 59(1), Jan. 1998, pp. 382-406.

Saxena, Sadhna, Limits and consequences of literacy programmes. *Economic and Political Weekly* 28 (8-9) 20-27 Feb. 1993, pp. 321-322.

Saroja, N., Technology application for adult literacy, some constraints. *Progressive Educational Herald* (Annual Number) 9(1) Oct. 1994, pp. 29-39.

Sen, Amartya, Beyond liberalization : Social opportunity and human capability. *Other Side.* 26 Nov. 1994, pp. 10-21.

Seth, M. (*et al.*), Groups interaction among women participants of a functional literacy programme in Delhi: A study. *Indian Journal of Adult Education.* 44(10) Oct. 1983, pp. 24-28.

Seth, Mridula, Communications and extension through literacy: development of a primer. *Indian Journal of Adult Education.* 52(3), Jul.-Sep. 1991, p. 6674.

Shah, A.B. and Susheela Bhan *(ed.)*, Non-formal education and the NAEP. Bombay, Oxford University, 1980.

Shah, Anupama and Hazarika, Sultana, Assessing Community needs. *Social Welfare*, 39(9) Dec.-1992, pp. 11-12.

Shah, S.Y., Adult education in the Eighth Plan : Same issues. *University News* 30 (51) 21 Dec. 1992 p. 1245.

Shah, S.Y., Each one teach one : Launch's materials and methods. IAEA, New Delhi, 1991, xii, p. 212.

Sharma, B., Adult education, New Delhi, Mittal, 1992, p. 88.

Sharma, O.P., Continuing education for neo literates. *Indian Journal of Adult Education.* 55 (4) Oct. - Dec. 1994, pp. 46-49.

Sharma, R.D., Importance of audio-visual technology in non-formal education. *Progress of Education* 64 (9) Apr. 1990, pp. 218-19+.

Sharma, Sita Ram, Development of adult education in India, Akashdeep, Delhi, 1990, p. 616.

Shaw, E.C., Reading new readers in rural areas. Lucknow, Saksharasa Niketan, 1950.

Shirur, Rajani R., Development through non-formal education rhetoric and realities. *Indian Journal of Adult Education* 55(1) Jan.-Mar. 1994, pp. 55-59.

Shri Prakash (*et al.*), A decomposition model of growth of literacy in India. *Journal of Educational Planning Act Administration*. 5 (2) Apr. 1991, pp. 117-42.

Shukla, B.B. and Behusia, R.K., The role of public libraries in adult literacy programme. *Indian Journal of Information, Library and Society*. 3(1-2) Mar.-Jun., 1990, pp. 149-152.

Shukla, S., Literacy and Development. *Indian Journal of Adult Education* 52 (3), Jul.-Sep. 1991, pp. 5-11.

Sinha, V.N.P. (*et al.*), Levels and trends of literacy in India. *National Geographer*. 29(2), Dec. 1994, pp. 89-97.

Sood, Meenakshi, Pre-requisite for development. *Social welfare* 41 (7) Oct. 1994, pp. 24-25.

Srinivasan, R., Association between per capita income and literacy for Indian States. *Educational Review* 96 (3) Mar. 1990, pp. 49-51.

Srivastava, I.C., Literacy and rural development, *Prasar*, 18(3) Oct.-Dec. 1991, pp. 33-37.

Srivastava, Onkar Nath, On creating a fully literate world. *University News*, 29 (44) 4 Nov. 1991, pp. 1-2.

Subba Rao, D., New Dimensions to adult literacy. *Social Welfare* 25(4) Dec. 1948.

Sundarapandian, M., Total literacy, campaigns in India—Review. *Indian Journal of Adult Education* 54(4), Oct.-Dec. 1993, pp. 16-24.

Tantry, G.N., Human rights and adult education. *Prasar* 19(3-4) Oct.-Dec. 1992, Jan.-March 1993, pp. 40-46.

Total Literacy Campaigns. *Progressive Educational Herald*. 6(4) Jul. 1992, pp. 33-37+.

Total Literacy Campaigns : Some guidelines. *Indian Journal of Adult Education*. 52 (4) Oct.-Dec. 1991, pp. 28-37.

Total Literacy Campaigns as National Strategy : A time to pause and think. *Indian Journal of Adult Education* 52(3), Jul.-Sep. 1991, pp. 5-11.

The training of adult educators and the university system in India : Themes, techniques and issues. *Indian Journal of Adult Education* 52(1-2), Jan.-Jun. 1991, pp. 15-21.

Tripathi, Bhanwar Lal, Educating the adults. *Rural India* 25(2) Feb. 1962, pp. 57-59.

Tripathi, Virendra, Post literacy in total literacy campaign. *Prasar:* 18(4) Jan.-March 1992, pp. 13-16.

Uniyal, M.P. and Shah, Beena, Dynamics of motivation for adult learners. *Indian Journal of Adult Education*. 44(10) Oct. 1983, pp. 3-5+.

Vanaja, V., Where are the women? Review of adult education is primers. *Economic and Political Weekly* 29(12) 1994, p. 665.

Vashishtha, U.C., (*et al.*) Post literacy : A pre-requistic for literacy. *Asian Journal of Psychology and Education* 28 (5-6), Aug.-Sep. 1995, pp. 34-39.

Veeraraghavan, J., Motivation and adult education. *Indian Journal of Adult Education*, Apr.-May, 1974.

Vidyapati, Nehru and literacy. *University News* 28(10), 5 Mar. 1990, pp. 1-3.

Viyahabharathy, M. and Portia, D.R., Adult education—Its impact upon democracy. *Educational Review* 90 (3), Mar. 1984, pp. 53-55.

Warier, K.U., Ernakulam blazes total literacy trail. *New Age*. 38(8), 25 Feb. 1990, pp. 6+.

Yadav, D.P., Trends in Indian adult education. *Indian Journal of Adult Education*, Apr.-May, 1974.

INDEX